Acts of the Apostles

✝ Catholic Commentary on Sacred Scripture

Acts
of the Apostles

William S. Kurz, SJ

Baker Academic

a division of Baker Publishing Group
Grand Rapids, Michigan

Published by Baker Academic
a division of Baker Publishing Group
P.O. Box 6287, Grand Rapids, MI 49516-6287
www.bakeracademic.com

Printed in the United States of America

Library of Congress Cataloging-in-Publication Data

Kurz, William S., 1939–
    Acts of the Apostles / William S. Kurz, SJ.
        pages   cm. — (Catholic commentary on sacred scripture)
    Includes bibliographic references and index.
    ISBN 978-0-8010-3633-0 (pbk.)
    1. Bible. Acts—Commentaries. 2. Catholic Church—Doctrines. I. Title.
    BS2625.53.K87   2013
    226.6′0uu—dc23   2013033612

Nihil obstat:
Dr. Patrick Russell
Censor librorum

Imprimatur:
Most Rev. Jerome E. Listecki
Archbishop of Milwaukee
May 10, 2013

The *nihil obstat* and *imprimatur* are official declarations that a book or pamphlet is free of doctrinal or moral error. There is no implication that those who have granted the *nihil obstat* or the *imprimatur* agree with the content, opinions, or statements expressed therein.

In keeping with biblical principles of creation stewardship, Baker Publishing Group advocates the responsible use of our natural resources. As a member of the Green Press Initiative, our company uses recycled paper when possible. The text paper of this book is composed in part of post-consumer waste.

20 21 22 23 24 25 26   12 11 10 9 8 7 6

Contents

Illustrations

Editors' Preface

The Church has always venerated the divine Scriptures just as she venerates the body of the Lord. . . . All the preaching of the Church should be nourished and governed by Sacred Scripture. For in the sacred books, the Father who is in heaven meets His children with great love and speaks with them; and the power and goodness in the word of God is so great that it stands as the support and energy of the Church, the strength of faith for her sons and daughters, the food of the soul, a pure and perennial fountain of spiritual life.

Second Vatican Council, *Dei Verbum* 21

Were not our hearts burning while he spoke to us on the way and opened the scriptures to us?

Luke 24:32

The Catholic Commentary on Sacred Scripture aims to serve the ministry of the Word of God in the life and mission of the Church. Since Vatican Council II, there has been an increasing hunger among Catholics to study Scripture in depth and in a way that reveals its relationship to liturgy, evangelization, catechesis, theology, and personal and communal life. This series responds to that desire by providing accessible yet substantive commentary on each book of the New Testament, drawn from the best of contemporary biblical scholarship as well as the rich treasury of the Church's tradition. These volumes seek to offer scholarship illumined by faith, in the conviction that the ultimate aim of biblical interpretation is to discover what God has revealed and is still speaking through the sacred text. Central to our approach are the principles taught by Vatican II: first, the use of historical and literary methods to discern what the biblical authors intended to express; second, prayerful theological reflection to understand the sacred text "in accord with the same Spirit by whom it was written"—that is, in light of the content and unity of the whole Scripture, the living tradition of the Church, and the analogy of faith (*Dei Verbum* 12).

The Catholic Commentary on Sacred Scripture is written for those engaged in or training for pastoral ministry and others interested in studying Scripture to understand their faith more deeply, to nourish their spiritual life, or to share the good news with others. With this in mind, the authors focus on the meaning of the text for faith and life rather than on the technical questions that occupy scholars, and they explain the Bible in ordinary language that does not require translation for preaching and catechesis. Although this series is written from the perspective of Catholic faith, its authors draw on the interpretation of Protestant and Orthodox scholars and hope these volumes will serve Christians of other traditions as well.

A variety of features are designed to make the commentary as useful as possible. Each volume includes the biblical text of the New American Bible Revised Edition (NABRE), the translation approved for liturgical use in the United States. In order to serve readers who use other translations, the most important differences between the NABRE and other widely used translations (RSV, NRSV, JB, NJB, and NIV) are noted and explained. Each unit of the biblical text is followed by a list of references to relevant Scripture passages, Catechism sections, and uses in the Roman Lectionary. The exegesis that follows aims to explain in a clear and engaging way the meaning of the text in its original historical context as well as its perennial meaning for Christians. Reflection and Application sections help readers apply Scripture to Christian life today by responding to questions that the text raises, offering spiritual interpretations drawn from Christian tradition, or providing suggestions for the use of the biblical text in catechesis, preaching, or other forms of pastoral ministry.

Interspersed throughout the commentary are Biblical Background sidebars that present historical, literary, or theological information, and Living Tradition sidebars that offer pertinent material from the postbiblical Christian tradition, including quotations from Church documents and from the writings of saints and Church Fathers. The Biblical Background sidebars are indicated by a photo of urns that were excavated in Jerusalem, signifying the importance of historical study in understanding the sacred text. The Living Tradition sidebars are indicated by an image of Eadwine, a twelfth-century monk and scribe, signifying the growth in the Church's understanding that comes by the grace of the Holy Spirit as believers study and ponder the Word of God in their hearts (see *Dei Verbum* 8).

A map and a Glossary are located in the back of each volume for easy reference. The glossary explains key terms from the biblical text as well as theological or exegetical terms, which are marked in the commentary with a cross (†). A list of Suggested Resources, an Index of Pastoral Topics, and an Index of Sidebars are included to enhance the usefulness of these volumes. Further resources, including questions for reflection or discussion, can be found at the series website, www.CatholicScriptureCommentary.com.

It is our desire and prayer that these volumes be of service so that more and more "the word of the Lord may speed forward and be glorified" (2 Thess 3:1) in the Church and throughout the world.

Peter S. Williamson
Mary Healy
Kevin Perrotta

Abbreviations

†	indicates that the definition of a term appears in the glossary
ACCS	Ancient Christian Commentary on Scripture, New Testament, vol. 5, *Acts*, ed. Francis Martin and Evan Smith (Downers Grove, IL: InterVarsity, 2006)
ANF	*Ante-Nicene Fathers*
Catechism	*Catechism of the Catholic Church* (2nd ed.)
JB	Jerusalem Bible
Lectionary	*The Lectionary for Mass* (1988/2000 USA Edition)
LXX	†Septuagint
NABRE	New American Bible Revised Edition (2011)
NIV	New International Version
NJB	New Jerusalem Bible
NRSV	New Revised Standard Version
NT	New Testament
OT	Old Testament
PL	Patrologia latina, ed. J.-P. Migne (Paris, 1844–64)
REB	Revised English Bible
RSV	Revised Standard Version
RSVCE	Revised Standard Version Catholic Edition

Books of the Old Testament

Gen	Genesis	1 Kings	1 Kings	2 Macc	2 Maccabees
Exod	Exodus	2 Kings	2 Kings	Job	Job
Lev	Leviticus	1 Chron	1 Chronicles	Ps	Psalms
Num	Numbers	2 Chron	2 Chronicles	Prov	Proverbs
Deut	Deuteronomy	Ezra	Ezra	Eccles	Ecclesiastes
Josh	Joshua	Neh	Nehemiah	Song	Song of Songs
Judg	Judges	Tob	Tobit	Wis	Wisdom
Ruth	Ruth	Jdt	Judith	Sir	Sirach
1 Sam	1 Samuel	Esther	Esther	Isa	Isaiah
2 Sam	2 Samuel	1 Macc	1 Maccabees	Jer	Jeremiah

Lam	Lamentations	Amos	Amos	Zeph	Zephaniah
Bar	Baruch	Obad	Obadiah	Hag	Haggai
Ezek	Ezekiel	Jon	Jonah	Zech	Zechariah
Dan	Daniel	Mic	Micah	Mal	Malachi
Hosea	Hosea	Nah	Nahum		
Joel	Joel	Hab	Habakkuk		

Books of the New Testament

Matt	Matthew	1 Tim	1 Timothy
Mark	Mark	2 Tim	2 Timothy
Luke	Luke	Titus	Titus
John	John	Philem	Philemon
Acts	Acts of the Apostles	Heb	Hebrews
Rom	Romans	James	James
1 Cor	1 Corinthians	1 Pet	1 Peter
2 Cor	2 Corinthians	2 Pet	2 Peter
Gal	Galatians	1 John	1 John
Eph	Ephesians	2 John	2 John
Phil	Philippians	3 John	3 John
Col	Colossians	Jude	Jude
1 Thess	1 Thessalonians	Rev	Revelation
2 Thess	2 Thessalonians		

Introduction

The Acts of the Apostles fulfills a unique role in the New Testament. Written as a sequel to the Gospel of Luke by the same author (Acts 1:1), Acts continues the Gospel by recounting how Jesus' mission was carried on by his disciples after he ascended into heaven. It provides the only narrative link we possess of the transition between Jesus' ministry, death, and resurrection to the spread of the Church beyond its Jewish origins to reach other nations. In addition, the canonical placement of Acts between the four Gospels and Paul's Letters enables Acts to introduce and situate those letters. Without Acts we would have no way to reconstruct the historical context of Paul's Letters or to establish some key dates within which his ministry took place.

Luke's second volume builds on what Jesus "began to do and teach" during his earthly ministry (Acts 1:1, literal translation). The Gospel covered all that Jesus *began* to do and teach. By implication, this sequel treats what Jesus *continues* to do and teach through his followers, after he was taken up to heaven and poured out his Holy Spirit on them. It describes how Jesus' mission is carried on by his followers, who spoke and acted in his name after they were empowered by the Holy Spirit. But Jesus' saving mission to all nations is not yet fully accomplished even with the apostles' ministry narrated in Acts. The narrative abruptly stops with Paul in house arrest in Rome, proclaiming the kingdom of God and teaching about the Lord Jesus Christ. The reason why the ending of Acts is deliberately left open-ended is to engage its readers. Inspired by the words and deeds of Paul and other followers of Jesus, Christians today are to carry on Jesus' mission even in the twenty-first century and until Jesus returns.

We disciples, who like the first Christians have been empowered by the Holy Spirit, are called to give ongoing witness to Jesus and his saving message to the ends of the earth. By recounting the climactic events of that story which took place in the first century, Luke's Gospel and Acts update the biblical story of salvation that began in the Old Testament. That story of salvation is *to be continued* by Jesus through us until he returns at the end of world history.

Who Wrote Luke and Acts?

Although the author is not named within Acts itself, the earliest surviving manuscripts of Luke's Gospel contain the superscription "according to Luke." Church traditions as early as the second century attribute both the Gospel and Acts to Luke, a traveling companion of Paul in his later journeys. Many scholars have debated, doubted, or denied this tradition, often because the theology in Acts does not always clearly correspond to Paul's own theological emphases. The tone of Acts differs especially from the sharpness of Paul's early controversies, as in Galatians, against the necessity of Jewish circumcision and the Mosaic law for salvation.

More recently, there is a growing acceptance that Luke probably was the author. The following conclusions seem reasonable. In the prologue of the Gospel (Luke 1:1–4), the author writes in the first person as "I." He concedes that he is not the first to write a Gospel: "Many have undertaken to compile a narrative of the events that have been fulfilled among us" (Luke 1:1). Nor does he claim that he himself is an eyewitness of Jesus' ministry. Rather, he says that "those who were eyewitnesses from the beginning and ministers of the word have handed them down to us" (v. 2). He then clarifies his own role. "I too have decided, after investigating everything accurately anew, to write it down in an orderly sequence for you, most excellent Theophilus" (v. 3). His purpose for writing to Theophilus is "so that you may realize the certainty of the teachings you have received" (v. 4). His Gospel is to confirm Christian oral traditions about Jesus by providing a carefully structured account of Jesus' life, ministry, death, and resurrection.

In the prologue to the Acts of the Apostles, the same author addresses the same Theophilus and refers back to his Gospel: "In the first book, Theophilus, I dealt with all that Jesus began to do and teach" (Acts 1:1, literal translation). So far, all the author has told us is that he is a Christian and not one of the original witnesses to Jesus. He makes no claim to have been present at Pentecost or in the earliest days of Paul's mission. Later in Acts, however, he uses the first-person "we" in several passages, implying that he was present at some of the events he is narrating. The first hint that the author was a companion of Paul is in Troas after Paul's vision of a Macedonian asking for help, when he writes that after Paul had seen the vision, "*we* sought passage to Macedonia at once, concluding that God had called us to proclaim the good news to them" (Acts 16:10, italics added). Several times thereafter, he employs first-person-plural pronouns, implying that he was a companion and eyewitness on some of Paul's journeys.

These claims of being present on some of Paul's later missions, beginning especially in Macedonia and Philippi, correspond to the references to Luke in Paul's Letters (Col 4:14; 2 Tim 4:11; Philem 24) and to the early Christian tradition that Luke was a Gentile companion of Paul. The "we" passages appear only after Paul's first missionary journey (Acts 13–14) and the †Jerusalem Council (Acts 15), so Luke claims to have been a companion only on Paul's later travels, well after all Paul's heated controversies about faith and circumcision (see Gal 2:1–5:12). This could explain why those early Pauline emphases are less prominent in Acts. It is the later Paul whom Luke knew personally.

Luke implies that although he was with Paul on his later journeys, including his journey to Rome in chains (28:14–15, after which "we" is no longer mentioned), he was not present at Paul's trials or final Roman imprisonment. Luke thus calls attention to similarities between Paul and his Lord Jesus, who was accompanied by his disciples on the journey to Jerusalem, but who faced his actual trials, final imprisonment, and crucifixion alone, without their presence or support.

With most of the Fathers and Church tradition, it makes sense to accept the traditional and simplest interpretation—that the author, Luke, was present at some events in the latter half of Acts. Although some scholars still treat the matter as historically insoluble, Joseph Fitzmyer has dealt with all the positions pro and con and has concluded that the most plausible historical explanation of the "we" passages, beginning with Acts 16:10, is that they are credible indications by the author of Acts that he actually was present on some of Paul's travels.[1] Although Acts has some theological differences from Paul's Letters, or has details about the †Judaizing controversies that are hard to reconcile with

---

1. See especially the introduction of Joseph A. Fitzmyer, *The Acts of the Apostles*, Anchor Bible 31 (New York: Doubleday, 1998), 98–103 and 580. Compare Ben Witherington III, *The Acts of the Apostles: A Socio-Rhetorical Commentary* (Grand Rapids: Eerdmans, 1997), 480–86; and C. K. Barrett, *A Critical and Exegetical Commentary on the Acts of the Apostles*, 2 vols. (Edinburgh: T&T Clark, 1994–98), 2:xxv–xxx and 773. Luke Timothy Johnson, *The Acts of the Apostles*, Sacra Pagina 5 (Collegeville, MN: Liturgical Press, 1992), 296–97, discusses the main possibilities without giving a strong opinion.

Paul's own accounts in Galatians, these can be partially explained if Acts was written at a later time, when the controversies were no longer burning questions.

For Whom Was Acts Written?

Both the Gospel of Luke and Acts are addressed to Theophilus. This common name in Greek means "lover of God," which could be a symbolic reference to all Christians. However, it seems likely that Luke was following the Greek and Roman practice of dedicating his writing to a patron of some sort and that Theophilus was an actual person to whom Luke dedicated his two-volume narrative. If so, Theophilus may have been a wealthy Christian, host of a house church, or a Christian leader who helped Luke get his two volumes copied and distributed (today we would say "published"). It can be presumed that the Gospel and Acts were meant for the Church and for Christians at large, and that Theophilus was someone who helped Luke to accomplish this goal.

When Was Acts Written?

The narrative ends with Paul's two-year house imprisonment in Rome, without reporting what happened to Paul at the end of those two years. However, Luke would not have known that Paul's imprisonment lasted "two full years" (Acts 28:30) without also knowing what happened to Paul at the end of that time, whether he was condemned and martyred or whether he was set free and continued his travels. (We know from Rom 15:24 that Paul had intended to go to Spain after visiting Rome: "I hope to see you in passing as I go to Spain.")

Luke's silence about Paul's fate at the end of Acts, therefore, is probably not because it had not yet befallen him but because the focus of Acts is not on the life of Paul. It is on the spread of the saving message of Jesus "to the ends of the earth." Luke deliberately ends on a high note, showing that the spread of God's word is not held back even by Paul's confinement. The book ends with an affirmation that even under house arrest, Paul continues to proclaim the kingdom and teach about Jesus Christ "with complete assurance and without hindrance" (Acts 28:31).

In Luke's account of Jesus' end-times discourse on the Mount of Olives, Jesus refers to events that would precede the destruction of the Jerusalem temple. He prophesies that there will be false prophets, wars, and natural disasters, "but it will not immediately be the end" (Luke 21:9). He adds, "Before all this happens, however, they will seize and persecute you, they will hand you over to the synagogues and to prisons, and they will have you led before kings and governors because of my name" (Luke 21:12). This period of persecution prophesied in Luke 21:12–19 is fulfilled in Acts when it befalls Stephen, James, Peter, Paul, and others.

Luke 21:20–24 then refers to the destruction of Jerusalem (which occurred in AD 70) as her "time of punishment" (v. 22), when her inhabitants will be slaughtered or taken captive to all the †Gentiles. This period of Jewish captivity after Jerusalem's destruction will last "until the times of the Gentiles are fulfilled" (v. 24). The implication is that after the fall of Jerusalem, when the Jews are scattered throughout the Roman world in exile, the Church's evangelization of Gentiles will increase dramatically. After that period will come the final cosmic signs and return of the Son of Man in judgment at the very end of the world (Luke 21:25–27). Most scholars date the death of Paul between AD 64 and 67, shortly before Jerusalem's destruction in 70. If, as many think, Luke wrote the Gospel and Acts after the destruction of Jerusalem, Luke may thus have regarded himself as living in the post-Jerusalem "times of the Gentiles," though Acts does not make explicit reference to that period.

Theological Themes

The framework for Luke's narrative is the biblical story of God's saving actions for his people, which began in the Old Testament and came to climactic fulfillment in Jesus' life, death, and resurrection. The Acts of the Apostles is a decisively new chapter in this story. In Acts the messianic age has dawned, and God is present in the world in a new way through the activity of Jesus and the Holy Spirit in the Church.

Through summaries, quotations, allusions, and echoes from the Old Testament, Luke places us distinctly within Scripture's perspective on God's plan of salvation. We read what happens to Jesus and the apostles within the overall narrative of a God who created all things "good" (Gen 1:31). However, human sin and rebellion infected the good creation with evil, alienating humans from their loving Creator. God initiated his plan to rescue estranged humanity through the people he formed from the seed of Abraham and accomplished this plan through the Messiah and Son of God sprung from their stock. Acts frequently refers back to Abraham, Moses, David, and the prophets to ground its narrative in the fulfillment of God's ancient promises.

One special theme in both Luke and Acts is that first Jesus (Luke 2:32) and then, in imitation of him, his followers such as Paul and Barnabas (Acts 13:47) exercise the role of the Servant of the Lord. The theme of the servant is rooted in the biblical depiction of Moses as God's servant in the exodus (Num 12:7). The prophet Isaiah develops this theme, describing a humble Servant of the Lord to whom God says: "It is too little . . . for you to be my servant, / to raise up the tribes of Jacob, / and restore the survivors of Israel; I will make you a light to the nations, / that my salvation may reach to the ends of the earth" (Isa 49:6). Luke understands this prophecy as fulfilled in both Jesus and his followers, who are to be "a light to the nations, that you may bring salvation to the ends of the earth" (Acts 13:47, author's translation). Although Jesus ministered primarily to his fellow Jews, the disciples in Acts specifically reached out to Gentiles ("the nations") as well as to Jews. As in the book of Isaiah, so also in Acts, this ministry to Gentiles includes a strong proclamation that there is only one God. This theme of †monotheism is depicted in Paul's occasionally humorous conflicts with idolatry and superstition.

Perhaps the principal theme in Acts is that Jesus' followers are his witnesses, who like him are filled with the Holy Spirit and empowered to speak and act in his name. The risen Jesus prophesies their witness in Acts 1:8, which is a skeleton outline of the plot of Acts: "You will receive power when the holy Spirit comes upon you, and you will be my witnesses in Jerusalem, throughout Judea and Samaria, and to the ends of the earth."[2]

Reading Acts Today

Today we find Acts to be a fascinating historical account of the beginning and initial spread of the Church through the witness of founding heroes like Peter, Stephen, Philip, Paul, and their coworkers. But Acts is not meant merely to inform us about the ancient church. It provides a paradigm for the life and mission of the Church today. As Pope Paul VI wrote in his apostolic letter on evangelization, Acts "bears witness to a privileged and in a sense exemplary moment of [the Church's] missionary effort which will . . . leave its mark on the whole history of the Church."[3] In the heroes of the earliest Church, we see models of how the risen Lord acts in and through his people today and of how we can respond to the Spirit's promptings.

Acts depicts the Church as filled with missionary dynamism. Apostles, deacons, prophets, and ordinary believers are all used powerfully by the Spirit to

2. Readers may discern other themes in Acts by considering the entries in the Index of Pastoral Topics beginning on p. 390.
3. *On Evangelization in the Modern World* (*Evangelii Nuntiandi*), 51.

draw others to Christ, and even to do signs and wonders in his name. Luke also portrays the character traits essential for sharing in Christ's mission: love of God and others, willingness to suffer for the sake of the gospel, obedience to the Holy Spirit, courage, faithfulness, endurance, boldness, and fervent intercessory prayer. Acts can thus renew our understanding of the evangelistic vocation of the Church and of our call to evangelize as individual believers in Christ. As Pope Paul VI stated, "Evangelizing is in fact the grace and vocation proper to the Church, her deepest identity. She exists in order to evangelize."[4] Saint John Paul II wrote even more strongly in a letter to all the Christian faithful: "We must rekindle in ourselves the impetus of the beginnings and allow ourselves to be filled with the ardor of the apostolic preaching which followed Pentecost. We must revive in ourselves the burning conviction of Paul, who cried out: 'Woe to me if I do not preach the Gospel' (1 Cor 9:16)."[5]

Another reason that Acts is timely today is that the cultural context in which the Church finds herself is in some ways more like that of the first-century Church than it has been at any time since. Vast numbers of people in contemporary society are ignorant of Christ and of the biblical worldview. Many are living a pagan, hedonistic lifestyle—not unlike the Gentiles whom Paul encountered in his missionary journeys throughout the Roman Empire. Social patterns often run counter to basic values such as the dignity of the person, the sanctity of life, or the Christian vision of marriage, sexuality, and family. Christians often find themselves subject to state pressure to conform to a secular agenda, and publicly witnessing to Christ sometimes provokes mockery, hostility, or even persecution.

As Christians we believe that Acts, like the entire Bible, is the word of God in human language. To understand what Luke, the inspired human author, intended, we employ historical-critical methods to uncover the meaning of the book in its first-century setting. Understanding the original sense helps us avoid †eisegesis, naively reading our contemporary biases into the Bible. On the other hand, because we recognize God as the ultimate author of the Bible, we understand Acts as God's word to us and to all Christians. We accept it as authoritative for our own lives and for our witness to the world.

Catholics interpret Acts within the context of the whole of Sacred Scripture as it has been elucidated in the Church's creeds, dogma, worship, sacraments, and tradition; we take into account the perspective of saints, scholars, and Church teaching, both ancient and modern. Unlike some early practitioners of

---

4. Ibid., 14.
5. *Novo Millennio Ineunte* (*At the Beginning of the New Millennium*), 40.

historical criticism, we do not regard dogma as obstructing our understanding of the Bible, but rather as shedding light on it. Studying this inspired account of the earliest years of the Church increases our faith in the power of God, raises our expectations of what God can do in and through us, and helps us understand how the Spirit and his gifts can operate in the lives of all who commit themselves to the Church's mission of evangelization.

Outline of Acts

Plan of Acts: Witness to Jesus in Jerusalem, Judea, and Samaria, and to the Ends of the Earth (1:8)

    I. Preface (1:1–2)

   II. Commission and Empowerment of the Disciples (1:3–2:13)

       A. Jesus' Farewell and Commission to Witness (1:3–8)

       B. Jesus' Ascension (1:9–11)

       C. Prayer in the Upper Room (1:12–14)

       D. Replacement of Judas (1:15–26)

       E. Pentecostal Empowerment by the Spirit (2:1–13)

  III. The Word of God in Jerusalem (2:14–8:4)

       A. Peter's Inaugural Address to Jews in Jerusalem (2:14–41)

       B. First Summary: Life in the Jerusalem Church (2:42–47)

       C. Peter's Healing of a Lame Man and Temple Speech (3:1–26)

       D. Peter and John before the Sanhedrin and Prayer of the Community (4:1–31)

       E. Second Summary: Sharing in Community Life (4:32–35)

       F. Positive and Negative Examples of This Sharing (4:36–5:11)

       G. Third Summary: Apostles' Signs and Wonders (5:12–16)

       H. Apostles before the Sanhedrin (5:17–42)

       I. Expansion of Community Leadership: The Seven (6:1–7)

       J. Stephen's Ministry, Discourse, and Martyrdom (6:8–8:1a)

       K. Persecution and Scattering of Disciples from Jerusalem (8:1b–4)

  IV. The Word of God in Judea and Samaria (8:5–12:25)

       A. Philip Evangelizes in Samaria and Judea (8:5–40)

    4. Paul before the Sanhedrin, Transfer to Caesarea (22:30–23:35)

    5. Trial before Felix and Imprisonment at Caesarea (24:1–27)

    6. Paul Appeals to Caesar, Relates His Call to Festus and Agrippa (25:1–26:32)

F. Journey to Rome, Shipwreck, Final Testimony in Rome (27:1–28:31)

    1. Sea Journey to Rome, Storm, Shipwreck (27:1–44)

    2. Arrival in Rome, House Arrest and Testimony (28:1–31)

Open Ending of Acts (28:30–31): "He remained for two full years in his lodgings. He received all who came to him, and with complete assurance and without hindrance he proclaimed the kingdom of God and taught about the Lord Jesus Christ."

Luke's Introduction to Acts

Acts 1:1–11

Luke's Gospel left off in the middle of the action. The risen Jesus ascended into heaven after commissioning his followers to preach in his name to all nations. He had instructed them to wait in Jerusalem and promised that he would send the Holy Spirit to empower them. But before reporting this event, Luke's Gospel ends with the disciples' worshiping God in the temple. Readers might wonder how Jesus' promise would come true and how his commission would be carried out. Here at the beginning of Acts, Luke resumes his account, retelling the last scene of the previous installment to bring the readers back into the flow of the story.

A Sequel to the Gospel Story (1:1–2)

¹In the first book, Theophilus, I dealt with all that Jesus did and taught ²until the day he was taken up, after giving instructions through the holy Spirit to the apostles whom he had chosen.

NT: Luke 1:1–4; 24:45–51
Catechism: "all that Jesus did and taught," 512
Lectionary: Acts 1:1–11: Ascension of the Lord (Years A–C)

1:1–2   Luke's reference to his Gospel as **the first book** highlights that Acts is a second book or sequel that continues the story begun in the Gospel. He first addresses **Theophilus** directly (see Luke 1:3). Though we know nothing about

25

Theophilus, most scholars believe he was the patron, the person of means and influence who helped Luke get his Gospel published and distributed. His name has a further possible significance. In Greek, *Theo-philos* means "lover of God." Thus Theophilus can stand symbolically for all readers of Acts, lovers and beloved of God.

Luke summarizes the content of his Gospel as **all that Jesus did and taught** before his ascension. A literal translation of the Greek would be "all that Jesus *began* to do and teach" (RSV, NIV). This remarkable phrase clarifies why Luke sees a sequel as necessary. If the Gospel narrates all that Jesus *began* to do and teach, this volume recounts what Jesus will *continue* to do and teach through the ministry of his disciples when they are filled with his Spirit.

The Gospel of Luke reported Jesus' activities **until the day he was taken up** to heaven in his ascension. Before this final departure he gave **instructions through the holy Spirit**[1] **to the apostles whom he had chosen,**[2] to equip them further for their leadership role. We know the risen Jesus' instructions included an explanation of why it had been necessary for Israel's Messiah to suffer and die and then be raised (Luke 24:26–27, 46–47). We may suppose his instructions included guidance on leading the Church after his ascension.

Jesus Prepares His Apostles for His Departure (1:3–5)

---

[3]**He presented himself alive to them by many proofs after he had suffered, appearing to them during forty days and speaking about the kingdom of God.** [4]**While meeting with them, he enjoined them not to depart from Jerusalem, but to wait for "the promise of the Father about which you have heard me speak;** [5]**for John baptized with water, but in a few days you will be baptized with the holy Spirit."**

OT: Isa 44:2–3; Ezek 39:29; Joel 3:1–2
NT: Luke 3:16; 24:49; John 16:12–13; Acts 13:30–31; 1 Cor 15:3–8
Catechism: appearances of the risen Jesus, 641–44; Jesus' ascension, 659–64; promise of the Holy Spirit, 729
Liturgy: Acts 1:3–8: confirmation; Acts 1:1–11: ascension of the Lord (Years A–C)

1. The NAB does not capitalize "holy," presumably to indicate that the Holy Spirit was not yet a fixed title for the Third Person of the Trinity.
2. The Greek syntax is ambiguous and scholars disagree as to whether the phrase "through the Holy Spirit" goes with "giving instructions" (as in the NAB, NRSV, NIV) or with "chose the apostles" (as in the NJB), that is, whether Luke describes the Spirit as influencing Jesus' final instructions or his choice of the apostles. The context seems to support the majority of translations, which prefer the former interpretation.

After addressing Theophilus directly, Luke resumes his story. First he re- 1:3
counts what Jesus did between his resurrection and ascension. Luke's Gospel
reported Jesus' ascension into heaven (Luke 24:51) but left the timing vague.
Now Luke clarifies that time frame: after Jesus' resurrection and before his
ascension, he spent forty days in preparing his disciples for his departure and
their future mission.

Luke emphasizes that Jesus **presented himself alive to them by many proofs**.
According to Luke's Gospel, the risen Jesus not only appeared to the apostles
but also let them touch him and ate some fish before them so they could be assured he was truly risen and not a ghost or spiritual apparition (Luke 24:36–43).
Those who encountered the risen Lord did not need arguments to be fully
convinced that he is alive (see sidebar).[3] Acts explicitly notes that the risen
Jesus showed himself only to his followers, who then had to witness to others about his resurrection (Acts 13:30–31). He will show himself to all people
only at his return for judgment at the end of the world (Luke 21:26–27). Thus,
although Jesus' appearances were incontestable proofs for the apostles who
saw him, later Christians depend by faith on the testimony of those apostolic
witnesses that the Jesus who "suffered, died, and was buried" (Nicene Creed)
is now truly risen and alive.[4]

The **forty days** are the period between Jesus' resurrection and ascension.
Jesus' many post-resurrection appearances (1 Cor 15:3–8) and further instruction of his disciples took place during this time (except for the later
appearance to Paul, who stresses the uniqueness of his own case in 1 Cor
15:8). Later †Gnostic heretics would claim that this period of post-Easter appearances extended to eighteen months, apparently to make more plausible
their claim that the risen Jesus revealed a whole new secret religion to them.[5]
Such later heresies illustrate how providential is Acts's mentioning a definite
endpoint—Jesus' visible ascension after forty days—after which no more appearances were to be expected.

The number forty calls to mind biblical events in which God's people received
divine revelation: the forty days when Moses received the law on Mount Sinai
and the forty years when God led Israel in the desert (Exod 24:18; Deut 8:2).
Just as the number forty appeared at the birth of the nation of Israel and its
instruction, so too it marks the birth and instruction of the Church. Moreover,

---

3. See Jaroslav Pelikan, *The Acts of the Apostles*, Brazos Theological Commentary on the Bible (Grand Rapids: Brazos Press, 2005), 96–98 on "Miracles as 'Signs.'"
4. Compare Richard Bauckham, *Jesus and the Eyewitnesses: The Gospels as Eyewitness Testimony* (Grand Rapids: Eerdmans, 2006).
5. Irenaeus, *Against Heresies* 1.3.2 [*ANF* 1:319]; Pelikan, *Acts*, 39.

Miracles: Proofs or Signs?

BIBLICAL BACKGROUND

Are the miracles in Acts proofs that compel belief or signs that require some further explanation to be understood? Luke is aware of both kinds of evidence, which are described by the Greek philosopher Aristotle (fourth century BC). In his *Rhetoric*, Aristotle distinguishes between two legal terms: a "sign" (*sēmeion*), evidence needing further explanation to be fully persuasive in court; and a "proof" (*tekmērion*), self-evident judicial proof not needing any explanation. Aristotle's example of a sign is a bloody knife that is insufficient to convict the accused without further evidence that the knife was found with him. His example of a proof is a birth more than nine months after a husband's absence in the army: the timing proves that the child is not the husband's.

The word Luke uses for "proofs" of Jesus' resurrection in Acts 1:3 is *tekmērion*. Thus Luke regards the multiple appearances of the risen Jesus as self-evident proofs to the apostles that Jesus is alive after his death. Luke treats most other miracles not as self-evident *proofs* but as *signs* that require explanation or evidence to be persuasive. For example, Peter's healing of a lame man is a "sign" (4:22) because it requires Peter's explanation to be understood. The healing was caused not by Peter's power but by the "God of Abraham," who glorified Jesus by raising him from the dead and healed this lame man through faith in Jesus' name (3:12–16). The signs done by the disciples in Jesus' name attest that Jesus is alive and are an invitation to faith in him, but faith always remains a free decision.

---

just as Jesus underwent forty days of preparation for his earthly ministry (Luke 4:1–2), his disciples are now prepared for their mission during the same length of time. By emphasizing the number forty, Luke underlines that the life of Jesus is relived in the Church.

During this interval, the risen Jesus continued to teach his followers about the **kingdom of God**, which had also been his principal message during his earthly ministry. The kingdom of God is the fulfillment of Israel's hope that God would one day fully manifest his sovereignty over the whole world, beginning with Israel (see Isa 24:23; 52:7). Even with this additional teaching, the apostles' response in verse 6 will show that their understanding of God's kingdom remained limited.[6]

---

6. Luke presumes that his readers know what "kingdom of God" means, for he does not define it either in his Gospel or in Acts (Joseph A. Fitzmyer, *The Acts of the Apostles*, Anchor Bible 31 [New York: Doubleday, 1998], 199).

Before taking any action, the apostles are to wait until they are empowered   by the Spirit from on high, since only then will they have the divine grace and power they need to carry out their daunting commission. As Jesus' farewell address in the Gospel of John indicates, he had more to teach his disciples than they could understand without the aid of the Spirit (John 16:12–13). Here the risen Jesus enjoins them **not to depart from Jerusalem, but to wait for "the promise of the Father . . . for John baptized with water, but in a few days you will be baptized with the holy Spirit."** Jesus thus reinforces his command in Luke 24:49: "I am sending the promise of my Father upon you; but stay in the city until you are clothed with power from on high."

The promise that believers would be "baptized with the holy Spirit" is one of the most frequently repeated prophecies in the New Testament.[7] John had contrasted his own baptism in water with the baptism of the mightier One to come: "I am baptizing you with water. . . . He will baptize you with the holy Spirit and fire" (Luke 3:16). The word "baptize" in Greek means to dip, drench, or immerse in water. It recalls the biblical promises that in the final times God would pour out his Spirit like water on thirsty ground.[8] The phrase "baptized with the holy Spirit" conveys a vivid image of what would soon occur. The disciples would receive a far greater baptism than that of John; they would be immersed in God's own divine life! This promise will be realized at Pentecost, and then in Christian baptism, which involves both water and the Spirit's indwelling and empowerment. In Acts 2 Luke will describe how this baptism with the Spirit fills the disciples with God's love, life, power, and insight into his work in the world.

Reflection and Application (1:3–5)

It is impossible to exaggerate the importance for Christian belief and practice of the insistence that Jesus is alive (Acts 1:3). He is not merely a "historical Jesus" who lived and died in the first century. Jesus presented himself as alive to the apostles, no more to die, and he is still alive today and forever.

Christian faith is grounded in the eyewitness testimony of the apostles who encountered Jesus alive after his death. This faith has been confirmed from the first century till now by the Church's experience of Jesus as alive and present to us in our worship, prayer, and communal life. From the very beginning of Christianity, Christians have baptized new believers "in the name of the Father,

---

7. It is announced by John the Baptist in all four Gospels (Matt 3:11; Mark 1:8; Luke 3:16; John 1:33) and by Jesus himself here in Acts 1:5 and is recalled by Peter in Acts 11:16. See also Jesus' promises of the Holy Spirit (the Paraclete or Advocate) in John 14:15–17, 25–26; 15:26; 16:7–15.
8. See Isa 32:15; 44:2–3; Ezek 39:29; Joel 3:1; Zech 12:10.

Rediscovering the Baptism with the Holy Spirit

LIVING TRADITION

Commenting on Jesus' promise that the disciples would be "baptized with the holy Spirit," Pope Benedict XVI noted that Acts presents Pentecost as the fulfillment of that promise and therefore "the crowning moment of Jesus' whole mission." The pope explained that the grace of Pentecost is not confined to the past but is a gift to be desired, prayed for, and rediscovered today:

> In effect, Jesus' whole mission was aimed at giving the Spirit of God to men and baptizing them in the "bath" of regeneration. This was realized through his glorification (cf. John 7:39), that is, through his death and resurrection: Then the Spirit of God was poured out in a superabundant way, like a waterfall able to purify every heart, to extinguish the flames of evil and ignite the fire of divine love in the world. . . .
>
> Today I would like to extend this invitation to everyone: Let us rediscover, dear brothers and sisters, the beauty of being baptized in the Holy Spirit; let us be aware again of our baptism and our confirmation, sources of grace that are always present. Let us ask the Virgin Mary to obtain a renewed Pentecost for the Church again today, a Pentecost that will spread in everyone the joy of living and witnessing to the Gospel.[a]

a. Benedict XVI, *Regina Coeli* message, May 11, 2008.

and of the Son, and of the holy Spirit" (Matt 28:19). From the beginning Christians have experienced the presence of the living Jesus in their midst, especially in their celebration of the Eucharist, as he promised: "Behold, I am with you always, until the end of the age" (Matt 28:20).[9]

Mission to the Whole Earth (1:6–8)

---

⁶When they had gathered together they asked him, "Lord, are you at this time going to restore the kingdom to Israel?" ⁷He answered them, "It is not for you to know the times or seasons that the Father has established by his own authority. ⁸But you will receive power when the holy Spirit comes upon you, and you will be my witnesses in Jerusalem, throughout Judea and Samaria, and to the ends of the earth."

---

9. See Larry W. Hurtado, *Lord Jesus Christ: Devotion to Jesus in Earliest Christianity* (Grand Rapids: Eerdmans, 2003).

OT: 2 Sam 7:16; Isa 43:10–12; 49:6; Dan 7:27
NT: Matt 28:19–20; Luke 2:30–32; 24:49; Acts 13:47
Catechism: the Church founded on the apostles, 857–60; coming of the kingdom, 672–73; out-pouring of the Spirit, 1287
Lectionary: Acts 1:1–11: Ascension of the Lord (Years A–C); Acts 1:3–8: Confirmation

The disciples' question raises concerns that will reappear in various ways in Acts: what, when, and for whom is God's **kingdom**? The disciples probably have in mind God's promises to restore the royal kingdom of David (Jer 23:5–6; Amos 9:11–12), which had been defunct since the sixth century BC. Many of their Jewish contemporaries expected that the †Messiah would reestablish the political kingdom of Israel and overthrow the oppressive Roman government. It may be that the disciples had such an understanding of the restoration of Israel. But Jesus uses the question as an opportunity to further expand their understanding of God's kingdom. Jesus' preaching of the kingdom of God throughout his public ministry was rooted in the Hebrew understanding of God the Creator as having dominion over not only his own Jewish people but also all people (Tob 13:11; Ps 99:1–2; Isa 49:6). Jesus taught his disciples to pray, "Your kingdom come," that is, "Your will be done, on earth as in heaven" (Matt 6:10). God's kingdom is wherever Jesus himself is present and God's will is loved and obeyed. Here Jesus indicates that the kingdom will be restored not by military or political conquest but by establishing his kingship in human lives through the witness of his disciples (v. 8). Jesus already reigns as king (Acts 2:34–36), although his kingdom will be fully and visibly realized only at the end of history.

1:6

Jesus puts off the disciples' question about a specific time for the restoration of Israel's kingdom with a simple answer: **"It is not for you to know the times or seasons."** Questions about God's timetable were often raised by Jews in the first century (and continue to be asked by Christians today), but Jesus refuses to answer this question. His disciples will receive God's power, not to exercise political authority, but to be his witnesses. And their testimony will not be related to Israel as a nation, but to God's saving authority over all nations.

1:7

"But you will receive power when the holy Spirit comes upon you," Jesus further explains. This power from the Spirit will give them the courage and guidance to be able to witness to Jesus. Jesus' promise of the Spirit's empowerment calls the disciples back from their concerns about "times or seasons" to his previous command to wait for "the promise of the Father," the promise that they "will be baptized with the holy Spirit" (vv. 4–5). Just as Jesus' own baptism in the Jordan, when the Spirit descended on him, inaugurated his public ministry

1:8

Fig. 1. The initial spread of the gospel: from Jerusalem throughout Judea and Samaria (Acts 1:8).

(Luke 3:21–22), so the apostles' baptism in the Spirit at Pentecost will launch their ministry. Up to this point the apostles have been afraid and hidden behind locked doors (John 20:19). The coming of the Spirit will break the crippling power of all such fear.

Jesus' promise, **"You will be my witnesses,"** introduces a major theme in Acts. Christian faith is grounded in the testimony of the apostles, both to Jews (Acts 2:32; 3:15; 4:33; 5:29–32) and to Gentiles (10:39–42; 13:30–31). The apostles had walked with Jesus, seen his mighty acts, recognized him as God's Messiah, and encountered him alive from the dead. Once they are empowered by the Spirit at Pentecost, they will boldly proclaim what they have seen and heard, becoming witnesses to God's saving acts in history.

Verse 8 functions as a skeleton table of contents, identifying the major events in Acts. The apostles' witness to Jesus will begin **in Jerusalem** after they have received the Holy Spirit (Acts 2–7). It later will spread out through **Judea and Samaria** (Acts 8–12), extending to the Mediterranean coast through Peter. Peter will be the first to preach to Gentiles (Acts 10–11). Finally, Paul will bring the witness all the way to Rome (Acts 13–28), the center of the empire, from where it can radiate out to **the ends of the earth**. The "ends of the earth" does not refer to a geographical locality but means that the mission is unlimited in scope.[10]

10. See Kenneth Duncan Litwak, *Echoes of Scripture in Luke-Acts: Telling the History of God's People Intertextually*, Journal for the Study of the New Testament: Supplement Series 282 (London, New York: T&T Clark International, 2005), 152–53.

The Mission of the Servant of the Lord

Jesus' commission to the apostles to be his witnesses "to the ends of the earth" (Acts 1:8) is an echo of God's commission to his servant in Isa 49:6: "I will make you a light to the nations, that my salvation may reach to the ends of the earth." The prophet Isaiah often wrote about this Servant of the Lord whose mission was to be God's witness to the †Gentiles. The servant embodies the vocation of Israel that began with Abraham (Gen 12:3): to be a blessing to all nations by bringing them knowledge of the one true God (see Isa 43:10–13; 44:8).

The mission of the Servant of the Lord is fulfilled in Jesus. At Jesus' presentation in the temple, Simeon prophesied that Jesus was "a light for revelation to the Gentiles, and glory for your people Israel" (Luke 2:30–32, echoing Isa 49:6). After his resurrection Jesus applies the servant's mission to his apostles, who are to witness to all nations about God's gift of salvation in him (Acts 1:8). Paul and Barnabas later ascribe the same mission of the Servant of the Lord to themselves: "For so the Lord has commanded us, 'I have made you a light to the Gentiles, that you may be an instrument of salvation to the ends of the earth'" (Acts 13:47). The missionary vocation of Israel, to testify to all nations that the Lord is the one God and savior of all, finds fulfillment in the Church, †eschatological Israel.

Reflection and Application (1:6–8)

Jesus' command that the apostles *wait* until they receive the Holy Spirit's power (Luke 24:49; Acts 1:4–5, 8) is significant not only for the apostolic Church but also for the Church today. Aware of the great needs of the world and a multitude of ministry opportunities, we can be tempted to rush out and try to accomplish things on our own rather than waiting for the Holy Spirit's empowerment and guidance. But merely human resources cannot accomplish the supernatural mission that God has given the Church.

Recent popes have summoned all Catholics to a "new evangelization," to bring the good news of Christ anew not only to distant non-Christian lands but also to the secularized post-Christian societies of the West. Saint John Paul II wrote of the urgency of this task: "I sense that the moment has come to commit all of the Church's energies to a new evangelization. . . . No believer in Christ, no institution of the Church, can avoid this supreme duty: to proclaim Christ to all peoples."[11] In order to carry out this great task, Catholics today are

---

11. *Redemptoris Missio*, 3.

as much in need of the presence and power of the Holy Spirit as were the first Christians. Indeed, Pope Paul VI insisted that "the Holy Spirit is the principal agent of evangelization," since "it is He who impels each individual to proclaim the Gospel, and it is He who in the depths of consciences causes the word of salvation to be accepted and understood."[12] It follows that in order to carry out the new evangelization, the Church needs a new Pentecost. In his visit to the United States in 2008, Pope Benedict XVI prayed: "Let us implore from God the grace of a new Pentecost for the Church in America. May tongues of fire, combining burning love of God and neighbor with zeal for the spread of Christ's Kingdom, descend on all present!"[13]

Many of the Church's prayers to the Spirit begin "Come, Holy Spirit!" Christians have already received the Holy Spirit in baptism and confirmation, yet are continually in need of a fresh outpouring of the Spirit to carry out the mission that God has entrusted to each one of us. With the spiritual power we too receive "when the holy Spirit comes upon" us, we in our own generation are able to continue the apostles' testimony that Jesus is risen and present among us.

Jesus' Ascension to Heaven and the Apostles' Mission on Earth (1:9–11)

[9]**When he had said this, as they were looking on, he was lifted up, and a cloud took him from their sight. [10]While they were looking intently at the sky as he was going, suddenly two men dressed in white garments stood beside them. [11]They said, "Men of Galilee, why are you standing there looking at the sky? This Jesus who has been taken up from you into heaven will return in the same way as you have seen him going into heaven."**

OT: Exod 24:15–18; 2 Kings 2:9–10; Dan 7:13–14
NT: Luke 21:27–28; John 16:7
Catechism: Jesus' ascension, 659–64; cloud as symbol of the Holy Spirit, 697
Lectionary: Acts 1:1–11: Ascension of the Lord (Years A–C)

Luke's description of Jesus' ascension looks backward to its Old Testament foreshadowings and forward to Jesus' prophesied return at the end of time. As the prophet Elijah was about to depart this earth, according to 2 Kings 2:9–10,

---

12. *Evangelii Nuntiandi*, 75.
13. Homily at St. Patrick's Cathedral, New York City, April 19, 2008.

Elisha asked him for a double share of his spirit. Elijah responded that this request would be granted only if Elisha saw him being taken into heaven. Elisha did see Elijah taken up in a flaming chariot, and consequently he received Elijah's spirit and power to work miracles. The apostles see Jesus being taken into heaven, recalling the confirming sign that Elisha had received. Readers can thus be assured that the apostles will receive Jesus' Spirit and work miracles as Jesus did in the Gospel. Likewise Moses imparted his spirit to his assistant Joshua before his departure, ensuring that Joshua would carry on his mission to lead Israel (Deut 34:9).[14] Such biblical allusions demonstrate the continuity between the Spirit-filled ministry of Jesus and that of his apostles and their successors. The scriptural theme of the passing on of Spirit-filled prophetic vocations—from Moses to Joshua, from Elijah to Elisha, and now from Jesus to his apostles—shows that succession of authority has always been part of God's saving plan.

As Moses ascended Mount Sinai in a cloud (Exod 19:16–20; 24:15–18) to receive the gift of the law and then give it to the people, so Jesus is now **lifted up** to heaven on a **cloud** to receive the gift of the Spirit and give it to his Church (see Acts 2:33). Often in Scripture a cloud represents God's presence (see Exod 13:21; 16:10). The angelic figures' appearing as **two men dressed in white garments** recall Moses and Elijah, who appeared with Jesus in the cloud at the transfiguration (Luke 9:29–35). **1:9**

As the disciples are **looking intently at the sky as he was going**, the two men chide them, **"Men of Galilee, why are you standing there looking at the sky?"** They remind the disciples that Jesus had prophesied his †parousia, his return in glory on a cloud at the end of the world (Luke 21:27–28): **"This Jesus who has been taken up from you into heaven will return in the same way as you have seen him going into heaven,"** that is, on a cloud. Jesus' ascending in a cloud alludes to Daniel's vision of "One like a son of man" coming on the clouds of heaven to receive everlasting dominion from God (Dan 7:13–14). Jesus had indicated that he himself is the Son of Man foreseen by Daniel who will come with power and glory (Luke 21:27). **1:10–11**

Jesus' ascension does not imply his absence from the Church. Rather, as Acts will show, he will be present and active in a new way through the Holy Spirit (see John 14:18). As his disciples speak and act "in his name," Jesus himself will be at work through them (see Acts 3:5–16).

---

14. According to Jewish tradition, Moses too had been taken up into heaven; see the Jewish apocryphal work *Ascension of Moses*.

Reflection and Application (1:9–11)

God provided that the apostles would receive the Spirit and power of Jesus so that his saving work could be continued through them. We can rely on the presence of that same Spirit and power in the Church today so that through us God can extend his saving work to our generation also. Because we, like the apostles, have assurance that Jesus will return at the end of the world, we should not regret his physical absence after the ascension (John 16:7), but focus instead on his presence through the Spirit and on the mission he has entrusted to us. Although we look forward to Jesus' coming in glory, we are not to focus on the "times or seasons" when he will return. Nor are we to get distracted from serving our neighbors and witnessing to Jesus by elaborate speculation about how the end times will play out.[15]

15. See William S. Kurz, *What Does the Bible Say about the End Times? A Catholic View* (Cincinnati: St. Anthony Messenger Press, 2004), a Catholic reading of biblical end-times prophecy in response to the Left Behind novels by Tim LaHaye and Jerry B. Jenkins.

Prayer in the Upper Room

Acts 1:12–26

As the disciples await the coming of the Holy Spirit, they offer us a pattern for spiritual renewal in our homes, parishes, communities, and world. The pattern begins with obedience to the command of Jesus and continues with the fervent prayer of the gathered community. Their concerted prayer leads to their understanding of how Scripture applies to their situation and to divine guidance in finding a replacement for Judas. The disciples' prayer also prepares them for the coming of the Holy Spirit.

The Apostles and Mary Pray for the Holy Spirit (1:12–14)

¹²Then they returned to Jerusalem from the mount called Olivet, which is near Jerusalem, a sabbath day's journey away. ¹³When they entered the city they went to the upper room where they were staying, Peter and John and James and Andrew, Philip and Thomas, Bartholomew and Matthew, James son of Alphaeus, Simon the Zealot, and Judas son of James. ¹⁴All these devoted themselves with one accord to prayer, together with some women, and Mary the mother of Jesus, and his brothers.

OT: Gen 13:8; 14:16; 29:15; Deut 19:15; Isa 2:2–4
NT: Luke 6:13–16; 8:1–3; 22:14–38; John 19:26–27; Acts 3:1–11; Gal 3:28
Catechism: Mary praying with the Church, 726, 2617, 2673; prayer for the Holy Spirit, 1310, 2623
Lectionary: Our Lady of the Rosary; Seventh Sunday of Easter (Year A)

1:12 The eleven remaining apostles immediately obey the angels' command to stop gaping after the ascended Jesus and to follow Jesus' directives (v. 11). After they return **to Jerusalem,** they go **to the upper room** to pray. Jesus had told them to wait in Jerusalem, which the Old Testament portrays as the future location of God's special blessings on both Jews and Gentiles (Ps 87; Isa 2:2–4). It is unclear whether the upper room is the one where the Last Supper took place (Luke 22:12). It may be the house of Mary, John Mark's mother, where disciples later gathered to pray (Acts 12:12), or some other place in Jerusalem. In Acts, upper rooms are places where Jesus' resurrection power is displayed (see 9:36–41; 20:8–10).

This is the first mention in Acts of the **mount** from which Jesus ascended, **Olivet,** or Mount of Olives, which is close enough to **Jerusalem** that one can walk from it to the city without violating Jewish limitations on travel on the **sabbath.**[1] In Luke 24:50 Bethany is named as the site of the ascension, and Luke 19:29 clarifies that Bethany is on the Mount of Olives.

1:13 Luke repeats the names of the eleven remaining apostles, recalling Jesus' choice of the Twelve in Luke 6:13–16. The first two pairs of brothers called by Jesus are listed first—**Peter and John and James and Andrew.** But instead of pairing them as brothers—Peter and Andrew, James and John (as in Luke 6:14)—Luke first names the three who are most prominent in Acts, in order of their importance. Peter and John are Jesus' primary witnesses in Acts 3–5; James will be the first apostle to be martyred (Acts 12:2); Andrew will not be mentioned again. Two pairs come next in the list, **Philip and Thomas, Bartholomew and Matthew.** With the omission of the twelfth, Judas Iscariot, the last three are mentioned together, **James son of Alphaeus, Simon the Zealot, and Judas son of James.**

Luke emphasizes witness in pairs because Jesus sent out his apostles in pairs—the Twelve in Mark 6:7; the Seventy (or Seventy-two) in Luke 10:1. One reason Jesus may have done so is because, according to the law of Moses, legal testimony requires two witnesses (Deut 19:15; see 17:6). Luke later depicts the witnessing pairs Peter and John (Acts 3:1–11; 4:13) and Barnabas and Saul (Acts 11:25–30; 12:25; 13:2). Even today, it is a blessing and protection to be able to witness or minister in mutually supportive pairs rather than alone.

1:14 The eleven **devoted themselves with one accord to prayer.** A more literal translation would be that they "were persisting with one accord in prayer." Luke

1. Jews of Jesus' day were allowed to walk 2,000 cubits (less than a mile) on the Sabbath, according to rabbinic interpretation of Exod 16:29 and Num 35:5. See Joseph A. Fitzmyer, *The Acts of the Apostles,* Anchor Bible 31 (New York: Doubleday, 1998), 213.

calls attention to the *persistence* of the prayer of the earliest Jerusalem community (Acts 1:14; 2:42, 46; 6:4). Even more, he emphasizes that they prayed *together with one accord* (Greek *homothymadon*), just as at the sealing of the Old Covenant God's people had responded with one accord (*homothymadon*), "Everything the Lord has said, we will do" (Exod 19:8 LXX).[2] Such united prayer calls to mind Jesus' teaching in Matthew, "Where two or three are gathered together in my name, there am I in the midst of them" (18:20).

Luke goes out of his way to mention that the apostles were not alone in praying for the Spirit. They prayed **together with some women**. Because the coming of the Holy Spirit at Pentecost will bring about the birth of the Church, Luke emphasizes that not only the apostolic leaders but also a representative gathering of both men and women constituted the first Christian community. He prepared for this in his Gospel by mentioning that Jesus was accompanied in his travels not only by the Twelve but also by some women who sustained them from their means (Luke 8:1–3).

This emphasis on women as part of the original community at Pentecost also prepares for Peter's explanation in which he quotes the prophet Joel: "I will pour out a portion of my spirit upon all flesh. Your sons and your daughters shall prophesy" (Acts 2:17). Luke is noted for stressing the equal dignity not only of Jew and Gentile but also of male and female (as does Paul in Gal 3:28).

Luke goes out of his way to mention the presence of **Mary the mother of Jesus, and his brothers**. Mary was the first to receive the outpouring of the Holy Spirit (Luke 1:35). As the Holy Spirit overshadowed her to bring about the birth of Jesus, he will overshadow the 120 disciples at Pentecost to bring about the birth of the Church.

Reflection and Application (1:12–14)

The apostles, Mary, and other disciples' prayer for the Holy Spirit was vital preparation for their witness to Jesus' resurrection and for the birth of the Church. Luke presents the persistent, united communal prayer of these first members of the Church to us for imitation. If we want to find and do the will of God, we too, like the earliest followers of Jesus, should earnestly join our sisters and brothers in Christ, both clerical and lay, along with Jesus' mother Mary, in fervent and unified prayer for empowerment by the Holy Spirit.

The beginning of the twenty-first century has been marked by a revival of Catholic devotion to Mary. When Jesus confides his mother to "the disciple . . .

2. See sidebar on solidarity in fellowship and prayer, p. 86.

The Brothers of Jesus and Mary's Perpetual Virginity

LIVING TRADITION

At first reading, New Testament references to Jesus' brothers and sisters (see Mark 3:32) might give the impression that Mary had other children after Jesus. Yet from at least the second century onward, Christians expressed belief in Mary's perpetual virginity. Early Church Fathers such as Clement of Alexandria and Origen explained New Testament references to Jesus' brothers and sisters in other ways. They pointed out that Scripture refers to close relatives besides full siblings as "brother" or "sister." In Gen 13:8, Abraham refers to himself and his nephew Lot as "brothers" (NAB has "kindred," but both the original Hebrew and the Greek †Septuagint say "brothers"). Likewise in Gen 29:15 Laban calls his nephew Jacob his "brother" (NAB has "relative").

Two other biblical passages can be seen as counterevidence to the impression that Mary had other children. First, the story of the finding of the boy Jesus in the temple gives no hint that Joseph and Mary had any other children, either along on this pilgrimage or at home after Jesus returned with them "and was obedient to them" (Luke 2:51). Second, the dying Jesus entrusts his mother not to a blood relative but to his beloved disciple (John 19:26–27), implying that Mary had no other sons to whom to confide her. Thus there is biblical evidence (see also Catechism 500) to support the considerable extrabiblical testimony from the early Church for the doctrine of the perpetual virginity of Mary.

whom he loved" in John 19:25–27, that unnamed disciple stands for all who aspire to be Jesus' beloved disciples. Inspired by the example of Pope John Paul II and Mother Teresa of Calcutta, many students, seminarians, priests, and religious have been rediscovering traditional expressions of Marian piety such as the rosary and personal consecration to Jesus through Mary. Especially after the death of my own mother, I too have found myself turning more in prayer to Mary as my mother.

Choosing a Replacement for Judas (1:15–26)

¹⁵During those days Peter stood up in the midst of the brothers (there was a group of about one hundred and twenty persons in the one place). He said, ¹⁶"My brothers, the scripture had to be fulfilled which the holy Spirit spoke beforehand through the mouth of David, concerning Judas, who

was the guide for those who arrested Jesus. [17]He was numbered among us and was allotted a share in this ministry. [18]He bought a parcel of land with the wages of his iniquity, and falling headlong, he burst open in the middle, and all his insides spilled out. [19]This became known to everyone who lived in Jerusalem, so that the parcel of land was called in their language Akeldama, that is, Field of Blood. [20]For it is written in the Book of Psalms:

> 'Let his encampment become desolate,
>> and may no one dwell in it.'

And:

> 'May another take his office.'

[21]Therefore, it is necessary that one of the men who accompanied us the whole time the Lord Jesus came and went among us, [22]beginning from the baptism of John until the day on which he was taken up from us, become with us a witness to his resurrection." [23]So they proposed two, Joseph called Barsabbas, who was also known as Justus, and Matthias. [24]Then they prayed, "You, Lord, who know the hearts of all, show which one of these two you have chosen [25]to take the place in this apostolic ministry from which Judas turned away to go to his own place." [26]Then they gave lots to them, and the lot fell upon Matthias, and he was counted with the eleven apostles.

OT: Ps 69:26; 109:8
NT: Matt 27:3–10; Luke 22:30–32; 1 Tim 3:1
Catechism: witnesses to the resurrection, 642, 995; Judas, 597
Lectionary: Acts 1:15–17, 20a, 20c–26: Seventh Sunday of Easter (Year B); Feast of St. Matthias

Luke numbers the community members at **about one hundred and twenty**   **1:15**
persons, a round number that has symbolic significance.[3] Biblical Israel had twelve tribes. Later Jewish tradition considered ten men a *minyan*, or quorum, for communal prayer. The 120 members of the Christian community at prayer may symbolize a quorum of all twelve tribes of a restored Israel.

Peter is clearly the leader who presides over the proceedings and speaks for   **1:16–17**
the group. He asserts that Judas's betrayal and loss of ministry among the Twelve was foretold by Scripture (see Ps 41:10). By saying **the holy Spirit spoke**, Peter affirms the Jewish belief that Scripture is inspired by the Spirit (see Mark 12:36;

---

3. Luke often uses *about* to indicate a round number, sometimes as a historian's concession that he did not actually count the number of people, as in Luke 9:14, "Now the men there numbered about five thousand." Sometimes he uses *about* to relativize a number in order to introduce a biblical allusion. "About eight days" (instead of Matthew and Mark's "six days"), which introduces Luke's transfiguration account, foreshadows Jesus' resurrection on "the eighth day," the first day of the new week (Luke 9:28). See also Acts 19:7, "Altogether there were about twelve men."

2 Tim 3:16). The **scripture had to be fulfilled** about **Judas**, who had been one of the apostles but who guided **those who arrested Jesus**. This does not imply that Judas lacked free will but that God foreknew his betrayal and used it for the accomplishment of his plan. Judas had been **allotted a share** (*klēros*) **in this ministry**, but he forfeited this honor by his actions.

1:18–19   Although details of Judas's death and the purchase of the **Field of Blood** vary between this account and the version in Matt 27:3–10, both versions link Judas's betrayal for money and a field purchased with that money. They also share the point that Judas died after betraying Jesus and that his blood money was of no benefit to him. In **falling headlong**, or prostrate, Judas suffered the punishment of the wicked described in Wis 4:19.

1:20   As betrayer of Jesus, Judas removed himself from the rest of the Twelve. Peter quotes from two psalms that express the fate of the wicked: "**Let his encampment become desolate, and may no one dwell in it**" (quoting a version of Ps 69:26) and "**May another take his office**" (Ps 109:8). The Greek word for "office," *episkopē*, was later used by the early Christians to refer to a leadership position in the local church (see 1 Tim 3:1) and is the origin of the English word "episcopacy." Jesus promised the Twelve that in his kingdom "you will sit on thrones judging the twelve tribes of Israel" (Luke 22:30). The office vacated by the defecting Judas had to be filled because the apostolic number twelve is symbolic of the restored faithful Israel.

This is Peter's first act in fulfillment of Jesus' commission to him at the Last Supper: "I have prayed that your own faith may not fail; and once you have turned back, you must strengthen your brothers" (Luke 22:32). By initiating and leading the community's restoration of the original number of the Twelve, Peter begins to strengthen his brothers.

1:21–22   Judas's replacement among the twelve apostles had to meet a criterion: to be **a witness to his resurrection** the candidate must have **accompanied us the whole time the Lord Jesus came and went among us**. The period in question was Jesus' entire public ministry, **beginning from the baptism of John until the day on which he was taken up from us**.

1:23–26   The community **proposed two** candidates who met this criterion: **Joseph called Barsabbas** and **Matthias**. The ultimate choice, however, they left to the risen Jesus: "**You, Lord, who know the hearts of all.**" They prayed to Jesus to **show which one of these two** he had chosen to replace Judas in the **apostolic ministry**. Their method of discovering the risen Jesus' choice was to cast **lots**, a biblical method of seeking God's will, and especially of assigning the duties of priests (Luke 1:9).[4]

4. See Lev 16:8; Num 33:54; Josh 19:1–40; 1 Chron 24:3–5.

The Coming of the Holy Spirit and the Birth of the Church

Acts 2

In Luke's Gospel, Jesus' ministry was launched when the Holy Spirit descended upon him as he prayed after his baptism in the Jordan (Luke 3:21–22). Here in Acts, the Church's ministry now likewise begins when the Holy Spirit descends upon the one hundred twenty men and women gathered in the upper room in Jerusalem. The "promise of the Father" that Jesus instructed his followers to await (Acts 1:4; see Luke 24:49) is now bestowed. The mission of Jesus, to be light for the Gentiles and glory for God's people Israel (Luke 2:32), is to be perpetuated by his followers, who are now empowered by his Holy Spirit.

Pentecost: The Holy Spirit Comes (2:1–13)

¹When the time for Pentecost was fulfilled, they were all in one place together. ²And suddenly there came from the sky a noise like a strong driving wind, and it filled the entire house in which they were. ³Then there appeared to them tongues as of fire, which parted and came to rest on each one of them. ⁴And they were all filled with the holy Spirit and began to speak in different tongues, as the Spirit enabled them to proclaim.

⁵Now there were devout Jews from every nation under heaven staying in Jerusalem. ⁶At this sound, they gathered in a large crowd, but they were confused because each one heard them speaking in his own language. ⁷They were astounded, and in amazement they asked, "Are not all these

people who are speaking Galileans? ⁸Then how does each of us hear them in his own native language? ⁹We are Parthians, Medes, and Elamites, inhabitants of Mesopotamia, Judea and Cappadocia, Pontus and Asia, ¹⁰Phrygia and Pamphylia, Egypt and the districts of Libya near Cyrene, as well as travelers from Rome, ¹¹both Jews and converts to Judaism, Cretans and Arabs, yet we hear them speaking in our own tongues of the mighty acts of God." ¹²They were all astounded and bewildered, and said to one another, "What does this mean?" ¹³But others said, scoffing, "They have had too much new wine."

OT: Gen 11:1–9; Exod 19:16–19

NT: Luke 3:16; 1 Cor 12–14

Catechism: Pentecost, 731–41, 1287, 2623; fire as symbol of the Holy Spirit, 696

Lectionary: Acts 2:1–11: Pentecost Sunday (Years A–C); Acts 2:1–6, 14, 22b–23, 32–33: Confirmation

2:1–4   Luke's phrase **the time for Pentecost was fulfilled** indicates that the Spirit's coming is the accomplishment of God's plan of salvation. The term has the same connotation in Luke 9:51: "When the days for his being taken up were fulfilled," that is, when the moment arrived for Jesus to obey God's plan by journeying to Jerusalem to complete his saving mission through the cross and resurrection.

The Jewish Feast of Pentecost, or Weeks, fifty days after Passover, was one of the three great pilgrimage feasts of Israel (Deut 16:16). It was originally a harvest celebration but later also became a commemoration of God's giving of the covenant and the law on Mount Sinai. For Christians, the coming of the Holy Spirit fulfills this meaning of Pentecost. The celebration of the gift of the law now embraces the giving of the new law in the Spirit (Rom 8:2), the writing of the law on the heart (Jer 31:31–34; 2 Cor 3:2–6).

The Spirit came on the disciples when **they were all in one place together** and united in prayer (1:14). The Spirit's coming is manifested with observable signs: **a noise like a strong driving wind** and the appearance of **tongues as of fire** that rested on each of them. Throughout Scripture, wind is often a sign of the Spirit, since the same word (*pneuma* in Greek) means both wind and spirit. The loud noise, wind, and fire evoke the †theophanies on Mount Sinai to

Fig. 2. An image of Pentecost from the Rabbula Gospels, a sixth-century Syrian illuminated manuscript.

Wikimedia Commons

Moses (Exod 19:16–19) and Elijah (1 Kings 19:11–13). The sign of fire especially recalls the Baptist's prophecy that the One to come "will baptize you with the holy Spirit and fire" (Luke 3:16). Yet Luke most emphasizes the sign that **they were all filled with the holy Spirit** so that they **began to speak in different tongues**. In this context the Greek word *glossai*, literally, "tongues," is better translated as "other languages" (NRSV), since it was the ordinary word used for languages.

The listeners are astounded, because they all understand the Galilean speak-   2:5–10
ers in their respective languages: **"Are not all these people who are speaking Galileans? Then how does each of us hear them in his own native language?"** The countries mentioned cover most of the world that was known to first-century Palestine and symbolize the fact that the Church will embrace the whole world, transcending all barriers of race, class, and nation. They include the regions of Israel's historic enemies, **Mesopotamia** (the center of the Assyrian and Babylonian Empires) and **Egypt**, fulfilling God's promise that Israel's oppressors would one day turn and acknowledge the God of Israel as the true God (Ps 87:1–4; Isa 19:22–25).

The list refers to Jews from the †Diaspora who have relocated to Jerusalem, or Jews who have come there on pilgrimage for the Feast of Pentecost. Jesus promised his apostles that they would be his witnesses from Jerusalem to the ends of the earth (Acts 1:8), as had been prophesied concerning the Servant of the Lord in Isa 49. Their witnessing to God's mighty acts in many languages is an initial fulfillment of this promise.

The fact that Jews from many different nations all heard the disciples **speaking**   2:11
in our own tongues of the mighty acts of God portends that the ancient tragedy of Babel (Gen 11:1–9) is now being reversed. The people at Babel had arrogantly tried to "make a name" for themselves by building a tower to the heavens—symbolizing the human attempt to seek power, wealth, and security without any reference to God. In consequence God confounded the universal human language into many different languages, which made it impossible for them to complete that tower. Instead, they were scattered throughout the world as separate nations, each with its own language. At Pentecost, the Spirit-given ability of Jesus' disciples to speak in various languages signifies that God is beginning to overcome human divisions. Now the Spirit has miraculously enabled Jesus' followers to speak and be understood in many languages from all over the known world. The unifying power of the Spirit will be frequently demonstrated throughout Acts as people who would never before have associated with one another—Jews and Gentiles, slaves and prominent people, the upright and the formerly impious—share a common life of brotherhood and sisterhood in the Church.

Speaking in Tongues at Pentecost and in Corinth

BIBLICAL BACKGROUND

The tongues reported at Pentecost appear to be a unique phenomenon, different from the gift of tongues that St. Paul discusses in 1 Cor 12–14, and probably also from tongues in Acts 10:46; 19:6. At Pentecost the disciples are able to speak and be understood in many other languages. In contrast, Paul indicates that in common prayer at Corinth, speech in tongues is not understood by others without an additional gift of interpretation (1 Cor 14:2, 6–9, 13–19, 27–28). Paul affirms tongues as a charism for prayer and praise (1 Cor 14:4–5, 18), but since such a tongue is unintelligible and therefore not useful to the listeners, he urges the Corinthians to prefer the gift of prophecy, declaring messages that can strengthen the faith of others. The event of tongues at Pentecost *is* actually a form of prophecy, since it is proclaiming "the mighty acts of God"—what God has done in Jesus Christ—in a way that the listeners can understand (Acts 2:11).

2:12–13   This puzzling linguistic phenomenon causes the listeners' bewilderment and even garners some mocking comments: **"They have had too much new wine."** But there is irony in this mockery. In the Old Testament, new wine, or sweet wine, symbolized the joy and abundant blessings that God would give his people in the messianic age (see Joel 4:18 LXX;[1] Amos 9:13–14 LXX). Jesus hinted that he himself would give the "new wine" of divine life (Mark 2:22; see John 2:10). At Pentecost it becomes clear that the new wine is the Holy Spirit, the gift of God's love poured into human hearts (see Rom 5:5).

Although the whole crowd hears the diverse languages coming from a group of Galileans, their reactions differ widely, from being **astounded and bewildered**, to questioning, to scoffing accusations that the believers are drunk. Miraculous signs are an invitation to faith but often require an explanation of what they signify. Such an explanation is what Peter's speech will provide (Acts 2:14–36).

Reflection and Application (2:1–13)

This inspiring account of the Church's inception is a model for contemporary Christians. Christian identity today is likewise grounded in our receiving the Holy Spirit in baptism and confirmation. Christians are sometimes tempted to

1. In the †Septuagint numbering this is Joel 3:18.

The Sober Intoxication of the Spirit

The ironic accusation that the disciples at Pentecost are "filled with new wine" (Acts 2:13) was a favorite theme for the Fathers of the Church. St. Cyril of Jerusalem explained to a group of catechumens,

> They are not drunk in the way you might think. They are indeed drunk, but with the sober intoxication which kills sin and gives life to the heart and which is the opposite of physical drunkenness. Drunkenness makes a person forget what he knows; this kind, instead, brings understanding of things that were not formerly known. They are drunk insofar as they have drunk the wine of that mystical vine which affirms, "I am the vine, you are the branches" (John 15:5).[a]

St. Ambrose exclaimed in a hymn, "Let us drink with joy the sober intoxication of the Spirit!" and said to the newly baptized, "He who becomes intoxicated with wine staggers, but he who becomes intoxicated with the Holy Spirit is rooted in Christ. How truly excellent is this intoxication which produces the sobriety of the soul!"[b]

St. Augustine, preaching to the newly baptized at Easter, said,

> The Holy Spirit has come to abide in you; do not make him withdraw; do not exclude him from your heart in any way. He is a good guest; he found you empty and he filled you; he found you hungry and he satisfied you; he found you thirsty and he has intoxicated you. May he truly intoxicate you! The Apostle said, "Do not be drunk with wine which leads to debauchery." Then, as if to clarify what we should be intoxicated with, he adds, "But be filled with the Spirit, addressing one another in psalms and hymns and spiritual songs, singing and making melody to the Lord with all your heart" (Eph 5:18–19). Doesn't a person who rejoices in the Lord and sings to him exuberantly seem like a person who is drunk? I like this kind of intoxication. The Spirit of God is both drink and light.[c]

For these patristic writers, it is evident that the new wine of the Holy Spirit outpoured at Pentecost continues to be given in the Church, especially through the sacraments of baptism and confirmation.

a. Cyril of Jerusalem, *Catechetical Lectures*, 17.19, quoted in Raniero Cantalamessa, *Sober Intoxication of the Spirit*, trans. Marsha Daigle-Williamson (Cincinnati: Servant, 2005), 2–3.
b. Ambrose, *On the Sacraments* 5.3.17.
c. *Sermons* 225.4.

think they can be saved by their determination to cultivate virtue, by doctrinal orthodoxy, or by scrupulously following rules and commandments. The Pentecost event reminds us how indispensable the Holy Spirit is to our faith and salvation. The indwelling Holy Spirit bestows on us the theological virtues of faith, hope, and love, from which all other Christian virtues and actions follow

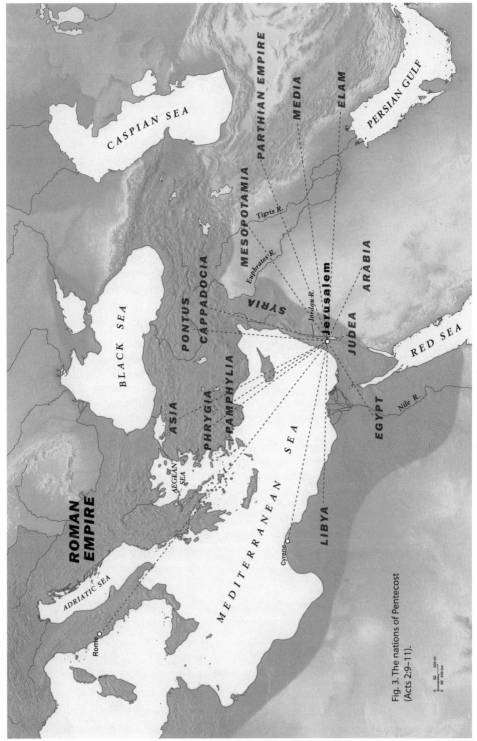

Fig. 3. The nations of Pentecost (Acts 2:9–11).

CASPIAN SEA

PARTHIAN EMPIRE

MEDIA

ELAM

PERSIAN GULF

MESOPOTAMIA

Tigris R.

Euphrates R.

ARABIA

PONTUS

CAPPADOCIA

SYRIA

Jordan R.

Jerusalem

JUDEA

RED SEA

BLACK SEA

ASIA

PHRYGIA

PAMPHYLIA

EGYPT

Nile R.

AEGEAN SEA

MEDITERRANEAN SEA

LIBYA

ROMAN EMPIRE

ADRIATIC SEA

Cyrene

Rome

0   50   100 mi
0   50   100 km

(Catechism 1812–13). The Spirit produces a particular kind of fruit in us (Gal 5:22–23), the character of Jesus.

The descent of the Spirit at Pentecost transformed the first followers of Jesus, who had previously hidden in fear from those responsible for Jesus' crucifixion and were unable to understand God's plan for a crucified Messiah (Luke 9:44–45; John 20:19). After the Holy Spirit's coming, they understood God's saving plan and were able to proclaim it boldly, even at the cost of beatings, imprisonment, and martyrdom. The charisms of prophecy and of speaking in tongues, as well as healings and miracles in the name of Jesus, were abundantly evident. The disciples were filled with joy and continual praise, even in the face of persecution. Today the Spirit is likewise needed to empower Christian life and ministry and to make it fruitful in bringing others to salvation.[2] Without the Holy Spirit, there are no Christians. Without the Holy Spirit, there is no Church.

Peter's Pentecost Speech (2:14–21)

[14]Then Peter stood up with the Eleven, raised his voice, and proclaimed to them, "You who are Jews, indeed all of you staying in Jerusalem. Let this be known to you, and listen to my words. [15]These people are not drunk, as you suppose, for it is only nine o'clock in the morning. [16]No, this is what was spoken through the prophet Joel:

[17]'It will come to pass in the last days,' God says,
　　'that I will pour out a portion of my spirit upon all flesh.
Your sons and your daughters shall prophesy,
　　your young men shall see visions,
　　your old men shall dream dreams.
[18]Indeed, upon my servants and my handmaids
　　I will pour out a portion of my spirit in those days,
　　and they shall prophesy.
[19]And I will work wonders in the heavens above
　　and signs on the earth below:
　　blood, fire, and a cloud of smoke.
[20]The sun shall be turned to darkness,
　　and the moon to blood,
　　before the coming of the great and splendid day of the Lord,
[21]and it shall be that everyone shall be saved who calls on the name of the Lord.' "

2. See Pope Paul VI, *Evangelii Nuntiandi*, 75.

OT: Joel 3:1–5; Num 11:29

NT: Luke 21:7–28; Acts 2:36; 3:19; 21:9

Catechism: prophecies of the Holy Spirit, 715; calling on the name of Jesus, 432, 2666

2:14–18   As spokesperson, **Peter stood up with the Eleven.** Chrysostom explains, "They expressed themselves through one common voice, and he was the mouth of all. The Eleven stood by as witnesses to what he said."[3] Peter begins by refuting their mistaken impression that the exuberant speech in many languages is a sign of drunkenness—a view that the early morning hour renders unlikely. Rather, these Pentecost phenomena fulfill **what was spoken through the prophet Joel.**

Peter adjusts a quotation from Joel. In place of "it shall come to pass" (Joel 3:1), he says **in the last days,** a phrase used by other biblical prophets.[4] Thus Peter explicitly declares that the outpouring of the Spirit signals the arrival of the last days, the †eschatological fulfillment toward which all Old Testament prophecies point. God promised that in the final days, **"I will pour out a portion of my spirit upon all flesh."** With the Israelites, God had poured out his Spirit on individual prophets, judges, and kings, but not on the whole people. In the wilderness, when God bestowed a portion of the Spirit on seventy elders, Joshua complained that two others had also received the Spirit and were prophesying even though they were not with the designated group. Moses responded, "Are you jealous for my sake? Would that all the people of the LORD were prophets! Would that the LORD might bestow his spirit on them all!" (Num 11:29). Centuries later, Joel and other prophets foretold that in the end times God would fulfill Moses' desire and bestow his Spirit on all the people.[5] Peter quotes Joel to announce that what the crowd is witnessing is indeed the longed-for outpouring of the Spirit on all flesh. Later in Acts it becomes clear that "upon all flesh" extends even beyond the people of Israel to include all nations.

Here is the observable result of this outpouring of God's Spirit, Peter claims: **"Your sons and your daughters shall prophesy, your young men shall see visions, your old men shall dream dreams. Indeed, upon my servants and my handmaids I will pour out a portion of my spirit in those days."** Joel prophesied that the Spirit would be bestowed on every category of people: men and women, old and young, slaves and free, who will all manifest prophetic words, visions, and dreams. Peter adds a phrase not found in Joel: **"and they shall prophesy,"** which is how he interprets the disciples' inspired speech in

3. *The Homilies of S. John Chrysostom on the Acts of the Apostles,* Part I, *Hom. I–XXVIII* (Oxford: John Henry Parker; London: F. and J. Rivington, 1851), "Homily IV, Acts ii.1,2," 60–61.

4. See Isa 2:2; Dan 2:28; Hosea 3:5.

5. Isa 44:1–5; Ezek 39:25–29; Zech 12:10.

Peter's Successor Speaks on Another Pentecost

On Pentecost 1998 Saint John Paul II addressed 500,000 pilgrims at St. Peter's Square in Rome. He spoke of the Church's rediscovery of its charismatic heritage at the Second Vatican Council and exhorted all Christians to open themselves to the Holy Spirit and his gifts:

> Whenever the Spirit intervenes, he leaves people astonished. He brings about events of amazing newness; he radically changes persons and history. This was the unforgettable experience of the Second Vatican Ecumenical Council during which, under the guidance of the same Spirit, the Church rediscovered the charismatic dimension as one of her constitutive elements: "It is not only through the sacraments and the ministrations of the Church that the Holy Spirit makes holy the people, leads them and enriches them with his virtues. Allotting his gifts according as he wills (cf. 1 Cor 12:11), he also distributes special graces among the faithful of every rank. . . . He makes them fit and ready to undertake various tasks and offices for the renewal and building up of the Church" (*Lumen Gentium*, 12). . . .
>
> Today, I would like to cry out to all of you gathered here in St. Peter's Square and to all Christians: Open yourselves docilely to the gifts of the Spirit! Accept gratefully and obediently the charisms which the Spirit never ceases to bestow on us! Do not forget that every charism is given for the common good, that is, for the benefit of the whole Church. . . .
>
> Today, from this upper room in St Peter's Square, a great prayer rises: *Come, Holy Spirit*, come and renew the face of the earth! Come with your seven gifts! Come, Spirit of Life, Spirit of Communion and Love! The Church and the world need you. Come, Holy Spirit, and make ever more fruitful the charisms you have bestowed on us. Give new strength and missionary zeal to these sons and daughters of yours who have gathered here. Open their hearts; renew their Christian commitment in the world. Make them courageous messengers of the Gospel, witnesses to the risen Jesus Christ, the Redeemer and Savior of man.

tongues. Later Luke will go out of his way to demonstrate that Christian prophets include women as well as men, such as Philip's "four virgin daughters gifted with prophecy" (Acts 21:9). This is part of Luke's pattern of including references to both men and women. God's Holy Spirit lives within every Christian and makes each one a son or daughter of God, empowered to act as God's servant in word and deed.

Joel prophesied that cosmic signs would accompany the Spirit's outpouring in the end times. Again the quotation in Acts adds words to Joel's prophecy. Peter emphasizes that the signs will be both cosmic signs in the heavens and

2:19–20

earthly signs here below by adding *above* and *below* to Joel 3:3: **"And I will work wonders in the heavens above and signs on the earth below."** Earthly "wonders" and "signs" recall the miracles that God worked through Moses to free the Israelites from slavery in Egypt (Exod 7:3; Deut 4:34) and the miracles worked by Jesus in his public ministry (v. 22). Wonders in the heavens are typical in biblical prophecies of the last day, the day when God would intervene in history to destroy evil and restore the fortunes of his people (Isa 13:10; Ezek 32:7; Rev 6:12).

Before the day of judgment, Joel describes images of destruction such as **blood, fire, and a cloud of smoke** and cosmic signs in the heavens such as **the sun** being **turned to darkness, and the moon to blood**. These details are similar to those in Jesus' end-times discourse: "There will be signs in the sun, the moon, and the stars, and on earth nations will be in dismay, perplexed by the roaring of the sea and the waves" (Luke 21:25). After these end-times cosmic signs, Joel foretells, there will be **the great and splendid day** (RSV "manifest day," NJB "terrible Day") **of the Lord.** The speech thus clearly distinguishes the *final day* (singular) of the Lord (v. 20) from the extended period of *final*

The "Final Days" before the "Final Day" of the Lord

BIBLICAL BACKGROUND

Luke's version of Jesus' end-times discourse (Luke 21:7–28) differentiates four stages: (1) a period of persecution and of testimony by the disciples (reported in Acts); (2) the destruction of Jerusalem (in AD 70, after the end of Acts); (3) the "times of the Gentiles" (Luke 21:24); and (4) the return of the Son of Man in judgment, accompanied by cosmic signs.

The period described in Acts, during which Jesus' first followers give testimony when persecuted (Luke 21:12–19), precedes the destruction of Jerusalem and the "times of the Gentiles," when "Jerusalem will be trampled underfoot by the Gentiles" (Luke 21:24). With many scholars, I think that Luke and Acts were written after the fall of Jerusalem, so that Luke's readers were living in these "times of the Gentiles" after Jerusalem's fall but before the cosmic signs that accompany the end of time (vv. 25–27). Since these cosmic signs have not yet occurred even in our days, we too are living in the "times of the Gentiles." According to Peter's speech in Acts 2, this entire period, from Pentecost until the final day, is the extended epoch of fulfillment of the Old Testament prophecies. Both the apostles after Pentecost and we today, therefore, are living in the "final days."

days (plural) with which the speech began (v. 17). The final days are the days in which Peter and his hearers (and Luke's readers) are living. The final day, the day of judgment, is still to come.

On the day of judgment, the day of the Lord, Peter proclaims, still quoting Joel, **"Everyone shall be saved who calls on the name of the Lord."** At this point in the speech, Peter has not yet argued that *Jesus* is the Lord (see Acts 2:36). However, readers already know that "the Lord," which in the Old Testament means the God of Israel, now refers to the risen Jesus. On the day of judgment, those will be saved from condemnation who in faith call on the name of Jesus, the Lord who is now fulfilling his promises to reconcile his alienated people.

2:21

Peter's Argument from Scripture That Jesus Is the Christ (2:22–32)

²²You who are Israelites, hear these words. Jesus the Nazorean was a man commended to you by God with mighty deeds, wonders, and signs, which God worked through him in your midst, as you yourselves know. ²³This man, delivered up by the set plan and foreknowledge of God, you killed, using lawless men to crucify him. ²⁴But God raised him up, releasing him from the throes of death, because it was impossible for him to be held by it. ²⁵For David says of him:

'I saw the Lord ever before me,
    with him at my right hand I shall not be disturbed.
²⁶Therefore my heart has been glad and my tongue has exulted;
    my flesh, too, will dwell in hope,
²⁷because you will not abandon my soul to the netherworld,
    nor will you suffer your holy one to see corruption.
²⁸You have made known to me the paths of life;
    you will fill me with joy in your presence.'

²⁹My brothers, one can confidently say to you about the patriarch David that he died and was buried, and his tomb is in our midst to this day. ³⁰But since he was a prophet and knew that God had sworn an oath to him that he would set one of his descendants upon his throne, ³¹he foresaw and spoke of the resurrection of the Messiah, that neither was he abandoned to the netherworld nor did his flesh see corruption. ³²God raised this Jesus; of this we are all witnesses.

OT: Deut 18:15; Pss 16; 110
NT: Mark 15:34; Luke 22:42

Catechism: Jesus' signs and wonders, 547–50; culpability for Jesus' death, 591, 597–99; Jesus' body preserved from corruption, 627

Lectionary: Third Sunday of Easter (Year A); Monday of the Octave of Easter

2:22–24   Peter addresses his listeners as **Israelites**, rather than Jews, to emphasize their membership in the people of God, to whom God's promises belong. He makes two proofs from Scripture. First he argues from Ps 16 that Jesus is the †*Christ*, the promised Messiah who would restore Israel, but not in the political manner often expected. Next he proves from Ps 110 that Jesus is the *Lord*. Peter begins by referring to **Jesus** of Nazareth as **a man commended to you by God with mighty deeds, wonders, and signs**. This reference to Jesus' miracles recalls the "signs and wonders" that God worked through Moses (Exod 7:3; Deut 7:19). Peter emphasizes Jesus' humanity by attributing the mighty deeds to God: **"which God worked through him in your midst."** Since God had also worked miracles through prophets like Moses and Elijah, Peter's argument so far demonstrates only that Jesus is God's servant.

Peter indicts his listeners for having crucified Jesus through **lawless men** (Roman Gentiles) even though God had endorsed him by these miraculous signs. Jesus' resurrection confirms that his death was part of **the set plan and foreknowledge of God**, as Jesus himself had foretold in his passion predictions (Luke 9:22, 44; 18:31–33). Luke repeatedly emphasizes that the death of the Messiah was always part of God's plan to save his people.[6] But Jesus' life was not to end with his death. God raised him, **releasing him from the throes of death, because it was impossible for him to be held by it**.

2:25   Peter uses Scripture to demonstrate for his Jewish audience that Jesus is the Messiah. He cites Ps 16, a psalm in which David expressed his trust and confidence in God:[7] **"I saw the Lord ever before me, with him at my right hand I shall not be disturbed."** As Peter points out below (vv. 29–31), in this psalm it is actually Jesus the Messiah who is speaking through the mouth of David. Jesus suffered anguish in anticipation of his passion. But after his struggle in the garden, when he submitted his human will to the Father's plan (Luke 22:42–44), he no longer was "disturbed" but exhibited serenity and courage, knowing that the Father would deliver him.

6. The Messiah's suffering was necessary in God's biblical plan of salvation, according to Luke 9:22; 13:33; 17:25; 24:7, 26, 44; Acts 17:3. God's plan also incorporated Judas's free decision to betray Jesus (Acts 1:16), and the necessity for Paul (Acts 9:16) and all Christians (Acts 14:22) to suffer as well as the Messiah.

7. The common Jewish understanding of the time was that David was author of most of the Psalms and had prophesied through them.

The Empty Tomb

BIBLICAL BACKGROUND

Luke would emphatically disagree with a statement sometimes heard today: "It would not affect my faith at all if Jesus' bones were found in his tomb." For Christian faith, the empty tomb is an essential sign of Jesus' resurrection. According to biblical anthropology, human beings are not souls who happen to inhabit bodies, but animated and thus ensouled bodies. Being raised from the dead means not just the continued existence of the soul but being raised as a complete human being, soul and body. Peter's argument that Ps 16 must refer to Jesus and not David unquestionably requires the evidence that Jesus' tomb had been found empty, in stark contrast to David's tomb, which remained "to this day." Similarly, St. Paul emphatically insists that Christian faith depends on the eyewitness testimony that Jesus has been raised from the dead, which means that he is no longer in his tomb (1 Cor 15:14–19).

2:26–28

Psalm 16 expresses Jesus' confident hope even during his passion that he would be raised from the dead: **"My flesh, too, will dwell in hope."** The reason for his hope follows: **"because you will not abandon my soul to the netherworld, nor will you suffer your holy one to see corruption."** The Jewish view was that physical decay began on the fourth day after death, as illustrated in Martha's comment that there would be an odor because Lazarus had been dead four days (John 11:39). But Jesus was raised on the third day—a sign that this prophecy that God's holy one "would not see corruption" was fulfilled in him! The psalm continues, **"You will fill me with joy in your presence."**

2:29–31

As Peter points out, Ps 16 cannot apply to David himself, because **his tomb is in our midst to this day**. This is in sharp contrast to Jesus' tomb, which was known to be empty (Luke 24:1–8). David's prophecy in Ps 16:10 quoted by Peter, "You will not abandon my soul to the netherworld," could not have applied to himself since he had been dead and buried for a thousand years. But because David **was a prophet and knew that God had sworn an oath to him that he would set one of his descendants upon his throne** (see Ps 132:11–12), he spoke rather of his descendant, Jesus: **he foresaw and spoke of the resurrection of the Messiah**.

2:32

If Jesus' body had, like David's, been known to still be in his tomb, Jesus' resurrection could have been easily disproved. But Peter's listeners do not dispute the fact that his tomb was empty. The empty tomb is *necessary* evidence of

Jesus' resurrection though it is not in itself *sufficient* to prove it.[8] Belief in Jesus' resurrection depends on the apostles' eyewitness testimony that he is alive: **of this we are all witnesses.**

Peter's Argument from Scripture That Jesus Is Lord (2:33–36)

[33]**Exalted at the right hand of God, he received the promise of the holy Spirit from the Father and poured it forth, as you [both] see and hear. **[34]**For David did not go up into heaven, but he himself said:**

> **"The Lord said to my Lord,**
> **'Sit at my right hand**
> ****[35]**until I make your enemies your footstool.'"**

[36]**Therefore let the whole house of Israel know for certain that God has made him both Lord and Messiah, this Jesus whom you crucified.**

OT: Ps 110
NT: John 7:37–39; 20:19–23; Acts 1:6–8; 1 Cor 15:22–28
Catechism: Jesus at God's right hand, 659; Jesus is Lord, 446–51, 746; culpability for Jesus' death, 591, 597–98
Lectionary: Acts 2:14a, 36–41: Fourth Sunday of Easter (Year A)

2:33   Peter's argument that Jesus is Lord (vv. 33–36) is parallel to his argument that Jesus is the †Christ (vv. 22–32). Although Peter's quotation of Ps 16 did not include the last line of the psalm, his audience undoubtedly knew what it said: "delights at your right hand forever" (Ps 16:11). Thus Peter continues to interpret the psalm when he says that Jesus' ascension is his glorification **at the right hand of God**, in heaven next to God and sharing his divine authority.[9]

Because Jesus **received the promise of the holy Spirit from the Father** in his own glorified human nature, he has now become the instrument for God's outpouring of the Spirit on humanity. Before Christ came, human beings were alienated from God by sin and could not receive the indwelling Spirit of God. But through Jesus' atoning death and resurrection, the gift of the Holy Spirit becomes possible (see John 7:39; 16:7). Jesus instructed the disciples to await the promised Holy Spirit in Jerusalem (Luke 24:49; Acts 1:4). Now, exalted with the Father, he has **poured it forth, as you [both] see and hear.** Thus Peter

8. See Catechism, 640.
9. The affirmation that Jesus is "at the right hand of God," sharing in God's divine authority, occurs in Mark 16:19; Luke 22:69; Acts 2:33; 5:31; 7:55–56; Rom 8:34; Col 3:1; Heb 10:12; 1 Pet 3:22.

explains the sights and sounds that the crowd experiences: the Lord Jesus, seated in divine glory at the Father's right hand, is pouring out the Holy Spirit on his disciples. The phrase "what you see and hear" emphasizes that the coming of the Spirit is a visible, unmistakable reality.

In verses 25–32 Peter argued that the prophecy of Ps 16, that the "holy one"   **2:34–35** would not "see corruption," applied not to David but to his descendent, Jesus the Messiah. Here he argues similarly from Ps 110. It is obvious that **David did not go up into heaven** to be at God's right hand because he is still in his tomb. But in this psalm David declares that **the Lord** (God) will tell **my Lord,** **"Sit at my right hand."** Peter observes that the psalm promises that not David but David's Lord, the Messiah, would sit at God's right hand **"until I make your enemies your footstool."** The risen Jesus is the Lord spoken of in the psalm, whose enemies are being placed under his feet by God. The early Church understood this last verse as a reference to Jesus' victory over all his enemies—sin, Satan and death—at the end of time (1 Cor 15:22–28; Heb 10:12–13).

Peter's combined conclusion to his arguments from Psalms 16 and 110 is that   **2:36** **God has made** Jesus **both Lord and Messiah.** The †synoptic Gospels all feature Jesus' question to his disciples, "But who do you say that I am?" (Luke 9:20), and Peter's climactic confession of faith in response: "You are the Messiah." Messiah (Hebrew *Mashiakh*), or Christ (Greek *Christos*), means "anointed one." Although the Jews expected that the Messiah would restore the kingdom of Israel (Acts 1:6), God's plan was that his Anointed would exercise a far greater kingship and bring a far superior salvation both to Jews and Gentiles (Luke 2:29–32).

The title "Lord" (Greek *kyrios*) is used throughout the Greek Old Testament to translate God's sacred name, Yahweh, which the Jews avoided pronouncing out of reverence. The New Testament continues to call God "the Lord." But the New Testament reveals something new: "the Lord" is also the risen Jesus, who as the Son shares in God's power and authority over the whole universe. In the Roman Empire, where "the lord" was a title for Caesar, the Christian confession that Jesus is Lord meant that Jesus alone, and not Caesar, is owed absolute loyalty and submission. Thus this confession of allegiance to a higher authority had cultural and political consequences and resulted in persecution for the early Christians, as for Christians in many parts of the world today.

Reflection and Application (2:33–36)

The early Church's confession of faith is summed up in the statement "Jesus Christ is Lord" (see Phil 2:11; 3:8). Jesus is Lord because he is risen and has conquered death forever! To confess that Jesus is Lord is to say that he is *my* Lord, my Savior, my King; that I have placed my life under his authority and that my whole destiny belongs to him. Thus St. Paul declares, "No one can say, 'Jesus is Lord,' except by the holy Spirit" (1 Cor 12:3). Paul expresses his own boundless joy and gratitude at this discovery: "I even consider everything as a loss because of the supreme good of knowing Christ Jesus my Lord" (Phil 3:8). For many Christians, Jesus is only a figure from the distant past. But the existential knowledge that Jesus is Lord, a living presence in our lives, is meant to be the inheritance of every Christian.

The People's Response to Peter's Witness (2:37–41)

³⁷Now when they heard this, they were cut to the heart, and they asked Peter and the other apostles, "What are we to do, my brothers?" ³⁸Peter [said] to them, "Repent and be baptized, every one of you, in the name of Jesus Christ for the forgiveness of your sins; and you will receive the gift of the holy Spirit. ³⁹For the promise is made to you and to your children and to all those far off, whomever the Lord our God will call." ⁴⁰He testified with many other arguments, and was exhorting them, "Save yourselves from this corrupt generation." ⁴¹Those who accepted his message were baptized, and about three thousand persons were added that day.

OT: Deut 32:5; Ps 78:8
NT: Matt 12:39; 28:18–20; Mark 1:15; Luke 3:15–16; Acts 1:4–5
Catechism: repentance and baptism, 1226, 1240, 1427
Lectionary: Acts 2:14a, 36–41: Fourth Sunday of Easter (Year A); Tuesday of the Octave of Easter; Acts 2:14a, 36–40a, 41–42: Christian initiation apart from the Easter Vigil

2:37–38   Listening to Peter's speech, the people are **cut to the heart**—a sign that the Holy Spirit has convicted their consciences of sin and opened their hearts to believe Peter's message. To their question what they are to do, Peter responds: **"Repent and be baptized"**—summing up the Christian call to conversion, which is grounded in Jesus' own message, "Repent and believe in the gospel" (Mark 1:15). Similar instructions will be given by Ananias at Paul's conversion: "Now, why delay? Get up and have yourself baptized and your sins washed away, calling upon his name" (Acts 22:16). Even though one aspect or the other may not be explicit, throughout Acts the response that the gospel requires is threefold: faith, repentance, and baptism.

In the New Testament, **forgiveness of sins** is closely linked with repentance. God desires to forgive all sinners, but his respect for human freedom necessitates that we accept his forgiveness by admitting and repenting of our guilt. This parallels a fact of human experience, that when a wrong has been committed but not acknowledged and renounced, even if the person who suffered the wrong is willing to forgive, reconciliation remains incomplete.[10]

Like the whole New Testament, Peter affirms that entrance into Christ's Church is through baptism, at least for everyone after the initial 120 on whom the Spirit first descended. A useful comment is offered by Raymond Brown: "Baptism as a public action is important. . . . Peter is portrayed as asking people to make a visible and verifiable profession of their acceptance of Jesus. This is tantamount to asking people to 'join up.' The basic Israelite concept is that God chose to save *a people*, and the renewal of the covenant on Pentecost has not changed that. There is a collective aspect to salvation, and one is saved as part of God's people."[11]

Christian converts are to be baptized **in the name of Jesus Christ**. Although some commentators hold that this expression is an alternative to the Trinitarian formula of baptism "in the name of the Father, and of the Son, and of the Holy Spirit" (Matt 28:19), I regard it less as a ritual formula than as Luke's emphasis on the converts' consecration to Christ, in distinction from John's baptism of repentance toward God (see Acts 18:25; 19:3–4).[12] To be baptized "in the name of Jesus" means to acknowledge that he is Lord and place one's life under his authority. Throughout Acts the apostles invoke the powerful name of Jesus in preaching (5:40; 9:27), healing (3:6; 9:34), casting out demons (16:18), and baptizing new believers (10:48).

Through baptism converts receive forgiveness of sins and **the gift of the holy Spirit** (see Col 2:12–13; 1 Pet 3:21). With this statement Peter establishes the link between baptism and receiving the Holy Spirit. The way to be filled with the power of the Holy Spirit, as were the first disciples at Pentecost, is by being joined to Christ through baptism. Unlike John's baptism in water, which signified repentance for forgiveness of sins (Luke 3:3; Acts 19:4), baptism in the name of Jesus also bestows the Holy Spirit, as John had prophesied, "He will baptize you with the holy Spirit and fire" (Luke 3:16; see Acts 1:5).

Peter ends his address by speaking of **the promise** (as in Luke 24:49 and Acts 1:4; 2:33) referring to God's gift of salvation expressed in the gift of the Spirit. God had promised through the prophets[13] to bestow his Spirit on Israel—**to you**

                   2:39

---

10. On repentance in Luke and Acts, see Luke 24:46–47; Acts 3:19; 8:20–24; 17:30–31; 26:20.
11. Raymond E. Brown, *Introduction to the New Testament*, Anchor Bible Reference Library (New York: Doubleday, 1997), 285–86.
12. See the Catechism 2, 232–34.
13. See Isa 32:15; 44:3; Ezek 11:19; 36:26–27; 37:14.

and to your children—but now, Peter declares, it reaches **to all those far off, whomever the Lord our God will call**. God's plan of salvation extends beyond his chosen people to Gentiles, whom God also intends to call. Although Peter invites his audience to respond, he here reminds them that God is the One who has taken the initiative in offering salvation.

2:40   The reference to **many other arguments** indicates that Luke has given us only a summary of Peter's address—a standard approach in ancient historical reports of speeches. The speech climaxes in Peter's exhortation to his listeners: **"Save yourselves from this corrupt generation."** The phrase "this corrupt generation" means the bad influences of a society that had in many ways turned away from God (see Deut 32:5; Ps 78:8).[14] The classic Old Testament example of a corrupt generation was the rebellious Israelites who perished in the desert after the exodus from Egypt. In the Gospels, Jesus compares his contemporaries who rejected him as Messiah to that disobedient desert generation (Luke 9:41; 11:29–32, 50–51).

2:41   The baptism of **about three thousand persons** is an impressive event that Luke presents as a marvelous beginning of the restoration of Israel under its risen Messiah. Luke later records another considerable growth to about five thousand Christians (4:4) and mentions further increase.[15] The continuous growth of the Church is sometimes described as the spread of "the word" (Acts 6:7; 13:49; 19:20), which implies that the primary way the Church grows is through the Spirit-filled proclamation of God's word, awakening faith in those who hear it.

Reflection and Application (2:14–41)

Peter's speech illustrates the importance of both faith and reason in the spread of Christianity. The startling transformation in Peter, from denying Jesus before a servant girl (Luke 23:56–57) to proclaiming him boldly to thousands in Jerusalem, is due to the empowerment of the Holy Spirit. To be shared with others, Christian faith must also be persuasively explained with the help of reason and argument, which is also done in the power of the Holy Spirit. Peter's speech illustrates an attractive mixture of testimony to his own experience and faith in God's word. It uses reasonable arguments to persuade listeners that the crucified Jesus is truly the Messiah and Lord promised in Scripture. Is our witness to friends and neighbors grounded in the power of God's Spirit, in personal experience of Jesus, in biblical revelation, and in reasonable explanation?

---

14. Deut 32:5 has "corrupt and depraved generation"; Ps 78:8 has "corrupt and rebellious generation" (my translations from the †Septuagint).

15. Acts 2:47; 5:14; 6:1, 7; 9:31; 11:21; 16:5.

The Life-Giving Waters of Baptism

The life-transforming gift of the Spirit at Pentecost was not for the original 120 disciples only. The Church continues to hold what Peter declared in Acts 2:38: that through baptism new believers are filled with the same divine Spirit who descended in the upper room. St. Cyprian of Carthage, a third-century Father of the Church, wrote a letter to his friend Donatus in which he gives eloquent testimony to the transformative effects of the Holy Spirit received in baptism:

> I went down into those life-giving waters, and all the stains of my past were washed away. I committed my life to the Lord; he cleansed my heart and filled me with the Holy Spirit. I was born again, a new man. Then in a most marvelous way all my doubts cleared up. I could now see what had been hidden from me before. I found I could do things that had previously been impossible. I saw that as long as I had been living according to my flesh, I was at the mercy of sin and my course was set for death, but that by living according to my new birth in the Holy Spirit, I had already begun to share God's eternal life. You know as well as I do what sins I died to at that moment, just as you know the gifts the Holy Spirit gave me along with my new life. . . .
>
> How tremendous is this freedom and the spiritual power the Lord has given us! Not only are we protected from harm, but we [also] are given authority over the whole force of the enemy who attacks us. When I look back on the darkness from which I have escaped, I can only praise and thank God for the love he has shown me. . . . We do not have to toil and sweat to achieve our own perfection, nor are money and influence needed to obtain the gift of the Holy Spirit. It is freely given by God, always available for us to use. Just as the sun shines and the day brings light, the stream irrigates the soil and rain waters the earth, so the heavenly Spirit pours himself into us.[a]

a. *Treatise to Donatus on the Grace of God*, paraphrased by Anne Field, *From Darkness to Light: What It Meant to Become a Christian in the Early Church* (Ann Arbor, MI: Servant Books, 1978), 190–92.

First Summary: Early Communal Life under the Apostles (2:42–47)

[42]They devoted themselves to the teaching of the apostles and to the communal life, to the breaking of the bread and to the prayers. [43]Awe came upon everyone, and many wonders and signs were done through the apostles. [44]All who believed were together and had all things in common; [45]they would sell their property and possessions and divide them among all according to each one's need. [46]Every day they devoted themselves to meeting together in the temple area and to breaking bread in their homes. They ate their meals with exultation and sincerity of heart, [47]praising God

and enjoying favor with all the people. And every day the Lord added to their number those who were being saved.

OT: Deut 34:11
NT: Acts 4:32–37; 5:12–16; 1 Cor 11:17–26
Catechism: apostles' teaching, 857; communal life, 949–53; breaking of bread, 1329, 1342; prayer, 2624–25
Lectionary: Second Sunday of Easter (Year A)

2:42   Those who believe and are baptized form a community. Acts 2:42–47 is the first of three summaries that describe the beginnings of the church in Jerusalem (with 4:32–35; 5:12–16). They depict an idyllic foundational stage in the Church's life intended to serve as an example.[16] This first summary portrays the Christian community after Pentecost as centered around the **teaching of the apostles**, which continues to be the foundation of Christian doctrine to this day. The new community is also founded on **the communal life** or fellowship (*koinōnia*) with one another, which is experienced especially through the **breaking of the bread**—the Eucharist and communal meals—and **prayers** together. This spiritual sharing is in turn the foundation for the material sharing of goods (vv. 44–45). As the Letters of Paul indicate, life in the church is a life of close brotherhood and sisterhood, which includes caring for one another's needs, celebrating joys together, and supporting one another in sorrow (see 1 Cor 12:25–26; Gal 6:1–2; Eph 5:18–20; Phil 2:3–4)—all of which is a crucial part of the Christian witness to the world. These four elements remain crucial for the life of the Church in future generations: the "teaching of the apostles," care for one another in community, "the breaking of the bread," and prayers.

2:43   Luke emphasizes the powerful impression the Christians made on others. **Awe** or reverent fear came upon everyone, especially because of the **wonders and signs** worked **through the apostles**. Like the teaching of Jesus (Acts 2:22), the teaching of his apostles is accompanied by mighty deeds that confirm the message. The wonders and signs done by the apostles are in fact done by the risen Jesus, who acts through them. They are *signs* because they signify the truth of the good news preached by the apostles, that Jesus is alive and is bringing

---

16. Skeptics have suggested that since Luke did not personally witness the early years of the Church in Jerusalem, his report of this period is fictional—too good to be true. While Luke clearly intends to present the Church after Pentecost as a model, there is no reason to doubt the overall veracity of the picture he paints. During his travels with Paul, Luke would have had plenty of contact with early members of the Jerusalem community, such as Silas, especially if Luke accompanied Paul to Jerusalem. Also, a careful reading of Acts' history of the Jerusalem Church reveals a certain realism about community problems as well as achievements.

The Fear of the Lord

BIBLICAL BACKGROUND

Luke's comment that "Awe [literally, fear] came upon everyone" (Acts 2:43) is an instance of the biblical theme of fear of the Lord. The signs and wonders worked by the apostles made it evident that God was present and acting in power, which caused people to be filled with reverent awe. Fear of the Lord in Scripture is not a servile terror but an appropriate attitude of reverence before God, which keeps us from sinning and produces repentance when we do sin (2 Cor 7:1). Paradoxically, fear of the Lord frees us from earthly fears such as anxiety over the disapproval of others. Moses exemplifies this paradox in exhorting the people, "*Do not be afraid*, for God has come only to test you and *put fear of him upon you* so you do not sin" (Exod 20:20). Fear of the Lord puts us in a position of recognizing God's holiness so that he is more free to act through us, since we are not approaching him presumptuously. It is one of the seven qualities of the Spirit-filled Messiah (Isa 11:1–3), traditionally recognized as the seven gifts of the Spirit. God's messianic people find delight in the fear of the Lord (see Isa 11:3).

about the kingdom of God. They are *wonders* because they call forth a response of awe, wonder, praise, and gratitude. They also recall the many signs and wonders that God worked through Moses during the exodus (Deut 34:11; Acts 7:36), indicating that in Jesus, God is accomplishing a new and greater act of deliverance.

All who believed were together, which indicates that they gathered often 2:44–45
in settings such as their homes and the temple (2:46). That they **had all things in common** indicates that their intense spiritual unity led to a sharing of material possessions. This sharing, in direct contrast to the human tendency toward possessiveness, is a powerful testimony to the presence of the kingdom inaugurated by Jesus.

Luke's portrayal of the early Christian community later became an inspiration for communal ownership of goods in monastic communities, in which monks literally surrender all worldly goods to the common account. Luke, however, does not indicate that all Christians practiced such strict sharing of goods. When Peter rebukes Ananias's dishonest claim about his land sale, he says, "While it remained unsold, did it not remain yours? And when it was sold, was it not still under your control?" (see Acts 5:4). Luke's words echo a well-known Hellenistic proverb about friendship: "Friends hold all things in common." The proverb declares that friends are willing to share all things when

The Church as Apostolic

As the early Christians "devoted themselves to the teaching of the apostles," so do Christians in every age. The Catechism (857) teaches that the Church is apostolic because she is founded on the apostles in three ways:

- She was and remains built on "the foundation of the Apostles" (Eph 2:20; Rev 21:14), the witnesses chosen and sent on mission by Christ himself (cf. Matt 28:16–20; Acts 1:8; 1 Cor 9:1; 15:7–8; Gal 1:1; etc.).

- With the help of the Spirit dwelling in her, the Church keeps and hands on the teaching (cf. Acts 2:42), the "good deposit," the salutary words she has heard from the apostles (cf. 2 Tim 1:13–14).

- The Church continues to be taught, sanctified, and guided by the apostles until Christ's return, through their successors in pastoral office: the college of bishops, "assisted by priests, in union with the successor of Peter, the Church's supreme pastor" (*Ad Gentes*, 5).

there is need, although usually they do not literally do so.[17] What did happen in the early Christian community was that some wealthy members would **sell their property and possessions**, as Barnabas did in Acts 4:36–37, to **divide them among all according to each one's need**. That is, those who had extra goods sold them to provide for the needs of the poor, especially widows and orphans (Acts 6:1). Among all the members was a bond of "friendship," mutual care, that was astounding and powerfully attractive to those who observed it.

2:46   The believers, who continued to consider themselves devout Jews, gathered to pray **in the temple area**, and they also broke bread **in their homes**. The **breaking** of **bread** refers to shared meals with fellow Christians, probably including the Eucharist, which were characterized by **exultation and sincerity of heart**. Before churches were built, Christians celebrated the Eucharist in homes, usually in connection with a common meal (see Paul's discussion of the Lord's Supper in 1 Cor 11:17–34).

2:47   The Christian community enjoyed **favor with all the people**, in this case the Jewish people. This emphasis on the positive impression Christians made on outsiders (see also Acts 4:33) brings to mind the boy Jesus, who advanced in

---

17. See Johnson's discussion of this proverb in Hellenistic writings and Philo, as well as of communities like Qumran that practiced strict community of goods not based on friendship ideals (Luke Timothy Johnson, *The Acts of the Apostles*, Sacra pagina 5 [Collegeville, MN: Liturgical Press, 1992], 58–59).

"wisdom and age and favor before God and man" (Luke 2:52). This good reputation contributed to the growth of the Church as **every day the Lord added to their number those who were being saved** (see Acts 2:21; 4:12; 16:30–31). Acts depicts the community life of the first Christians as having a powerful evangelizing impact.

Reflection and Application (2:42–47)

Luke's description of the early Church lays a challenge before us. To what degree do our parishes resemble the early Christian community in Jerusalem? Do our Sunday gatherings for the Eucharist express a communal life characterized by praying together, mutual support, shared meals, and other forms of fellowship? Does our parish spiritual life extend beyond Mass to sharing our lives with one another in small groups, Bible studies, and social and evangelistic outreaches? Such communal life leads to joy and an intense awareness of the presence of the Lord in our midst, which culminates in a rich celebration of the liturgy.

The example of the Jerusalem church teaches us to share our time, money, and goods with Christian brothers and sisters in need. Nor ought Christian generosity stop with Church members: it should extend to non-Christians as well. Paul says it well: "Let us do good to all, but especially to those who belong to the family of the faith" (Gal 6:10). Christian love, service, and generosity attract people to Jesus and the Church today just as they did in the Church's youth. The more Christians today live a Spirit-filled life, the more we can also expect signs and wonders of all kinds to take place among us.

Luke's summary of early Christian communal life portrays the beginnings of a Christian culture—a society and way of life founded on God's word and animated by the Holy Spirit. As recent Church teaching has emphasized, the goal of evangelization is that the good news would not only reach individuals but also penetrate and transform cultures, purifying and elevating those elements in them that are compatible with the gospel.[18] Today's Christianity, however, is often very individualistic. Even in some countries with large numbers of believers, there is a lack of Christian influence on laws and institutions, education, the sciences, entertainment, sports, or the arts. As Pope John Paul II stated, "A faith that does not affect a person's culture is a faith not fully embraced, not entirely thought out, not faithfully lived."[19] Indeed, "the split between the Gospel and culture is without a doubt the drama of our time. . . . Therefore, every effort must be made to ensure a full evangelization of culture."[20]

18. See Vatican II, *Gaudium et Spes*, 2.
19. *The Lay Members of Christ's Faithful People* (*Christifideles Laici*), 59.
20. Pope Paul VI, *Evangelii Nuntiandi*, 20.

Healing Spurs the Growth of the Church

Acts 3:1–4:4

In Acts 1:8 Jesus promises that, after receiving the Holy Spirit, the apostles would become his witnesses. Three elements of the Church's witness in Jerusalem stand out: first, ministry to the sick and the poor (Acts 3:1–10); second, preaching God's gift of salvation in Jesus (3:11–26); and third, faithfulness in the midst of persecution (4:1–4).

Peter Healing a Crippled Beggar (3:1–10)

¹Now Peter and John were going up to the temple area for the three o'clock hour of prayer. ²And a man crippled from birth was carried and placed at the gate of the temple called "the Beautiful Gate" every day to beg for alms from the people who entered the temple. ³When he saw Peter and John about to go into the temple, he asked for alms.

⁴But Peter looked intently at him, as did John, and said, "Look at us." ⁵He paid attention to them, expecting to receive something from them. ⁶Peter said, "I have neither silver nor gold, but what I do have I give you: in the name of Jesus Christ the Nazorean, [rise and] walk." ⁷Then Peter took him by the right hand and raised him up, and immediately his feet and ankles grew strong. ⁸He leaped up, stood, and walked around, and went into the temple with them, walking and jumping and praising God. ⁹When all the people saw him walking and praising God, ¹⁰they recognized him as the one who used to sit begging at the Beautiful Gate of the

temple, and they were filled with amazement and astonishment at what
had happened to him.

OT: Isa 35:6; Mal 3:20
NT: Matt 11:5; Mark 16:17–18; Luke 5:23–25
Catechism: Christ the physician, 1503–5; healing the sick, 1506–10; wonder and praise, 2640
Lectionary: Vigil of the Feast of Saints Peter and Paul (June 29); Wednesday of the Octave of
Easter

Although **Peter and John** are mentioned together (as throughout Acts 3–4),   **3:1**
the focus is on Peter as spokesperson.[1] Peter does all the talking and acting.
John's silent presence here is probably mentioned to emphasize that there is a
second witness to all that occurs. Jesus used to send out his disciples in pairs
(Luke 10:1).

The apostles go **to the temple area for the three o'clock hour of prayer** (literally, at the ninth hour),[2] the time of the daily evening sacrifice (Exod 29:38–39;
Dan 9:21). Jesus' first disciples did not abandon their Jewish religious practices
but continued to live as observant Jews.

They met a man **crippled from birth** at one of the temple gates, the **Beautiful**   **3:2–5**
Gate, who was placed there daily to beg for alms. The location of the Beautiful
Gate is uncertain, but it may have led from the outer court of the Gentiles into
the inner temple courts. Luke accents the contrast between the lame man, who
is **carried and placed** at the gate and **the people who entered the temple**.
The man is outside the temple not simply because he is lame but also because
he is a social outcast. If he were of a priestly family, his disability would have
excluded him from the priesthood (see Lev 21:16–18) and perhaps even from
the temple.[3]

The beggar asks Peter and John to give him **alms**. Luke reports that **Peter**
looked intently at him, then somewhat awkwardly adds, **as did John**, to remind
readers of John's presence. By saying, **"Look at us,"** Peter invites the lame man
to expectant faith.

First, Peter disappoints the beggar's hope for money from him: **"I have neither**   **3:6**
silver nor gold." Immediately, however, he offers him something immeasur-
ably better: **"but what I do have I give you: in the name of Jesus Christ the**

---

1. Peter and John are the two whom Jesus sent to prepare for the Passover (Luke 22:8). They are
also listed as those commissioned by the apostles to investigate the new developments in Samaria (Acts
8:14). Luke changes usual †synoptic order in the list of the Twelve, "Peter, James, and John," to "Peter,
John, and James" in Acts 1:13; Luke 8:51; 9:28 to highlight Peter and John as a team.
2. Since the first hour begins with sunrise (about 6:00 a.m.), the ninth hour is about 3:00 p.m.
3. See Mikeal C. Parsons, "The Character of the Lame Man in Acts 3–4," *Journal of Biblical Literature*
124 (2005): 306.

Nazorean, [rise and] walk."[4] Peter's words and actions echo those of Jesus in his healing of the paralytic: "Which is easier, to say, 'Your sins are forgiven,' or to say, 'Rise and walk'?" (Luke 5:23). Peter speaks of the ability to bring about the beggar's cure as something in his possession or under his influence: "what I do have." Yet the command to be healed is spoken in the name of Jesus Christ the Nazorean.[5] Throughout Scripture, those who ministered or prophesied "in the name of the Lord" did so as the Lord's authorized representatives (Deut 18:5; 1 Sam 17:45; Jer 26:9). To act "in the name of Jesus" means to act under his authority, united to him, invoking his presence and power. Thus this healing confirms the impression given at the beginning of Acts that Jesus would *continue* to speak and act through his disciples, and especially his apostles (Acts 1:1 refers to all that Jesus *began* to do and teach in his earthly ministry).

3:7–8   The healing is an instantaneous strengthening of the lame man's **feet and ankles** as Peter **raised him up**. Here and in verse 6 the verb for "raised" (Greek *egeirō*) is the same word used for Jesus' resurrection (Luke 24:34), hinting that the same Holy Spirit by whom Jesus was raised from the dead now raises up the lame man. Luke graphically accents the healed man's joy and excitement: he **leaped up, stood, and walked around**. The man's exhilaration is unmistakable as he goes **into the temple** with Peter and John, **walking and jumping and praising God.** His excitement is even more understandable because now he is entering the temple as part of the worshiping community instead of begging at the gate. For those who witness it, the healing is a sign that the messianic age has arrived, as God had promised: "Then will the lame leap like a stag" (Isa 35:6); "for you who fear my name, there will arise the sun of justice with its healing rays; / And you will gambol like calves out of the stall" (Mal 3:20).[6]

3:9–10   Although **all the people** refers directly to witnesses in the temple, it may also emphasize that those who wondered at the healing were Jews, to whom Acts frequently refers as "the people" (of God). They recognized the man **walking and praising God** in the temple as **the one who used to sit begging at the Beautiful Gate of the temple** but who had been unable to enter it. Their response was **amazement and astonishment** at his healing and his presence in God's house, the typical human response to seeing a mighty work of God (Luke 4:36; 5:9, 26).

4. Most manuscripts, patristic witnesses, and ancient translations include the words "rise and," though some early manuscripts omit it.

5. The term "Nazorean" could simply mean "of Nazareth" but may also be an allusion to the Davidic "shoot" (Hebrew *nezer*) that God promised would "sprout from the stump of Jesse" (Isa 11:1). "Nazoreans" may have been a Jewish term for Jesus' disciples before the term "Christians" became common (see Acts 11:26; 24:5).

6. Mal 3:20 in the Hebrew Old Testament and NAB is Mal 4:2 in the LXX and most English translations.

Healing the Sick

The Catechism (1503) explains that just as in the earthly ministry of Jesus, so in the Church today healings are signs of the presence of the kingdom:

> Christ's compassion toward the sick and his many healings of every kind of infirmity are a resplendent sign that "God has visited his people" (Luke 7:16; Matt 4:24) and that the Kingdom of God is close at hand. Jesus has the power not only to heal, but also to forgive sins (Mark 2:5–12); he has come to heal the whole . . . [person], soul and body; he is the physician the sick have need of (Mark 2:17). His compassion toward all who suffer goes so far that he identifies himself with them: "I was sick and you visited me" (Matt 25:36). His preferential love for the sick has not ceased through the centuries to draw the very special attention of Christians toward all those who suffer in body and soul. It is the source of tireless efforts to comfort them.

In 2000 the Congregation for the Doctrine of the Faith published an *Instruction on Prayers for Healing*, recognizing that such prayers remain a vibrant part of the Church's experience. Regarding "the desire for healing and prayer to obtain it," the document states:

> Presuming the acceptance of God's will, the sick person's desire for healing is both good and deeply human, especially when it takes the form of trusting prayer addressed to God. Sirach exhorts his disciple: "My son, when you are ill, delay not, but pray to God, who will heal you" (Sir 38:9). A number of the Psalms also ask for healing (cf. Pss 6; 37; 40; 87).
>
> Large numbers of the sick approached Jesus during his public ministry, either directly or through friends and relatives, seeking the restoration of health. The Lord welcomes their requests, and the Gospels contain not even a hint of reproach for these prayers. The Lord's only complaint is about their possible lack of faith: "If you can! Everything is possible to one who has faith" (Mark 9:23; cf. Matt 6:5–6; John 4:48).

Reflection and Application (3:1–10)

Throughout Acts, the proclamation of the good news is accompanied by healings and miracles done in the name of Jesus, who has divine power to do what is humanly impossible. During his earthly ministry, Jesus instructed his apostles "to proclaim the kingdom of God and to heal" the sick (Luke 9:2). Although miraculous healings are not necessary to faith, they play the important role of visibly manifesting the reality of the kingdom. They are signs demonstrating the truth of the gospel message: that God loves all people; that Jesus has won the victory over sin, sickness, and death; that he has come to heal and save. They thus dispose people's hearts to believe in the Lord Jesus, who is being proclaimed to them. Healings are also a foreshadowing of our ultimate salvation: being raised up, body and soul, to eternal life with God.

Some theologians, even some Church Fathers, have thought that miracles belonged primarily to the apostolic age. But miracles have continued to be a part of the Church's growth and life in every age, as illustrated especially in the lives of saints throughout Church history. Today the process of canonization—formally declaring a holy person to be a saint—requires evidence of miraculous healings through the saint's intercession. Besides these healings, evaluated according to strict criteria, there are many more ordinary examples of the Lord's healing people at shrines like Lourdes, in informal healing services, through the prayers of ordinary people, or through the Sacrament of the Sick. The world today has no less need of God's healing power than the first-century world in which the apostles preached.

Christian concern for the sick goes far beyond miraculous healings. Not only Jesus but also Peter and the other apostles showed compassion and tender care for the persons they healed. The Church shows compassion for the sick not only by praying for their healing but also by using natural means to ameliorate their condition through its many medical ministries.

Peter's Sermon Explaining the Healing (3:11–26)

[11]As he clung to Peter and John, all the people hurried in amazement toward them in the portico called "Solomon's Portico." [12]When Peter saw this, he addressed the people, "You Israelites, why are you amazed at this, and why do you look so intently at us as if we had made him walk by our own power or piety? [13]The God of Abraham, [the God] of Isaac, and [the God] of Jacob, the God of our ancestors, has glorified his servant Jesus whom you handed over and denied in Pilate's presence, when he had decided to release him. [14]You denied the Holy and Righteous One and asked that a murderer be released to you. [15]The author of life you put to death, but God raised him from the dead; of this we are witnesses. [16]And by faith in his name, this man, whom you see and know, his name has made strong, and the faith that comes through it has given him this perfect health, in the presence of all of you. [17]Now I know, brothers, that you acted out of ignorance, just as your leaders did; [18]but God has thus brought to fulfillment what he had announced beforehand through the mouth of all the prophets, that his Messiah would suffer. [19]Repent, therefore, and be converted, that your sins may be wiped away, [20]and that the Lord

may grant you times of refreshment and send you the Messiah already appointed for you, Jesus, [21]whom heaven must receive until the times of universal restoration of which God spoke through the mouth of his holy prophets from of old. [22]For Moses said:

> 'A prophet like me will the Lord, your God, raise up for you
>   from among your own kinsmen;
>   to him you shall listen in all that he may say to you.
> [23]Everyone who does not listen to that prophet
>   will be cut off from the people.'

[24]Moreover, all the prophets who spoke, from Samuel and those afterwards, also announced these days. [25]You are the children of the prophets and of the covenant that God made with your ancestors when he said to Abraham, 'In your offspring all the families of the earth shall be blessed.' [26]For you first, God raised up his servant and sent him to bless you by turning each of you from your evil ways."

OT: Deut 18:15–19; Isa 52:13–53:12

NT: Matt 21:33–46; Rom 9–11

Catechism: culpability for Jesus' death, 591, 597–98; Jesus' death in God's plan, 599–601; the name of Jesus, 430–35, 2666; Jesus' second coming, 673–74; the Church and Jews, 839–40

Lectionary: Acts 3:13–15, 17–19: Third Sunday of Easter (Year B); Acts 3:11–26: Thursday of the Octave of Easter

Luke emphasizes people's positive reaction to the miracle worked by Jesus' followers: **all the people** rushed **in amazement** toward the healed man, who was clinging to **Peter and John. Solomon's Portico** was a roofed colonnade that ran along the eastern wall of the temple complex. This colonnade was a favorite setting for Jesus to gather with his disciples (John 10:23), and it continued to be a gathering place for the early Church (Acts 5:12). | 3:11

Peter addresses **the people** as **you Israelites**. Use of their biblical name emphasizes their status as God's chosen people and descendants of Jacob, through whom God's promises to Abraham are being fulfilled. Peter reproaches them for staring at him and John as if the healing had occurred by their **own power or piety** (like Paul in Acts 14:15). They should not focus on the human instruments through whom God healed but on God himself, who declared in Exodus, "I am the LORD who heals you" (Exod 15:26). | 3:12

With the phrase **the God of our ancestors**, Peter emphasizes his shared Jewish identity with his listeners. The expression underscores the continuity between God's present action through the apostles and his former deeds for his people in the Old Testament. The God who is acting through the apostles | 3:13

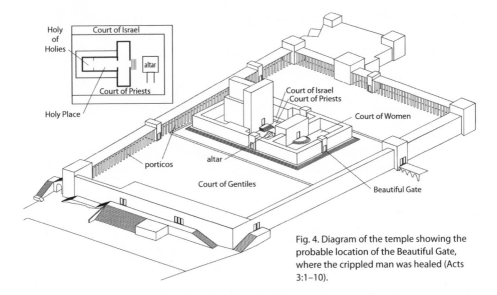

Fig. 4. Diagram of the temple showing the probable location of the Beautiful Gate, where the crippled man was healed (Acts 3:1–10).

is **the God of Abraham, [the God] of Isaac, and [the God] of Jacob** (see Luke 13:28; 20:37; Acts 7:32), who revealed himself to Moses at the burning bush (Exod 3:15). The same God who made promises to the patriarchs of Israel—the *only* God—continues to act through Jesus his Son.

This healing is a sign that God **has glorified his servant Jesus**, whom **you**, his Jewish compatriots, had rejected before Pilate (see John 1:11). Though "servant" can also be translated "child," here it alludes to Isaiah's prophecies of the Suffering Servant, who would suffer for the sins of the people but be glorified by God (Isa 52:13–53:12; Acts 8:32–35).

3:14–15   Peter calls Jesus the **Righteous One**, a title used by the centurion at the cross who recognized Jesus' innocence (Luke 23:47). In sharp contrast, the listeners had a **murderer**, Barabbas, **released** (Luke 23:18–19) and killed the **author of life**. The word for "author" can mean that Jesus is the cause or originator of life (see John 1:1–4) or that he is the pioneer or leader of life, inasmuch as he is the first to rise to life after death (see Col 1:18). Although the Jews who clamored for Jesus' crucifixion chose death over life, God reversed their decision and **raised him from the dead,** of which the apostles **are witnesses**.

3:16   Peter concludes his explanation of the healing of **this man, whom you see and know,** by declaring that it was done by the power contained in the **name** of Jesus, before whom all other powers give way (Eph 1:21; Phil 2:9–11). Biblically, a name represents the presence and power of the person named. As Old Testament priests blessed the people by invoking God's name over them (Num

6:27), Jesus' disciples healed the sick by invoking Jesus' name over them. **His name has made** the man **strong**.

It was **faith** in the name of Jesus that produced the man's **perfect health** (or "soundness in all parts of the body," which would also entail ritual cleanness), in the **presence** of numerous witnesses. This statement underscores the importance of faith in Jesus for healing, as frequently emphasized by Jesus (Luke 7:50; 8:48; 17:19; 18:42). Although there was no mention of the lame man's faith before his healing, his obedience to Peter's command (Acts 3:6–8) implies faith in what Peter said. A word spoken with confident faith in the name of Jesus, like Peter's command to the lame man to "rise and walk," has power to stir up faith in others.

Peter mentions the **ignorance** in which the Jerusalem Jews **acted** during Jesus' passion, as Jesus had prayed on the cross, "Father, forgive them, they know not what they do" (Luke 23:34).[7] But he implies that now the stakes are higher, since they can no longer claim ignorance. There is greater culpability for those who continue to reject Jesus after hearing the apostolic testimony that he has been raised from the dead. At the Areopagus in Athens, Paul later declares that "God has overlooked the times of ignorance, but now he demands that all people everywhere repent" (Acts 17:30).   **3:17**

Peter proclaims that **God** used their ignorant actions to bring to **fulfillment** all that he **had announced beforehand**, thus accomplishing his saving plan revealed in Scripture (see Luke 24:26, 46; Acts 17:3; 26:22–23). Peter does not specify particular Scripture passages foretelling that the **Messiah would suffer**, but he is probably alluding to Isaiah's prophecies of the Suffering Servant and the Psalms of David in which the psalmist cries out to God in his innocent suffering.[8]   **3:18**

The scandal of the Messiah's being crucified initially prevented Paul and other Jews from accepting Jesus as Messiah. In New Testament times, death by crucifixion was considered to be proof that the victim was cursed by God, since the law of Moses stated that "anyone hung on a tree is under God's curse" (Deut 21:23 NRSV). How could the Messiah be cursed by God? Only later did Paul come to understand that it was God's plan for the Messiah to suffer, as Jesus himself foretold, and that Jesus willingly took upon himself the curse of the law so that we could be freed from it. "Christ ransomed us from the curse of the law by becoming a curse for us" (Gal 3:13).

---

7. Although lacking in some important manuscripts, this part of the verse is fundamental to Luke's key themes of forgiveness for acts done in ignorance (see also Acts 7:60; 13:27).

8. Isa 42:1–9; 49:1–7; 50:4–11; 52:13–53:12; Pss 22; 55; 69; 88. See the commentary on Acts 2:29–31; see also Joshua W. Jipp, "Luke's Scriptural Suffering Messiah: A Search for Precedent, a Search for Identity," *Catholic Biblical Quarterly* 72, no. 2 (April 2010): 255–74.

3:19–21   Like his Pentecost speech (Acts 2:38), Peter's sermon here concludes with a call for his listeners to **repent** and **be converted** and a promise **that your sins may be wiped away**. To the pledge of forgiveness is added the further promise that **the Lord** God would grant **times of refreshment** or relief—probably referring to the spiritual refreshment that comes from the Holy Spirit.[9] The messianic age, or "last days" (Acts 2:17), has begun but will only be fully accomplished on the ultimate "great and splendid day of the Lord" (Act 2:20), when Jesus returns in power from heaven. Then will be the **times of universal restoration**, an †apocalyptic expression for God's end-time renewal of creation (see Gen 1:31), which has been spoiled by human sin. During the time of refreshment, which has begun but will not be fulfilled until the end of the world, Christians await the †parousia or coming of **the Messiah already appointed for you, Jesus**. Jesus' resurrection vindicates the claim that he is indeed the Messiah, as previously explained in Acts 2:22–36 (see Rom 1:1–4). Peter declares that these end times, the culmination of God's plan of salvation, were foretold in the Old Testament by **God . . . through the mouth of his holy prophets from of old**.

3:22–23   The quotation from Moses in verses 22–23 is a key not only to Luke's †Christology (his understanding of who Jesus is) but also to his †ecclesiology (his understanding of the Church) and his view of the relationship between the people of Israel and the new community of Jesus' followers. Moses promised the Israelites that **the Lord, your God**, will **raise up for you** a **prophet like me** (Deut 18:15). Peter proclaims that Jesus is that †prophet like Moses. The obvious meaning of "raise up" is that God would *call forth* a wonder-working prophet from the people, as he called Moses and Elijah.[10] But in light of what Peter knows happened to Jesus, a deeper meaning of "raise up" in the passage from Deuteronomy becomes clear: God would *raise from the dead* the prophet like Moses, and this meaning can only apply to Jesus (see v. 26).

Deuteronomy 18:15–20 emphasizes that the people must obey the prophet like Moses whom God will raise up, under pain of being **cut off from the people**. Here Peter interprets the prophecy to mean that the people of God, the Jews, are under absolute obligation to heed and obey Jesus, the prophet like Moses whom God has raised up: **to him you shall listen in all that he may say to you**. Some of the people to whom Peter is preaching rejected Jesus and had him

---

9. The verb for "refresh" can be used for relief from work (Exod 23:12) or the refreshment that comes from food, water, or a friend's kindness (Judg 15:19; 2 Sam 16:14; 2 Tim 1:16).

10. Elijah and, to a lesser extent, his disciple Elisha had been regarded as prophets like Moses because they were the only prophets besides Moses who were celebrated for working signs and wonders (1 Kings 17–2 Kings 13). The writing prophets, such as Isaiah, Jeremiah, and Hosea, were known primarily for their oracles, for accounts of their calls, and for some of their nonmiraculous prophetic signs, like Jeremiah's breaking a pot to emphasize his message.

killed (v. 15). But since they acted in ignorance (v. 17), they can now repent and be forgiven (v. 19). Peter is asserting that since God has resurrected this prophet like Moses and sent him to them through the preaching and miracles of the apostles, there is no longer an excuse for not listening to him. Those who do accept Jesus (5,000 men by Acts 4:4) become part of the restored people of God, in continuity with the people of God throughout the Old Testament.

After speaking of Jesus as the risen prophet like Moses whom the people   **3:24–25** must heed, Peter states that **all the prophets** in general **from Samuel and those afterwards, also announced these days**. Peter is expressing the Christian

The Church's Understanding of Judaism

LIVING TRADITION

Vatican Council II laid the foundations for a new understanding of Judaism and its relationship to the Church when it declared:

> As Holy Scripture testifies, Jerusalem did not recognize the time of her visitation, nor did the Jews in large number accept the Gospel; indeed not a few opposed its spreading. Nevertheless, God holds the Jews most dear for the sake of their fathers; He does not repent of the gifts He makes or of the calls He issues—such is the witness of the Apostle [Paul]. In company with the Prophets and the same Apostle, the Church awaits that day, known to God alone, on which all peoples will address the Lord in a single voice and "serve him shoulder to shoulder" (Zeph 3:9).[a]

Pope John Paul II further developed this understanding. In an address to the Jewish communities of Italy in 1986, he declared:

> The Church of Christ discovers its "links" with Judaism "by pondering its own mystery" (cf. *Nostra Aetate*). The Jewish religion is not "extrinsic" to us, but in a certain manner, it is "intrinsic" to our religion. We have therefore a relationship with it which we do not have with any other religion. You are our favored brothers and, in a certain sense, one can say our elder brothers.

As the Pontifical Biblical Commission has observed, the way toward further progress in Jewish-Christian relations "lies in avoiding a one-sided reading of biblical texts . . . and making instead a better effort to appreciate the whole dynamism that animates them, which is precisely a dynamism of love. In the Old Testament, the plan of God is a union of love with his people. . . . In the New Testament, God's love overcomes the worst obstacles; even if they do not believe in his Son whom he sent as their Messiah Savior, Israelites are still 'loved' (Rom 11:29). Whoever wishes to be united to God, must also love them."[b]

a. *Nostra Aetate (Declaration on the Relation of the Church to Non-Christian Religions)*, 4.
b. *The Jewish People and Their Sacred Scriptures in the Christian Bible*, 86.

conviction that the entire Old Testament speaks of Christ (see Luke 24:25–27). Finally, Peter's reference to his listeners as **children of the prophets and of the covenant** assures them that they are beneficiaries of God's irrevocable covenant with **Abraham** (Gen 22:18): **In your offspring all the families of the earth shall be blessed.** God is fulfilling his promise to make his chosen people Israel the source of blessing for the entire world.

3:26   Peter declares that God's raising of Jesus from death benefits first the Jews, who were the first to receive the gospel, then also Gentiles: **for you first** God raised **his servant and sent him to bless you.** This is the basis of Paul's pattern of preaching to Jews first and then to Gentiles (Acts 13:46; 26:20) and of his hopes that one day "all Israel will be saved" (Rom 11:26). For the New Testament, the Jews remain the people of God's promises. The condition for their receiving the blessing promised to Abraham is cooperating with the risen Jesus' **turning each of you from your evil ways.** Receiving God's blessing, whether one already belongs to God's chosen people or not, begins with repentance for one's sins, as Jesus himself preached: "This is the time of fulfillment. The kingdom of God is at hand. Repent, and believe in the gospel" (Mark 1:14–15).

Peter Is Arrested for Preaching the Resurrection (4:1–4)

---

[1]While they were still speaking to the people, the priests, the captain of the temple guard, and the Sadducees confronted them, [2]disturbed that they were teaching the people and proclaiming in Jesus the resurrection of the dead. [3]They laid hands on them and put them in custody until the next day, since it was already evening. [4]But many of those who heard the word came to believe and [the] number of men grew to [about] five thousand.

OT: Isa 26:19; Ezek 37:12; Dan 12:2
NT: Luke 20:37; 21:12
Catechism: persecution for faith, 769, 1808, 1816
Lectionary: Acts 4:1–12: Friday of the Octave of Easter

4:1–2   Luke moves rapidly from Peter's speech to the reaction it garners by highlighting an interruption from irate listeners (as at Nazareth in Luke 4, and later in Jerusalem when Paul is speaking in Acts 22). Here it is **the priests, the captain of the temple guard, and the Sadducees** who interrupt the speech. The †Sadducees were members of the priestly aristocracy in Jerusalem. As Luke explains elsewhere (Luke 20:27; Acts 23:6–8), they did not believe in a resurrection. Their annoyance is due to the disciples' **proclaiming in Jesus the resurrection of the dead**—a concise summary of the Christian †kerygma.

The priests, temple guard, and Sadducees arrest Peter and John and **put them in custody**. Despite their arrest, many of their listeners **came to believe**: counting only adult males, the **number of men grew to [about] five thousand** (see 2:41). Even when Jesus' witnesses are imprisoned, the word of God continues to spread and the number of believers continues to grow. Official sanctions cannot prevent a significant minority of Jews in Jerusalem from becoming followers of Jesus. On the contrary, as has often happened throughout Church history, the willingness of Christians to suffer for the name of Jesus leads to an even greater spread of the gospel. The growth of the Church is proving unstoppable, no matter what the authorities try to do to hinder it.

4:3–4

Bold Testimony and a New Outpouring of the Spirit

Acts 4:5–31

The reaction to the lame man's healing and Peter's explanation (Acts 3:1–26) was swift. On the one hand, many new believers joined the apostles. On the other hand, resistance by the †Sanhedrin, or Jewish high court, was also immediate. In Acts 4 Luke shows the apostles and their followers answering these challenges.

Witness before the Sanhedrin (4:5–12)

⁵On the next day, their leaders, elders, and scribes were assembled in Jerusalem, ⁶with Annas the high priest, Caiaphas, John, Alexander, and all who were of the high-priestly class. ⁷They brought them into their presence and questioned them, "By what power or by what name have you done this?" ⁸Then Peter, filled with the holy Spirit, answered them, "Leaders of the people and elders: ⁹If we are being examined today about a good deed done to a cripple, namely, by what means he was saved, ¹⁰then all of you and all the people of Israel should know that it was in the name of Jesus Christ the Nazorean whom you crucified, whom God raised from the dead; in his name this man stands before you healed. ¹¹He is 'the stone rejected by you, the builders, which has become the cornerstone.' ¹²There is no salvation through anyone else, nor is there any other name under heaven given to the human race by which we are to be saved."

OT: Ps 118:22

NT: Luke 12:8–12; 20:1–2; John 3:36; 14:6; 1 Tim 2:5
Catechism: salvation in Jesus alone, 161, 432; the Church's mission, 849–56
Lectionary: Acts 4:8–12: Fourth Sunday of Easter (Year B); St. Bernardine of Siena; Acts 4:1–12: Friday of the Octave of Easter

Luke emphasizes that the entire Jewish leadership is present to judge Peter **4:5–6** and John in this official gathering of the highest Jewish court, the Sanhedrin, the same court that had tried Jesus (Luke 22:66). The general term **leaders** probably refers to all the seventy-one members of the Sanhedrin, headed by the high priest: **elders**, **scribes**, and members of **the high-priestly class** (see Luke 9:22; 20:1). Among the high-priestly class, Luke first mentions **Annas the high priest**, actually a former high priest (AD 6–15) who was deposed by Rome but still esteemed by Jews. The actual high priest at that time was his son-in-law **Caiaphas** (see John 18:13). The Sanhedrin also included **John**, probably referring to Annas's son who became high priest after Caiaphas (in AD 36), **Alexander**, and other less known high priests.

The Sanhedrin leaders demand that Peter and John explain themselves: **"By** **4:7** **what power or by what name have you done this?"** This question was precisely what Peter had already answered before the Jewish crowd at the temple when he told them not to think that this healing was achieved "by our own power or piety" (Acts 3:12). Rather, the lame man was healed by faith in the name of Jesus (Acts 3:16).

Jesus instructed his disciples not to be afraid when they are brought to trial **4:8–10** for their faith: "When they take you before synagogues and before rulers and authorities, do not worry about how or what your defense will be or about what you are to say. For the holy Spirit will teach you at that moment what you should say" (Luke 12:11–12). Here, in fulfillment of Jesus' prophetic instructions, **Peter** is **filled with the holy Spirit** as he **answered them**. His response manifests Spirit-inspired wisdom and boldness. The same Peter who cowered before the challenge of a serving girl (Luke 22:56–57) now fearlessly confronts the Sanhedrin: **Leaders of the people and elders**. He implicitly reproaches them for interrogating him **about a good deed done to a cripple**, then solemnly proclaims to them and **to all the people of Israel** the cause of the healing: it was done **in the name of Jesus Christ the Nazorean**. Even though Jesus was the one whom **you**, the Sanhedrin, **crucified** by handing him over to Pilate with a capital charge (Luke 23:1–2), God reversed that action and **raised** him **from the dead**. Peter declares that **in his name**, Jesus' name, the lame man **stands before you healed**.

In this testimony Peter states the facts and, in so doing, reproves the Sanhe- **4:11** drin for opposing God's plan. Jesus is **the stone rejected by you, the builders,**

which has become the cornerstone. The Sanhedrin are the "builders" of Israel, yet they had rejected the Messiah, the cornerstone, or capstone, essential to the building's structure. In the Gospel, Jesus quoted this same line from Ps 118:22 to show that his rejection by the Jewish leaders was part of God's plan and to illustrate the divine reversal of human purposes (Luke 20:17–19). God raised up the crucified Jesus and made him the cornerstone of the new temple, the Church. The First Letter of Peter similarly refers to Jesus as "a living stone, rejected by human beings but chosen and precious in the sight of God" (1 Pet 2:4) and in 1 Pet 2:6 goes on to cite Isa 28:16:

> Therefore, thus says the Lord GOD:
> "See, I am laying a stone in Zion,
> a stone that has been tested,
> A precious cornerstone as a sure foundation;
> whoever puts faith in it will not waver."

4:12   Then Peter states something truly extraordinary when he solemnly declares, **"There is no salvation through anyone else,"** for God has not given human beings **"any other name under heaven . . . by which we are to be saved."** In fact, the meaning of the name Jesus (Hebrew *Yeshua*, a shortened form of *Yehoshua*) is "Yahweh saves." Peter's pronouncement is the most absolute and universal statement in Scripture of salvation in Jesus Christ alone.[1] The prophetic leader of the restored people of God proclaims to the Sanhedrin that God has made his Son the one provision for the salvation of the human race. Peter sets an example for Christians throughout the ages not to be afraid to present the Christian claim to those who do not yet believe.

Reflection and Application (4:5–12)

The time since Vatican II has seen much confusion about our obligations as Catholics regarding evangelization and interreligious dialogue. On the one hand, the New Testament is absolutely clear that Christians have an obligation to bear witness to Jesus Christ, the Savior of *all* peoples. While addressing the leaders of Judaism in Acts 4, Peter refuses to downplay the truth that "there is no salvation through anyone else" besides Jesus. He does not avoid proclaiming this message by hiding behind the notion that all religions have their own

1. For similar statements see Mark 16:15–16; John 3:36; 14:6; 1 Tim 2:5; 1 John 5:12.

Evangelizing All Nations

LIVING TRADITION

The word *catholic* comes from a Greek phrase meaning "according to the whole." The Catechism teaches that one reason the Church is called "catholic" is "because she has been sent out by Christ on a mission to the whole of the human race" (831). The Catechism goes on to explain the Church's missionary motivation (851):

It is from God's love for all . . . that the Church in every age receives both the obligation and the vigor of her missionary dynamism, "for the love of Christ urges us on" (2 Cor 5:14). Indeed, God "desires all . . . to be saved and to come to the knowledge of the truth" (1 Tim 2:4). . . . Salvation is found in the truth. Those who obey the prompting of the Spirit of truth are already on the way of salvation. But the Church, to whom this truth has been entrusted, must go out to meet their desire, so as to bring them the truth. Because she believes in God's universal plan of salvation, the Church must be missionary.

views. He directly challenges his listeners' unbelief and leaves it to them to accept or reject his message.

Unfortunately, in the centuries since then, anti-Semitic prejudice and false ideas about Jewish guilt for Jesus' crucifixion have often led to hostility between Christians and Jews. In efforts to avoid such interreligious hostility, many contemporary Christians refrain from witnessing about Jesus to Jews or members of other religions. To clarify the Church's teaching on this matter, in 2000 the Congregation for the Doctrine of the Faith published the document *Dominus Iesus*, which states that "The Catholic Church rejects nothing of what is true and holy in [other] religions. She has a high regard for the manner of life and conduct, the precepts and teachings, which, although differing in many ways from her own teaching, nonetheless often reflect a ray of that truth which enlightens all men." The document then affirms:

One can and must say that Jesus Christ has a significance and a value for the human race and its history which are unique and singular, proper to him alone, exclusive, universal, and absolute. Jesus is, in fact, the Word of God made man for the salvation of all. In expressing this consciousness of faith, the Second Vatican Council teaches: "The Word of God, through whom all things were made, was made flesh, so that as perfect man he could save all men and sum up all things in himself. The Lord is the goal of human history, the focal point of the desires of history and civilization, the center of mankind, the joy of all hearts, and the fulfillment of all aspirations. It is he whom the Father raised from the dead, exalted, and placed at his right hand, constituting him judge of the living and the dead." "It is precisely this uniqueness of Christ which gives him an absolute and universal significance whereby, while belonging to history, he remains history's center and goal: 'I am the Alpha and the Omega, the first and the last, the beginning and the end' (Rev 22:13)."

This statement, like Peter's in Acts 4:12, might be viewed as arrogant or unacceptable by people who disagree or who deny the existence of absolute truth. But it is not arrogant to share good news revealed by God that is critically important to people's eternal salvation.

On the other hand, it does indeed seem condescending and is ultimately both unfaithful to the truth and uncharitable for Christians to say, "I don't tell Muslims about Jesus. I help them to be better Muslims." What do *we* as Christians know about helping Muslims (or others of different religions) *be better Muslims*? Rather, we must say with Peter's offer: "What I do have I give you" (Acts 3:6). What we have is the good news that God became man in Jesus to save all people: "With your blood you purchased for God those from every tribe and tongue, people and nation" (Rev 5:9). Authentic missionary witness lovingly and noncoercively shares with others what we most value, regardless of whether some listeners will be annoyed by our message or even try to suppress it.

"Are We to Obey You Rather Than God?" (4:13–22)

[13]Observing the boldness of Peter and John and perceiving them to be uneducated, ordinary men, they were amazed, and they recognized them as the companions of Jesus. [14]Then when they saw the man who had been cured standing there with them, they could say nothing in reply. [15]So they ordered them to leave the Sanhedrin, and conferred with one another, saying, [16]"What are we to do with these men? Everyone living in Jerusalem knows that a remarkable sign was done through them, and we cannot deny it. [17]But so that it may not be spread any further among the people, let us give them a stern warning never again to speak to anyone in this name."

[18]So they called them back and ordered them not to speak or teach at all in the name of Jesus. [19]Peter and John, however, said to them in reply, "Whether it is right in the sight of God for us to obey you rather than God, you be the judges. [20]It is impossible for us not to speak about what we have seen and heard." [21]After threatening them further, they released them, finding no way to punish them, on account of the people who were

all praising God for what had happened. ²²For the man on whom this sign of healing had been done was over forty years old.

NT: Luke 21:12–15; Acts 5:29; 1 Cor 1:26–27; 1 John 1:1–3
Catechism: "what we have seen and heard," 425; praising God, 2639–43
Lectionary: Saturday of the Octave of Easter

The Sanhedrin members are **amazed** by the **boldness** in speech of these   **4:13–14**
uneducated fishermen. "Boldness" here refers to freedom and fearlessness in speaking. The Sanhedrin is surprised that common men who lack formal training in the law of Moses or in †rhetoric speak with such confidence and authority. Making the situation even more galling for the leaders is their recognition that Peter and John were **companions of Jesus,** literally, "they had been with Jesus." Jesus taught in the Gospel that the task of a disciple is first to "be with him" (Mark 3:14). Peter and John exhibit a Spirit-inspired courage, confidence, and authority that came from having spent time with Jesus. Even today, the boldness of Christians' testimony depends on their spending time with Jesus. The Sanhedrin thought that Jesus' death would free them from having to deal with his influence. Because of the irrefutable evidence of **the man who had been cured standing there with them, they could say nothing in reply** to Peter's bold proclamation.

The members of the Sanhedrin are befuddled, frustrated, and struggling to   **4:15–17**
limit the damage. Their consultation about Peter and John illustrates the powerlessness of Israel's old leadership to effectively counter the apostolic leaders of renewed Israel. Because the man's healing is public knowledge, they are forced to admit that it was a **remarkable sign** that **was done through** the apostles. Calling the healing a "sign," rather than a healing or marvel, invites reflection on what the sign signifies: in this case it means that Jesus is alive and acting through the disciples. Yet ironically the Sanhedrin members refuse to accept the evidence before them, just as during Jesus' public ministry (see John 12:37). They are determined that the apostles' witness **not be spread any further among the people** and that what they regard as a harmful message be suppressed. Yet their **warning** and attempt to silence the apostles is doomed to failure.

The Sanhedrin try to forbid Peter and John **to speak or teach at all in the**   **4:18**
name of Jesus, the name Peter has just said is the only one given by God for the salvation of the human race (4:12). This prohibition recalls the purpose of Acts as stated in the prologue: to continue the Gospel's account of "all that Jesus *began* to do and teach" (Acts 1:1, literal translation). What Jesus' disciples do, such as the healing of the lame man, and teach, such as the meaning of this sign "in the name of Jesus," is the risen Jesus' *continuing* to act and teach

through them. For the Sanhedrin to forbid preaching in the name of Jesus is the absurd equivalent to forbidding the risen Lord to continue to act and teach through his apostles.[2]

4:19   In reply, **Peter and John** challenge their judges with the rhetorical question **whether it is right in the sight of God for us to obey you rather than God**. Because Jesus had asserted the necessity of God's biblical plan (Luke 24:46–49) and directly commanded his disciples to be his witnesses (Acts 1:8), the apostles are under divine mandate to proclaim the gospel from Jerusalem to the ends of the earth. The Sanhedrin's attempt to silence them contradicts the solemn commission they have received from the Father through the Son, for which they have been empowered by the Holy Spirit.

4:20   It is obvious, therefore, that for the disciples **not to speak about what we have seen and heard** is simply not an option. Testimony to what one has seen and heard is the mark of an eyewitness, in contrast to mere hearsay testimony, which lacks probative value. Testimony based on both *seeing* and *hearing* corresponds closely to the description of Luke's Gospel as recounting "all that Jesus did and taught" (Acts 1:1), for which Luke relied on "eyewitnesses from the beginning and ministers of the word" (Luke 1:2). The apostles as eyewitnesses have *seen* what Jesus did and have *heard* his teachings. Christian belief is grounded in this apostolic eyewitness testimony. Analogously, contemporary Christian witness is more persuasive when it flows from one's personal encounter with the risen Jesus.

4:21–22 The powerlessness of Israel's old leadership remains vividly on display as they are reduced merely to **threatening** the apostles and have no choice but to release them. They cannot punish them because the people are **all praising God for what had happened**. Clearly the people are better able to recognize signs of God's action than the leaders, which suggests that the leaders have lost effective authority over God's people. Instead, the people are now heeding the apostles. The people's praising God for what they saw and heard functions as an implicit acknowledgment of the apostles as their new leaders. The healing of a man crippled from birth is an incontrovertible public event, a sign that wins the people's praise of God and respect for the apostles. The mention that the man was **over forty years old**, while underscoring the significance of the healing, may also be intended to recall Israel's forty years in the desert before their entrance into the promised land.

---

2. See the sustained demonstration in Keith Warrington, "Acts and the Healing Narratives: Why?," *Journal of Pentecostal Theology* 14, no. 2 (2006): 189–217; his thesis is stated on 189: "The healings indicate that Jesus is present among the believers. The ascension of Jesus does not indicate his absence. The healings are reminiscent of the way Jesus healed. It is as if he was performing them himself; in reality, he is."

Prayer of the Community (4:23–31)

²³After their release they went back to their own people and reported what the chief priests and elders had told them. ²⁴And when they heard it, they raised their voices to God with one accord and said, "Sovereign Lord, maker of heaven and earth and the sea and all that is in them, ²⁵you said by the holy Spirit through the mouth of our father David, your servant:

> 'Why did the Gentiles rage
> and the peoples entertain folly?
> ²⁶The kings of the earth took their stand
> and the princes gathered together
> against the Lord and against his anointed.'

²⁷Indeed they gathered in this city against your holy servant Jesus whom you anointed, Herod and Pontius Pilate, together with the Gentiles and the peoples of Israel, ²⁸to do what your hand and [your] will had long ago planned to take place. ²⁹And now, Lord, take note of their threats, and enable your servants to speak your word with all boldness, ³⁰as you stretch forth [your] hand to heal, and signs and wonders are done through the name of your holy servant Jesus." ³¹As they prayed, the place where they were gathered shook, and they were all filled with the holy Spirit and continued to speak the word of God with boldness.

OT: Ps 2:1–2
NT: Luke 23:12; John 20:19–23; Acts 2:29–31
Catechism: the Lord's anointed, 436–40; Jesus' death according to Scripture, 599–601
Lectionary: Saturday of the Octave of Easter; Mass for Persecuted Christians

The Christian community was in no way intimidated by the warnings of the **4:23–24** **chief priests and elders** that Peter and John reported. On the contrary, they broke into spontaneous and united prayer as they **raised their voices to God** and asked the all-powerful God to defeat the threats not only of Jewish leaders but also of world-ruling Romans. As before and after Pentecost (Acts 1:14; 2:46), they pray **with one accord**.

The community addresses God as **Sovereign Lord**, a term for God used elsewhere only by the prophet Simeon (Luke 2:29). Although this form of address may sound similar to the way pagan Greeks addressed their gods, when combined with **maker of heaven and earth and the sea and all that is in them** it expresses the biblical worldview. God has created the universe (Gen 1) and consequently has authority over it. The focus on God as creator and ruler of the

Solidarity in Fellowship and Prayer

BIBLICAL BACKGROUND

The expression "with one accord" (*homothymadon*) is frequent in Acts, describing the community's united prayer before Pentecost (1:14), their communal gatherings in the temple after Pentecost (2:46), their prayer for boldness (4:24), their togetherness in Solomon's portico (5:12), the unified attention of the Samaritans to Philip (8:6), and the unity at the Council of Jerusalem (15:25). In Rom 15:6 Paul prays "that with one accord [*homothymadon*] you may with one voice glorify the God and Father of our Lord Jesus Christ." The unity of Christians, especially in prayer and fellowship, builds the faith of members and attracts new believers, whereas disunity repels them.

universe is particularly appropriate here because God is ruler of both Jewish and Gentile authorities.

4:25–26   The core of the community's prayer is a quotation from Ps 2, which they apply to their present situation. This way of applying Scripture to a contemporary situation has been commonly used by both Jewish and Christian interpreters from that time to today. The disciples acknowledge that this psalm was spoken **by the holy Spirit through the mouth of our father David**. That is, the psalm is a prophecy uttered by David, the presumed author of many of the psalms, speaking for God because he was inspired by the Spirit (see Acts 2:30–31). The reference to David as God's **servant** applies to him the same designation that is used for all Israel's prophets, from Moses to Malachi: "all my servants the prophets" (Jer 7:25; see Isa 49:5).

The prayer quotes Ps 2:1–2: **"Why did the Gentiles rage and the peoples entertain folly? The kings of the earth took their stand and the princes gathered together against the Lord and against his anointed."** The disciples understand the psalm as foretelling the combined opposition to the Lord (God) and his anointed (Christ) by Jewish and Roman authorities. "The Gentiles" refers here to the Roman authorities and the "peoples" refers to the Jewish authorities. Further, "kings" is applied to Herod Antipas, ruler of Galilee, and "princes," or "rulers," to Pilate. Luke's is the only Gospel to mention that Pilate sent Jesus to be tried by Herod and that "Herod and Pilate became friends that very day" (Luke 23:12). At the same time, the reference to a hostile gathering of rulers alludes to the recent gathering of the Sanhedrin against Jesus' followers (Acts 4:5).

4:27–28   The prayer applies this united enmity of kings and rulers to those who **gathered in this city against your holy servant Jesus**, meaning Herod and

Pontius Pilate, together with the crowd that agitated for Jesus' death. The prayer proclaims that this persecution of Jesus by Jews in alliance with Romans was foreseen by God and used for his saving plan. In fact, their combined attack on God's anointed one achieved what God's **hand** and **will had long ago planned to take place**.

With this assurance that God's providence continues to be in control of all events, the Christians pray to God to **enable your servants** to act as prophets and **speak your word with all boldness**, as prophets do. Not only are the disciples not intimidated by the warnings of the Sanhedrin: they also pray to have even more boldness in proclaiming the gospel. **4:29**

In addition they ask that their bold prophetic witness be confirmed by God's direct action **to heal** and by **signs and wonders** worked **through the name of your holy servant Jesus**. The reference to "signs and wonders" recalls the miracles of God's servant Moses in the exodus from Egypt (Deut 34:11). The believers ask God to empower their prophetic witness to be like that of Moses and like that of the †prophet even greater than Moses, Jesus (Acts 3:22; 7:37). Their speaking God's word in Jesus' name with healings, signs, and wonders would in fact be the risen Jesus' continuing his prophetic ministry through them by the power of the Holy Spirit. **4:30**

In a scene reminiscent of Pentecost, the prayer of the disciples is answered immediately and sensationally. The shaking of their gathering **place** brings to mind the shaking of Mount Sinai (Exod 19:18) and the earthquakes expected before God's definitive action in the end times (see Isa 29:6; Luke 21:11; Rev 16:17–18). Like the first 120 disciples in the upper room at Pentecost, they are **all filled with the holy Spirit**. The immediate result is that they **continued to speak** (NIV, NRSV, RSV "spoke"; NJB, JB "began to proclaim") **the word of God with boldness**. Threatened by the old leadership of Israel, Jesus' disciples pray to the God who rules the universe for empowerment to witness even more boldly and powerfully than before. Filled with the Spirit in a new and deeper way, they do so testify. **4:31**

Reflection and Application (4:13–31)

Living as Christians today and witnessing to our faith and moral convictions is no easier for us than it was for the first disciples, who needed the Spirit's empowerment at Pentecost to come out from behind locked doors (John 20:19) to preach to the crowds. For example, it is sometimes difficult for pro-life medical students to be accepted into specializations like obstetrics and gynecology. Some medical schools may reject candidates who demonstrate a firm Catholic faith because of their resistance to unethical practices related to abortion, in vitro fertilization, embryonic stem cell research, euthanasia, and the like. It takes a clear commitment to Jesus and strength from the Holy Spirit to "obey God rather than any human authority" (see Acts 4:19; 5:29 NRSV) even at the cost of one's desired career. Nevertheless, empowered by the Holy Spirit and much prayer, many health-care aspirants are giving a bold and courageous witness to their faith and ethical convictions, regardless of their personal sacrifice.

Sharing of Goods: Two Contrary Examples

Acts 4:32–5:11

The community has just weathered external aggression from the Sanhedrin. Its idyllic unity and harmony are soon threatened from within. Satan's infiltration of two members undermines the unity of the Church under apostolic leadership. By contrast, Luke presents Barnabas as a positive example of sharing, to be emulated by Christians.

Second Summary: Life in the Christian Community (4:32–35)

³²**The community of believers was of one heart and mind, and no one claimed that any of his possessions was his own, but they had everything in common. ³³With great power the apostles bore witness to the resurrection of the Lord Jesus, and great favor was accorded them all. ³⁴There was no needy person among them, for those who owned property or houses would sell them, bring the proceeds of the sale, ³⁵and put them at the feet of the apostles, and they were distributed to each according to need.**

OT: Deut 15:4–11
NT: Acts 2:42–47
Catechism: private ownership, 2402–6; care for the poor, 2443–49; communion in spiritual goods, 949–53
Lectionary: Second Sunday of Easter (Year B); St. Peter Julian Eymard

This is the second summary of the life of the early Christian community   4:32
in Jerusalem. Like the first (Acts 2:42–47), it emphasizes the members' unity

and sharing of possessions. Although these two passages have inspired the communal ownership of goods in religious communities, their original meaning does not seem to be that the Jerusalem Christians were obligated to share their goods, since those who owned property were free to sell it or not (Acts 5:4). The absence of a requirement makes the Christians' free choice to share their possessions all the more powerful a sign of the presence of the Spirit in their midst.

Because of Luke's Hellenistic background, he uses an expression familiar in Hellenistic literature for sharing among friends: **they had everything in common**. Another common expression was that friends were of "one mind" (literally, "one soul"). Luke's addition of the heart makes the expression **one heart and mind** a more biblical phrase (see 1 Sam 2:35; 1 Chron 29:18; Ps 26:2). Luke's description has both Hellenistic and biblical resonances, thus appealing to his mixed audience of readers.

The remark that **no one claimed that any of his possessions was his own** was another common Hellenistic way of describing friendship. The Latino expression of hospitality *Mi casa es tu casa* ("My house is your house") has similar connotations, without literally meaning that the host's house actually belongs to the guest. What Luke's expressions indicate is the early Christians' genuine sense of being brothers and sisters who joyfully care for one another's needs. They shared not only material goods, but also spiritual goods such as faith and love, joys and sufferings, and the charisms and fruits of the Holy Spirit.[1] Such sharing was an important witness in the first century and remains so today.

4:33 This passage illustrates the authority of the apostles as the disciples lay proceeds at the apostles' feet (4:35, 37; 5:2). For Luke, administration of possessions is symbolic of authority in the community, as will be made significant in Acts 6:1–6.[2] Luke emphasizes the **great power** by which **the apostles bore witness to the resurrection of the Lord Jesus**. The apostles' miracles corroborated their testimony that Jesus is Lord (the same title the Old Testament gives to God), as attested by his resurrection. And all the Christians were both blessed by God and respected by humans. The expression **great favor was accorded them all** has a double reference, since the Greek word for "favor" (*charis*) also means "grace." The NAB seems to imply that the favor was human esteem (as in NJB, "accorded great respect," and REB, "held in high esteem"). But it could also refer to grace from God, as in most other translations (RSV, NRSV, NIV).

---

1. See the Catechism, 949–53.
2. See Luke Timothy Johnson, *The Literary Function of Possessions in Luke-Acts* (Missoula, MT: Scholars Press, 1977).

The reason why **there was no needy person among them** is the generosity   4:34–35
of other members of the Christian community. This phrase echoes Deut 15:4:
"since the LORD, your God, will bless you abundantly in the land the LORD,
your God, will give you, . . . there shall be no one of you in need." God links this
promise to Israel's obeying his commandments, and in particular, the instruction to remit all debts within the covenant community every seventh year (Deut
15:1–5). Now needy persons are lacking in the Jerusalem community because
of the Christians' Spirit-inspired readiness to share their resources with one
another; such active caring fulfills Old Testament legislation and obtains the
promised outcome of obedience to God's law, God's abundant blessing. This
fulfills the prophetic promise through Ezek 36:27–28 that God will bestow his
Spirit and thus enable his people to keep the law and experience his blessings.

Although the church in Jerusalem seems to have presumed private ownership of property, its members exercised a form of sharing in which those with
property or houses contributed the **proceeds** from land they sold, which were
then **distributed** to poorer individuals **according to need**. The phrase **at the
feet of the apostles** implies the apostles' authority over the money put into
the common fund. Since whoever administers a group's money influences the
endeavors in which the group engages, the phrase can be interpreted more
broadly to illustrate the authority of the apostles over all the affairs of the community. It also implies that the members trusted the apostles' discernment in
distributing the funds where they were most needed. At this point the common
fund was administered by the apostles, though that monetary authority will be
delegated to "the Seven" in Acts 6.

Putting Contributions at the Feet of the Apostles (4:36–5:11)

[36]Thus Joseph, also named by the apostles Barnabas (which is translated
"son of encouragement"), a Levite, a Cypriot by birth, [37]sold a piece of
property that he owned, then brought the money and put it at the feet of
the apostles.

[1]A man named Ananias, however, with his wife Sapphira, sold a piece of
property. [2]He retained for himself, with his wife's knowledge, some of the
purchase price, took the remainder, and put it at the feet of the apostles.
[3]But Peter said, "Ananias, why has Satan filled your heart so that you lied
to the holy Spirit and retained part of the price of the land? [4]While it remained unsold, did it not remain yours? And when it was sold, was it not
still under your control? Why did you contrive this deed? You have lied

not to human beings, but to God." [5]When Ananias heard these words, he fell down and breathed his last, and great fear came upon all who heard of it. [6]The young men came and wrapped him up, then carried him out and buried him.

[7]After an interval of about three hours, his wife came in, unaware of what had happened. [8]Peter said to her, "Tell me, did you sell the land for this amount?" She answered, "Yes, for that amount." [9]Then Peter said to her, "Why did you agree to test the Spirit of the Lord? Listen, the footsteps of those who have buried your husband are at the door, and they will carry you out." [10]At once, she fell down at his feet and breathed her last. When the young men entered they found her dead, so they carried her out and buried her beside her husband. [11]And great fear came upon the whole church and upon all who heard of these things.

OT: Deut 6:16; Dan 13:55, 59
NT: Luke 4:12
Catechism: authority in the Church, 894–96; tempting God, 2118–19; lying, 2482–87

Luke now gives back-to-back positive and negative illustrations of the community practice of laying sale proceeds at the feet of the apostles: the inspiring model of Barnabas (Acts 4:36–37) and the frightening example of Ananias and Sapphira (5:1–11).

4:36   Barnabas is introduced as a model of the community's sharing of goods to help poor members. His given name is **Joseph**, but **the apostles** give him a new name, **Barnabas**, which is used in the rest of Acts. Luke explains that in †Aramaic, the language then spoken in Palestine, Barnabas means **son of encouragement**.[3] The Greek word for encouragement, *paraklēsis*, is related to *paraklētos*, a title for the Holy Spirit (John 14:16, 26), which means advocate, consoler, intercessor, and counselor. The new name reflects the apostles' recognition of Barnabas's character. He will live up to the meaning of his name when he encourages the Jerusalem Christians to welcome their former persecutor, Paul (Acts 9:26–27), and later, when he enlists Paul to help him nurture the first community comprised of both Jews and Gentiles, in Antioch (11:22–26; see sidebar on Barnabas, p. 189).

4:37   Barnabas was from the tribe of Levi and a native of Cyprus, which may have been the location of his property. His action exemplifies Luke's statement that the early believers sold their property and shared the proceeds with the needy of the Church (4:34–35). Barnabas **sold a piece of property that he owned,**

---

3. *Bar* means "son" in Aramaic, but the linguistic foundation for the translation "son of encouragement" is unclear.

92

then brought the money and put it at the feet of the apostles. The key phrase "at the feet of the apostles" is used three times in five verses (4:35, 37; 5:2), emphasizing the apostles' leadership role in the Church.

The positive example of Barnabas is followed immediately by the negative example of **Ananias** and **his wife Sapphira**. The contrasting examples are linked by the term **however** (or "but," RSV and NRSV). Ananias ostensibly performed the same action as Barnabas: he **sold a piece of property**. However, he secretly **retained for himself some of the purchase price** and put the rest **at the feet of the apostles**. In Titus 2:10 the same Greek verb meaning "retain for oneself" can refer to a slave's embezzling from his master. Although technically this couple did not embezzle, their lie about the portion of the funds contributed to the community has some analogies to embezzling. In the Greek Old Testament, the same verb is used for stealing gold vessels from the temple (2 Macc 4:32) and for the thievery of Achan, who took and hid goods that were dedicated to the Lord (Josh 6:24; 7:1). Achan's disobedience resulted in God's refusal to help the Israelites until they removed the sinner from their midst. Although Ananias and Sapphira's crime differed from that of Achan, it did involve similar deceit and met a similar punishment.

5:1–2

Luke emphasizes the wife's complicity with her husband in this deception by mentioning it twice. In verse 1 Ananias sold the property "with his wife Sapphira." In verse 2 he withheld some of the proceeds also **with his wife's knowledge**. Because she shared the same severe punishment as her husband, Luke is careful to indicate that she was equally guilty of the sin of lying to and testing (v. 9) the Holy Spirit.

Peter, as Spirit-filled head of the community, confronts **Ananias** with his sinful deception. Peter underscores the gravity of the offense by attributing it to **Satan**, who has **filled** Ananias's **heart**—a striking contrast to the frequent mention of disciples who are "filled with the Holy Spirit."[4] Behind human actions, Luke often recognizes the influence of the Holy Spirit or the evil spirit, Satan. That Satan filled Ananias's heart means that he allowed Satan's evil counsels to dominate his actions. Luke also made a similar claim about Judas: "Then Satan entered into Judas" (Luke 22:3).

5:3

What was the sin that would warrant the sinners' being struck dead on the spot? The essence of the sin is mentioned in Peter's accusation to Ananias: he **lied to the holy Spirit**. Lying to God insinuates that God is not all-knowing, that God can be deceived. In effect, this denies that God is God! Dishonesty and impure motives in Christians can also hinder others from coming to faith

4. See Luke 1:15, 41, 67; Acts 2:4; 4:8, 31; 6:5; 7:55; 11:24; 13:9, 52.

in Christ, of which Paul was keenly aware (2 Cor 4:2; 1 Thess 2:3). The way the couple lied to the Holy Spirit was that they deceptively **retained part of the price of the land** from the amount they gave to the apostles, perhaps desiring the appearance of generosity without the cost entailed.

5:4   Peter asks, **"Why did you contrive this deed?"** The Greek literally says, "Why did you put this deed *in your heart*?" Although the couple thought they were duping the apostles, they **have lied not to human beings, but to God**. Peter is making the remarkable claim that lying to the church and its Spirit-filled apostolic leadership is the equivalent of lying to God. Since God generally exercises his authority through his Spirit-filled Church and its leaders, it is important to respect the human representatives who stand in his place.

Peter's questions enable us to see that the couple's sin lay not in holding back money from the sale, but in doing so while claiming otherwise. Peter clearly indicates that the couple was under no obligation either to sell their property or to give the proceeds to the apostles. **"While it remained unsold, did it not remain yours?"** If one chose to sell and donate some of the money to the common fund, one was still free to keep part of the proceeds: **"When it was sold, was it not still under your control?"** Instead, the couple chose to pretend that they were doing what Barnabas had done, placing the entire amount at the feet of the apostles. Their greed is compounded by religious hypocrisy, which Jesus severely condemned (Matt 23:13–33).

5:5–6   Peter did not utter any direct judgment or curse. **When Ananias heard these words** challenging his deceit, which only the Holy Spirit within Peter could have enabled him to detect, **he fell down and breathed his last,** literally, "expired." The Spirit exposed the couple's lie and executed judgment on Ananias, removing him from the body of the Church. As a result, **great fear came upon all who heard of it**. Not only did this shocking death cause fear at the time, but it also remains quite disturbing to readers even unto our day. The narrative ends on a note of finality, with a brief mention of the community's **young men** wrapping, carrying out, and burying Ananias.

5:7–11   Because of the narrow focus of this story as a cautionary negative example, it leaves gaps about the burial of Ananias and how Sapphira could be ignorant of his death. Such details are irrelevant to the main point, which is to demonstrate the equal complicity and sin of Sapphira as a reason for her identical punishment. She is identified as Ananias's **wife**, who arrives **about three hours** later, still **unaware of what had happened**. She is like a witness in court who has been outside the courtroom during the testimony of other witnesses, so that the court can see to what extent her account corresponds to previous testimony.[5] Like a judge, Peter questions her and gives her an opportunity to admit the truth: **"Tell me, did you sell the land for this amount?"** She repeats the same amount that her husband had falsely claimed. **Peter** then confronts her with her own lie and her complicity with the lie told by her husband: **"Why did you agree to test the Spirit of the Lord?"**

Here the sin is a kind of blasphemy, **to test the Spirit of the Lord**. To test the Spirit (or "tempt," RSV; "put to the test," NRSV, JB, NJB) is similar to the sin that Satan tried to get Jesus to commit in the desert (Luke 4:12, quoting Deut 6:16). Peter's charge probably refers to testing the Spirit of the Lord *Jesus*, for Luke had declared that the risen Jesus "received the promise of the holy Spirit from the Father and poured it forth" on his disciples (Acts 2:33). It was the Spirit of Jesus whom the couple had put to the test, and the Spirit of Jesus in Peter immediately exposed their sinful deceit.

Peter's prophetic announcement to Sapphira, **"Those who have buried your husband are at the door, and they will carry you out,"** is the first time she is informed of Ananias's death. Her fate is identical to her husband's: **At once, she fell down at his feet and breathed her last** (literally, "expired"), then was carried out and buried **beside her husband**. A major reason for this account is expressed in the final line: **And great fear came upon the whole church and upon all who heard of these things.** This is Luke's first use of the word "church" (Greek *ekklēsia*, "assembly"), which accents the continuity with God's people Israel, since the same term *ekklēsia* is used in the †Septuagint for the assembly of God's people Israel in the desert with Moses (Deut 31:30 LXX; see Acts 7:38). The lesson drawn from this incident by the Church and others who heard of it is fear of the Lord and a profound awareness of the potential consequences of sin against God.

Reflection and Application (4:32–5:11)

Many readers from earliest Christian times unto today have found the Ananias and Sapphira incident abhorrent. To some, it paints a harsh picture of God. However, this feeling is sometimes influenced by a tendency to minimize the gravity of sin or excuse it for all kinds of psychological or sociological reasons. The story brings out the truth that serious sins can have devastating consequences. In the New Testament, judgments for grave sin can include excommunication or removal from the Church (see 1 Cor 5:1–5, 13; 1 Tim 1:20), which

---

5. In a similar way Daniel questions segregated false witnesses in Susanna's trial (Dan 13:45–64).

only confirms what the individual has in reality chosen. The community's life, unity, and holiness may sometimes require removing from its midst obstinate sinners or those who cause others to sin, as in Jesus' "millstone" saying (Mark 9:42; see Catechism 1463). Such temporal penalties are always for the sake of leading a sinner to repentance and thereby sparing that person eternal punishment (see 1 Cor 5:5).

Signs and Wonders and Trials

Acts 5:12–42

The power of the Holy Spirit in the apostles and early believers continues to produce an amazing growth of the Church in Jerusalem, the first stage of witness for which Jesus had commissioned the apostles (Acts 1:8). The Spirit's mighty signs and wonders through the apostles attract large crowds for healing. This generates further conversions and increasing numbers of believers. The rapid growth, however, also attracts intense opposition from the former leaders of God's people, the Sanhedrin.

Third Summary: Signs and Wonders of the Apostles (5:12–16)

[12]Many signs and wonders were done among the people at the hands of the apostles. They were all together in Solomon's portico. [13]None of the others dared to join them, but the people esteemed them. [14]Yet more than ever, believers in the Lord, great numbers of men and women, were added to them. [15]Thus they even carried the sick out into the streets and laid them on cots and mats so that when Peter came by, at least his shadow might fall on one or another of them. [16]A large number of people from the towns in the vicinity of Jerusalem also gathered, bringing the sick and those disturbed by unclean spirits, and they were all cured.

OT: Exod 7:3; Deut 6:22; Jer 32:20–21; Dan 6:28
NT: Mark 6:56; Luke 9:11; Acts 4:30; 19:11–19
Catechism: healing of the sick, 1506–10
Lectionary: Second Sunday of Easter (Year C)

Fig. 5. Model of the temple showing Solomon's Portico, where the early Christians gathered (Acts 3:11; 5:12).

5:12   This third summary of the life of the early Church (after 2:42–47; 4:32–35) focuses on God's power being exercised through **many signs and wonders ... done among the people at the hands of the apostles**. In this passage "the people" refers to God's Jewish people, who are witnessing signs and wonders reminiscent of those worked by Moses at the time of their birth as a nation (Deut 6:22; Jer 32:20–21). These miracles greatly increased the apostles' credibility and helped to fortify their influence on the people, no matter what the Sanhedrin did to hinder them. Most translations, including the NAB, interpret the next sentence to mean that believers **were all together in Solomon's portico**, although the Greek is ambiguous.[1] Luke continues to stress the Christians' unity more strongly than most translations indicate. The Greek word *homothymadon* means not merely that the apostles were physically "together," but that they were one in heart and purpose (see sidebar, p. 86).

5:13   **None of the others dared join them**. The "others" probably refers to Jews who were afraid to join the Christians because of their awe at the powerful works done at the apostles' hands, including reports of the fate of Ananias and

---

1. But some scholars consider that "they" refers to the apostles, and "the others" in v. 13 refers to the believers in general. See Luke Timothy Johnson, *The Acts of the Apostles*, Sacra pagina 5 (Collegeville, MN: Liturgical Press, 1992), 95; and Joseph A. Fitzmyer, *The Acts of the Apostles*, Anchor Bible 31 (New York: Doubleday, 1998), 328.

Sapphira (Acts 5:11).[2] Yet **the people esteemed them** (or "highly regarded them," NIV). Wonder-working tends to lead to both attraction and fearful avoidance, as in Jesus' ministry (see Mark 5:15–17, 21).

The RSV and NRSV read "believers were added to the Lord," whereas the NAB, NJB, and others refer to **believers in the Lord** who were added to **them** (the Greek of v. 14 does not actually use the word "them"). In either case, multitudes of newcomers joined the Christian community. Despite the fear that kept many from daring to join the Christians in such a public place as the temple portico, the Church grew more than ever. As often in the Bible, the passive expression **were added** indicates action by God: *God* added the **great numbers of men and women** to the Church.

5:14

So great was the faith and excitement among the new believers, and probably also among other witnesses of the apostles' miracles, that **they even carried the sick out into the streets and laid them on cots and mats.** Their hope was that if even Peter's **shadow might fall on one or another of them**, they might be healed. This depiction is the first of several in Acts in which healings occur through material objects or physical proximity (see Acts 9:17; 19:11–12; 20:10). Although such healings can look like magic (see Acts 8:4–24), later narratives clarify that the power working through the Christians is God's, and they are only his human instruments. By contrast, in magic the focus is on the human control and manipulation of spiritual powers (see Acts 8:9–11; 13:6–8; 19:19).

5:15

As was the case in the ministry of Jesus, and as occurs even today with people who have a reputation for spiritual healing, large crowds **gathered** to the apostles from the whole **vicinity of Jerusalem**. They brought the **sick and those disturbed by unclean spirits** for healing and deliverance, **and they were all cured.** This third summary of the life of the early Christian community concludes by exhibiting the power of the Holy Spirit as working mightily in the apostles to heal, which provided a massive evangelizing momentum for the early Church. Healings throughout Church history, including today, continue to demonstrate God's reality, power, and love in ways that attract nonbelievers to Christianity.

5:16

Reflection and Application (5:12–16)

Today, as in the first century, healings give a powerful thrust to the work of evangelization because they attract people's attention to the risen Lord and

2. But "the others" could refer to Christians who were reluctant to join the apostles in the public area of Solomon's Portico from fear of the Sanhedrin.

vividly demonstrate his authority over all the evils that afflict human life. They reveal God's love and compassion for the sick and his desire to restore fallen humanity to the fullness of life, both spiritually and physically. As in Jesus' public ministry, healings of the sick also function as prophetic signs, anticipating the ultimate healing that will occur at the resurrection of the dead.

Like the early Christians in Acts 4:29–30, we should ask the Lord to increase such signs and wonders, which strengthen the faith of believers as well as draw new members to the Church. As Pope John XXIII prayed, "O Divine Spirit, renew your wonders in this our day as by a new Pentecost."

Arrest, Release by an Angel, Arrest Again (5:17–26)

[17]Then the high priest rose up and all his companions, that is, the party of the Sadducees, and, filled with jealousy, [18]laid hands upon the apostles and put them in the public jail. [19]But during the night, the angel of the Lord opened the doors of the prison, led them out, and said, [20]"Go and take your place in the temple area, and tell the people everything about this life." [21]When they heard this, they went to the temple early in the morning and taught. When the high priest and his companions arrived, they convened the Sanhedrin, the full senate of the Israelites, and sent to the jail to have them brought in. [22]But the court officers who went did not find them in the prison, so they came back and reported, [23]"We found the jail securely locked and the guards stationed outside the doors, but when we opened them, we found no one inside." [24]When they heard this report, the captain of the temple guard and the chief priests were at a loss about them, as to what this would come to. [25]Then someone came in and reported to them, "The men whom you put in prison are in the temple area and are teaching the people." [26]Then the captain and the court officers went and brought them in, but without force, because they were afraid of being stoned by the people.

OT: Ps 34:7; Jer 7:2
NT: Luke 20:6, 19; Rom 8:31
Catechism: bearing witness to Christ even under persecution, 2471–74

5:17–18   The popularity of the apostles with the crowds arouses the **jealousy** of **the high priest** and the **party of the Sadducees**. In Luke-Acts, the †Sadducees are among the chief opponents of the message, first of Jesus and then of the apostles. These members of the priestly aristocracy had a great deal of power within the Jewish leadership. In another effort to stop the work of the apostles, they again arrest them **and put them in the public jail** (as in Acts 4:1–3). This reaction of jealousy or envy toward those favored by God, as with Joseph's brothers in Genesis (see Acts 7:9), is a common theme in Scripture and is described by Matthew and Mark as one of the reasons the chief priests had Jesus put to death (Matt 27:18; Mark 15:10).

This time God immediately intervenes and overturns the Sadducees' efforts. **5:19–20** Through an angel—ironically, for the Sadducees did not believe in the existence of angels (Acts 23:8)—God frees the apostles from **prison**. The **angel of the Lord** commands the released apostles to return to the **temple area** and **tell the people** of Israel **everything about this life**. The directive accents the urgency of continuing to preach the gospel, despite human attempts to silence it. The term for the content of the apostles' preaching, "this life," is unusual. It seems to refer to the experience of a whole new life among Jesus' disciples that results from his resurrection and the apostles' ministry—a converted life on earth that is the beginning of eternal life.[3]

Luke goes on to portray the comical contrast between the freed apostles as **5:21** teaching in **the temple early in the morning,** and the solemn convening of the **Sanhedrin, the full senate of the Israelites**, who send to the now-empty **jail to have them brought in**. Luke uses humor to highlight the contrast between the powerful ministry of the apostles and the powerlessness of the assembled old leadership of Israel.

The report that the **court officers** could not find their prisoners underlines **5:22–24** the miraculous element in the apostles' escape. Although **the jail** was **securely locked and the guards stationed outside the doors**, the officers **found no one inside**. At this turn of events, the perplexity of the **captain of the temple guard and the chief priests** is described by the same Greek word (*diaporeō*, to be bewildered or utterly **at a loss**) that is used for the crowds while hearing many languages at Pentecost (Acts 2:12).

The futility of the Sanhedrin's efforts to hinder the progress of the gospel is **5:25** further emphasized by the report: **"The men whom you put in prison are in the temple area and are teaching the people."** The apostles are audaciously preaching even in the temple, which is under the authority of the very chief priests who are trying to stop them. As St. Paul wrote, "If God is for us, who can be against us?" (Rom 8:31). Paul also declared that even when he was in prison, "the word of God is not chained" (2 Tim 2:9).

---

3. See John 17:3. Luke refers to Jesus as "the author of life" (Acts 3:15) and to Christian conversion as "life-giving repentance" (Acts 11:18). Those who believe the gospel are "destined for eternal life" (Acts 13:48).

5:26   The Sanhedrin sends **the captain and the court officers** to bring the apostles in once again. The weakening of their effective authority, however, is underscored by Luke's observation that the officers **brought them in, but without force, because they were afraid of being stoned by the people**—as occurred in Jesus' own life (Luke 20:6, 19). The people are plainly more sympathetic to the apostles than to the officers who are arresting them.

Reflection and Application (5:17–26)

Beginning with Cain's murder of Abel and the patriarchs' selling of their brother Joseph into slavery (Gen 4:2–8; 37:11–28), Scripture depicts religious jealousy as a grave spiritual danger that can lead to yet graver sin. It can cause those who succumb to it to oppose God's servants, resist God's purposes, and even fight against God himself.[4] In Acts, Luke depicts the Jewish religious leaders and others as persecuting Christians out of jealousy (5:17; 13:45; 17:5). But religious jealousy can just as easily occur among Christians. The Letters of Paul frequently warn us to guard against jealousy and its destructive effects in the body of Christ.[5]

"We Must Obey God Rather Than Men" (5:27–32)

---

²⁷**When they had brought them in and made them stand before the Sanhedrin, the high priest questioned them,** ²⁸**"We gave you strict orders [did we not?] to stop teaching in that name. Yet you have filled Jerusalem with your teaching and want to bring this man's blood upon us."** ²⁹**But Peter and the apostles said in reply, "We must obey God rather than men.** ³⁰**The God of our ancestors raised Jesus, though you had him killed by hanging him on a tree.** ³¹**God exalted him at his right hand as leader and savior to grant Israel repentance and forgiveness of sins.** ³²**We are witnesses of these things, as is the holy Spirit that God has given to those who obey him."**

OT: Deut 21:22–23; Ps 110:1
NT: Heb 1:13; 2:9–10; 12:1–2; Gal 3:13
Catechism: obeying God rather than men, 2242–43; culpability for Jesus' death, 591, 597–98
Lectionary: Acts 5:27–32, 40b–41: Third Sunday of Easter (Year C)

---

4. See Num 11:28–29; 12:1–10; 16:1–35; Pss 73:2–3; 106:16; Ezek 35:11.
5. Rom 13:13; 1 Cor 3:3; 2 Cor 12:20; Phil 1:15; 1 Tim 6:4–5; see also James 3:14–16.

The members of the **Sanhedrin** act as if they still have unchallenged authority over the apostles, ordering them to **stand before** the court while **the high priest** interrogates them. The high priest refers to the Sanhedrin's earlier solemn command (4:18) as **strict orders** that the apostles must **stop teaching in that name**. The phrase "that name" suggests that the high priest is reluctant even to mention the name of Jesus, which has been shown to have great power (Acts 3:16; 4:10). He accuses the apostles of having ignored the Sanhedrin's prohibition and **filled Jerusalem with** their **teaching**. He also charges them with wanting **to bring this man's blood upon us**, that is, attributing to the leaders bloodguilt for the death of Jesus the Messiah. Acts does show the apostles as repeatedly indicting the leaders for their part in the killing of Jesus, but for the sake of calling them to repentance and faith.[6] One cannot invite others to new life without speaking truthfully about their wrongdoing and summoning them to repent for it (see Mark 1:14–15).

5:27–28

The response of **Peter and the apostles** is emphatic: **"We must obey God rather than men."** Jesus' command to preach the gospel (Acts 1:8) overrules the Sanhedrin's command to keep quiet about it. This repeats an unambiguous statement of principle that appeared earlier in the form of a question (Acts 4:19). When human laws contradict God's laws, believers are called to obey God even if disobeying human authority will cost them social advancement, their livelihood, or their lives. Peter's statement has become a rallying cry in many situations in which people are pressured to violate their consciences by human laws or commands.

5:29

Verses 30–31 illustrate the principle that God prevails over human authority. Peter contrasts the Sanhedrin's action, **"You had him killed by hanging him on a tree,"** with the action of **God**, who vindicated **Jesus** by raising him from the dead. God further **exalted** Jesus **at his right hand** (Acts 2:32–36), an expression from Ps 110:1 that signifies being given a share in God's own divine majesty and power.[7]

5:30–31

Peter here says that Jesus has been exalted **as leader and savior**, using different terms from "Lord and Messiah" appearing elsewhere for his exaltation

---

6. Peter accuses the Jews of Jerusalem (Acts 2:36) and the Jewish leaders (Acts 4:10) of crucifying Jesus and asking that a murderer, Barabbas, be released to them instead (3:14). In Matthew's account of the passion, the Jewish crowd cries out to Pilate, "His blood be upon us and upon our children" (Matt 27:25), an acceptance of responsibility for Jesus' death that ironically is also a cry for mercy, since the blood of Jesus is the source of redemption and the forgiveness of sins (Matt 26:28; Acts 20:28; Rom 3:25).

7. Being "at the right hand" means sharing in a ruler's power and honor in Ps 16:11; 45:10; Zech 6:13. Jesus testifies before the Sanhedrin that he will sit at God's "right hand" (Luke 22:69), alluding to Ps 110:1. The early Christians often used this phrase to express the divine power and authority of the risen Jesus (Acts 2:33–34; 5:31; 7:56; Rom 8:34; Eph 1:20; Heb 1:3, 13; 8:1; 10:12; 1 Pet 3:22).

The "Curse" of "Hanging on a Tree"

BIBLICAL
BACKGROUND

Peter's reference to "hanging him on a tree" in Acts 5:30 (see also 10:39) draws on the Jewish interpretation of a text in the Law of Moses. Deuteronomy 21:22–23 mandates that "if a man guilty of a capital offense is put to death and you hang him on a tree, his corpse shall not remain on the tree overnight. You must bury it the same day; anyone who is hanged is a curse of God. You shall not defile the land which the LORD, your God, is giving you as a heritage." This text originally referred to the corpse of a criminal who had been executed, probably by stoning, which afterward was hung on a tree as a warning to others. Deuteronomy is saying that because God's curse, his judgment, rests on an evildoer who has been executed, his body should not remain on display. Later the curse of being hung on a tree was applied to crucifixion, the cruel form of execution that Jews suffered at the hands of the Persians and later the Romans. The expression came to refer not only to hanging a corpse on a tree but also to fastening someone alive by nails or ropes to a wooden cross (thus using the word "tree" figuratively), there to suffer torment until finally dying. St. Paul in Galatians shows how Jesus willingly suffered this curse on our behalf: "Christ ransomed us from the curse of the law by becoming a curse for us, for it is written, 'Cursed be everyone who hangs on a tree'" (Gal 3:13).

(Acts 2:36). The Greek word for leader, *archēgos*, can mean "prince" (NIV) or "author" (Acts 3:15 NAB), but here it more likely means the "first to go along a path"; that is, Jesus is the first to pass through death to life and thus is the pioneer for all those who will one day be raised from the dead.[8]

In the Old Testament and much of the New Testament, the term "savior" is usually applied to God, but for the early Church it also became a title for Jesus. For those Christians who had a Gentile background, such as many of the original readers of Acts, "savior" was a more familiar term than Messiah (Christ) since it was often used of the Roman emperor. Both here and in Acts 13:23, the context clearly refers to Jesus as savior of **Israel**, though the New Testament also affirms that Jesus is savior of the whole world (John 4:42; 1 John 4:14). Here Peter speaks as a fellow Israelite to the Sanhedrin and chief priests by referring to the **God of our ancestors**, whom they all worship. He explains that the way Jesus saves Israel is by granting **repentance and forgiveness of sins**. Peter is saying that the risen Jesus is now offering

8. Jesus is called *archēgos* four times in the New Testament: Acts 3:15; 5:31; Heb 2:10; 12:2. See Fitzmyer, *Acts*, 286.

the opportunity to repent and be forgiven, extending this offer to those in Israel who will respond.

After insisting that God has established Jesus as leader and savior of Israel, the same Jesus whom the Jewish leaders arranged to have crucified, Peter ends by emphasizing the apostles' credentials to give this testimony: **"We are witnesses of these things,"** that is, of Jesus' death, his resurrection, and the consequent outpouring of the Holy Spirit. That God has exalted Jesus is evidenced by the healings worked through the apostles and by their previous testimony. Not only are the apostles witnesses, but also **the holy Spirit that God has given to those who obey him.** Peter is saying that the Holy Spirit testifies within the hearts and minds of Christians to the truth of what he is preaching. The Spirit's irrefutable testimony was experienced most recently in the healing of the lame man (Acts 3), the event that first provoked the Sanhedrin to arrest the apostles. In addition, Peter implies, those who believe in Jesus have been given the Spirit because they obey God (see Acts 5:29), whereas the Sanhedrin leaders have not received the Spirit because they do not obey God.

5:32

Reflection and Application (5:27–32)

Along with Jesus' directive to "repay to Caesar what belongs to Caesar and to God what belongs to God" (Matt 22:15–21), Peter's statement that "we must obey God rather than any human authority" (Acts 5:29 NRSV) is foundational for the Christian understanding of conscience and good citizenship. Based on these two passages, the Catechism teaches that Catholics should be good citizens, but that "the citizen is obliged in conscience not to follow the directives of civil authorities when they are contrary to the demands of the moral order, to the fundamental rights of persons or the teachings of the Gospel" (2242). In many parts of today's world certain civil authorities or laws violate human dignity or improperly restrict the Church's freedom to evangelize and speak out on moral matters. Under the guidance of their bishops, Catholics should prayerfully discern how to resist such abuses of authority.

Gamaliel: Beware of Fighting against God (5:33–42)

---

[33]**When they heard this, they became infuriated and wanted to put them to death. [34]But a Pharisee in the Sanhedrin named Gamaliel, a teacher of the law, respected by all the people, stood up, ordered the men to be put outside for a short time, [35]and said to them, "Fellow Israelites, be careful what**

you are about to do to these men. ³⁶Some time ago, Theudas appeared, claiming to be someone important, and about four hundred men joined him, but he was killed, and all those who were loyal to him were disbanded and came to nothing. ³⁷After him came Judas the Galilean at the time of the census. He also drew people after him, but he too perished and all who were loyal to him were scattered. ³⁸So now I tell you, have nothing to do with these men, and let them go. For if this endeavor or this activity is of human origin, it will destroy itself. ³⁹But if it comes from God, you will not be able to destroy them; you may even find yourselves fighting against God." They were persuaded by him. ⁴⁰After recalling the apostles, they had them flogged, ordered them to stop speaking in the name of Jesus, and dismissed them. ⁴¹So they left the presence of the Sanhedrin, rejoicing that they had been found worthy to suffer dishonor for the sake of the name. ⁴²And all day long, both at the temple and in their homes, they did not stop teaching and proclaiming the Messiah, Jesus.

OT: Isa 30:10; Lam 3:37
NT: Matt 5:10–12; Luke 6:22–23; John 19:1; Rom 5:3; 2 Cor 12:10; James 1:2; 1 Pet 4:13–16
Catechism: persecution for faith, 769, 1808, 1816
Lectionary: Acts 5:27–32, 40b–41: Third Sunday of Easter (Year C)

5:33–35   Predictably, Peter's refusal to obey the Sanhedrin and stop preaching Jesus so **infuriated** the majority that they **wanted to put them to death**. From their perspective, the apostles' preaching Jesus was leading the people astray from Jewish religion, for which the punishment was stoning (see Deut 13:6–10). However, **Gamaliel**, a highly **respected** rabbi who had been Paul's teacher (Acts 22:3), counsels caution.

5:36–37   Gamaliel cites examples of other quasi-messianic movements that died out with the killing of their founders because they were not from God. His two examples, **Theudas** and **Judas the Galilean at the time of the census**, are also mentioned by the Jewish historian Josephus, a contemporary of Luke.⁹ Both had stirred up rebellion against Rome, and both were killed and their followers **disbanded** and **scattered**, so that their movements **came to nothing**.

5:38–39   Gamaliel asserts that if the Christian movement is of human origin, it will destroy itself. However, if it comes from God, the Sanhedrin **will not be able to destroy them** and may even find itself **fighting against God**. Gamaliel's principle is not only a guide for the council's practical action. Retrospectively

9. According to Josephus, Judas's rebellion took place during the tax census ordered by Caesar Augustus in AD 6 (not the census of Jesus' birth, Luke 2:1). Josephus places Theudas's movement much later than Judas's and later than the events of Acts 5, in AD 45–46. See Josephus, *Antiquities of the Jews* 17.271–72; 18.1–10; 20.97–99; Fitzmyer, *Acts*, 339–40.

Fig. 6. A model of the temple as it looked in the first century.

it also provides evidence that the Church was indeed from God, since the Sanhedrin was not able to destroy it.

Though the leaders **were persuaded by** Gamaliel not to stone the apostles, they nevertheless **flogged** them and, uselessly, **ordered them to stop speaking in the name of Jesus** before dismissing them. Not only did this pain and humiliation not deter the apostles in the least, but they also rejoiced in having **been found worthy to suffer dishonor for the sake of the name** of Jesus. Jesus had taught that persecution is cause for rejoicing (Matt 5:10–12), a principle that the early Christians took to heart.[10] Their rejoicing at dishonor was completely counter to the strong emphasis on personal honor in the Greco-Roman world. In those times dishonored Romans often committed suicide, but the apostles rejoiced in the dishonor by which they identified with Jesus. Their dedication to Jesus was stronger than their cultural antipathy to shame. They persisted in **teaching and proclaiming the Messiah, Jesus**, both publicly **at the temple and** privately **in their homes**.

5:40–42

Reflection and Application (5:33–42)

The rapid growth of the Church as portrayed in Acts, despite all efforts by the Sanhedrin to obstruct it, is remarkable. Although Luke certainly emphasizes the

10. See Acts 16:25; Rom 5:3; Col 1:24; James 1:2; 1 Pet 2:19–21.

miraculous deeds worked through the apostles, the unstoppable momentum of the Christian movement is clearly also due to the apostles' zeal to announce the good news and their refusal to let any intimidation, threats, or even beatings and imprisonment deter them from witnessing to Jesus. Christians would do well to consider what could happen in the developed world today if we fervently asked the Holy Spirit to kindle a similar zeal in us.

The Ordination of the Seven and the Preaching of Stephen

Acts 6:1–15

The rapid expansion of the Church under the powerful ministry of the apostles hits a speed bump in Acts 6, but the resolution of that difficulty leads to an important development for the future of the Church and its ordained ministry.

The Twelve Expand Church Leadership (6:1–7)

¹At that time, as the number of disciples continued to grow, the Hellenists complained against the Hebrews because their widows were being neglected in the daily distribution. ²So the Twelve called together the community of the disciples and said, "It is not right for us to neglect the word of God to serve at table. ³Brothers, select from among you seven reputable men, filled with the Spirit and wisdom, whom we shall appoint to this task, ⁴whereas we shall devote ourselves to prayer and to the ministry of the word."

⁵The proposal was acceptable to the whole community, so they chose Stephen, a man filled with faith and the holy Spirit, also Philip, Prochorus, Nicanor, Timon, Parmenas, and Nicholas of Antioch, a convert to Judaism. ⁶They presented these men to the apostles who prayed and laid hands on them. ⁷The word of God continued to spread, and the number of the disciples in Jerusalem increased greatly; even a large group of priests were becoming obedient to the faith.

OT: Num 8:10; 27:18; Isa 1:17

NT: Luke 6:13–16; 10:1; 1 Tim 3:8–13
Catechism: deacons, 1554, 1569–71
Lectionary: Fifth Sunday of Easter (Year A)

6:1   The continuing growth of the Church did not come without growing pains. As the **number of disciples** grew, so did complaints. The complaints ran along the lines of linguistic tensions within the community. The newer minority group, the †**Hellenists**, were †Diaspora Jews who spoke Greek, used the Greek translation of the Old Testament (the †Septuagint) as their Bible, and had lived outside of Palestine but then had migrated to Palestine and were now members of the Jerusalem Christian community. The majority group were the **Hebrews**, Jews native to Palestine who spoke †Aramaic, a Semitic language closely related to Hebrew, and whose Bible was primarily the Hebrew Old Testament.

These ethnic complaints were precipitated by practical matters. The minority Hellenists complained that their **widows were being neglected in the daily distribution** of food and financial assistance. Luke previously showed that within the community of believers those who had extra property sold some of it and presented the proceeds to the apostles, who distributed the money or goods to those in need (4:34–35). The Old Testament frequently urges care for those most vulnerable, especially widows and orphans. The prophets emphasize that justice and mercy to the poor are grave obligations of God's people, more important than temple sacrifices (see Isa 1:11–18; 58:6–12; Amos 8:3–7).

6:2   The complaints from the aggrieved minority are not ignored by those in authority, **the Twelve.** They **called together the community of the disciples** to ensure the participation of the whole church in resolving the problem, and then announced their proposed solution. A most generous solution it is, for all the new officeholders they appoint have Greek names and thus apparently are members of the complaining minority group, the Hellenists. We have seen how the placing of goods for distribution "at the feet of the apostles" symbolizes the apostles' authority (Acts 4:35, 37; 5:2). Now this newly appointed group of seven, all apparently Hellenists, share in the apostles' authority over the community.

The Greek word that most translations render as "distribution" in verse 1 is *diakonia*, whose general meaning is "service" or "ministry." The related verb *diakoneō*, to serve at table (or "wait on," NRSV, NIV), is used in the apostles' response to the complaints: **"It is not right for us to neglect the word of God to serve at table."** Both the verb "to serve" and the noun "service" or "ministry" can refer to all kinds of ministries, whether preaching the word or serving at

The Origin and Functions of Christian Deacons

Although Acts 6:1–6 does not call the seven new officeholders "deacons"—in fact, one of them is later identified as "Philip the evangelist, who was one of the Seven" (Acts 21:8)—nevertheless they are ordained by the apostles to fulfill a role of service in the community. At first the apostles may have had a narrower vision of what the diaconate would entail. The stated reason for their ordination is to "serve at table," to oversee the daily distribution of food and financial assistance. But two of the seven are then portrayed as exercising powerful ministries of preaching and healing. Philip's evangelizing activity was precipitated by the martyrdom of Stephen, which in turn resulted from Stephen's preaching. Whatever the apostles may have originally had in mind, the Church recognized the action of the Holy Spirit through Stephen and Philip and thereby came to realize that God's plan for deacons is not limited to caring for the poor of the Christian community, as important as that is, but also entails evangelizing, teaching, and sacramental ministry.

Other New Testament writings clearly identify an ordained group of ministers called deacons, an early form of what later became the order of deacons. Philippians 1:1 refers to "bishops and deacons" (rendered "overseers and ministers" in the NAB), and the letter in part concerns the Philippians' material assistance to Paul, which may have been the responsibility of the deacons. However, at the time when the New Testament was written, the vocabulary for ordained Christian ministers was still developing.

St. Ignatius, who according to Eusebius was martyred around AD 107–8, provides the earliest explicit list of the traditional three orders of bishop, priest, and deacon, probably based on the Old Testament priestly hierarchy of high priest, priests, and Levites. In his letter *To the Philippians*, Ignatius greets the members of the church, "especially if they are at one with the bishop and the presbyters and deacons who are with him, who have been appointed by the mind of Jesus Christ, whom he . . . securely established by his Holy Spirit." Later Ignatius refers to the one Eucharist of a local church and "one altar, just as there is one bishop, together with the presbytery and the deacons, my fellow servants."[a]

a. Ignatius of Antioch, *To the Philippians*, proem and 4, in *The Apostolic Fathers: Greek Texts and English Translations*, ed. and rev. Michael W. Holmes (Grand Rapids: Baker Academic, 1999), 131, 177, 179. See also M. H. Shepherd, "Deacon," in *The Interpreter's Dictionary of the Bible*, ed. George A. Buttrick (Nashville: Abingdon, 1962), 1:785–86.

table. The apostles distinguish the administration of temporal goods from their evangelizing and teaching, which they must not neglect. Both, however, are important ministries in the Church.

The Catechism on Deacons

According to Catholic teaching, "the divinely instituted ecclesiastical ministry is exercised in different degrees by those who even from ancient times have been called bishops, priests, and deacons" (Catechism, 1554; see *Lumen Gentium*, 28). All three degrees are conferred by ordination, that is, by the sacrament of Holy Orders. The Catechism describes the ministry of deacons as follows (1570):

> Deacons share in Christ's mission and grace in a special way. The sacrament of Holy Orders marks them with an *imprint* ("character") which cannot be removed and which configures them to Christ, who made himself the "deacon" or servant of all. Among other tasks, it is the task of deacons to assist the bishop and priests in the celebration of the divine mysteries, above all the Eucharist, in the distribution of Holy Communion, in assisting at and blessing marriages, in the proclamation of the Gospel and preaching, in presiding over funerals, and in dedicating themselves to the various ministries of charity.

The Church has traditionally viewed this episode as the origin of the order of deacons. Although Acts does not use the noun for deacon (*diakonos*), the English term *deacon* comes from the same Greek root as the terms in these two verses. In most New Testament uses, *diakonos* has the general meaning of "servant," but in some texts it has the specialized sense of ordained deacons, such as 1 Tim 3:8–13, which treats of the qualifications to be deacon. The ordination of the seven in Acts 6:1–7 marks an important turning point in the Church's expansion of ordained ministry.

6:3–4   The Twelve do not even select the seven candidates themselves. They instruct the members of the community, **"Select from among you seven reputable men."** These men needed to have both natural and spiritual gifts. On the natural level, they were to be reputable, that is, men held in good standing among the people. They should also be individuals whose lives were guided by the Holy **Spirit** and whose conduct was characterized by **wisdom**. This spiritual requirement would bear fruit in the ministry of the new officeholders Stephen and Philip, which would clearly go beyond "serving at table" (v. 2) or even handling community finances and distribution of aid. Their ministry would also include preaching, teaching, and healing (Acts 6:8–8:13), as did that of the apostles themselves.

The seven candidates chosen by the community are appointed **to this task** of distributing the community's goods, **whereas** the Twelve will **devote** themselves **to prayer and to the ministry of the word**. It is significant that in the apostles' priorities, the ministry of the word comes second to the responsibility to pray.

This implies that worshiping God, interceding for his people, and listening to the Holy Spirit are the primary means by which they receive what they will proclaim to others. Although prayer and the ministry of the word reflect the core of the apostles' mission, the continuing narrative makes it clear that such activities will not be carried out exclusively by them, for the activities of Stephen and Philip also are a ministry of the word.

All seven candidates presented by the **whole community** to the **apostles** are named, but only the first two listed, **Stephen** and **Philip**, will play significant roles in the rest of Acts. One, **Nicholas of Antioch**, is called **a convert** (RSV, NRSV "proselyte"), which means that he was born into a non-Jewish family but converted **to Judaism** and was circumcised. Presumably all the others were raised as Jews in a Hellenistic environment.

6:5

The believers **presented these men to the apostles** to be ordained as ministers for service to the community, and the apostles **prayed and laid hands on them**. Here the apostles are following the example of Jesus, who prayed before selecting the Twelve (Luke 6:12–16). Laying on of hands is a gesture often used in Scripture to ordain or consecrate someone to ministry, such as the Levites (Num 8:10), Joshua (Num 27:18), and Timothy (1 Tim 4:14). It is also the means of imparting the Holy Spirit (8:17; 9:17; 19:6).

6:6

A brief summary of the life of the early Church follows this ordination account: **The word of God continued to spread** (RSV, NIV "increased"). One of the principal themes of Acts is the unstoppable spread of the word of God, no matter what its obstacles or new situations into which it is carried. Luke reports church growth beyond the five thousand mentioned in Acts 4:4, but from now on, the numbers are left indefinite: **the number of the disciples in Jerusalem increased greatly**.[1] The next observation is somewhat surprising: **even a large group of priests were becoming obedient to the faith**. Earlier "the priests, the captain of the temple guard, and the Sadducees" had been the apostles' fiercest opponents (Acts 4:4). Therefore the conversion of a large group of priests is unexpected. As even former opponents are converted, the word of God is becoming irresistible in its growth.

6:7

Reflection and Application (6:1–7)

The extension of ordained Christian authority beyond the Twelve, and the powerful preaching and arrest of one of the seven newly ordained ministers,

---

1. Acts 2:41, 47; 4:4; 5:14; 6:7; 12:24; 19:20. See Luke Timothy Johnson, *The Acts of the Apostles*, Sacra pagina 5 (Collegeville, MN: Liturgical Press, 1992), 107.

Stephen—these events mark important steps in the growth of the Church. The apostles' appointment of members of an aggrieved minority, the Hellenists, to oversee this aspect of community life that aroused their complaints is an inspiring model of magnanimous pastoral leadership. Their example cautions us against tolerating cliques in communities or parishes, in-groups that inevitably lead to resentful "outsiders" and a divisiveness that destroys genuine community. In Acts 6 the apostles are models of responsive and nondefensive listening to grievances of those under their authority. The apostles' wise response to the criticisms of their ministry contributed to the continued growth and spread of the Church.

Accusation against Stephen (6:8–15)

[8]Now Stephen, filled with grace and power, was working great wonders and signs among the people. [9]Certain members of the so-called Synagogue of Freedmen, Cyrenians, and Alexandrians, and people from Cilicia and Asia, came forward and debated with Stephen, [10]but they could not withstand the wisdom and the spirit with which he spoke. [11]Then they instigated some men to say, "We have heard him speaking blasphemous words against Moses and God." [12]They stirred up the people, the elders, and the scribes, accosted him, seized him, and brought him before the Sanhedrin. [13]They presented false witnesses who testified, "This man never stops saying things against [this] holy place and the law. [14]For we have heard him claim that this Jesus the Nazorean will destroy this place and change the customs that Moses handed down to us." [15]All those who sat in the Sanhedrin looked intently at him and saw that his face was like the face of an angel.

OT: Exod 34:29–30
NT: Luke 12:11–12; 21:12–15; 2 Cor 3:7–9
Catechism: blasphemy, 2148; bearing false witness, 2464, 2575–76
Lectionary: Acts 6:8–10; 7:54–59: Feast of St. Stephen

6:8   The reference to **Stephen** as **filled with grace and power** and to his **working great wonders and signs among the people** underlines Stephen's similarity to Jesus. Jesus grew in "grace" as a child (Luke 2:52, "favor" in NAB; see Luke 2:40), he spoke with "grace" in his inaugural sermon at Nazareth (Luke 4:22, "gracious word" in NAB), and did "wonders and signs" (Acts 2:22). Through these parallels Luke shows that the pattern of Jesus' life is reproduced in his disciples through the Holy Spirit. Stephen's activity also resembles the miracles

of the apostles (Acts 4:22), and the wonders and signs of Moses in the exodus
(in Stephen's speech, 7:36).

Stephen seems to have focused his preaching especially on †Hellenistic Jews   6:9–10
like himself. The **so-called Synagogue of Freedmen** consisted of Jews from
outside Israel: **Cyrenians, . . . Alexandrians, and people from Cilicia and
Asia** who had relocated to Jerusalem. These Hellenistic Jews were, like Stephen
himself, more likely to read their Bible in Greek than in Hebrew. The response
of some of them is aggressive: they **came forward and debated with Stephen**.
However, as Jesus promised his disciples in Luke 12:12 ("the holy Spirit will
teach you at that moment what you should say") and 21:15 ("for I myself shall
give you a wisdom in speaking that all your adversaries will be powerless to
resist or refute"), **they could not withstand the wisdom and the spirit with
which he spoke**.

When the Hellenistic Jews become frustrated in arguing with Stephen, they   6:11–12
resort to false witnesses, just as occurred in Jesus' trial (Mark 14:56). They
instigate some people to accuse Stephen of **speaking blasphemous words
against Moses and God**. Charges of blasphemy were also made against Jesus,
including the implied indictment for blasphemy in Luke 22:70–71, when the
Sanhedrin condemned Jesus after he refused to deny that he was Son of God.
With these false charges, Stephen's opponents stir up **the people, the elders,
and the scribes**. They are thus able to bridge the gap between ordinary Jewish
people and their leaders that had repeatedly frustrated the Sanhedrin's previous
efforts to incarcerate the apostles. They **seized him** (the word connotes forceful arrest) **and brought him before the Sanhedrin**. Thus one of the Hellenists
whom the apostles had just ordained meets the same fate as they, being summoned to trial before the Jewish leadership.

The **false witnesses** present two sets of false charges, one against Stephen   6:13–14
and the other including allegations about Jesus. The charges against Stephen
are dire: **"This man never stops saying things against [this] holy place and
the law."** That is, they accuse him of blaspheming against the two great Jewish institutions, the temple (often called "the place" or "the holy place") and
the law of Moses. Later Acts will present what Stephen actually says concerning the temple and the law in his defense speech before the Sanhedrin (Acts
7:44–51). Here, the charges against Stephen are augmented by charges against
Jesus, namely, that Stephen had further claimed, **"This Jesus the Nazorean will
destroy this place and change the customs that Moses handed down to us."**
This accusation is very similar to the false claim at Jesus' own trial: "We heard

him say, 'I will destroy this temple made with hands and within three days I will build another not made with hands'" (Mark 14:58).

6:15   Before Stephen begins his defense, the Sanhedrin members all **looked intently at him**, as those in the synagogue had looked at Jesus before his inaugural address in Luke 4:20. Paul uses the same term to refer to the Israelites' looking at the radiant face of Moses (2 Cor 3:7, 13). Here God's intervention on Stephen's behalf is revealed in that **his face was like the face of an angel**. That is, his face was shining, as angelic "faces" were perceived to be. Stephen's radiant face recalls Moses after he came down from Mount Sinai (Exod 34:29–30) and Jesus as he spoke with Moses and Elijah at the transfiguration (Luke 9:29–31). As Moses' face shone after seeing God, Stephen's face shone on seeing the glorified Son of Man (see Acts 7:55–56).

Before Stephen can even begin his defense against their false charges, God is silently testifying to him by manifesting heavenly glory on his face.

Reflection and Application (6:8–15)

Readiness to accept persecution. The powerful witness of the newly ordained Stephen reminds us that successes in Christian ministry, especially in defending the faith against outsiders' attacks, can lead to opponents' frustration, anger, and even persecution. The very Spirit-endowed invincibility of Stephen in arguments with his challengers provided the occasion for his persecution by them and eventually his martyrdom by stoning. Stephen was filled with grace and power, wisdom and the Holy Spirit, which he needed in order to have the courage to proclaim the gospel even at the cost of his life. As we likewise pray for the Holy Spirit to bring success in our ministries, let us also imitate the willingness of Stephen and the prophets to be rejected for this very prophetic ministry. Both the teachings of Jesus and the example of Stephen, the first witness to die for him, remind us that with power and wisdom, the Spirit also brings us the courage to endure persecution gracefully in imitation of Christ.

Stephen's Overview of Biblical History

Acts 7:1–53

This long speech by Stephen shows how persecution plays an increasing role in the spread of the gospel. Stephen was accused by Hellenistic Jews of speaking against Moses, the temple, the law, and even God (Acts 6:11, 13). His response is to give a summary of the history of Israel, beginning with Abraham. It is a history that Stephen's opponents already know well, but the way he retells it is full of typological hints and clues for interpreting the present time.

Stephen's Speech: The Patriarchs (7:1–16)

¹Then the high priest asked, "Is this so?" ²And he replied, "My brothers and fathers, listen. The God of glory appeared to our father Abraham while he was in Mesopotamia, before he had settled in Haran, ³and said to him, 'Go forth from your land and [from] your kinsfolk to the land that I will show you.'

⁴"So he went forth from the land of the Chaldeans and settled in Haran. And from there, after his father died, he made him migrate to this land where you now dwell. ⁵Yet he gave him no inheritance in it, not even a foot's length, but he did promise to give it to him and his descendants as a possession, even though he was childless.

⁶"And God spoke thus, 'His descendants shall be aliens in a land not their own, where they shall be enslaved and oppressed for four hundred years; ⁷but I will bring judgment on the nation they serve,' God said, 'and after that they will come out and worship me in this place.' ⁸Then he gave

him the covenant of circumcision, and so he became the father of Isaac, and circumcised him on the eighth day, as Isaac did Jacob, and Jacob the twelve patriarchs.

⁹"And the patriarchs, jealous of Joseph, sold him into slavery in Egypt; but God was with him ¹⁰and rescued him from all his afflictions. He granted him favor and wisdom before Pharaoh, the king of Egypt, who put him in charge of Egypt and [of] his entire household. ¹¹Then a famine and great affliction struck all Egypt and Canaan, and our ancestors could find no food; ¹²but when Jacob heard that there was grain in Egypt, he sent our ancestors there a first time. ¹³The second time, Joseph made himself known to his brothers, and Joseph's family became known to Pharaoh. ¹⁴Then Joseph sent for his father Jacob, inviting him and his whole clan, seventy-five persons; ¹⁵and Jacob went down to Egypt. And he and our ancestors died ¹⁶and were brought back to Shechem and placed in the tomb that Abraham had purchased for a sum of money from the sons of Hamor at Shechem."

OT: Gen 11:31; 12:1–4; Pss 78; 105
NT: Luke 1:73–75; 24:27
Catechism: Abraham, 59–64; Joseph, 312
Lectionary: Feast of St. Stephen

7:1–3   After the false accusations against Stephen, the **high priest**, acting as judge, interrogates him: **"Is this so?"** Stephen begins his defense positively with a brief rhetorical attempt to win the good graces of his hearers. As a fellow Jew he acknowledges their kinship and common religious heritage by calling them **my brothers and fathers** and by referring inclusively to **our father Abraham**. Although the setting and opening remarks are that of a defense speech against formal charges in court, this speech is more an overview of the biblical story of salvation, as the foundation for the story of Jesus, than an answer to specific charges against Stephen. It is in the biblical tradition of summaries of salvation history.[1]

Stephen begins his account with an unusual title for God, who appeared to Abraham: **the God of glory**. This phrase is found elsewhere in Scripture only in Ps 29:3, "The God of glory thunders, the LORD, over the mighty waters." God's glory is the visible manifestation of his holiness and majesty through his great deeds. God appeared to Abraham **while he was in** his native city of Ur in **Mesopotamia**, in modern-day Iraq. Some details in Stephen's recounting of biblical history differ slightly from those in Genesis. But God's challenging mission

---

1. See Josh 24; Ezek 20:5–44; Neh 9:7–31; Pss 78; 105.

to Abraham is essentially the same as in Gen 12:1: **"Go forth from your land and [from] your kinsfolk to the land that I will show you."** By commanding Abraham to set out without yet knowing where he was to go, God asked of him a radical trust and dependence.

Abraham obeyed God in leaving the land where he was living. Stephen shortens the story, attributing the move from the **land of the Chaldeans** to **Haran** under Abraham's father Terah (Gen 11:31), to God's direct command to Abraham. After Terah **died** in Haran, God made Abraham **migrate** to the **land** of Canaan.   `7:4`

However, God left Abraham as a sojourner in the land. Abraham did not own the land even after his arrival there. Rather, God continued to test his faith: **he gave him no inheritance in it**, only his **promise to give it to him and his descendants as a possession**. Abraham's faith was tested even more extremely, for at the time of God's promise he **was childless** and without any hope of descendants through Sarah.   `7:5`

God's promises to Abraham were set far in the future and included predictions of adverse circumstances for his **descendants** in the meantime. God foretold that not only would Abraham's descendants be **aliens in a land not their own**, but there they also would be **enslaved and oppressed for four hundred years** (Gen 15:13–14). Only after these centuries of hardship would they receive their promised inheritance in the land of Israel. As the psalmist declares to God, "A thousand years in your eyes are merely a day gone by" (Ps 90:4). God's plan of salvation unfolds over long periods of time.   `7:6`

God further promised that he would **bring judgment on the nation** that enslaved them, Egypt, and **after that** the Israelites would **come out and worship me in this place**. This sentence combines God's promise to Abraham with his later promise to Moses (Exod 3:23), where "this place" means Mount Sinai. But for Stephen and his listeners, "this place" can also refer specifically to the Jerusalem temple (see Acts 6:13). Luke's Gospel emphasizes that in Jesus, after even more centuries, God fulfilled his promise that Abraham's descendants would freely worship him without fear from oppressors (Luke 1:73–75). The oppressors encountered by both Jesus and his followers are not only human persecutors but also spiritual enemies: Satan and his minions.[2] Thus a large part of the ministry of both Jesus in the Gospel and his disciples in Acts involves   `7:7`

---

2. See Susan R. Garrett, "Exodus from Bondage: Luke 9:31 and Acts 12:1–24," *Catholic Biblical Quarterly* 52, no. 4 (1990): 656–80. She argues that the exodus from bondage achieved by Jesus and his followers in Luke-Acts is primarily an †eschatological and cosmic victory over Satan and his bondage (see Luke 10:18).

freeing many people from the grip of demonic oppression.[3] Paul later declares that he was sent to the Gentiles "that they may turn . . . from the power of Satan to God" (Acts 26:17–18).

7:8   God confirmed his promises by giving Abraham **the covenant of circumcision**, that is, the †covenant of which the circumcision of male Israelites was to be the visible sign (Gen 17:11). God's promises began to be fulfilled when, despite Abraham and Sarah's childlessness and advanced age, Abraham **became the father of Isaac**. In fidelity to the covenant, Abraham **circumcised him on the eighth day**. His descendants likewise kept the covenant, **Isaac** doing the same for his son **Jacob**, and **Jacob** for his sons, **the twelve patriarchs**.

7:9–12   A particularly significant chapter in Stephen's overview of God's saving deeds is his account of **Joseph**, who was **sold . . . into slavery in Egypt** by his **jealous** brothers, the other **patriarchs**. The Joseph story emphasizes how God used the evil done to Joseph by his brothers to bring salvation from famine for those same brothers. It clearly serves as a foreshadowing of Christ's passion, in which God used the far greater evil done to Jesus to bring a far greater salvation to the very people who killed him.

Although Joseph suffered grievously at the hands of his brothers, their crime was used by God to place him in a position from which he could save others, even his brothers and their families. In Joseph's dire need, **God was with him and rescued him from all his afflictions**. By granting him **favor and wisdom before Pharaoh**, God caused Joseph to be **put in charge of Egypt** and Pharaoh's **entire household**. He became the steward or prime minister responsible for distributing food rations during the **famine** that **struck all Egypt and Canaan.** When the Jews' **ancestors could find no food** and were facing starvation, **Jacob** sent his sons to Egypt to buy grain. During this **first** visit, the brothers did not recognize Joseph (Gen 42:8). Stephen is hinting that in a similar way, Jesus' Jewish "brothers" did not recognize him in the "first visit"—their encounter with him during his public ministry.

Peter's Pentecost speech in Acts 2 recounted how God overcame the murder of Jesus along plot lines similar to those of the Joseph story. Although Jesus' own people had turned him over to the Romans to be crucified, God rescued him from death, not by sparing him death but by raising him from the dead. God raised up Jesus so that he could send his disciples to save the very people who turned him over to the Romans, as well as all people.

7:13–16   **The second time** refers to the second trip to Egypt by Joseph's brothers to seek provisions. This time, **Joseph made himself known to his brothers, and**

3. Luke 4:35, 41; 8:2, 33; 9:1, 42; 10:17; 11:14, 20; 13:32; Acts 8:7; 16:16–18.

Jesus the New Joseph

BIBLICAL BACKGROUND

Although the Joseph story (Gen 37–50) is mentioned only rarely in the New Testament, Joseph is one of the most striking biblical †types of Jesus. Like Jesus, Joseph was a son loved by his father but envied by his brothers (fellow children of Israel). He foretold his future glory, was sent out by his father, and sought his brothers until he found them. Jesus was conspired against, betrayed by those close to him, stripped of his robe, cast down, and sold for pieces of silver. He was thirty years old when he began his life's work. He became a servant, was tempted and did not sin, was falsely accused, foretold the future, and was a revealer of secrets. He was raised to high honor, forgave his brothers, gave bread to a famished world, and became a savior to all.

Joseph's family became known to Pharaoh (Gen 45:1–4). Again Stephen is giving his listeners clues to interpret the present time: the listeners' opportunity for a second "visit" with Jesus comes through his presence in his disciples through the Holy Spirit, as they make him known through the proclamation of the gospel.

Joseph sent **for his father Jacob** to bring **his whole clan, seventy-five persons to Egypt.**[4] After settling there, Jacob **died** and was **brought back to Shechem** to **the tomb that Abraham had purchased.**[5]

Reflection and Application (7:1–16)

Through the centuries Abraham has been held up as a powerful example of faith in God's providence and guidance. Abraham's amazing response to God's challenging call is the reason he has become an exemplar of faith among both Jews and Christians (see Rom 4:11–16; Heb 11:8). God asked not only that Abraham be willing to leave land and kinsfolk, but also that he set out with no known destination, believing that along the way God would provide guidance to "the land that I will show you." In Christian spirituality Abraham's call in Gen

---

4. The Hebrew version of Gen 46:27 and Exod 1:5 mentions only seventy persons, but the †Septuagint has 75, perhaps counting Joseph's grandsons and great-grandsons who were born in Egypt.

5. The NAB note to Acts 7:2 points out these further discrepancies between Genesis and Stephen's version in Acts 7:16: thus Gen 50:13 has Jacob buried in Machpelah near Hebron, rather than at Shechem. And Gen 33:19 and Josh 24:32 say that Jacob, not Abraham, purchased the land in Shechem. Narrating from memory and condensing multiple events into one account might account for these discrepancies.

12 has thus become a foundational model for surrendering to God's vocational call, responding in trust that the Spirit will guide us along the way to a future that only God knows. For example, a bride and groom pronounce their vows to be faithful to each other "for better or for worse, for richer or for poorer, in sickness and in health, till death do us part." Like Abraham, Christian spouses entrust themselves not only to each other but also to the providence of the God who leads them into an unknown "land" and future together.

Stephen's Speech: Moses' First Visit and Rejection (7:17–29)

[17]"When the time drew near for the fulfillment of the promise that God pledged to Abraham, the people had increased and become very numerous in Egypt, [18]until another king who knew nothing of Joseph came to power [in Egypt]. [19]He dealt shrewdly with our people and oppressed [our] ancestors by forcing them to expose their infants, that they might not survive. [20]At this time Moses was born, and he was extremely beautiful. For three months he was nursed in his father's house; [21]but when he was exposed, Pharaoh's daughter adopted him and brought him up as her own son. [22]Moses was educated [in] all the wisdom of the Egyptians and was powerful in his words and deeds.

[23]"When he was forty years old, he decided to visit his kinsfolk, the Israelites. [24]When he saw one of them treated unjustly, he defended and avenged the oppressed man by striking down the Egyptian. [25]He assumed [his] kinsfolk would understand that God was offering them deliverance through him, but they did not understand. [26]The next day he appeared to them as they were fighting and tried to reconcile them peacefully, saying, 'Men, you are brothers. Why are you harming one another?' [27]Then the one who was harming his neighbor pushed him aside, saying, 'Who appointed you ruler and judge over us? [28]Are you thinking of killing me as you killed the Egyptian yesterday?' [29]Moses fled when he heard this and settled as an alien in the land of Midian, where he became the father of two sons."

OT: Exod 1–3
NT: Luke 1:69–75; 19:41–44
Catechism: Moses, 62, 204–10, 2574–77

7:17–19   Stephen's account is structured into periods of history, arranged especially according to God's promises and their fulfillment. After the Joseph story situated the Israelites in Egypt, Stephen introduces the story of Moses as the **fulfillment of the promise** made **to Abraham** hundreds of years earlier (Gen 15:5). As

God had promised Abraham descendants numerous as the stars, the Israelites **increased and become very numerous in Egypt**. Meanwhile **another king who knew nothing of Joseph came to power**. For political reasons this later Pharaoh tried to control the increase of this alien group of Hebrews, whose rapid growth was perceived as a threat to Egyptian rule. Stephen reports that this new king even **oppressed [our] ancestors by forcing them to expose their infants, that they might not survive**. The stage is set for the story of Moses.

One of the charges made against Stephen was "We have heard him speaking   7:20–22 blasphemous words against Moses and God" (Acts 6:11). Stephen's favorable narrative about Moses belies such a charge. His tale of Moses even adds extra positive details beyond the Hebrew version in Exodus. The first addition is from the Greek Old Testament, which describes the baby Moses as **extremely beautiful,** intensifying the more simple "goodly" in the Hebrew (Exod 2:2). After Stephen recounts the rescue and adoption of the exposed baby Moses by **Pharaoh's daughter**, he adds from later Jewish traditions that she had Moses **educated [in] all the wisdom of the Egyptians**. Thus Moses became **powerful in his words and deeds**. This parallels the Luke 24:19 description of "Jesus the Nazarene, who was a prophet mighty in deed and word." Stephen's account of Israelite history can hardly be considered "blasphemous words against Moses" (see 6:11).

Stephen recounts Moses' life in three forty-year segments. He portrays Moses   7:23–25 as a prophetic savior who is twice disowned by his own people. Moses' first rejection came when he was **forty years old,** when he stopped the beating of a fellow Hebrew **by striking down the Egyptian** (Exod 2:11–12). Stephen's account emphasizes the biblical theme of the rejection of prophets by God's people. Although God called prophets to deliver his people from oppression, all too often the people refused to accept the message of those whom God sent to them. In this case, Moses **assumed** that his compatriots **would understand that God was offering them deliverance through him**, but **they did not understand**. Jesus faced a similar lack of understanding when he wept over a Jerusalem about to be destroyed "because you did not recognize the time of your visitation" (Luke 19:41–44).

The **next day**, when Moses tried to **reconcile** some **fighting** Hebrews, the **one**   7:26–29 **who was harming his neighbor** rejected his intervention: **"Who appointed you ruler and judge over us?"** At the man's mention of how Moses had **killed the Egyptian**, Moses feared the deed was known to the Egyptians. He **fled when he heard this and settled as an alien in the land of Midian**. This was the first of two rejections of Moses as prophet and leader by his fellow Hebrews.

Reflection and Application (7:17–29)

That Egyptian wisdom helped Moses become "powerful" (v. 22) is an example of how human learning can supplement divine revelation in preparing people to preach and prophesy. This example can help counter the prejudice of some scholars who question the appropriateness of employing Greek or Latin thought to articulate Christian doctrine: if God used Egyptian learning to prepare Moses, why not Greek or Latin learning to articulate biblical revelation? It also illustrates the mutually supporting roles of faith and reason, and the way that secular learning can foster and strengthen faith. As a Jesuit, I was trained first in the classical humanities and in philosophy, which provided a strong foundation for my theology studies in preparation for the priesthood.

Stephen's Speech: Moses' Second Sending
to the People (7:30–38)

---

³⁰"Forty years later, an angel appeared to him in the desert near Mount Sinai in the flame of a burning bush. ³¹When Moses saw it, he was amazed at the sight, and as he drew near to look at it, the voice of the Lord came, ³²'I am the God of your fathers, the God of Abraham, of Isaac, and of Jacob.' Then Moses, trembling, did not dare to look at it. ³³But the Lord said to him, 'Remove the sandals from your feet, for the place where you stand is holy ground. ³⁴I have witnessed the affliction of my people in Egypt and have heard their groaning, and I have come down to rescue them. Come now, I will send you to Egypt.' ³⁵This Moses, whom they had rejected with the words, 'Who appointed you ruler and judge?' God sent as [both] ruler and deliverer, through the angel who appeared to him in the bush. ³⁶This man led them out, performing wonders and signs in the land of Egypt, at the Red Sea, and in the desert for forty years. ³⁷It was this Moses who said to the Israelites, 'God will raise up for you, from among your own kinsfolk, a prophet like me.' ³⁸It was he who, in the assembly in the desert, was with the angel who spoke to him on Mount Sinai and with our ancestors, and he received living utterances to hand on to us."

OT: Exod 3:4–12; 4:1–17; Deut 18:15
NT: Mark 12:26; Gal 3:19; Heb 2:2
Catechism: the burning bush, 204–9, 724, 2575, 2777

7:30–34   **Forty years later**, Moses began a second attempt to deliver his people from Egyptian bondage, this time not on his own initiative but as sent by God. Stephen recounts that **an angel appeared** to Moses, although the voice that addressed him from the bush was **the voice of the Lord**. In reporting †theophanies, appearances of God, Scripture often mentions angels in place of God, based on the understanding that human beings cannot survive direct contact with the all-holy God.[6] The angel appears to him **in the desert near Mount Sinai in the flame of a burning bush**. When the Lord speaks to Moses, he identifies himself as **the God of your fathers, the God of Abraham, of Isaac, and of Jacob**, linking what he would do through Moses with his promises to the patriarchs.

Moses displays the typical human reaction to a †theophany: **trembling** with fear, he does **not dare to look at** the burning bush. Scripture portrays such awe as the natural response to an awareness of the infinite chasm between the holy Creator God and human beings, his creatures. The Lord instructs Moses on how to show reverence for his presence: **"Remove the sandals from your feet, for the place where you stand is holy ground."** God reminds Moses of his constant providence and concern for his people, saying that he has **witnessed the affliction** of his **people in Egypt** and **heard their groaning**. The plight of the people has moved God to action: **"I have come down to rescue them."**

However, according to God's usual biblical pattern, he rescues his people not only by direct divine action but also through his chosen human instruments, in this case, Moses. **"Come now, I will send you to Egypt."** But it was not easy for Moses to face returning to Egypt, from which he had fled for his life some forty years earlier. Stephen does not mention Moses' repeated evasions and excuses in Exod 3:11–4:14. Nor does he describe how God finally lost patience with Moses' excuses but allowed him to take as spokesperson his brother, Aaron, who was an eloquent speaker (Exod 4:14–17). Unlike the book of Exodus, Stephen's focus is not on Moses' reluctance to accept his prophetic mission but on the *people's* failure to accept his mission.

Stephen reminds his listeners that the people had already rejected Moses' leadership once before. With ironic echoes, he uses almost the same titles to describe their earlier rejection of Moses, **"Who appointed you *ruler and judge?*,"** and God's sending of Moses to them in this second instance, **"This Moses . . . God sent as [both] *ruler and deliverer.*"** The people's earlier rejection of a deliverer does not prevent God from sending the same deliverer back to them.   7:35-37

Stephen reports that God sent Moses **through the angel who appeared to him in the bush**, again identifying God's appearance with that of his angelic agent. He quickly summarizes the exodus events: Moses **led** the people **out,**

---

6. In Exod 33:20 God tells Moses, "You cannot see my face, for no one can see me and live." See also Gen 32:31 (30 NRSV); Judg 13:22; Isa 6:5; John 1:16–18.

performing wonders and signs in **Egypt, at the Red Sea, and in the desert for forty years**. Stephen's emphasis on Moses' twice trying to save the people builds up to his climactic repetition of Moses' prophecy in Deut 18:15: "**God will raise up for you . . . a prophet like me**"—a prophecy that clearly points forward to the resurrection of Jesus.

Stephen's narrative is meant to reveal that Moses is a †type of Jesus, the fulfillment of God's promise to raise up a †prophet like Moses. Like Moses, Jesus took action to save his people a second time after their first rejection of him. Jesus' second attempt to save his people is through his witnesses, who are empowered by the Holy Spirit after his resurrection (Acts 2:33). Like Moses, Jesus works wonders and signs, both in his earthly life and later through his Spirit-filled disciples, including Stephen himself (Acts 6:8). Stephen's emphasis on Jesus as the prophet like Moses (Deut 18:15) is another mark of his high esteem for Moses, which rebuts the charge that he had blasphemed Moses (Acts 6:11).

7:38 Again Stephen speaks of Moses as interacting with an **angel** rather than with God himself as reported in Exodus. It is from this angel that Moses **received living utterances to hand on to us**, that is, the law of Moses, which is the foundation of the Jewish religion. A Jewish tradition held that God had given the law through the mediation of angels (Acts 7:53; Gal 3:19; Heb 2:2).[7] Stephen's emphasis on angels rather than God is preparing for his final accusation of his Jewish listeners: "You received the law as transmitted by angels, but you did not observe it" (Acts 7:53). Perhaps he is implying that what God is giving in Jesus is greater than the law given through angels, and thus the stakes in rejecting it are higher (see Heb 2:2).

Stephen's Speech: The Second Rejection of Moses (7:39–50)

[39]"**Our ancestors were unwilling to obey him; instead, they pushed him aside and in their hearts turned back to Egypt,** [40]**saying to Aaron, 'Make us gods who will be our leaders. As for that Moses who led us out of the land of Egypt, we do not know what has happened to him.'** [41]**So they made a calf in those days, offered sacrifice to the idol, and reveled in the works of their hands.** [42]**Then God turned and handed them over to worship the host of heaven, as it is written in the book of the prophets:**

> '**Did you bring me sacrifices and offerings
> for forty years in the desert, O house of Israel?
> [43]No, you took up the tent of Moloch**

7. See also *Jubilees* 1.29; Philo, *On Dreams* 1.141–43; Josephus, *Antiquities of the Jews* 15.136.

and the star of [your] god Rephan,
the images that you made to worship.
So I shall take you into exile beyond Babylon.'

[44]"Our ancestors had the tent of testimony in the desert just as the One who spoke to Moses directed him to make it according to the pattern he had seen. [45]Our ancestors who inherited it brought it with Joshua when they dispossessed the nations that God drove out from before our ancestors, up to the time of David, [46]who found favor in the sight of God and asked that he might find a dwelling place for the house of Jacob. [47]But Solomon built a house for him. [48]Yet the Most High does not dwell in houses made by human hands. As the prophet says:

> [49]"The heavens are my throne,
> What kind of house can you build for me?
> says the Lord,
> or what is to be my resting place?
> [50]Did not my hand make all these things?'"

OT: Exod 32:1–6; 1 Kings 8:27; Ps 115:4–8; Isa 44:12–17; 66:1–2; Bar 6:1–72; Ezek 20:7–8
NT: Matt 5:34–35; John 4:21
Catechism: idolatry, 2112–14; the temple, 583–86
Lectionary: Acts 7:44–50: Anniversary of the Dedication of a Church

Still identifying with his Jewish listeners, Stephen reports: **Our ancestors**   7:39–41
were unwilling to obey Moses. **In their hearts** they **turned back to Egypt**—
that is, they reverted to the idolatry that they had practiced in Egypt (see Ezek
20:7–8). They demand, **"Make us gods who will be our leaders,"** on the excuse
that they **do not know what has happened to that Moses who led us out of
the land of Egypt.** Their request to Aaron for a calf is both a rejection of Moses
as their leader and the grave sin of idolatry. Losing trust in the invisible God—
and losing patience when God does not act according to their timetable—the
people revert to the behavior of their unbelieving neighbors and put their
trust instead in images that are more tangible. They worship the calf they have
made, offering **sacrifice to the idol** and reveling **in the works of their hands.**
Stephen's language strongly echoes the condemnations by the prophets of the
Israelites' worship of lifeless idols that they themselves had made and that were
completely impotent to help them.[8]

Stephen's speech links the people's sin with God's punishment by using the   7:42–43
same word. The sin occurred when the people "turned" back to Egypt in their

---

8. See, for instance, 1 Sam 12:20–21; Isa 2:8; 44:12–17; 66:1–2; Bar 6:1–72.

hearts (v. 39), which led to their making the calf to worship. Therefore, their punishment came about when **God turned and handed them over to worship the host of heaven** (v. 42).[9] God is portrayed as surrendering the Israelites to their own wickedness (as in Rom 1:24, 26, 28), worshiping not only the original molten calf but later also false gods like stars and their governing spirits (2 Kings 17:16; 21:3; 23:4–5; Jer 19:13).

Stephen explains this idolatrous worship by citing **the book of the prophets**, the first-century title for the twelve minor prophets, Hosea to Malachi. His quotation is almost verbatim from the †Septuagint translation of Amos 5:25–27, adding only the reason why they made **images**, that is, **to worship** them. Amos charges that even during their **forty years in the desert**, the Israelite sacrifices were not to God but rather involved **the tent of Moloch and the star of [your] god Rephan, the images that you made to worship**.

This charge seems to compress multiple epochs of idolatry.[10] The Israelite temptation to immolate children to Moloch is evidenced from as early as Leviticus (Lev 18:21) to as late as one of the last Davidic kings, Josiah (2 Kings 23:10). It is not clear who the god Rephan is, but reference to the star of Rephan relates this idolatry to God's "handing them over to worship the host of heaven" (v. 42). What is clear is that Stephen's speech accuses the exodus generation of worshiping several false gods—the calf, Moloch, and Rephan—rather than God. He also merges various punishments for worship of false gods—the sinful first generation's forty years' wandering in the desert with Moses, and the much later **exile beyond Babylon**.[11]

7:44   Stephen contrasts the tent of Moloch (v. 43) with the **tent of testimony in the desert**. This tent was a portable shrine that housed the ark of the covenant and served as God's dwelling place among his people, where God made himself present for them to worship him and seek his guidance. The **One who spoke to Moses** probably refers to God. God **directed** Moses **to make** the **tent of testimony** according to **the pattern he had seen** (Exod 25:8–9, 40). As the Letter to the Hebrews observes, this implies that there is a heavenly sanctuary of

---

9. Fitzmyer traces the term "hosts of heaven" to 1 Kings 22:19; Jer 7:18; Neh 9:6, denoting either the stars or the spirits "thought to govern their movements" (Joseph A. Fitzmyer, *The Acts of the Apostles*, Anchor Bible 31 [New York: Doubleday, 1998], 381).

10. The compression seems to occur already in the †Septuagint, which Stephen is citing. The Septuagint puts the verb "carry away" in the aorist tense rather than the future tense, implying a past event—that is, the Israelites were already carrying the idolatrous images during their desert journey.

11. C. K. Barrett, *A Critical and Exegetical Commentary on the Acts of the Apostles*, 2 vols. (Edinburgh: T&T Clark, 1994–98), 1:370–71. Other than the calf incident (Exod 32), Old Testament reports do not specify that Israelites practiced idolatrous worship in the desert. However, the idolatry could have taken place during the people's forty-year punishment of desert exile.

which the earthy tent is only a copy (Heb 8:5). Because God revealed to Moses the pattern that he was to follow, this tent was in full accord with God's will.

The Israelites **brought** the tent into the promised land **with Joshua.** The   7:45–47
time from Joshua, Moses' lieutenant and successor, to Samuel the prophet, the last judge before the kings, is known as the period of the judges. Under the judges the common **ancestors** of Stephen and his hearers offered sacrifice and sought God's guidance at the tent of testimony. This continued **up to the time of David.** The speech then draws a contrast between David's desire to **find a dwelling place for the house of Jacob** (2 Sam 7) and Solomon's actual construction of a house for God.[12] Even though David **found favor in the sight of God,** his request to build a temple for God was not granted. **But Solomon built a house for him.** Stephen implies that unlike Moses' construction of the tent of testimony, Solomon's building the temple (1 Kings 6) may not have been entirely according to God's will. Solomon made a house for the God who does not dwell in houses made by humans, instead of the tent in which God had previously manifested his presence.

Stephen explains why God did not need Solomon's building:[13] **"The Most**   7:48–50
High does not dwell in houses made by human hands." Stephen not only implies that the tent sufficed as a place for Israelites to consult and worship their God as he traveled in their midst; he also quotes **the prophet** Isaiah (Isa 66:1–2) to invoke the principle of God's transcendence. God has the **heavens** as his dwelling, and **the earth** as his **footstool.** What **resting place** appropriate for God can be made by human hands,[14] since everything in creation was already made by God's **hand?** Stephen's speech is not condemning the temple as such but is exposing the attempt to domesticate God that is implied in some people's attitudes toward the temple.

Solomon himself, at the dedication of his temple, had admitted that no humanly built temple could be God's actual house: "If the heavens and the highest heavens cannot contain you, how much less this house which I have built!" (1 Kings 8:27). It is true that humans crave some material location at which they can focus their prayer and inquiry into God's will, such as the tent

---

12. Most older manuscripts have "house of Jacob," but some corrections in these manuscripts and some later manuscripts have "God of Jacob," which is the Greek translation of Ps 132:5 ("dwelling place for the *God* of Jacob") to which this phrase alludes.

13. Many OT texts and even Jesus and Christians continued, of course, to show reverence for the temple. But Jesus also referred to his body as the new temple, replacing the destroyed temple (as in John 2:19–21).

14. "Made by human hands" is frequently used in Scripture as a negative term for idols. A close paraphrase of the term appears in Acts 7:41, when the people sacrificed to the calf as idol (see Exod 32) "and reveled in the works of their hands."

of testimony had been and as the temple also was during its existence, for Luke repeatedly mentions Christians' praying there. But the temple could not be an adequate house for the transcendent God. Thus its destruction (probably before Acts was written) did not make it impossible to consult and worship God, because God is with his people everywhere, as he was with Moses in the desert and with Paul in Corinth (Acts 18:9–10).

Stephen's Prophetic Indictment (7:51–53)

[51]"You stiff-necked people, uncircumcised in heart and ears, you always oppose the holy Spirit; you are just like your ancestors. [52]Which of the prophets did your ancestors not persecute? They put to death those who foretold the coming of the righteous one, whose betrayers and murderers you have now become. [53]You received the law as transmitted by angels, but you did not observe it."

OT: Exod 33–34; Deut 9–10; 31; Dan 12:1
NT: Luke 11:47; 13:34; Gal 3:19; Heb 2:2
Catechism: resisting the Holy Spirit, 1864

7:51–52   Throughout Stephen's entire review of biblical history, he has referred to "*our* ancestors," emphasizing his solidarity with his listeners. However, in his conclusion he suddenly separates himself from them and applies to them Moses' prophetic criticism of the desert generation: **"You stiff-necked people"** (Exod 32:9; often in Exod 33–34; Deut 9–10; 31). Stephen's reference to their being **uncircumcised in heart and ears** implies that, although they are circumcised in the flesh as belonging to God, their hearts do not correspond but remain alienated from God's ways (see Deut 10:16). Moses promised that God would circumcise their hearts and those of their descendants "so that you will love the LORD, your God, with your whole heart and your whole being, in order that you may live" (Deut 30:6). The expression "uncircumcised in ears" occurs in Scripture only here. By analogy, it refers to the people's refusal to listen to God, to whom they are supposed to be dedicated by their circumcision.

No longer in solidarity with his listeners, Stephen now accuses them in words that echo Isa 63:10: **"You always oppose the holy Spirit."** He no longer speaks of "our ancestors." It is now **your ancestors** who persecuted **the prophets** and killed **those who foretold the coming of the righteous one,** Jesus, whose **betrayers and murderers you have now become.** These charges are similar to Jesus' indictment of the scribes in Luke 11:47–48: "Woe to you! You build the memorials of the prophets whom your ancestors killed. Consequently, you bear witness and give consent to the deeds of your ancestors."

Stephen's claim that the **law** the people accepted was **transmitted by angels** is a Jewish tradition that in no way denigrated the law's value. Ancient Jews had a lofty view of angels as God's agents, mediators of the covenant and the law (Gal 3:19; Heb 2:2), and members of the heavenly court around God's throne (Job 2:1; Ps 89:6; Tob 12:15). Stephen's speech affirms the holiness and authority of the law and the gravity of sins against it. Even though the law was given by angels to instruct Israel in God's ways, Stephen tells his Jewish listeners, **"You did not observe it."** Their failure to observe the law is seen especially in their persecution of the prophets and even of the one whom the prophets foretold: Jesus. Stephen thus turns their accusation that he disrespected the law back against them.

      7:53

Reflection and Application (7:1–53)

Stephen's speech is a fascinating example of the typological interpretation of the Old Testament, that is, interpreting Israel's history in a manner that shows how it points forward in hidden ways to the fulfillment of God's plan in Christ. The Gospel of Luke recounts the story of the two disciples on the road to Emmaus, to whom the risen Jesus explains how the Scriptures foretold his passion: "Beginning with Moses and all the prophets, he interpreted to them what referred to him in all the scriptures" (Luke 24:25–27). Luke does not give us the content of Jesus' explanation—surely the greatest of all Bible studies! But here in Acts 7 we have a clear example of how the early Christians understood the events and words of the Old Testament as a foreshadowing of Christ. Jesus is the new Joseph, rejected by his brothers but exalted by God as savior of his people; he is the new Moses, who delivers his people from bondage and leads them into the promised land; he is the new Solomon, builder of the true temple of God. Although Stephen's interpretive moves are subtle and understated, his first-century Jewish audience would have easily caught his meaning: the story of Israel is one great prophecy of the coming of God's Messiah, Jesus, in the fullness of time. This understanding has been the foundation for spiritual interpretation of the Old Testament throughout Christian tradition (see Catechism 117–18). As the Catechism expresses it, quoting Hugh of St. Victor, "All sacred Scripture is but one book, and this one book is Christ, 'because all divine Scripture speaks of Christ, and all divine Scripture is fulfilled in Christ'" (134).

Martyrdom, Persecution, and Mission

Acts 7:54–8:40

Stephen's martyrdom and the following persecution of believers in Jerusalem not only fail to hinder the spread of God's word and the witness to the risen Jesus but actually accelerate that outreach.

Stephen's Martyrdom (7:54–8:1a)

[54]When they heard this, they were infuriated, and they ground their teeth at him. [55]But he, filled with the holy Spirit, looked up intently to heaven and saw the glory of God and Jesus standing at the right hand of God, [56]and he said, "Behold, I see the heavens opened and the Son of Man standing at the right hand of God." [57]But they cried out in a loud voice, covered their ears, and rushed upon him together. [58]They threw him out of the city, and began to stone him. The witnesses laid down their cloaks at the feet of a young man named Saul. [59]As they were stoning Stephen, he called out, "Lord Jesus, receive my spirit." [60]Then he fell to his knees and cried out in a loud voice, "Lord, do not hold this sin against them"; and when he said this, he fell asleep.

[8:1]Now Saul was consenting to his execution.

OT: Exod 33:18–23; Lev 24:16; Job 16:9; Pss 35:16; 37:12; 112:10
NT: Luke 4:28–29; 23:34, 46; Acts 9:1–2
Catechism: Jesus at God's right hand, 659; prayer of intercession, 2634–36; love of enemies, 1825, 1933, 2844
Lectionary: Feast of St. Stephen; Acts 7:55–60: Seventh Sunday of Easter (Year C)

It is no surprise that when Stephen accused his listeners of opposing the   7:54–55
Holy Spirit, killing the prophets, and not keeping the law (Acts 7:51–53), **they
were infuriated** and **ground their teeth at him** in murderous rage. Because
Stephen was **filled with the holy Spirit**, he was permitted, when he **looked up
intently to heaven**, to see **the glory of God and Jesus standing at the right
hand of God**. The verb "to look intently" is a favorite expression of Luke's, which
connotes intense expectation or rapt attention to what one is seeing.[1] Stephen
saw "the glory of God" rather than seeing God directly, since, as Scripture often
emphasizes, no human being can see God face-to-face: "My face you cannot
see, for no man sees me and still lives" (Exod 33:20).[2] However, Stephen can
and did look directly on the glorified Jesus.

Stephen witnesses to the Sanhedrin that he is having a heavenly vision: 7:56
"Behold, I see the heavens opened." This is a common expression for reports
of visions, especially end-time visions like that of John in Revelation: "I had a
vision of an open door to heaven" (Rev 4:1). Stephen says that he sees **the Son of
Man standing at the right hand of God**. In the Gospels, Jesus frequently refers
to himself as "Son of Man," but this is the only biblical text in which someone
else calls him Son of Man. The expression identifies Jesus as the exalted figure
of Daniel's vision, "One like a son of man" who appears before the throne of
God and receives glory and universal dominion (Dan 7:13–14).[3]

What Stephen saw was partly what the Sanhedrin would expect in heavenly visions, namely, the glory of God. The other part was challenging to
them: Jesus, the Son of Man, standing at the right hand of God—implying
that Jesus is the messianic king to whom God has given everlasting dominion! Jesus had prophesied before the same Sanhedrin during his own trial,
"But from this time on the Son of Man will be seated at the right hand of
the power of God" (Luke 22:69). This claim led the Sanhedrin to respond,
"Are you then the Son of God?" and to condemn him for blasphemy (Luke
22:70; see Mark 14:64).

Why is Jesus *standing* instead of "seated at the right hand" (Luke 22:69)? Of
many suggested possibilities, Jesus' standing could indicate that he has risen
to welcome Stephen, who with his dying breath will entrust his life to his Lord
(v. 59). Jesus' standing could also be a posture of intercession, since "he lives
forever to make intercession" for us (Heb 7:25). In John's heavenly vision, Jesus

---

1. Luke 4:20; 22:56; Acts 1:11; 3:4, 12; 6:15.
2. See Gen 16:13; 32:30; Deut 5:24; Judg 6:22; 13:22; Isa 6:5; John 1:18; 1 Tim 6:16.
3. Daniel's vision is also applied to Jesus in Rev 14:14.

The Exalted Son of Man

BIBLICAL
BACKGROUND

Jesus' references to his exaltation as Son of Man and Stephen's statement in Acts 8:55 draw on a vision described in the book of Daniel:

> As the visions during the night continued, I saw
> coming with the clouds of heaven
>   One like a son of man.
> When he reached the Ancient of Days
>   and was presented before him,
> He received dominion, splendor, and kingship;
>   all nations, peoples and tongues will serve him.
> His dominion is an everlasting dominion
>   that shall not pass away,
>   his kingship, one that shall not be destroyed. (Dan 7:13–14)

Both the Gospels and Stephen's vision identify Jesus as the Son of Man described in Daniel. He is the glorious king, exalted at God's right hand, who is given everlasting dominion over all nations and peoples.

appears as the Lamb, standing as if slain in the center of God's throne (Rev 5:6–14).[4]

7:57–58   The members of the Sanhedrin **covered their ears** at what they regarded as blasphemy, refusing to listen to Stephen's prophetic witness. Thus they ironically confirmed Stephen's accusation that they were "uncircumcised in heart and ears" (Acts 7:51). They rushed upon Stephen **together** in violence—an ironic contrast to the Christians' togetherness in fellowship and prayer (Acts 2:46; 4:24; 5:12). Jesus' crucifixion outside the city of Jerusalem (Luke 23:33) was foreshadowed by the attempt of the Nazarenes to kill him outside Nazareth (Luke 4:29). Similarly here, the Sanhedrin took Stephen and **threw him out of the city**. They **began to stone him**, which was the biblical penalty for blasphemy: "Take the blasphemer outside the camp, and . . . let the whole community stone him" (Lev 24:14).[5]

4. See Luke Timothy Johnson, *The Acts of the Apostles*, Sacra pagina 5 (Collegeville, MN: Liturgical Press, 1992), 139. Angelic beings stand in God's presence, such as Gabriel (Luke 1:19) and the seraphim (Isa 6:2). Another possibility Johnson and others mention is that Jesus is standing in judgment, as in Isa 3:13, "The LORD rises to accuse, stands to try his people." Psalm 82 begins, "God stands in the assembly of the gods, and in the midst he judges gods" (translation mine).

5. Roman law reserved capital punishment to be authorized by Roman authorities (see John 18:31). So how could the Sanhedrin stone Stephen? At least three possibilities have been proposed. Some speculate that this act was the equivalent of a lynching that Stephen's opponents got away with due to popular

The Christians had laid goods "at the feet of the apostles" as an acknowledgment of their leadership role in the Church (Acts 4:35, 37; 5:2); likewise here **the witnesses laid down their cloaks at the feet of a young man named Saul.**[6] By this parallel, Luke seems to hint that Saul had some kind of responsible role among Stephen's executioners. The fact that "Saul was consenting to his execution" (Acts 8:1) and soon afterward took a leadership role in persecuting Christians (Acts 8:3; 9:1–2; 22:5) seems to confirm some such responsibility.

Luke describes Stephen's martyrdom by emphasizing how closely Stephen's death follows the pattern of Jesus' death. Both Jesus and Stephen forgave their executioners. Jesus asked his Father, "Forgive them, they know not what they do" (Luke 23:34); Stephen asks the risen **Lord Jesus** not to **hold this sin against them**. Stephen's fierce prophetic rebuke of his judges seems not to have embittered his spirit: he desires their good. In another parallel, Jesus surrendered his spirit to the Father when dying: "Father, into your hands I commend my spirit" (Luke 23:46). Stephen hands his spirit over to Jesus: **"Lord Jesus, receive my spirit."** Stephen is the first Christian martyr, and his martyrdom imitates the way Jesus himself died for us on the cross.

7:59–60

The fact that **Saul** was **consenting to his execution** includes Saul explicitly among those for whom Stephen intercedes, praying that the Lord Jesus will not hold this sin against them (Acts 7:60). Just as Jesus' forgiveness of the Jerusalem mob standing near his cross (Luke 23:34) laid the groundwork for Peter's offer of mercy to the Jerusalem crowd at Pentecost (Acts 2:37–38), so Stephen's intercession for Saul prepares the way for Saul's conversion and call in Acts 9.

8:1

Reflection and Application (7:54–8:1a)

Stephen's martyrdom has remarkable parallels to the passion of Jesus. Like Jesus, Stephen is filled with the Holy Spirit (7:55) and undergoes a transfiguration before his passion (Acts 6:15). He indicts the leaders of Israel for their hard-heartedness (7:51), is cast out of the city (7:58), begs forgiveness for his murderers (7:60), and at the moment of death echoes the words of Jesus but

---

outrage at his alleged offense. Some think the event occurred during an interregnum in AD 36–37, when Pilate went to Rome to answer charges brought against him. Finally, some think that blasphemy against the temple, of which Stephen was accused, belonged to a narrow category of exceptions for which the Jews were allowed to impose capital punishment.

6. This expression gives us a rough idea of when Saul, also called Paul, was born. The Greek word for young man, *neanias*, referred to a man between the ages of 24 and 40. In Philem 9 Paul describes himself as "an old man," *presbytēs*, usually referring to someone over 50. If the stoning of Stephen occurs in the mid-30s and Philemon was written about AD 60, Paul was likely born in the first decade of the first century.

now addresses Jesus himself: "Receive my spirit" (7:59). Luke emphasizes these parallels to show that the ultimate work of the Holy Spirit is to reproduce in Christians the life of Jesus—to conform them more and more closely to Christ both in life and in death (see Rom 8:29).

Stephen, like Jesus, met hatred and lethal violence with understanding, love, and forgiveness. He turned the other cheek (Luke 6:29) and personally embodied nonviolence, even in the face of appalling brutality. Stephen's death, like that of Jesus, thus provides a model for us as believers not only to stand up for our beliefs, but also to put into practice Jesus' command to forgive our enemies (Matt 5:44; Mark 11:25). Perhaps the most challenging moment of our lives will be when we, like Jesus and Stephen, are staring death in the face—from whatever cause, whether sickness, age, accident, or violence. From my priestly experience at several deathbeds, I find it amazing how tenaciously people cling to life, even when unconscious. Fear of death truly is one of our greatest human fears (see Heb 2:15). Jesus and Stephen model for us how to surrender our lives to our Father (and to our Lord Jesus) when it is our time to die: "Father, into your hands I commend my spirit" (Luke 23:46). This surrender at our last moment can be considerably facilitated by our frequent acts of surrender to God's loving providence in all the trials and anxieties we encounter each day. The more we practice surrendering our daily cares to God our loving Father, the easier it will be to commend our spirit to him at death.

Persecution of the Church (8:1b–3)

On that day, there broke out a severe persecution of the Church in Jerusalem, and all were scattered throughout the countryside of Judea and Samaria, except the apostles. ²Devout men buried Stephen and made a loud lament over him. ³Saul, meanwhile, was trying to destroy the Church; entering house after house and dragging out men and women, he handed them over for imprisonment.

NT: John 15:20; 16:2; Acts 22:4; 26:10; Gal 1:13; Phil 3:6; 1 Tim 1:13
Catechism: persecution for faith, 769, 1808, 1816

8:1   Stephen's martyrdom occasions the outbreak of **severe persecution of the Church in Jerusalem**. Because of this persecution, **all were scattered throughout the countryside of Judea and Samaria.** Although this looks like a setback, God will use this dispersal of believers as an instrument for the dissemination of God's word and the growth of the Church (Acts 8:4–8). Thus ironically it will activate the next step in the fulfillment of Jesus' prophecy to his apostles, "You will be my witnesses in Jerusalem, throughout Judea and Samaria, and to the ends of the earth" (Acts 1:8). Luke's final remark, **except the apostles**, prompts a question: why are the apostles able to remain in Jerusalem unharmed? It seems that †Hellenistic Jewish Christians like Stephen are the primary target of persecutors' ire in Jerusalem. Hebrew-speaking Jewish Christians like the apostles were pursued less aggressively.

The apostles' remaining in Jerusalem highlights another irony. Although it was to the apostles that Jesus had prophesied, "You will be my witnesses . . . throughout Judea and Samaria, and to the ends of the earth," the witnessing in Samaria and Judea was not initiated by the apostles themselves but by others such as Philip, one of the Seven (see Acts 6:1–6). The next evangelizing work mentioned in Acts will be by the converted persecutor Saul (Acts 9). Peter's witness beyond Jerusalem will be first reported in Acts 10–12. The apostles may have chosen to remain in Jerusalem despite the persecution because they recognized the importance of preserving the stability of the first community as a reference point for the wider Church, especially in its early phase. For instance, the apostles are able to send Peter and John from the mother church of Jerusalem to confirm Philip's work in Samaria when they hear about his missionary success there (Acts 8:14–17).

Luke portrays the human side of Stephen's martyrdom in the **loud lament over him** uttered by the **men** who **buried Stephen**. Even a glorious martyrdom entails deep human suffering among those who loved the individual. Our faith in the victory of those who die for Jesus does not eliminate our grief at losing someone we love in this life.

8:2

Luke draws special attention to Saul's fanaticism in carrying out the persecution that followed Stephen's martyrdom. He portrays **Saul** as an activist who **was trying to destroy the Church, entering house after house and dragging out men and women**, handing them over **for imprisonment**. The Greek verb for "trying to destroy" is a powerful word that can mean devastate or ravage. This portrait of uncompromising harassment will be confirmed by Paul's statements in Acts 22:4 and 26:10. In his own letters Paul states, "I persecuted the church of God beyond measure and tried to destroy it" (Gal 1:13) and "In zeal I persecuted the church" (Phil 3:6), though he does not give details about breaking into houses and imprisoning Christian men and women. After his conversion Paul himself endured the same kind of suffering he had inflicted (Acts 16:23; 2 Cor 11:23–24; Phil 1:14). Jesus had prophesied to his disciples, "They will hand you over to the synagogues and to prisons" (Luke 21:12).

8:3

The Scattering: Philip in Samaria (8:4–8)

---

⁴**Now those who had been scattered went about preaching the word.** ⁵**Thus Philip went down to [the] city of Samaria and proclaimed the Messiah to them.** ⁶**With one accord, the crowds paid attention to what was said by Philip when they heard it and saw the signs he was doing.** ⁷**For unclean spirits, crying out in a loud voice, came out of many possessed people, and many paralyzed and crippled people were cured.** ⁸**There was great joy in that city.**

OT: Isa 35:1, 6
NT: Matt 10:1, 23; Luke 6:18–19; 9:2; John 4:39–41
Catechism: exorcism, 1673
Lectionary: Acts 8:5–8, 14–17: Sixth Sunday of Easter (Year A)

8:4–5   Luke shows that God continues to work his saving plan even through apparent setbacks. Here the persecution that forced disciples out of Jerusalem, which can certainly be regarded as a defeat for them on the human level, is directly used by God to spread his word of salvation. The very disciples **who had been scattered went about preaching the word.** The followers of Jesus evidently regarded evangelization as a natural response to new circumstances, unexpected though they were. **Philip**, the second Hellenist named after Stephen in the list of those designated as leaders by the apostles (Acts 6:5), is the first missionary mentioned. He took the word to **Samaria**, where he **proclaimed the Messiah to them.** Samaria was part of the area belonging to the northern kingdom of Israel, which split off from Judah after Solomon's reign (1 Kings 12). The ten tribes of the northern kingdom were exiled into Assyria in 722 BC, and their land was repopulated with non-Israelites. By New Testament times, Jews regarded Samaritans as mixed-blood heretics who refused to worship in the temple at Jerusalem (see John 4:20). Philip's mission is the first reported mission beyond Jerusalem, fulfilling what Jesus had prophesied in Acts 1:8.

8:6–8   Verse 6 repeats one of Luke's favorite expressions to highlight the unity among those who heard the word preached by Philip: **with one accord.**⁷ The **signs** that Philip **was doing** moved the Samaritan **crowds** to **pay attention** to his preaching. Luke mentions especially Philip's exorcisms and physical healings: **unclean spirits** cried out **in a loud voice** when they **came out of many possessed people**; there were also healings of **many paralyzed and crippled people.** All these wondrous signs worked by Philip resulted in **great joy in**

7. Greek *homothymadon*, as in Acts 1:14; 2:46; 4:24; 5:12; 15:25; etc.

that city. Luke often emphasizes the joy that follows Jesus' mighty deeds and the conversion of sinners (Luke 15:7, 23–24; 19:37; Acts 13:52). However, the following incident with Simon the magician illustrates that the presence of authentic signs and wonders does not guarantee an appropriate response.

Simon the Magician and Philip (8:9–13)

⁹**A man named Simon used to practice magic in the city and astounded the people of Samaria, claiming to be someone great. ¹⁰All of them, from the least to the greatest, paid attention to him, saying, "This man is the 'Power of God' that is called 'Great.'" ¹¹They paid attention to him because he had astounded them by his magic for a long time, ¹²but once they began to believe Philip as he preached the good news about the kingdom of God and the name of Jesus Christ, men and women alike were baptized. ¹³Even Simon himself believed and, after being baptized, became devoted to Philip; and when he saw the signs and mighty deeds that were occurring, he was astounded.**

OT: Exod 7:11; 8:14; Deut 18:10–12
NT: Matt 24:24; Acts 3:12; 14:11; Rev 13:13–14
Catechism: magic, 2115–17; signs and wonders, 547–50; faith and baptism, 1226

Philip's signs attract the same Samaritan crowds who had been in awe of **Simon**, a local occult practitioner whose **magic** had **astounded** them. After narrating Philip's miracles, Luke provides background on Simon's apparently similar activities and his reputation. Luke emphasizes how this Samaritan magician promoted himself as **someone great**. He got the Samaritans, **from the least to the greatest**, to pay **attention to him**, as they also pay attention to Philip's preaching because of Philip's signs. The crowds even proclaimed Simon as the **"Power of God" that is called "Great."** Although the precise meaning of these titles is not clear, Luke's general point is. Not only did Simon promote himself as an important religious figure, but also the Samaritan crowds treated him as embodying divine power.

8:9–10

Luke repeatedly contrasts Christian miracles with non-Christian magic and presents the wonders done in Jesus' name as overcoming superstition and magical arts, which in the ancient world involved not just sleight of hand but occult practices as well.[8] Practitioners of magic like Simon Bar-Jesus treated wonder-working power as something they personally manipulated and for

8. See Peter's rebuke of Simon (Acts 8:20–23), Paul's rebuke of and imposition of temporary blindness on the magician Bar-Jesus (13:6–11), Paul's exorcism of a slave girl with an oracular spirit (16:16–18),

St. Justin Martyr on Simon the Magician

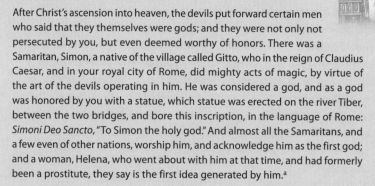

LIVING TRADITION

One of the Church's earliest martyrs is St. Justin Martyr, a Greek-speaking philosopher from Samaria who converted to Christianity and was killed about AD 150. According to Justin, the Samaritan magician Simon continued practicing magic after the incident narrated in Acts 8. Writing to a Roman audience in his *First Apology*, Justin recounts:

> After Christ's ascension into heaven, the devils put forward certain men who said that they themselves were gods; and they were not only not persecuted by you, but even deemed worthy of honors. There was a Samaritan, Simon, a native of the village called Gitto, who in the reign of Claudius Caesar, and in your royal city of Rome, did mighty acts of magic, by virtue of the art of the devils operating in him. He was considered a god, and as a god was honored by you with a statue, which statue was erected on the river Tiber, between the two bridges, and bore this inscription, in the language of Rome: *Simoni Deo Sancto*, "To Simon the holy god." And almost all the Samaritans, and a few even of other nations, worship him, and acknowledge him as the first god; and a woman, Helena, who went about with him at that time, and had formerly been a prostitute, they say is the first idea generated by him.[a]

a. *First Apology* 26, in Alexander Roberts et al., *The Ante-Nicene Fathers* (Oak Harbor, WA: Logos Research Systems, 1997), 1:171. For other patristic views of Simon, see Johnson, *Acts*, 146–47.

which they could take credit. In contrast, Peter insisted that neither his power nor his piety was responsible for healing the lame man (Acts 3:12), and Paul had to urge the pagans at Lystra not to attribute divine honor to him after his healing of a lame man (Acts 14:8–18). Wonders done at the hands of Christians were worked not by them but by Jesus, in whose name they were acting.

8:11–13   Luke compares the superstitious **attention** the Samaritans gave Simon, who **had astounded them by his magic for a long time**, with their beginning **to believe Philip** and his preaching of **the good news**. The content of Philip's preaching was both **the kingdom of God**, which had been the central theme of Jesus' own preaching in the Gospel (see Luke 4:43; 8:1), and **the name of Jesus Christ**, the powerful name by which the reality of the kingdom is made present and effective.

Philip soon won over those who had formerly been fascinated by Simon's magic, so that Samaritan **men and women alike were baptized**. Philip's

the fiasco of the itinerant Jewish exorcists (19:13–16), and the burning of books of magic in Ephesus (19:17–19).

preaching and miracles won over **even Simon himself,** who **believed,** was **baptized,** and **became devoted to Philip.**[9] However, the main reason Luke gives for Simon's association with Philip is his astonishment and admiration for Philip's **signs and mighty deeds.** Simon later attempts to buy divine power from Peter (v. 19), which suggests that here he was probably regarding Philip primarily as another magician, more powerful than himself.

The Apostles, the Spirit, and Simon the Magician (8:14–25)

[14]Now when the apostles in Jerusalem heard that Samaria had accepted the word of God, they sent them Peter and John, [15]who went down and prayed for them, that they might receive the holy Spirit, [16]for it had not yet fallen upon any of them; they had only been baptized in the name of the Lord Jesus. [17]Then they laid hands on them and they received the holy Spirit.

[18]When Simon saw that the Spirit was conferred by the laying on of the apostles' hands, he offered them money [19]and said, "Give me this power too, so that anyone upon whom I lay my hands may receive the holy Spirit." [20]But Peter said to him, "May your money perish with you, because you thought that you could buy the gift of God with money. [21]You have no share or lot in this matter, for your heart is not upright before God. [22]Repent of this wickedness of yours and pray to the Lord that, if possible, your intention may be forgiven. [23]For I see that you are filled with bitter gall and are in the bonds of iniquity." [24]Simon said in reply, "Pray for me to the Lord, that nothing of what you have said may come upon me." [25]So when they had testified and proclaimed the word of the Lord, they returned to Jerusalem and preached the good news to many Samaritan villages.

OT: 2 Kings 5:15–16; Isa 55:1
NT: Matt 10:8; Luke 3:16; Acts 3:6; 9:17–18; 1 Tim 6:5
Catechism: baptism and the Holy Spirit, 1226; confirmation, 1285–1305; simony, 2121
Lectionary: Acts 8:5–8, 14–17: Sixth Sunday of Easter (Year A); Acts 8:1bc, 4, 14–17: Confirmation

The original leaders of the Church, **the apostles in Jerusalem,** followed up this marvelous acceptance of **the word of God** in **Samaria** by sending **them Peter and John.** The apostles may have wanted to observe firsthand and give their approval of this new outreach beyond the bounds of Judaism. The two apostles **prayed for** the new converts, **that they might receive the holy Spirit** and thus

8:14–17

---

9. The Greek for "became devoted to" is *proskartereō*, with a basic meaning "stay with." It can also mean "associate closely with" or "adhere firmly to" someone.

141

complete their initiation into the Church. Luke underlines apostolic authority in the early Church by stressing the continuity between the first conversions in Jerusalem at the hands of the apostles and the laying on of hands by Peter and John, which completed the incorporation of the Samaritans into the Church.

8:18–19   **Simon** is so impressed by the powerful manifestations of **the Spirit** in those on whom **the apostles** have laid their **hands** that he misinterprets their action as a potent form of magic, to which he would like to buy access. He offers the apostles **money** in exchange for spiritual power: **"Give me this power too, so that anyone upon whom I lay my hands may receive the holy Spirit."** The sin of simony, the buying or selling of church offices or other spiritual goods, is named after this corrupt action of Simon.

8:20–22   Simon's proposition leads to Peter's harsh rebuke, **"May your money perish with you, because you thought that you could buy the gift of God with money."** This illustrates the essential distinction between magic and God's gifts. Magic is something the practitioner can control through methods or techniques, and

---

Baptism and God's Freedom in Giving the Spirit

BIBLICAL BACKGROUND

Luke reports some variety in the relationship between baptism and the receiving of the Holy Spirit. After the initial outpouring of the Spirit on the 120 disciples at Pentecost, Peter declares that the way to receive the same gift of the Spirit is through repentance and baptism (Acts 2:38). Luke likewise implies that Saul's baptism and receiving of the Spirit occurred on the same occasion (9:17–18). Here in Acts 8 the outpouring of the Spirit occurs in a separate step *after* baptism, when the apostles lay hands on the new converts, bringing the baptismal gift to its full realization. Similarly, some disciples in Ephesus received only the baptism of John, but when Paul baptizes them in the name of Jesus and lays hands on them, they receive the Spirit (19:5–6). On the other hand, the Spirit falls on Cornelius and his friends *before* baptism as an extraordinary sign of God's will to save Gentiles (Acts 10:44–48).

Catholic tradition has interpreted these texts to mean that a person receives the Holy Spirit initially in baptism and then in a fuller way through the laying on of hands at confirmation (see Living Tradition sidebar). At the same time, the Cornelius event illustrates God's freedom in pouring out his Holy Spirit whenever he chooses. Even in Cornelius's case, however, Peter's subsequent directive to have the new converts baptized indicates the necessity of incorporating believers fully into the body of Christ through the sacraments.

The Holy Spirit and the Sacrament of Confirmation

LIVING TRADITION

The apostles' practice of laying hands on new believers to impart the Holy Spirit, as here in Acts 8, is regarded by Catholic tradition as the origin of the sacrament of confirmation, which completes baptism and "in a certain way perpetuates the grace of Pentecost in the Church" (Catechism, 1288). The Catechism emphasizes the Holy Spirit's action and the powerful effects of this sacrament.

> Confirmation brings an increase and deepening of baptismal grace, . . . roots us more deeply in the divine filiation which makes us cry, "Abba! Father!," . . . unites us more firmly to Christ, . . . increases the gifts of the Holy Spirit in us, . . . renders our bond with the Church more perfect, . . . gives us a special strength of the Holy Spirit to spread and defend the faith by word and action as true witnesses of Christ, to confess the name of Christ boldly, and never to be ashamed of the Cross." (1303)

Those entrusted with preparing young people for confirmation can help them to await the gift of the Spirit with great faith and expectancy by teaching them about the outpourings of the Holy Spirit in Acts and their effects on the lives of the early Christians.

---

can even buy. To debase the gift of God to the level of magical practices is a form of blasphemy. Because Simon treated the gift of the Spirit as a commodity, Peter tells him that his **heart is not upright** and he has **no share or lot in this matter**—that is, in the benefits of the gospel—because he has not really repented of his attachment to the occult.

Simon neither denies nor admits to Peter's harsh charge: **"You are filled with bitter gall and . . . in the bonds of iniquity."** Instead of repenting of and confessing his sin, **Simon** merely asks Peter to **pray** for him that he be spared the punishment Peter threatened. Simon may still be thinking in terms of the relative power of competing magicians, his and the apostles'. **8:23–24**

The incident ends abruptly without resolution regarding Simon. Luke reports instead that the apostles Peter and John completed their mission of testifying to Jesus and proclaiming **the word of the Lord**. Afterward **they returned to Jerusalem**. On their way, however, they further evangelized the Samaritans as they **preached the good news to many Samaritan villages**. Luke thus shows the apostles as not only endorsing the mission to the Samaritans—the people whom the Jews considered outsiders to God's covenant—but also contributing **8:25** to it. He also shows the power of the gospel to overcome deep historic enmity between peoples.

Reflection and Application (8:14–25)

Through the centuries the Church has continued to incorporate new believers into Christ and impart the Holy Spirit through the sacraments of initiation: baptism, confirmation, and the Eucharist. Acts shows the powerful effect these sacraments can have in the life of a believer. To be baptized into Christ and receive his Holy Spirit is a radically life-transforming event with perceptible outward effects: a personal knowledge of Jesus as Lord, joy in his salvation, overflowing praise and thanksgiving, eagerness to know and follow his teaching, zeal to proclaim the gospel, and service to others through various charisms of the Spirit. Yet how many baptized and confirmed Catholics today manifest these effects? If such sacramental fruitfulness is lacking, the reason may be that many who received the sacraments as young children have never personally appropriated the divine life they received by surrendering their whole lives to the lordship of Jesus Christ.[10] In addition, various other obstacles may have hindered their sacramental preparation, such as inadequate understanding, unrepented sin, or an environment of lukewarm faith.[11] As the Catechism teaches, "The sacraments act *ex opere operato* (literally, 'by the very fact of the action's being performed'), by virtue of the saving work of Christ, accomplished once for all. . . . Nevertheless, the fruits of the sacraments also depend on the disposition of the one who receives them" (1128). The dispositions needed for the sacraments to bear fruit include faith in Jesus, turning from sin, an understanding of the gifts that God intends for his people, and the desire to do God's will. If someone who was baptized as an infant grows up in a vibrant community of faith, the effects of the sacraments unfold naturally as these dispositions develop. But if a person does not acquire these dispositions, the grace they received remains bound or dormant.

Acts can serve as an impetus for those responsible for sacramental preparation to do everything possible to help candidates believe, repent, desire, and expect the full outpouring of the Holy Spirit in their lives as it was experienced in the early Church. For those already baptized and confirmed, Acts can awaken a

10. See John Paul II, *On Catechesis in Our Time*, 19.

11. In the part of his *Summa theologica* devoted to baptism (III, QQ. 66–71), Thomas Aquinas indicates the importance of proper dispositions and preparation for the efficacy of baptism. He specifically mentions repentance and faith, devotion, sincerity, instruction, exorcism, follow-up after baptism, responsible and knowledgeable godparents, and desire. See also Augustine, *Sermons* 269.2.

new desire to experience the full effects of these sacraments by acquiring the needed dispositions and by praying persistently in accord with the promise of Jesus: "Ask and you will receive; seek and you will find; knock and the door will be opened to you. . . . If you then, who are wicked, know how to give good gifts to your children, how much more will the Father in heaven give the holy Spirit to those who ask him?" (Luke 11:9–13).[12]

Philip and the Ethiopian (8:26–40)

[26]Then the angel of the Lord spoke to Philip, "Get up and head south on the road that goes down from Jerusalem to Gaza, the desert route." [27]So he got up and set out. Now there was an Ethiopian eunuch, a court official of the Candace, that is, the queen of the Ethiopians, in charge of her entire treasury, who had come to Jerusalem to worship, [28]and was returning home. Seated in his chariot, he was reading the prophet Isaiah. [29]The Spirit said to Philip, "Go and join up with that chariot." [30]Philip ran up and heard him reading Isaiah the prophet and said, "Do you understand what you are reading?" [31]He replied, "How can I, unless someone instructs me?" So he invited Philip to get in and sit with him. [32]This was the scripture passage he was reading:

> "Like a sheep he was led to the slaughter,
>   and as a lamb before its shearer is silent,
>   so he opened not his mouth.
> [33]In [his] humiliation justice was denied him.
>   Who will tell of his posterity?
>   For his life is taken from the earth."

[34]Then the eunuch said to Philip in reply, "I beg you, about whom is the prophet saying this? About himself, or about someone else?" [35]Then Philip opened his mouth and, beginning with this scripture passage, he proclaimed Jesus to him. [36]As they traveled along the road they came to some water, and the eunuch said, "Look, there is water. What is to prevent my being baptized?" [[37]][38]Then he ordered the chariot to stop, and Philip and the eunuch both went down into the water, and he baptized him. [39]When they came out of the water, the Spirit of the Lord snatched Philip away, and the eunuch saw him no more, but continued on his way rejoicing.

---

12. Programs available to help bring alive the graces of baptism and confirmation include the Life in the Spirit Seminar, Cursillo, the Alpha Course, and Philip Course.

⁴⁰**Philip came to Azotus, and went about proclaiming the good news to all the towns until he reached Caesarea.**

OT: Deut 23:2; Ps 87:4; Isa 53:7–8; 56:3–7
NT: Mark 16:16; Luke 24:25–27, 32; Acts 21:8; 1 Pet 2:21–25
Catechism: help of angels, 334–36; the Suffering Servant in Isaiah, 601, 713–14; evangelization, 904–5
Lectionary: Christian initiation apart from the Easter Vigil

8:26–29
After Philip's ministry in Samaria, the **angel of the Lord** called **Philip** to travel **south** toward **Gaza**, and he immediately **got up and set out**. On the way he encountered an **Ethiopian eunuch** returning home after he **had come to Jerusalem to worship**. Eunuchs were castrated men, whom ancient monarchs often employed as guardians of the royal harem (see 2 Kings 9:32; Jer 41:16, translated "court officials" by NAB) or in other official posts.[13] This eunuch had an important post as **court official of the Candace, the queen of the Ethiopians, in charge of her entire treasury**. Like many Gentiles in the ancient world, he was drawn to Judaism and had come to believe in the one God whom the Jews worshiped. As a eunuch he was barred from becoming a full member of God's people and entering the inner courts of the temple (Deut 23:2).

But through Isaiah, God had promised that in the messianic age foreigners who believe, and even eunuchs, would be welcomed into the temple as members of God's people (Isa 56:3–7). The Old Testament also foretells that "Ethiopia will stretch out its hands to God" (Ps 68:31 NJB [32 NAB]) and that all peoples would "call upon the name of the LORD, to serve him with one accord; / From beyond the rivers of Ethiopia . . . they shall bring me offerings" (Zeph 3:9–10). By faith in Jesus this Ethiopian eunuch will be baptized, receive the Spirit, and become a full-fledged member of God's people (vv. 36–38).

God's purpose for this meeting is for Philip to evangelize the eunuch. When Philip hears him **reading the prophet Isaiah** aloud **in his chariot**, the **Spirit** commands Philip to **join** him. Although it was an angel of the Lord who first called Philip to travel beyond Samaria, it was the Spirit who commanded him to join the Ethiopian.[14] In both cases, Luke portrays God himself as directing Philip's actions, indicating the depth of God's care for this man and for the salvation of the Gentiles.

---

13. The term "eunuch" was sometimes used more broadly to refer to a royal official who was not literally castrated. For instance, Gen 39:1 in both Hebrew and Greek uses the term "eunuch" for the married official Potiphar.

14. This alternation between angel and Spirit exemplifies the biblical pattern in which God is portrayed as mysteriously present and acting even when he does so through the ministry of angels (see, for example, Exod 3:2–6; 33:2, 14; Judg 6:12, 14).

Fig. 7. Portion of the Isaiah Scroll (one of the Dead Sea Scrolls) dating to the second or third century BC; shown here is part of Isaiah 53, which the Ethiopian eunuch was reading (Acts 8:30–33).

When **Philip** asks him, **"Do you understand what you are reading?"** the man   8:30–31
replies, **"How can I, unless someone instructs me?"** This exchange expresses an
important theme in Luke-Acts: to understand the Scriptures fully, one must be
taught by someone who knows how the Scriptures have been fulfilled in Jesus.
As the disciples on their way to Emmaus could not understand the Scriptures
without the help of the risen Jesus, who explained to them how all the various
parts of the Old Testament referred to himself (Luke 24:25–27, 32), so this man
cannot understand the Isaiah passage unless someone instructs him. He invites
Philip into his chariot to teach him.

Unlike the Emmaus account, where Luke leaves us in the dark about which   8:32–33
biblical passages Jesus referred to, here he quotes a passage from the Greek translation of Isaiah (53:7–8). This passage is from one of Isaiah's Suffering Servant
songs, describing an unnamed servant of God who suffers in silence for the sins
of the people (Isa 52:13–53:12). The early Church recognized this as a prophetic
foreshadowing of the passion of Jesus.[15] As this servant **was led to the slaughter**, he kept silence **like a sheep** or **a lamb before its shearer**. Moreover, **justice
was denied** this humiliated servant. Instead, **his life** was **taken from the earth**.

15. See, for instance, the allusions to this passage in Mark 10:45; John 12:38; Rom 10:16; 1 Pet 2:21–25.

The Greek for "taken" (in Acts and in the †Septuagint version of Isa 53:8, which it is quoting) can mean either "lifted up" or "done away with." This permits a double meaning when interpreted in light of Christ: he was "taken from the earth" in the sense of being "done away with" in death, but has been "lifted up" from the earth, from his grave, by resurrection. In a similar way the Gospel of John refers to Jesus' passion as his being "lifted up," both in the torture of crucifixion and in the exaltation of his resurrection (John 12:32–33).

8:34–35   The eunuch's question whether **the prophet** was referring to **himself** or to **someone else** reflects a common interpretive procedure in the ancient world. One could either focus on a text's original meaning (in this case, the Ethiopian suggests that Isaiah was referring to himself), or on a prophetic meaning beyond what the author may have intended. In a similar way, Peter argued that Ps 16 refers not to the prophet David himself but to his future messianic descendant (Acts 2:25–31).[16]

Philip responds by **beginning with this scripture passage** as a basis from which to proclaim **Jesus**. Previously Philip had evangelized Samaritan crowds by preaching with signs and wonders. Now he evangelizes this individual by showing how Jesus fulfills the Scriptures. Luke portrays both as important ways of proclaiming the good news.

8:36–38   Philip must have given the eunuch a full explanation of how one becomes a Christian, for when the **eunuch** spotted water near the **road**, he pointed to it and asked, **"What is to prevent my being baptized?"** Until then, even if he desired to convert to Judaism, he was barred from full membership in God's people (Deut 23:2). Now he sees there is no longer anything to hinder him! His faith in Jesus was enough for him to be incorporated into the people of God through baptism. The eunuch stopped the **chariot**, they both **went down into the water**, and Philip **baptized him**. They thereby fulfilled another prophecy of Isaiah:

> The foreigner joined to the LORD should not say,
> "The LORD will surely exclude me from his people";
> Nor should the eunuch say,
> "See, I am a dry tree."
> For thus says the LORD:
> To the eunuchs who keep my sabbaths,
> who choose what pleases me,
> and who hold fast to my covenant,

---

16. The Essenes at Qumran, a first-century Jewish sect, similarly interpreted numerous passages as prophesying their leader, the "Teacher of Righteousness."

I will give . . . a monument and a name
Better than sons and daughters. . . .
And the foreigners who join themselves to the LORD,
to minister to him,
To love the name of the LORD,
to become his servants. . . .
Them I will bring to my holy mountain
and make them joyful in my house of prayer. (Isa 56:3–7)

Immediately upon coming **out of the water, the Spirit of the Lord snatched**   8:39–40
Philip away. The Spirit had guided Philip to evangelize and baptize this foreign official, and now the Spirit transfers him to his next mission at **Azotus**, on the seaside road between Gaza and Joppa, and on to **Caesarea**, where he will be living when we next meet him in Acts 21:8. This baptism of the eunuch is an example of how Luke uses individual events to illustrate the general pattern of the rapid spread of the gospel. The **eunuch** in turn **saw** Philip **no more** but journeyed on home to Ethiopia, **rejoicing** at his baptism and acceptance into God's covenant people.

Reflection and Application (8:26–40)

Obeying the Spirit. Luke portrays Philip as an evangelist who is guided by the Spirit in extraordinary ways. Even if we are not literally "snatched away" from one place to another, Philip's example can awaken in us a more expectant faith in the Holy Spirit's active guidance in our lives and ministry. Philip, like Peter and Paul (see Acts 10:19; 16:6–10), was attuned to the Spirit's voice and quickly obeyed his promptings. For us too, obeying the Spirit brings a fruitfulness that goes beyond what is possible by our own resources (see John 14:12; 15:8–10).

The word of God is not chained. God is often forced to "write straight with crooked lines" to accomplish his saving plan. Neither the killing of Stephen, the persecution of Christians in Jerusalem, the Samaritan misinterpretation of Christian miracles as magic, or even the status of being a eunuch—none of these could hinder God's plan to spread the good news of salvation to all nations and all classes of individuals, from Jerusalem to the ends of the earth. When we are faced with bad news and failures, Acts reminds us not to lose heart. Our hope lies not in human success but in God, for whom nothing is impossible (Matt 19:26; Luke 1:37).

Paul's Conversion and Baptism

Acts 9:1–22

In the divinely empowered growth of the Church in Acts, Paul's conversion from rabid persecutor to zealous witness called to speak the word of God "to the ends of the earth" (Acts 13:47) is pivotal.[1] The risen Jesus is able to reverse the persecuting zeal of Saul to make of him perhaps the Church's greatest evangelizer and theologian.

Saul's Conversion (9:1–9)

[1]Now Saul, still breathing murderous threats against the disciples of the Lord, went to the high priest [2]and asked him for letters to the synagogues in Damascus, that, if he should find any men or women who belonged to the Way, he might bring them back to Jerusalem in chains. [3]On his journey, as he was nearing Damascus, a light from the sky suddenly flashed around him. [4]He fell to the ground and heard a voice saying to him, "Saul, Saul, why are you persecuting me?" [5]He said, "Who are you, sir?" The reply came, "I am Jesus, whom you are persecuting. [6]Now get up and go into the city and you will be told what you must do." [7]The men who were traveling with him stood speechless, for they heard the voice but could see no one. [8]Saul got up from the ground, but when he opened his eyes he could see nothing; so they led him by the hand and brought him to

---

1. I will generally use the name "Saul" when Acts does, and "Paul" after Acts begins using that name (Acts 13:9, except in later references to his conversion) and when discussing his letters, which always use "Paul."

Damascus. [9]For three days he was unable to see, and he neither ate nor drank.

OT: Exod 3:7; Dan 10:7
NT: John 16:2; Acts 22:3–16; 26:9–20; 1 Cor 15:9; Gal 1:11–17; 1 Tim 1:13
Catechism: conversion of heart, 1430–33; call to conversion, 545, 1036, 1427–29
Lectionary: Acts 9:1–22: Feast of the Conversion of St. Paul (Jan. 25)

Saul's conversion is so important that Acts will recount it three times, each time bringing out different aspects or emphases (9:1–19; 22:3–22; 26:4–23). This double repetition underscores the huge role that Paul played in spreading the gospel.

9:1-2

This first report of Saul's encounter with the risen Jesus immediately follows the description of Philip's mission. Luke links this momentous event with his earlier report of Saul's persecuting activity (Acts 8:1–3) with the word "still": **Saul, still breathing murderous threats**. . . . Saul's fierce hostility to Christianity is mentioned repeatedly in Acts and in his own letters.[2]

Luke explains that Saul received authorization from the **high priest** to extradite Jewish **disciples of the Lord** from **the synagogues in Damascus** for punishment in **Jerusalem**. Another historical example of such extradition power is 1 Macc 15:16–21, in which the Romans grant such authority to the high priest. Saul seeks permission to seize **any men and women** belonging to **the Way**, which implies that he thinks they deserve punishment as a reprehensible Jewish sect.[3] The term †"the Way" was the earliest name for Christianity.[4] It refers to the fact that following Jesus is a whole way of life, and it alludes to the biblical expression "the way of the Lord," meaning a way of life that is pleasing to God and in keeping with his covenant.[5]

Saul is brought up short in his **journey** to **Damascus** by a sudden appearance of the risen Jesus. Luke narrates this event in language reminiscent of Old Testament †theophanies—overwhelming experiences of the presence and holiness of God. Saul is intercepted by a **light from the sky** (or "light from heaven," RSV, NRSV, NIV). Biblical †theophanies are often accompanied by heavenly light (see Ezek 1:4, 7, 13; Dan 10:5–6), as was Jesus' transfiguration (Luke 9:29–31). Because of the shock from this light, Saul **fell to the ground**

9:3

2. See Acts 22:4–8; 26:9–15; Gal 1:13; Phil 3:5–6; 1 Tim 1:13–16.
3. See also Acts 24:14.
4. Within the Bible, only Acts uses this expression for the Christian movement (see especially 18:25–26; 19:9, 23; 24:5, 14, 22). "The Way" is analogous to the Jewish term *halakah*, which refers to the laws, customs, and traditions that guide daily Jewish life.
5. See Acts 18:25; Gen 18:19; Judg 2:22; 2 Kings 21:22; Isa 40:3; Ezek 33:17, 20.

(there is no mention of his falling off a horse, and it seems unlikely since v. 8 says that Saul's companions lead him into Damascus by hand).

9:4–5   Saul hears a heavenly voice call his name twice, **"Saul, Saul,"** just as occurred in the Old Testament when God had an urgent command, mission, or promise for figures like Abraham, Jacob, Moses, and Samuel.[6] The voice from the heavenly light challenges him: **"Why are you persecuting me?"** Mystified, **Saul** asks the identity of his heavenly visitor: **"Who are you, sir?"** Although Saul does not know who his visitor is, he is certainly aware that he is from heaven. The context, therefore, calls for the more exalted translation "Lord" (NIV, NJB, JB, RSV, NRSV) rather than "sir" for the Greek *kyrios*.

The response, **"I am Jesus, whom you are persecuting,"** is earth-shattering to Saul for two reasons. First, Jesus of Nazareth, whom Saul thought was not only dead but also cursed by God (see Deut 21:22–23; Gal 3:13), and for this reason could not possibly be the Messiah, is alive and risen from the dead! Saul has become an eyewitness to the risen Jesus, as were the other apostles (see 1 Cor 15:4–8).

Second, the risen Jesus identifies himself with those who believe in him, whom Saul is persecuting. Saul discovers that to lay a hand on Jesus' followers is to lay a hand on Jesus himself. This self-identification of Jesus with his disciples later became the foundation for Paul's theology of the Church as the "body of Christ," one of his central themes (Eph 4:12; see 1 Cor 12:12–30).

9:6   The Lord instructs Saul to **go into the city**, Damascus, where he **will be told what** he **must do**. Saul's conversion is at the same moment his commissioning as an apostle and witness to Christ. Although the Lord sovereignly initiates this commission, he leaves its implementation to the ministry of the Church in the person of Ananias.

9:7   Luke emphasizes that only Paul both saw and heard the vision, not the **men who were traveling with him**, who **heard the voice** (or "the sound," NIV) **but could see no one**. This exemplifies the New Testament emphasis on reliable testimony as requiring that a witness both *saw* and *heard* that to which the witness testifies, that is, it cannot be just hearsay.[7] Later Paul will emphasize that what qualifies him as an apostle is the fact that he saw the risen Lord (1 Cor 9:1).

9:8   When Saul gets **up from the ground**, he discovers that he can **see nothing**, since the light from the vision has blinded him. Ironically, this persecutor—who had intended to lay hands on Christian captives, bind them, and lead them

---

6. See Gen 22:11; 46:2–3; Exod 3:4; 1 Sam 3:7–10.
7. See Luke 7:22; Acts 4:20; 22:15; John 3:32; and especially the insistence on personal witness in 1 John 1:3: "What we have seen and heard we proclaim now to you, so that you too may have fellowship with us."

back to Jerusalem—must himself be helplessly **led by the hand** into the city of **Damascus.**

Saul's blindness lasts **three days,** during which **he neither ate nor drank.**   9:9
The three days may be intended to allude to the interval between Jesus' death and resurrection. Saul's physical and spiritual darkness parallels the emotional and spiritual desolation of Jesus' followers between his death and resurrection. During this period Saul was taking in the magnitude of what had happened to him and reevaluating his whole life in a new light. He now realized that he had made a terrible mistake. When he thought he was doing the will of God, he was blaspheming and persecuting God's Messiah, resisting the Holy Spirit, and opposing God (see Acts 7:51; 1 Cor 15:9; Gal 1:13; 1 Tim 1:13). His righteousness and religious zeal now appear for what they were: *self*-righteousness, arrogance, and stubborn self-will. At the same time, Saul's heart was captured by the Lord. In his Letter to the Philippians he wrote of this momentous event: "Whatever gains I had, these I have come to consider a loss because of Christ. More than that, I even consider everything as a loss because of the supreme good of knowing Christ Jesus my Lord. For his sake I have accepted the loss of all things and I consider them so much rubbish, that I may gain Christ and be found in him" (Phil 3:7–9). Fasting, a traditional sign of penitence, is Saul's instinctive response to his encounter with the Lord and a preparation for his baptism and further enlightenment.

Saul's Baptism (9:10–19a)

¹⁰There was a disciple in Damascus named Ananias, and the Lord said to him in a vision, "Ananias." He answered, "Here I am, Lord." ¹¹The Lord said to him, "Get up and go to the street called Straight and ask at the house of Judas for a man from Tarsus named Saul. He is there praying, ¹²and [in a vision] he has seen a man named Ananias come in and lay [his] hands on him, that he may regain his sight." ¹³But Ananias replied, "Lord, I have heard from many sources about this man, what evil things he has done to your holy ones in Jerusalem. ¹⁴And here he has authority from the chief priests to imprison all who call upon your name." ¹⁵But the Lord said to him, "Go, for this man is a chosen instrument of mine to carry my name before Gentiles, kings, and Israelites, ¹⁶and I will show him what he will have to suffer for my name." ¹⁷So Ananias went and entered the house; laying his hands on him, he said, "Saul, my brother, the Lord has sent me, Jesus who appeared to you on the way by which you came, that you may regain your sight and be filled with the holy Spirit." ¹⁸Immediately things

like scales fell from his eyes and he regained his sight. He got up and was baptized, [19]and when he had eaten, he recovered his strength.

OT: Isa 6:8; 55:8–9; Tob 11:13
NT: John 16:33; Acts 14:22; 22:12–16; 26:9–20; Col 1:24; 2 Tim 1:8
Catechism: baptism, 1214–16; faith and baptism, 1226; suffering with Christ, 618
Lectionary: Acts 9:1–22: Feast of the Conversion of St. Paul (Jan. 25)

9:10   **Ananias**, the **disciple in Damascus** whom God sent to remove Saul's blindness, is God's chosen instrument for incorporating Saul into the Church through baptism. Ananias and **Saul** receive an unusual reciprocal vision of each other, similar to the reciprocal vision that Peter and Cornelius will have in Acts 10. The Lord appears to Ananias and calls him by name **in a vision**, but he calls his name only once, **"Ananias"** (compared to the double "Saul, Saul" in v. 4).[8] In an exemplary biblical response to a divine call, Ananias answers, **"Here I am,"** just as Isaiah had responded to God's invitation (Isa 6:8; see also Gen 46:2; Exod 3:4; 1 Sam 3:4). The Lord who appears here to Ananias is the risen Jesus, who is addressed as **Lord**, the Old Testament name for God (Acts 9:13–17).

9:11–12   **The Lord** Jesus directs Ananias with great detail to the **street called Straight** and to **the house of Judas**, to seek out **a man from Tarsus named Saul**. Jesus reveals that Saul is **praying** and that he too is seeing a vision, in which **Ananias** comes in and lays hands on him for him to **regain his sight**. Saul's vision is a mirror image of Ananias's vision.

9:13–15   **Ananias** balks at this mission because he knows Saul's reputation as a persecutor of the Lord's **holy ones in Jerusalem**. Worse, Saul is now in Damascus with **authority** to arrest **all who call upon** Jesus' **name**. It could be dangerous to reveal one's belief in Jesus to this persecutor. There is a touch of irony in Ananias's trying to inform **the Lord** about Saul's actions when the Lord already has a plan to change Saul from persecutor to chosen evangelist. Ananias's objections are overruled by the Lord: **"Go, for this man is a chosen instrument of mine to carry my name before Gentiles, kings, and Israelites."** God is clearly in charge of this event, and his ways are not our ways (Isa 55:8–9).

In the Gospel of Luke, Simeon prophesied that Jesus had been sent as "a light for revelation to the Gentiles, and glory for your people Israel" (Luke 2:32). Saul is being sent to proclaim Jesus to the same groups. The addition of "kings" recalls Jesus' prophecy to his disciples: "They will seize and persecute you, they will hand you over to the synagogues and to prisons, and they will have you led before kings

---

8. In Luke-Acts, Jesus' calling a name twice has a reproachful connotation: "Martha, Martha" (Luke 10:41); "Jerusalem, Jerusalem" (Luke 13:34); "Simon, Simon" (Luke 22:31).

and governors because of my name" (Luke 21:12). Later in Acts, Luke will show Paul indeed witnessing to Christ before governors and kings (13:7; 26:1–30) and to both Gentiles and Jews in cities throughout the empire (9:20; 14:1; 22:1–21).

Jesus concludes his response to Ananias by explicitly foretelling how much Saul **will have to suffer for my name**. This former persecutor will now himself be asked to endure persecution for Jesus' sake. Both Acts and Paul's own letters attest to the fulfillment of this prophecy, for example, by his being stoned at Lystra (Acts 14:19) and being beaten and imprisoned at Philippi (16:19–24). The last chapters of Acts are devoted to Paul's imprisonments and trials, from his arrest in Jerusalem (21:30–33) to his house arrest in Rome, at the end of the book (28:16–31). Paul's Letters also have many references to his sufferings, which he endured joyfully for the sake of Christ (Col 1:24).[9]

9:16

Some scholars have seen the role of Ananias as conflicting with Paul's own statement in Gal 1:11–12: "I want you to know, brothers, that the gospel preached by me is not of human origin. For I did not receive it from a human being, nor was I taught it, but it came through a revelation of Jesus Christ." However, Acts 9 shows that Paul did not receive the gospel, the good news about Jesus' resurrection, from Ananias, but from personally encountering the risen Jesus. Luke's statement implying that Saul would be instructed by a member of the Church (Ananias) about how to respond to the revelation of Jesus can be reinforced by another of Paul's autobiographical narratives: "I handed on to you as of first importance what I also received: that Christ died for our sins in accordance with the scriptures; that he was buried; that he was raised on the third day in accordance with the scriptures" (1 Cor 15:3). There Paul appears to be citing a creed that he had been taught, either by Ananias or some other Christian, in his baptismal instruction after he had seen the risen Christ.[10] Thus the initial divine revelation, which he received directly from God, was supplemented by the teaching he received through the mediation of the Church.

Accepting Jesus' explanation and obeying his command, **Ananias** lays **hands** on Saul and addresses the former fierce persecutor as **my brother**, welcoming him into the Christian community. He reports, **"The Lord has sent me, Jesus who appeared to you, . . . so that you may regain your sight and be filled with the holy Spirit."** First Saul is healed from his blindness, a sign of his inner spiritual enlightenment. The **scales** coming off his **eyes** remind us of the cataracts

9:17–19

---

9. See, for instance, Rom 8:18; 1 Cor 4:11–13; 2 Cor 1:2–11; 4:8–10; 11:23–28; Phil 3:7–11; 2 Tim 2:8–13.

10. The Greek expressions he uses, "what I also received" (*paralambanō*), and now "handed on to you" (*paradidōmi*), are both technical expressions used for receiving and passing on tradition, in Paul's case possibly the earliest baptismal creed.

AJ Alfieri-Crispin/Wikimedia Commons

Fig. 8. Mosaic of St. Paul in
Veria, Greece (location of
ancient Beroea).

peeling off blind Tobit's eyes (Tob 11:13). Then after he is filled with the **holy
Spirit** and **baptized**, Saul breaks his fast, eats, and recovers **his strength**.

Saul Preaches in Damascus (9:19b–22)

He stayed some days with the disciples in Damascus, [20]and he began at
once to proclaim Jesus in the synagogues, that he is the Son of God. [21]All
who heard him were astounded and said, "Is not this the man who in Jerusalem ravaged those who call upon this name, and came here expressly
to take them back in chains to the chief priests?" [22]But Saul grew all the
stronger and confounded [the] Jews who lived in Damascus, proving that
this is the Messiah.

OT: Ps 2:7
NT: Gal 1:23–24; Phil 3:6–7; 1 Tim 1:12–13
Catechism: Jesus the Son of God, 441–45, 470–78; Jesus the Messiah, 436–40
Lectionary: Acts 9:1–22: Feast of the Conversion of St. Paul (Jan. 25)

Saul lost no time in fulfilling his new mission to witness to Jesus. During **9:19b–20** the period in which he remained **with the disciples in Damascus**, he began **at once** to preach and proclaim the **Jesus** whose followers he had previously persecuted. He directly confronted the Jews, his former allies, **in the synagogues**, announcing that Jesus **is the Son of God**. The Church would later fully articulate the theological meaning of "Son of God" in declarations such as the Nicene Creed. But even here in Acts, Saul is preaching much more than the Old Testament understanding of the Davidic king as an adopted son of God (Ps 2:7). Luke's Gospel already hinted at the fuller meaning of Son of God in Gabriel's message that Jesus would be conceived by the Holy Spirit, that is, that he would have no human father (Luke 1:32–35).

Luke emphasizes the radical change in Saul by quoting the exclamation of **9:21** those **who heard him**: "**Is not this the man who in Jerusalem ravaged those who call upon this name** [of Jesus]**?**" Is not his purpose here in Damascus to extradite them **in chains to the chief priests?** In Gal 1:23, Paul cites the same response to his transformation: "The one who once was persecuting us is now preaching the faith he once tried to destroy." The astonished reactions underline how humanly unbelievable was Saul's transformation—as astounding as the previously crippled beggar's walking and leaping in the temple (Acts 3:8–10).

The term used to describe **Saul** as growing **stronger** (*endynamoō*) is the same **9:22** Greek word Paul uses to describe Abraham, who was empowered to believe (Rom 4:20), and to exhort Christians to "be strong" in the Lord (Eph 6:10). In the power of the Holy Spirit, Saul **confounded** the **Jews** in **Damascus** by means of convincing biblical demonstrations, **proving** that Jesus is **the Messiah**. Saul was especially equipped to make effective proofs from Scripture since he himself had needed to make a 180–degree turn in his own biblical interpretation. He had been convinced that Jesus could not be the Messiah because he had died the death of crucifixion and was under its curse (Deut 21:23). By seeing Jesus alive, he was compelled to accept that Jesus is indeed the Messiah who has freely taken our curse upon himself (Gal 3:13).

Reflection and Application (9:1–22)

Jesus' choices of human instruments to do his work are unpredictable and surprising. First he chooses fishermen and other "uneducated, ordinary men" (Acts 4:13). Then he chooses Saul, a highly trained and distinguished Pharisee (Acts 22:3; Phil 3:4–6) who is convinced that Jesus' followers are spreading blasphemy and is fanatical in persecuting them.

Young people considering a priestly, religious, or lay vocation sometimes think, "I am not worthy." Acts makes clear that Jesus does not seek out the worthy to be his priests, religious, missionaries, or lay evangelists. Luke even quotes Jesus as saying that he came not for the healthy but the sick, not to call the righteous but sinners (Luke 5:31–32).[11] Paul said of himself, "I was once a blasphemer and a persecutor and an arrogant man" (1 Tim 1:13)—clearly one of the sinners Jesus came to call. Worthiness is unquestionably not the prerequisite for being called by the Lord. Rather, by his grace the Lord *makes us worthy* for whatever task he calls us to.

---

11. The RSV (and NRSV) word order, which follows the Greek word order, is clearer than the NAB at Luke 5:32: "I have not come to call the righteous, but sinners to repentance."

Saul's Escape; Peter's Healing of Aeneas and Tabitha

Acts 9:23–43

The brief narratives in this section may seem to lack a unifying theme, yet together they provide a transition from one crucial event—the conversion of Saul—to one that is equally crucial—the conversion of Cornelius. Cornelius's conversion will be a major pivot point in the plot of Acts, for it will mark a shift from evangelization of *Jews* directed by the apostles to evangelization of *Gentiles* spearheaded by Paul. Thus the episodes in this short section bring us to the brink of the Church's historic development from being entirely Jewish to embracing all peoples of the world.

Saul Visits Jerusalem (9:23–30)

[23]After a long time had passed, the Jews conspired to kill him, [24]but their plot became known to Saul. Now they were keeping watch on the gates day and night so as to kill him, [25]but his disciples took him one night and let him down through an opening in the wall, lowering him in a basket.

[26]When he arrived in Jerusalem he tried to join the disciples, but they were all afraid of him, not believing that he was a disciple. [27]Then Barnabas took charge of him and brought him to the apostles, and he reported to them how on the way he had seen the Lord and that he had spoken to him, and how in Damascus he had spoken out boldly in the name of Jesus.

²⁸**He moved about freely with them in Jerusalem, and spoke out boldly in the name of the Lord.** ²⁹**He also spoke and debated with the Hellenists, but they tried to kill him.** ³⁰**And when the brothers learned of this, they took him down to Caesarea and sent him on his way to Tarsus.**

OT: Judg 16:2; 1 Sam 19:12
NT: 2 Cor 11:32–33; Gal 1:15–24; 1 Pet 3:15
Catechism: persecution, 769, 1808, 1816; bearing witness to Christ, 2471–74
Lectionary: Acts 9:26–31: Fifth Sunday of Easter (Year B)

9:23   After his conversion Saul spent **a long time** in Damascus, seeking to convince the †Hellenistic Jews who lived there that Jesus was the Messiah (v. 22). Because of this, those **Jews conspired to kill him**, as Saul himself and the Hellenistic Jews of Jerusalem had killed Stephen. Paul himself reports in Gal 1:17–18 that after his conversion, "I went into Arabia and then returned to Damascus. Then after three years I went up to Jerusalem." Paul does not say why he went to Arabia, but a common conjecture is that he went for solitude to pray over his meeting with the risen Jesus and to revise everything he understood in light of his discovery that Jesus is the Messiah. Others speculate that Paul continued his preaching there. Paul does not say where in Arabia he went or how long he was there before returning to Damascus. Although most commentators seem to presume Paul was there almost the whole three years, his statement could even more naturally be understood as referring to a short time in Arabia and then a stay in Damascus of almost three years.

9:24–25   The novelistic details of Paul's enemies watching the city **gates day and night so as to kill him**, and his escape through a lowered **basket**, are confirmed as factual by Paul himself in 2 Cor 11:32–33, though he names the "governor under King Aretas" as the one guarding the city gates. Both accounts agree that Paul escaped when **his disciples took him** to **an opening in the wall** of the city, lowering him in a basket in humiliating helpless flight. Paul's flight is reminiscent of the Israelite spies' escape from Jericho with the help of Rahab, who let them down by a rope through a window in the city wall (Josh 2:15).

9:26–28   After his arrival in **Jerusalem**, Saul **tried to join the disciples**. The Jerusalem disciples naturally avoided him out of fear, **not believing that he was a disciple**. It took the mediation of **Barnabas** to incorporate Saul into the Jerusalem church. Barnabas **took charge** of Saul to facilitate his acceptance and introduced him **to the apostles**, who were still leaders in Jerusalem. He related to them the story of Saul's vision of **the Lord** and his subsequent bold witness **in the name of Jesus**. Paul considered it essential to remain in unity

Augustine: Paul Preserved Himself for the Sake of the Church

LIVING TRADITION

Explaining that Paul's escape in a basket was not a matter of cowardice, Augustine wrote:

> He would not have fled from the snares laid for him by the prince [King Aretas], his persecutor, except that he wished to save himself for others who needed him, and that is why he said, "But I am pulled between the two: having a desire to be dissolved and to be with Christ, a thing by far the better; but to abide still in the flesh is needful for you." (Phil 1:23–24)[a]

a. *Letters* 228, *The Fathers of the Church* (New York: Fathers of the Church, Inc., 1956), 32:147.

with the original apostles (see especially Acts 15 and Paul's collection from Gentile Christians for the poor of the Jerusalem community in 1 Cor 16:1–3). Because of Barnabas, Saul was thereafter able to associate **freely with them in Jerusalem**. There he **spoke out boldly in the name of the Lord**, as he had done in Damascus.

The focus of this account, which highlights Paul's acceptance by the apostles in Jerusalem, differs from Paul's emphasis in Gal 1:15–20, where to some degree he minimizes his contact with the apostles in Jerusalem in order to emphasize that his apostleship came directly from Christ and was therefore as authentic as that of the Twelve. Although details of the accounts here and in Galatians 1 are difficult to harmonize, the main facts of the two reports can in general be reconciled.[1] It is unclear to what extent Paul's fifteen-day private visit with Peter and James (Gal 1:18) may coincide with Barnabas's introduction of Saul to the apostles and Saul's witness to Jesus in Jerusalem described here in Acts 9. In any case, Saul's bold speech in Jerusalem was not to last long, as the following verses make clear.

When Saul **spoke and debated with the Hellenists**, they reacted the same **9:29–30** way as those in Damascus: **they tried to kill him.** But also as in Damascus, this plot against Saul became known. Therefore his fellow Christians **took him down to Caesarea**, and in that port city they put him on a ship **to Tarsus**, his hometown in the province of Cilicia in Asia Minor.

1. See especially Luke Timothy Johnson, *The Acts of the Apostles*, Sacra pagina 5 (Collegeville, MN: Liturgical Press, 1992), 173–74, where he discusses both the minor disagreements between the two accounts and the more substantial agreements between them (also 170–73). Compare Joseph A. Fitzmyer, *The Acts of the Apostles*, Anchor Bible 31 (New York: Doubleday, 1998), 437–41.

The Church at Peace (9:31)

---

[31]The church throughout all Judea, Galilee, and Samaria was at peace. It was being built up and walked in the fear of the Lord, and with the consolation of the holy Spirit it grew in numbers.

OT: Josh 21:44; 1 Chron 22:18; Ps 111:10

NT: Acts 6:7; Rom 15:13; 1 Cor 3:9; Col 1:10; Jude 20

Catechism: peace, 1829, 1832; consolation, 769; fear of the Lord, 1303, 2144–45

9:31   After reporting that Saul had been sent away safely to his home city of Tarsus following plots against his life, Luke inserts a summary. The **church** has now been freed from the hostility of †Hellenistic Jews aroused by Paul's preaching. In all three regions of Palestine—**Judea, Galilee, and Samaria**—the church enjoys a time of **peace** and of **being built up** and living **in the fear of the Lord Jesus.** This is the first and only mention of the existence of the church in Galilee (which illustrates the selective nature of Luke's history). Until this point, Luke has reported on the growth of the Church in Jerusalem and Samaria; only now will he report on Peter's ministry in Judea (vv. 32–43).

Luke attributes the fact that the church in these regions **grew in numbers** to **the consolation of the holy Spirit**. The Greek term for consolation (*paraklēsis*) is related to Paraclete, the title Jesus gives the Holy Spirit in John 14:16, and expresses the Spirit's work of aiding, comforting, and encouraging the church. The numerical growth of the church through the work of the Spirit is a major recurring theme in Acts.

Peter Heals Aeneas at Lydda (9:32–35)

---

[32]As Peter was passing through every region, he went down to the holy ones living in Lydda. [33]There he found a man named Aeneas, who had been confined to bed for eight years, for he was paralyzed. [34]Peter said to him, "Aeneas, Jesus Christ heals you. Get up and make your bed." He got up at once. [35]And all the inhabitants of Lydda and Sharon saw him, and they turned to the Lord.

OT: 1 Kings 17:17–24; 2 Kings 4:32–37

NT: Luke 5:17–26; 7:11–16; 8:49–56; Acts 3:6–10

Catechism: evangelization, 2044, 2472; healing the sick, 1506–10

After Luke's summary about the peace and growth of the church, he abruptly shifts focus from Paul to Peter, giving accounts of Peter's healing and preaching in Lydda, Sharon, and Joppa—Judean towns and regions near the Mediterranean Sea. The risen Jesus continues to act through his disciples by the Holy Spirit, which he has poured out on them (Acts 2:33).

The occasion for Peter's healing activity is his visitation of Christian churches **through every region** of Judea. When the Jerusalem Christians were scattered by persecution (as by Saul in Acts 8:1–3), the apostles remained in Jerusalem. But now, perhaps because the church in Jerusalem is at peace (Acts 9:31), Peter and the other apostles feel that the Jerusalem community is secure enough that they can now venture out to attend to the needs of the churches in the surrounding area. Luke refers to the disciples **in Lydda** as **the holy ones** (or "saints," RSV, NRSV; "God's holy people," NJB). This ancient way of Christians referring to one another is a reminder that through faith, baptism, and the indwelling of the Holy Spirit, Christians belong to God and need to conduct themselves in a manner that corresponds to this fact. 9:32–34

In the church in Lydda, Peter meets **Aeneas**, a man who is **paralyzed** and has been **confined to bed for eight years**. Peter boldly declares to him: **"Jesus Christ heals you."** Then he simply commands him, **"Get up and make your bed,"** which Aeneas does **at once**. Peter speaks with a conviction that Jesus is present and acting through him. His direct command to Aeneas is similar to Jesus' healing commands, but his preceding statement "Jesus Christ heals you" makes clear that he is speaking not by his own initiative but in the name of Jesus. Here as elsewhere, Luke makes clear that whereas Jesus heals by his own authority (Luke 5:20–25), his disciples do so by *his* authority (Acts 3:12–13).

Luke emphasizes that this healing of Aeneas had an extraordinary evangelizing impact in Judea. When **all the inhabitants of Lydda and Sharon saw** the healed Aeneas, **they turned to the Lord** Jesus. 9:35

Peter Restores Tabitha to Life (9:36–43)

36Now in Joppa there was a disciple named Tabitha (which translated means Dorcas). She was completely occupied with good deeds and alms-giving. 37Now during those days she fell sick and died, so after washing her, they laid [her] out in a room upstairs. 38Since Lydda was near Joppa, the disciples, hearing that Peter was there, sent two men to him with the request, "Please come to us without delay." ³⁹So Peter got up and went with them. When he arrived, they took him to the room upstairs where all the widows came to him weeping and showing him the tunics and cloaks that Dorcas had made while she was with them. ⁴⁰Peter sent them all out and knelt down and prayed. Then he turned to her body and said, "Tabitha, rise up." She opened her eyes, saw Peter, and sat up. ⁴¹He gave her his hand and raised her up, and when he had called the holy ones and the widows, he presented her alive. ⁴²This became known all over Joppa, and many came to believe in the Lord. ⁴³And he stayed a long time in Joppa with Simon, a tanner.

OT: 1 Kings 17:17–24; 2 Kings 4:32–37; Tob 4:10; 12:8–9; Sir 29:12
NT: Mark 5:38–43; Luke 7:11–16; 8:51–56
Catechism: almsgiving, 1969, 2447, 2462–63

9:36-37   After the healing of Aeneas, Peter does an even greater miracle for a devout widow, whose name Luke gives in †Aramaic, **Tabitha**, and in its Greek translation, **Dorcas**. Both words mean "gazelle." Luke emphasizes her **good deeds and almsgiving**, that is, sharing material goods with others as children of the same heavenly Father.² After describing Tabitha's sickness, death, and the **washing** of her body, Luke reports that **they laid [her] out in a room upstairs** (reminiscent of the "upper room" where the Holy Spirit first came in power: Acts 1:13; 2:1–4).

9:38-39   The **disciples** in **Joppa** heard **that Peter was** in nearby **Lydda**, so they **sent two men** to ask him to **come** to them **without delay**. Peter did so and was taken to the room upstairs. Luke focuses on the grief of the **widows** who were **weeping and showing** the clothes **that Dorcas had made** while alive—showing them to Peter or, more likely, to God as a way of interceding for Dorcas. The widows' reaction to Dorcas's death speaks eloquently of their love for her and of her generosity to the poor during her lifetime.

9:40-41   Peter's actions are very similar to those of Jesus in raising the daughter of Jairus (Matt 9:24–25; Mark 5:40–41). Like Jesus, **Peter sent** the weeping bystanders **out** of the room, perhaps because they were a hindrance to an atmosphere of faith that was needed for the miracle.³ He then commanded the dead

---

2. Luke strongly emphasizes the Christian practice of almsgiving. See, for instance, Luke 11:41; 12:33; Acts 10:2, 4, 31; 24:17.

3. Luke 8:51 does not state that Jesus put the mourners out (compare Matt 9:24–25; Mark 5:40) but says, "He allowed no one to enter with him except Peter and John and James, and the child's father and mother." The Gospels frequently emphasize the importance of faith in Jesus' miracles, both negatively (Matt 13:58; Mark 6:5–6) and positively (Luke 7:50; 8:48; 17:19; 18:42; see also Acts 14:9).

Almsgiving Delivers from Death

LIVING TRADITION

St. Cyprian of Carthage, a third-century bishop and martyr, taught that the raising of Tabitha shows that "almsgiving delivers from death" (Tob 12:9).

Peter was called to the dead body; and when he, with an apostle's kindness, had come without delay, the widows stood round him weeping and petitioning, showing cloaks and coats and all the garments they had received from her, and interceding for the dead woman, not by their own words but by her deeds. Peter knew that what was asked for in such a manner could be obtained, and that Christ's aid would not fail the pleading widows, because in clothing them Tabitha had clothed Him. Having knelt down and prayed, as a fit advocate for widows and the poor, having lifted to the Lord the prayers entrusted to him, turning to the body, . . . Peter said, "In the name of Jesus Christ, Tabitha, arise." He who had said in the Gospel that whatever is asked in his name will be granted did not fail to give his aid to Peter at once. Death is suspended and the spirit given back. As all wonder and are astonished, the body lives again and takes new breath in this world. Such was the miracle wrought by the merits of mercy, such was the power of just works. She who had bestowed the means of life on suffering widows merited to be recalled to life through the widows' intercession.[a]

a. Cyprian, *Works and Almsgiving* 5.

person to **rise** and presented her to those who were grieving their loved one. Whether or not Luke's readers would have caught the wordplay, Peter's command **"Tabitha, rise up"** (*Tabitha qumi* in Aramaic) sounds much like Jesus' command in Mark 5:41, *Talitha koum*, "Little girl, rise up!"[4] Luke continues to show that what the apostles do and say in Acts is continuing what "Jesus did and taught" in the Gospel (Acts 1:1). This occurs as they exercise great faith, confident in Jesus' power and in their own authority to speak and act in his name under the leading of the Holy Spirit.

This account ends, as do many accounts of miracles in Luke-Acts, with mention that the deed **became known**, in this case, **all over Joppa**. The raising of this widow led **many** to come **to believe in the Lord** Jesus. This remarkable deed confirmed Peter's testimony that Jesus is indeed alive and has power to save and even to raise from the dead. Meanwhile, Peter remained **a long time in Joppa with Simon, a tanner**.

9:42–43

4. The parallel in Luke 8:54 does not include the Aramaic transliteration but simply translates, "Child, arise!"

Pope Benedict on Healing and the Apostolic Mission

LIVING TRADITION

In *Jesus of Nazareth*, Pope Benedict XVI writes, "Healing is an essential dimension of the apostolic mission and of Christian faith in general." It can even be said that Christianity is a "therapeutic religion—a religion of healing. When understood at a sufficiently deep level, this expresses the entire content of redemption."[a] Jesus' and the disciples' works of healing are visible signs of Christ's work of salvation, which ultimately is a healing of humanity's deepest wound—the wound of original sin and our consequent alienation from God. "Whoever truly wishes to heal man must see him in his wholeness and must know that his ultimate healing can only be God's love."[b]

a. Joseph Ratzinger (Pope Benedict XVI), *Jesus of Nazareth* (San Francisco: Ignatius Press, 2007), 176.
b. Ibid., 177.

Reflection and Application (9:36–43)

These short reports about Paul and Peter remind us that although the growth and spread of Christianity takes place through human instruments, on a deeper level it is the work of the Holy Spirit. Only the divine power of the Spirit could change Saul from persecutor to proclaimer of the gospel. Only by the power of the Spirit could Peter heal the lame Aeneas and raise the dead widow Tabitha to life. The Church's ministry and growth takes place today through an enormous variety of human instruments, including ourselves. Still, the principal agent of the Church's outreach remains the Holy Spirit. Only in the power of the Spirit are contemporary "apostles to the Gentiles" able to attract others to Christ by their preaching and their loving deeds, whether great or small. Our access to this power of the Spirit is grounded in the fact that Jesus is exalted at the right hand of God and has poured out his Spirit on us (Acts 2:33; Catechism 1266, 1274, 2017).

The Conversion of Cornelius

Acts 10:1–11:18

In Acts 10–11 Luke relates how God acted sovereignly to demonstrate beyond any doubt that Gentiles too are offered salvation through faith in Christ. Through an extraordinary series of divine interventions, Peter finds himself preaching the good news to a Gentile audience for the first time, at the house of the centurion Cornelius. God then dramatically pours out his Spirit on the assembled listeners in what is sometimes called the "Gentile Pentecost."

The interrelated events of the conversion of Cornelius, the Jewish-Christian reaction to that conversion, and its consequences, constitute a turning point in Acts. They also help readers today understand the original difficulties that Jewish Christians, beginning with Peter himself, had in clarifying how the Gentiles are to fit into God's holy people and how their Jewish brothers and sisters are to relate to them. To understand these difficulties will require some consideration of what it meant to first-century Jews to be a holy people singled out from the profane world for their holy God. Vital for Jewish distinctiveness from the pagan world were their perceptions of what is clean and unclean.

The Vision of Cornelius (10:1–8)

¹Now in Caesarea there was a man named Cornelius, a centurion of the Cohort called the Italica, ²devout and God-fearing along with his whole household, who used to give alms generously to the Jewish people and pray to God constantly. ³One afternoon about three o'clock, he saw plainly

167

in a vision an angel of God come in to him and say to him, "Cornelius." [4]He looked intently at him and, seized with fear, said, "What is it, sir?" He said to him, "Your prayers and almsgiving have ascended as a memorial offering before God. [5]Now send some men to Joppa and summon one Simon who is called Peter. [6]He is staying with another Simon, a tanner, who has a house by the sea." [7]When the angel who spoke to him had left, he called two of his servants and a devout soldier from his staff, [8]explained everything to them, and sent them to Joppa.

OT: Tob 12:8–9, 12; Ps 141:2; Dan 9:21
NT: Luke 1:11–12; 7:1–10
Catechism: help of angels, 334–36; almsgiving, 1969, 2447, 2462–63
Lectionary: Acts 10:1, 33–34a, 37–44: Confirmation

10:1–2   The story begins **in Caesarea** with **Cornelius**, a **centurion**, that is, a Roman army officer usually in charge of a hundred soldiers. Luke identifies his **cohort** as the **Italica** to provide concrete historical detail that helps identify this centurion. As a centurion, Cornelius was a Roman citizen. Like the centurion in Luke 7:1–10 who had built a synagogue for the Jews, Cornelius gave **alms generously to the Jewish people**. Both centurions were influenced by the Jewish people among whom they were stationed. Besides being well disposed toward them, they were also drawn toward Jewish belief in the one God revealed in Scripture. Further, Cornelius was accustomed to **pray to God constantly**, an indication

---

Almsgiving in the *Didache*   LIVING TRADITION

The *Didache* is an early Christian catechetical document, usually dated to the late first or early second century (around AD 50–120). It gives evidence of how Christians continued to emphasize generosity and almsgiving as Jesus had (Matt 6:1–18).

> "Give to everyone who asks you, and do not demand it back," for the Father wants something from his own gifts to be given to everyone. Blessed is the one who gives according to the command, for such a person is innocent. . . . But it has also been said concerning this: "Let your alms sweat in your hands until you know to whom to give them." (*Didache* 1.5–6)
>
> As for your prayers and almsgiving and all your actions, do them all just as you find it in the Gospel of our Lord. (*Didache* 15.4)[a]

a. Translation modified from *The Apostolic Fathers: Greek Texts and English Translations*, ed. and rev. Michael W. Holmes (Grand Rapids: Baker Books, 1992, 1999), 251, 253, 267.

that he and **his whole household** were **devout**. Prayer and almsgiving were emphasized both in Judaism (see Tob 12:8–9) and in early Christianity (see Jesus' teaching on alms, prayer, and fasting in Matt 6:1–18). Luke also describes Cornelius as **God-fearing**. There is evidence that in the first century there were many †God-fearing Gentiles, that is, people who adopted Jewish beliefs and practices without actually becoming Jews.

That Cornelius practiced Jewish forms of prayer is illustrated by the fact that he had a **vision** while he was praying **about three o'clock** (literally, "about the ninth hour of the day"), which was the time of Jewish evening prayer and sacrifice.[1] In a **vision** he sees **an angel of God** coming **to him** and calling his name, **Cornelius**. The scene recalls the biblical prophet Daniel, who also had an angelic visitation while in prayer at the time of the evening sacrifice (Dan 9:21).

10:3

Cornelius's reaction was to be **seized with fear** (Greek *emphobos*, "terrified" or "in terror," RSV, NRSV, NJB). He **looked intently** at the angel, as the Sanhedrin had looked intently at Stephen's face, which was "like the face of an angel" (Acts 6:15), and as Stephen had looked intently at "the glory of God and Jesus standing at the right hand of God" (Acts 7:55).

10:4

Cornelius asks, **"What is it, sir?"** The Greek for "sir" is *kyrios*, the Old Testament title "Lord," often used for God or God's messenger or angel. Since Cornelius was staring in terror at an angel, the translation "Lord" seems to express the meaning better than "sir." The angel responds that Cornelius's **prayers and almsgiving** have been regarded as a **memorial offering**. This combines two biblical ideas. The first is that prayer and almsgiving can be an acceptable substitute for animal sacrifices, which could be offered only in the Jerusalem temple (see Ps 141:2; Tob 4:11; 12:12; Sir 45:16). The second is that God accepts such offerings as a memorial or *reminder* that moves him to act on behalf of the offerer. Here Cornelius's prayers and righteous deeds have **ascended** and pleased God, who now will bestow an extraordinary blessing in return.

The **angel** commands Cornelius to **send some men** from Caesarea to nearby **Joppa and summon one Simon who is called Peter**. The angel informs the messengers that Peter is **staying** with **another Simon, a tanner,** whose **house** is **by the sea**. Right after the angel's departure, Cornelius sends a pair of his household **servants and a devout soldier from his staff**, men who share his faith in the God of Israel and can well present his request to Peter in Joppa.

10:5–8

---

1. See Exod 29:38–39; Dan 9:21; Acts 3:1.

The Vision of Peter (10:9–23a)

---

[9]The next day, while they were on their way and nearing the city, Peter went up to the roof terrace to pray at about noontime. [10]He was hungry and wished to eat, and while they were making preparations he fell into a trance. [11]He saw heaven opened and something resembling a large sheet coming down, lowered to the ground by its four corners. [12]In it were all the earth's four-legged animals and reptiles and the birds of the sky. [13]A voice said to him, "Get up, Peter. Slaughter and eat." [14]But Peter said, "Certainly not, sir. For never have I eaten anything profane and unclean." [15]The voice spoke to him again, a second time, "What God has made clean, you are not to call profane." [16]This happened three times, and then the object was taken up into the sky.

[17]While Peter was in doubt about the meaning of the vision he had seen, the men sent by Cornelius asked for Simon's house and arrived at the entrance. [18]They called out inquiring whether Simon, who is called Peter, was staying there. [19]As Peter was pondering the vision, the Spirit said [to him], "There are three men here looking for you. [20]So get up, go downstairs, and accompany them without hesitation, because I have sent them." [21]Then Peter went down to the men and said, "I am the one you are looking for. What is the reason for your being here?" [22]They answered, "Cornelius, a centurion, an upright and God-fearing man, respected by the whole Jewish nation, was directed by a holy angel to summon you to his house and to hear what you have to say." [23]So he invited them in and showed them hospitality.

OT: Gen 7:1–3; 15:12; Lev 11:1–31; Ezek 1:1; Dan 6:11
NT: Mark 7:18–19; Luke 7:2–5; 2 Cor 12:2–4; Eph 3:4–6; Rev 19:11
Catechism: Jesus and the law, 577–82, 592; new law fulfilling the old, 1967–68

10:9–10   According to Luke, Peter's vision took place the **next day**, as the messengers from Cornelius were **on their way**, which emphasizes that their two visions were related to each other. Luke underscores Peter's hunger as he awaited his midday meal, which gives an added intensity to his vision of food. As he prayed **he fell into a trance**, an altered state of consciousness.[2]

10:11–12   **He saw heaven opened** is a standard biblical expression to signal the beginning of a heavenly vision (see Ezek 1:1; Rev 19:11). Peter's vision was of **all the earth's four-legged animals and reptiles and the birds of the sky**. Even

---

2. The term "trance" (Greek *ekstasis*) is uncommon for visions in the New Testament (but see Acts 22:17), but occurs several times in the †Septuagint (such as Adam in Gen 2:21 and Abraham in Gen 15:12).

though God had called all the animals "good" (Gen 1:21, 25), he differentiated them into **clean** and **unclean** in the law given through Moses (Lev 11:1–31; see Gen 7:1–3).[3] By these laws, animals that were ritually unclean were forbidden to Jews as food.

The heavenly voice tells Peter to **slaughter and eat**. But Peter protests that, as **10:13–14** a faithful Jew, he has always avoided eating foods that are forbidden as **unclean** or **profane** according to the law of Moses. Why could **Peter** not simply have picked out some of the **clean** animals to eat? According to the Mosaic law, clean foods or persons can be made unclean by contact with what is unclean.[4] Thus even the clean animals on the sheet in Peter's vision, because of their proximity to the unclean creatures, would be "profane" and therefore not to be eaten. Peter has avoided eating not only what is explicitly declared unclean, but also anything contaminated by contact with the unclean.

The heavenly response, **"What God has made clean, you are not to call** **10:15–16** **profane,"** does not explain how God has made any of these animals clean. That will be clarified fully only after this twice-repeated vision, when Peter finally comes to realize that the distinction between clean and unclean foods symbolizes the far more important distinction between Jews as clean and Gentiles as unclean—a distinction that has now been removed in Christ (Acts 10:28). The fact that the same vision appears **three times** underscores not only its importance but perhaps also how difficult it is for Peter to understand it.

Clarification of Peter's **doubt** or "perplexity" **about the meaning of the** **10:17–20** **vision** began that very moment with the arrival at **Simon's house** of **the men** **sent by Cornelius.** Luke emphasizes that **Peter was pondering the vision** while the messengers from Cornelius were **inquiring** about Peter's presence there. In response to Peter's pondering, **the Spirit** spoke to him in prayer: **"There** **are three men here looking for you."** The Spirit told Peter to **"accompany** **them without hesitation, because I have sent them."** Peter's observance of the traditional Jewish prohibition against associating with Gentiles (see v. 28) was thus overridden by God's own initiative in commanding Peter to go with the men.

---

3. See Lev 10:10, "You must be able to distinguish . . . between what is unclean [Greek *akathartos*] and what is clean [*katharos*]."

4. Some scholars regard "unclean" (*akathartos*) and "profane" (*koinos*) as synonymous in this passage (Joseph A. Fitzmyer, *The Acts of the Apostles*, Anchor Bible 31 [New York: Doubleday, 1998], 453–55; Luke Timothy Johnson, *The Acts of the Apostles*, Sacra pagina 5 [Collegeville, MN: Liturgical Press, 1992], 184–85). However, Mikeal C. Parsons, *Acts*, Paideia: Commentaries on the New Testament (Grand Rapids: Baker Academic, 2008), 150, 146–47, translates *koinos* as "contaminated" (by contact with what is unclean). In this interpretation, "unclean" refers to the animals that were intrinsically unclean (such as reptiles), and "profane" refers to the clean animals that were contaminated by contact with the unclean.

10:21–23a   **Peter** immediately obeyed, met the **men**, and asked them why they had come.
Their answer was a narrative about how **a holy angel** had directed **Cornelius** to
invite Peter **to his house** and **hear** what he had to say. As in a similar request on
behalf of another **centurion** (Luke 7:4–5), these men emphasize that Cornelius
is **an upright and God-fearing man, respected by the whole Jewish nation**.
Peter also realizes that for this proposed meeting, Cornelius has been directed
by an angel as he himself has been commanded by the Holy Spirit, so the whole
affair is divinely orchestrated. This breaks down any remaining hesitation he
had as a Jew about showing **them hospitality** as Gentiles. How incredibly coun-
tercultural this was will become clearer in the following passages.

Peter and Cornelius (10:23b–33)

The next day he got up and went with them, and some of the brothers
from Joppa went with him. ²⁴On the following day he entered Caesarea.
Cornelius was expecting them and had called together his relatives and
close friends. ²⁵When Peter entered, Cornelius met him and, falling at his
feet, paid him homage. ²⁶Peter, however, raised him up, saying, "Get up. I
myself am also a human being." ²⁷While he conversed with him, he went in
and found many people gathered together ²⁸and said to them, "You know
that it is unlawful for a Jewish man to associate with, or visit, a Gentile,
but God has shown me that I should not call any person profane or unclean. ²⁹And that is why I came without objection when sent for. May I ask,
then, why you summoned me?"

³⁰Cornelius replied, "Four days ago at this hour, three o'clock in the
afternoon, I was at prayer in my house when suddenly a man in dazzling
robes stood before me and said, ³¹'Cornelius, your prayer has been heard
and your almsgiving remembered before God. ³²Send therefore to Joppa
and summon Simon, who is called Peter. He is a guest in the house of
Simon, a tanner, by the sea.' ³³So I sent for you immediately, and you were
kind enough to come. Now therefore we are all here in the presence of
God to listen to all that you have been commanded by the Lord."

OT: Dan 10:12; Sir 29:12
NT: Acts 11:3; 14:15; 15:9; Phil 4:18; 1 Thess 2:13; Rev 19:10
Catechism: Gentiles in God's plan, 60, 674, 755, 781
Lectionary: Acts 10:25–26, 34–35, 44–48: Sixth Sunday of Easter (Year B)

10:23b–26   **The next day** Peter **went with them** to **Caesarea**, along with **some of the**
Christian **brothers from Joppa**. Later, Luke will clarify that these brothers

were Jewish Christians (10:45). Peter was **met** by **Cornelius**, along with **his relatives and close friends**, his household and guests. The number of guests Cornelius had gathered, not yet knowing who Peter was or what he would say, is an indication of his great faith, like that of the centurion in the Gospel (Luke 7:2–10). Cornelius fell at Peter's **feet** in **homage** (the Greek *proskyneō* literally means "bow down to kiss" someone's feet or the ground, thus "worship"). This gesture is similar to the misunderstanding that would later be shown by pagans who try to sacrifice to Paul and Barnabas at Lystra (Acts 14:11–18). But **Peter** makes sure to forestall such confusion. He immediately **raised** Cornelius **up** and emphasized that he **also** was only **a human being**.[5]

The Greek term for **unlawful** (*athemitos*) is more common in secular Greek writings than in the Bible or other Jewish sources. Because Peter is talking not to Jews but to Gentiles, he uses a term familiar to them to remind them that a **Jewish man** would normally never **associate with, or visit, a Gentile**. This prohibition does not come directly from the Old Testament but from oral tradition. It is attested in *Jubilees*, a Jewish †intertestamental writing (composed between the periods of the Old and New Testaments): "Separate yourself from the gentiles, and do not eat with them, and do not perform deeds like theirs. And do not become associates of theirs. Because their deeds are defiled, and all their ways are contaminated, and despicable, and abominable."[6]

10:27–30

But **God has shown** Peter in his vision (Acts 10:9–16) that he **should not call any person profane or unclean**. Here in his visit to Cornelius, Peter recognizes the main point of his food vision—that it applies more to persons than to food. He now realizes that people are not to be treated as unclean in themselves. Nor should he fear contamination by contact with them (see above on vv. 13–14). This explains why Peter **came without objection** to this Gentile gathering. This recognition had incalculable significance for the Church, for it was an essential prerequisite for bringing Gentiles into the Church in full communion with Jewish members. Only thus could Jewish and Gentile Christians gather to worship and celebrate the Eucharist together. As Paul explains in Ephesians, Jesus "made both one and broke down the dividing wall of enmity" between Jews and Gentiles (Eph 2:14).

In response to Peter's question, **"May I ask, then, why you summoned me?"** **Cornelius** repeats the story about his vision that Luke reported in Acts 10:3–6. The fact that he **was at prayer** at **three o'clock**, a special time for Jewish prayer

---

5. Greek *anthrōpos*, "human" as a species, with RSV, JB, NJB, NIV; see NRSV "mortal."
6. *Jubilees* 22.16, in *The Old Testament Pseudepigrapha*, ed. James H. Charlesworth (Garden City, NY: Doubleday, 1985), 2:98. See also C. K. Barrett, *A Critical and Exegetical Commentary on the Acts of the Apostles*, 2 vols. (Edinburgh: T&T Clark, 1994–98), 1:515.

and sacrifices, underscores his admiration for Judaism. Luke had identified the one who appeared to Cornelius as simply "an angel of God" (Acts 10:3). Cornelius now describes him as **a man in dazzling robes**. In biblical appearances of heavenly beings, bright or dazzling clothes are a sign of divine glory. At the transfiguration, Jesus' "face changed in appearance and his clothing became dazzling white" (Luke 9:29); at the empty tomb "two men in dazzling garments appeared" to the women (Luke 24:4); and after Jesus' ascension, "suddenly two men dressed in white garments stood beside them" (Acts 1:10).

10:30–33   With slight variations, Cornelius reports the message from his angelic messenger narrated earlier (10:4–6): "**Your prayer has been heard and your almsgiving remembered before God.**" When Luke repeats a story, he tends to vary the wording slightly, probably for variety. The angel had instructed Cornelius to **send** for **Simon, who is called Peter,** with very specific directions as to where Peter was to be found. Cornelius concludes, "**I sent for you immediately,**" adding graciously, "**and you were kind enough to come.**" Cornelius shows his expectant faith in declaring, "**We are all here**" awaiting Peter's message **in the presence of God**, indicating a prayerful setting. They are there to **listen** with open minds and hearts, expecting that Peter's message will contain **all** that he has **been commanded by the Lord.** Such eager reception by listeners of one's message as coming from God would warm the heart of any preacher! It is also evidence of the expectant faith that disposes people's hearts to receive the Holy Spirit.

Peter's Speech (10:34–43)

[34]Then Peter proceeded to speak and said, "In truth, I see that God shows no partiality. [35]Rather, in every nation whoever fears him and acts uprightly is acceptable to him. [36]You know the word [that] he sent to the Israelites as he proclaimed peace through Jesus Christ, who is Lord of all, [37]what has happened all over Judea, beginning in Galilee after the baptism that John preached, [38]how God anointed Jesus of Nazareth with the holy Spirit and power. He went about doing good and healing all those oppressed by the devil, for God was with him. [39]We are witnesses of all that he did both in the country of the Jews and [in] Jerusalem. They put him to death by hanging him on a tree. [40]This man God raised [on] the third day and granted that he be visible, [41]not to all the people, but to us, the witnesses chosen by God in advance, who ate and drank with him after he rose from the dead. [42]He commissioned us to preach to the people and

testify that he is the one appointed by God as judge of the living and the dead. ⁴³To him all the prophets bear witness, that everyone who believes in him will receive forgiveness of sins through his name."

OT: Deut 10:17–18; Lev 19:15; 2 Chron 19:6–7; Sir 35:11–14

NT: Luke 24:40–43; Rom 2:11–12; 14:9–12; James 2:1–4

Catechism: salvation outside the Church, 776, 846–48; Jesus anointed by the Spirit, 438, 486; judge of the living and dead, 678–79

Lectionary: Acts 10:34–38: Baptism of the Lord (Year A); Acts 10:34a, 37–43: Mass of Easter Sunday; Mass for the Dead during Easter season; Acts 10:25–26, 34–35, 44–48: Sixth Sunday of Easter (Year B); Acts 10:1, 33–34a, 37–44: Confirmation

The phrase **Peter proceeded to speak** is, literally, "Peter opened his mouth and said" (RSV), an expression used for solemn discourses under the inspiration of the Holy Spirit (see Matt 5:2; Acts 8:35). The biblical maxim that **God shows no partiality**, literally, "is no respecter of persons," plays a significant role in the theology of both Luke-Acts and Paul. Here Peter applies it to the belief that God wants not only his chosen people but also people **in every nation** to be saved. God is a just judge: **whoever fears him** and **acts uprightly**, literally, "does justice," regardless of their national origin, **is acceptable to him**. To fear God is to reverence and obey him, which is to do what is upright and just. As impartial judge, God will in turn approve and accept such good people and their behavior and show them the way to salvation. Even in the Old Testament, Isa 56:6–7 applies this principle explicitly to Gentiles, though still presupposing that their sacrifices will take place in the Jerusalem temple:

> And foreigners who join themselves to the LORD,
>   to minister to him,
> To love the name of the LORD,
>   to become his servants—
> All who keep the sabbath without profaning it
>   and hold fast to my covenant,
> Them I will bring to my holy mountain
>   and make them joyful in my house of prayer;
> Their burnt offerings and their sacrifices
>   will be acceptable on my altar,
> For my house shall be called
>   a house of prayer for all peoples. (Isa 56:6–7)

10:34–35

Immediately after proclaiming that God does not show partiality but accepts all who sincerely follow their consciences, Peter goes on to insist that **Jesus Christ** is indispensable in God's saving plan. He is the Messiah of Israel, **who**

10:36

"God Shows No Partiality"

BIBLICAL
BACKGROUND

The expression "show no partiality" is based on the Greek noun *prosōpolēmptēs*, literally, "respecter of persons." It derives from the Old Testament expression "to lift up the face," that is, to show favor to someone. It refers especially to favoritism in court rulings. Deuteronomy 10:17–18 declares that God is no respecter of persons; that is, he is impartial: "The LORD, your God, is the God of gods, the Lord of lords, the great God, mighty and awesome, who has no favorites, accepts no bribes; who executes justice for the orphan and the widow, and loves the resident alien, giving them food and clothing." Paul makes it into a theological principle regarding God's judgment of both Jews and Gentiles: "There is no partiality with God. All who sin outside the law will also perish without reference to it, and all who sin under the law will be judged in accordance with it" (Rom 2:11–12).

Like God himself, his people are also to show no partiality: "You shall not act dishonestly in rendering judgment. Show neither partiality to the weak nor deference to the mighty, but judge your neighbor justly" (Lev 19:15). Newly appointed judges are instructed, "And now, let the fear of the LORD be upon you. Act carefully, for with the LORD, our God, there is no injustice, no partiality, no bribe-taking" (2 Chron 19:7; see Sir 35:11–14). This maxim is applied to Jesus even by his enemies: "Teacher, we know that what you say and teach is correct, and you show no partiality, but teach the way of God in accordance with the truth" (Luke 20:21). James 2:1–4 uses the phrase to urge Christians to impartial treatment of fellow members of the Church, rich and poor alike.

is now also **Lord of all** nations (as Peter proclaimed at Pentecost, Acts 2:36). Peter had insisted to the Jewish leaders, "There is no salvation through anyone else, nor is there any other name under heaven given to the human race by which we are to be saved" (Acts 4:12; see 15:17).

Peter refers to the **word** that God **sent to the Israelites**, that **he proclaimed peace through Jesus Christ**.[7] This preaching of the good news was done first by Jesus during his public ministry, then by his witnesses (as reported in vv. 37–39). The biblical meaning of "peace" (*shalom* in Hebrew) is not only the absence of conflict but also the fullness of relationship with God and enjoyment of his covenant blessings that those who are reconciled to him can now receive. An

---

7. The Greek of these verses is difficult, and the NAB, RSV, and NRSV all move **You know** forward from v. 37 to v. 36, treating the two verses as in apposition, the second explaining and developing the first. NIV repeats "You know" before both verses. NJB translates the Greek more literally, with "You know" only before v. 37.

emphasis on peace runs through Luke-Acts. Peace was part of Israel's messianic expectation, as seen in Zechariah's canticle declaring that God would "guide our feet into the path of peace" (Luke 1:79). The angels at Jesus' birth announced "peace to those on whom his favor rests" (Luke 2:14). The crowd proclaimed peace during Jesus' triumphal entry into Jerusalem (Luke 19:38). This messianic peace promised by the prophets (see Isa 52:7; Nah 2:1 [= 1:15 NRSV]; Hag 2:9) is experienced by the Church (Acts 9:31) and by those who come to faith in Jesus or are healed by him (Luke 7:50; 8:48).

10:37 Peter summarizes Christ's ministry as taking place **all over Judea, beginning in Galilee** (here Luke seems to treat Galilee as part of the province of Judea).

Salvation outside the Church

LIVING TRADITION

The Catechism summarizes and applies the teaching of Vatican Council II on the possibility of salvation outside the Church. It begins by explaining that "all salvation comes from Christ the Head through the Church which is his Body." The Church is necessary for salvation, since "the one Christ is the mediator and the way of salvation; he is present to us in his body which is the Church." Since Jesus himself asserted the necessity of faith and baptism (Mark 16:16; John 3:5), "they could not be saved who, knowing that the Catholic Church was founded as necessary by God through Christ, would refuse either to enter it or to remain in it" (846; see *Lumen Gentium*, 14).

This statement, however, is "not aimed at those who, through no fault of their own, do not know Christ and his Church." Those who "seek God with a sincere heart" and with the help of God's grace try to do his will as they know it through their conscience—such persons may also "achieve eternal salvation" (847; see *Lumen Gentium*, 16). However, *Lumen Gentium* cautions:

> But very often, deceived by the Evil One, men have become vain in their reasonings, have exchanged the truth of God for a lie and served the world rather than the Creator (cf. Rom 1:21, 25). Or else, living and dying in this world without God, they are exposed to ultimate despair. Therefore, commanded by the Lord to "preach the Gospel to every creature" (Mark 16:15), the Church zealously fosters the missions.[a]

The Catechism (848) supplements this position by saying that God, in ways known only to himself, can lead those inculpably ignorant of the gospel to saving faith; yet this fact does not exempt the Church from "the obligation and also the sacred right to evangelize all men" (*Ad Gentes* 7; see Heb 11:6; 1 Cor 9:16).

a. Flannery translation, 1981.

Skipping Jesus' infancy (Luke 1–2), Peter focuses on Jesus' public life **beginning in Galilee after the baptism that John preached**. Peter uses a shorthand expression that combines John's preaching of repentance with his ritual act of baptizing people, which together were an indispensable preparation and catalyst for the public ministry of the Messiah. John's baptism of Jesus, when the Father affirmed him as his beloved Son, was at the beginning of Jesus' public ministry (Luke 3:21–22).

10:38   Like Luke's Gospel (3:22; 4:1), Peter emphasizes that **God anointed Jesus ... with the holy Spirit and power**. Although the Spirit was with Jesus from his conception (Luke 1:35), at his baptism the Spirit empowered Jesus' human nature for his ministry of preaching, healing, and exorcisms, just as the Spirit empowers the Church for ministry in Acts. Fortified by the Spirit and divine power, Jesus **went about doing good and healing all those oppressed by the devil**. Peter's explanation that **God was with him** emphasizes the presence of the Triune God with and in Jesus' humanity. Luke's emphasis on Jesus' humanity—rather than on his divinity, which John's Gospel more frequently accentuates—shows that Jesus worked miracles not only as God, as stressed in John, but also as a Spirit-empowered man, who is therefore a model for all his disciples. This enables Luke and Acts to underline the continuity between wonder-working prophets like Moses and Elijah, the miraculous prophetic ministry of Jesus, and the miracles of his Spirit-empowered followers like Peter, Stephen, and Paul in Acts. Peter and others imitated Jesus' healings as part of their prophetic witness to God's saving message; so such works are likewise possible for Spirit-empowered Christian readers of Luke-Acts.

10:39   In Acts 1:8, the risen Jesus prophesied that his followers would "be my witnesses." So now, Peter proclaims, **"We are witnesses of all that he did both in the country of the Jews and [in] Jerusalem."** Because Peter is speaking to Gentiles in Caesarea, a largely Gentile area on the Mediterranean coast of Palestine, he refers to "the country of the Jews" as if it were an alien land. His mention of Jerusalem focuses especially on the Jews' putting Jesus **to death** there **by hanging him on a tree**, an Old Testament phrase that by New Testament times was applied to crucifixion (see Acts 5:30).

10:40–41   Peter's sermon reaches its climax with the early Christian creedal statement **"This man God raised [on] the third day."**[8] As confirmation of Jesus' resurrection, Peter focuses not on the empty tomb but on the testimony of **us, the witnesses chosen by God in advance.** He testifies that Jesus did not appear **to all the people, but to us** only. The risen Jesus will not be seen by his enemies

---

8. Paul makes a similar declaration in 1 Cor 15:4.

or unbelievers, nor even by the vast majority of followers, until his return at the end of the world, when "they will see the Son of Man coming in a cloud with power and great glory" (Luke 21:27). Until then, "we walk by faith, not by sight" (2 Cor 5:7).

Peter declares that Jesus **commissioned us to preach to the people and testify** to him. This speech to Gentiles differs from Peter's earlier speech to Jews, where he had cited the resurrection to argue, "Therefore let the whole house of Israel know for certain that God has made him both Lord and Messiah" (Acts 2:36). To Gentiles, who would not be familiar with Jewish messianic prophecies, he cites the fact of the resurrection to argue that Jesus **is the one appointed by God as judge of the living and the dead.** Paul's speech to the Athenians will similarly refer to the risen Jesus as universal judge on the last day (Acts 17:31).

10:42

Christian belief in the risen Jesus is also grounded in **all the prophets** of the Old Testament, who **bear witness** to Jesus (see sidebar). That is, faith in the resurrection is based on both the living witness of apostles who saw Jesus risen and on the Old Testament prophecies. The aim of both the testimony of eyewitnesses and the prophecies is that every believer in Jesus **will receive forgiveness of sins through his name.** The essence of salvation is that people's sins are forgiven by invoking Jesus' name, because of all that he has accomplished on their behalf.[9]

10:43

The Baptism of Cornelius (10:44–49)

[44]While Peter was still speaking these things, the holy Spirit fell upon all who were listening to the word. [45]The circumcised believers who had accompanied Peter were astounded that the gift of the holy Spirit should have been poured out on the Gentiles also, [46]for they could hear them speaking in tongues and glorifying God. Then Peter responded, [47]"Can anyone withhold the water for baptizing these people, who have received the holy Spirit even as we have?" [48]He ordered them to be baptized in the name of Jesus Christ. [49]Then they invited him to stay for a few days.

OT: Num 11:25–29; 1 Sam 16:13; 19:23–24
NT: Acts 2:1–4; 8:36; 1 Cor 12:4–11; Gal 3:14, 27; Eph 2:11–16
Catechism: necessity of baptism, 1257; gift of the Spirit, 797–98, 2670–72; gift of tongues, 2003
Lectionary: Acts 10:25–26, 34–35, 44–48: Sixth Sunday of Easter (Year B)

9. See Luke 3:3; 24:47; Acts 5:31; 13:38; 26:18.

10:44   At this point Peter's speech is interrupted by the Holy Spirit! Luke has included everything he wanted to mention in the speech. There is an interesting parallel with Jesus' sermon at Nazareth (Luke 4:28–29) and Paul's speech in Jerusalem (Acts 22:22).[10] All three of these interruptions take place after a mention of outreach to Gentiles: with the speeches by Jesus and Paul, the interruptions stem from Jewish anger at the idea; in the present case the cause of the interruption is **the Holy Spirit** himself, descending on Gentiles before the preacher can invoke his coming. The Spirit interrupts while **Peter was still speaking these things**, by falling upon **all who were listening to the word**. The verb **fell upon** suggests a sudden and dramatic coming. These Gentile listeners evidently believe Peter's testimony, but before they can even respond, God's Spirit directly intervenes by entering and empowering them, as he had done at Pentecost to the disciples in the upper room (Acts 2:1–4). This dramatic intervention recalls God's promise in Isaiah, "Before they call, I will answer; while they are yet speaking, I will hear" (Isa 65:24).

10:45–46   Here for the first time Luke specifies that the **believers who had accompanied Peter** to the home of Cornelius were **circumcised** Jewish Christians. They **were astounded that the gift of the holy Spirit should have been poured out on the Gentiles also**. Gentiles were not members of God's chosen people. Although Jews knew that Israel was called to be a "light to the nations" (Isa 49:6; see 42:6; 60:1–3), most expected that that would happen by Gentiles joining the chosen people, being circumcised, and keeping the law of Moses. Yet these uncircumcised Gentiles had obviously been filled with the Spirit of God. The evidence from which Peter and his companions arrived at this understanding was hearing these Gentiles' **speaking in tongues and glorifying God**, just as had happened to Jewish believers at Pentecost, who "were all filled with the holy Spirit and began to speak in different tongues" (Acts 2:4). The gift of the Holy Spirit is evident in its effects in the recipients, such as tongues and prophecy (see Acts 19:6), which Paul will call gifts of the Spirit (see 1 Cor 12:4–11). For the New Testament, the Holy Spirit's coming on believers is not something imperceptible, to be accepted only on faith, but observable, sometimes even dramatic (see Gal 3:2–5; Heb 2:4). On this occasion it caused the Jewish believers who were present to expand their limited conception of God's plan and be docile to his purposes.

10:47–49   Peter's leadership is decisive in this momentous development. His response to the surprising outpouring of the Spirit on his Gentile listeners is to obey

---

10. Parsons, *Acts*, 155, has a fuller list of other such artificially interrupted speech in Acts, including 17:32; 23:7; 26:24. Acts 11:15 is Peter's report of this interruption in 10:44.

Fig. 9. The baptism of Cornelius, from a fourth-century sarcophagus.

Holly Hays / Art History Images

God's obvious guidance and fully incorporate them into the Church without further ado: **"Can anyone withhold the water for baptizing these people . . . ?"** Because they **have received the holy Spirit even as we have**, what objection could anyone raise to God's evident will to accept them fully as fellow Christians? The Ethiopian eunuch had raised a similar question to Philip: "What is to prevent my being baptized?" (Acts 8:36). Here there would normally have been even greater resistance to baptizing a whole group of uncircumcised Gentiles. Luke makes it clear that it is God's own direct action of giving his Spirit to these Gentiles that overrides all objections that would prohibit baptizing them. For they now have the same Spirit as the Jewish believers. This confirms Peter's realization that "God has shown me that I should not call any person profane or unclean" (Acts 10:28). These Gentiles too are now adopted sons and daughters of God and members of the body of Christ, God's Son.

The Baptism of Cornelius Explained (11:1–18)

¹Now the apostles and the brothers who were in Judea heard that the Gentiles too had accepted the word of God. ²So when Peter went up to Jerusalem the circumcised believers confronted him, ³saying, "You entered the house of uncircumcised people and ate with them." ⁴Peter began and explained it to them step by step, saying, ⁵"I was at prayer in the city of Joppa when in a trance I had a vision, something resembling a large sheet coming down, lowered from the sky by its four corners, and it came to me. ⁶Looking intently into it, I observed and saw the four-legged animals of the earth, the wild beasts, the reptiles, and the birds of the sky. ⁷I also heard a voice say to me, 'Get up, Peter. Slaughter and eat.' ⁸But I said, 'Certainly not, sir, because nothing profane or unclean has ever entered my mouth.' ⁹But a second time a voice from heaven answered, 'What God

has made clean, you are not to call profane.' ¹⁰This happened three times, and then everything was drawn up again into the sky. ¹¹Just then three men appeared at the house where we were, who had been sent to me from Caesarea. ¹²The Spirit told me to accompany them without discriminating. These six brothers also went with me, and we entered the man's house. ¹³He related to us how he had seen [the] angel standing in his house, saying, 'Send someone to Joppa and summon Simon, who is called Peter, ¹⁴who will speak words to you by which you and all your household will be saved.' ¹⁵As I began to speak, the holy Spirit fell upon them as it had upon us at the beginning, ¹⁶and I remembered the word of the Lord, how he had said, 'John baptized with water but you will be baptized with the holy Spirit.' ¹⁷If then God gave them the same gift he gave to us when we came to believe in the Lord Jesus Christ, who was I to be able to hinder God?" ¹⁸When they heard this, they stopped objecting and glorified God, saying, "God has then granted life-giving repentance to the Gentiles too."

OT: Lev 10:10; 11:47
NT: Acts 15:7–11; Gal 5:6; Eph 2:11–13; 3:4–6; Col 3:11
Catechism: Church as "catholic," 830–38; salvation of households, 1655–57
Lectionary: Solemnity of Saints Peter and Paul

11:1–3   Acts 11 repeats the Cornelius story reported in Acts 10 from the distinct perspective of Peter, with minor variations and with more focus and brevity. Like the triple telling of Saul's conversion (in Acts 9 and through Paul's speeches in Acts 22 and 26), the conversion of Cornelius is told three times (in Acts 10 and through Peter's speeches in Acts 11 and 15), an indication of the importance Luke attributes to it. It was a world-changing event.

News of the Cornelius event reached **the apostles** and the †**brothers**, that is, both the apostolic leaders and the church at large, **in Judea**, especially in the vicinity of Jerusalem (some distance from Caesarea, which was on the Mediterranean seacoast). All indications are that they regarded favorably what had happened: **the Gentiles too had accepted the word of God.**

However, some believers were disturbed by these events. After **Peter** returned to **Jerusalem, the circumcised believers confronted him.** They did not question Peter's accepting and baptizing the Gentiles. Their accusation was **"You entered the house of uncircumcised people and ate with them."** According to the Jewish understanding, a Jew would become contaminated by such interaction, since the food served in Gentile homes would have been raised and prepared without regard for ritual purity (see above on Acts 10:27–29). If meat was served, it might include flesh that was forbidden under the Levitical regulations. Moreover, since table fellowship was regarded as a kind of spiritual sharing with others, eating with Gentiles could be seen as colluding in idolatry.[11] Some Jewish Christians feared that converted pagans, even though they had come to faith in Christ, could still blemish the community's holiness by regressing back to (or never fully getting beyond) idolatrous pagan practices to which they had been accustomed, such as eating meat sacrificed to idols (see 1 Cor 8–10).[12] This concern will be dealt with more explicitly in Acts 15.

Peter's speech justifying his actions contains elements of argumentation common to Greek †rhetoric, such as the citing of witnesses, signs, and a conclusion in the form of a rhetorical question. But Peter defends his behavior primarily by telling his story. He **explained** it **step by step** (*kathexēs*, literally, "in order" or "in an orderly sequence," the same expression used in Luke 1:3 to describe the Gospel narrative). 11:4–6

In his account of what happened, **Peter** in his own words repeats what Luke has previously narrated in Acts 10. He states that he **was at prayer** and that **in a trance** he experienced **a vision** from heaven—a vision he describes as **something resembling a large sheet** that was **lowered** to him **from the sky by its four corners**. It contained earth's various **animals**, namely, **the wild beasts, the reptiles, and the birds**.

A **voice** told Peter: **"Slaughter and eat"** these animals. In refusing the unclean food, Peter was not being a hyperlegalist but obeying the law revealed through Moses (see Lev 11) and imitating heroic Jews of the past who were loyal to God's law at great cost. Daniel had shown great courage in refusing the king's food (Dan 1:8), as had Judas Maccabeus in avoiding defiled food imposed by Hellenistic persecutors (2 Macc 5:27). Their example and the standard they upheld help to explain why such a dramatic divine intervention was needed to open the early Jewish Christians to full communion with Gentiles in the Church. Thus Peter objected against this command, because **nothing profane or unclean has ever entered my mouth** (see above on Acts 10:14). But the **voice from heaven** answered, **"What God has made clean, you are not to call profane."** The command, Peter's objection, and the heavenly response took place **three times**, indicating God's emphasis on its importance. 11:7–10

Peter gives the number of messengers **from Caesarea** as **three men**. He leaves out minor details to simply report that the messengers appeared **at the house** 11:11–14

---

11. Johnson, *Acts*, 197.
12. See Robert W. Wall, "Reading Paul with Acts: The Canonical Shaping of a Holy Church," in *Holiness and Ecclesiology in the New Testament*, ed. Kent E. Brower and Andy Johnson (Grand Rapids: Eerdmans, 2007), 129–47, who interprets from the perspectives of both Paul (especially 1 Corinthians) and Acts (especially Acts 15) the dangers to a mixed Jewish-Gentile Christian community from eating meat sacrificed to idols and from pagan forms of sexual immorality (*porneia*).

where we were. Peter went with them because he was directly commanded by the **Spirit** to **accompany them without discriminating** or arguing. For Peter not to go to Cornelius would have been disobedience to God's explicit command.

Peter includes in his action the **six brothers** with him (identified as "circumcised believers" in Acts 10:45). With Peter, these Jewish brothers **entered the man's house**, where they learn of Cornelius's own vision of an **angel**, who commanded him to **summon Simon, who is called Peter**. This time the purpose of the summons is reported, namely, that Peter should **speak words to you by which you and all your household will be saved**. By preaching the gospel, Peter would invite them to salvation in Jesus Christ through faith and baptism.

11:15–18   Peter omits the content of his speech, emphasizing only that **the holy Spirit fell upon them as it had among us at the beginning**, recalling the day of Pentecost when the Spirit filled the disciples and empowered them with tongues and prophecy (Acts 2). It would be a mistake to understand **as I began to speak** literally (see 10:34–43). Peter's point is to emphasize that the Spirit acted before he had completed all that he had intended to say and before he could make any personal decisions about what action to take regarding his Gentile listeners.

The dramatic outpouring of the Spirit recalled to Peter's mind **the word of the Lord** reported at the beginning of Acts (1:5), when the risen Jesus prophesied that **John baptized with water but you will be baptized with the holy Spirit**, as the Baptist himself had also prophesied (Luke 3:16). Peter thus recognized the Spirit's coming on his Gentile listeners as their being baptized with the Holy Spirit, in contrast to John's baptism **with water**. Pentecost had been extended to the Gentiles! The Jerusalem church, then, should be able to see that this event, fulfilling the prophecies of the Baptist and of Jesus, was part of God's saving plan.

Peter concludes with a compelling rhetorical question. **"If then God gave** the Gentiles **the same gift he gave to us** Jewish believers—namely, the Holy Spirit—**who was I to be able to hinder God?"** God himself has made the matter indisputably clear: his gift of salvation and divine life is for the Gentiles too. This question silences all protests: **they stopped objecting**, literally, "they kept silent."

The community's second reaction is one often emphasized in Luke-Acts. They **glorified God**, as people did repeatedly in response to Jesus' mighty deeds.[13] They are convinced by Peter's explanation and enthusiastically conclude that **God** has **granted** the same **life-giving repentance**—literally, "repentance unto life"—**to the Gentiles too**. "Repentance unto life" is a way of summing up Christian conversion: turning away from sin and instead receiving God's gift of his own divine life. The Gentiles had received the Spirit as they listened in

13. Luke 5:25–26; 7:16; 13:13; 17:15; and see Luke 23:47; Acts 10:46.

faith to Peter's preaching and converted to the Lord and his life-giving ways. Since God has treated the Gentile converts the same as he had earlier treated the Jewish followers of Jesus, their initial objections are replaced by praise of God and his saving plan.

Reflection and Application (11:1–18)

These accounts in Acts 10–11 make it clear that God extends his offer of salvation not only to his original chosen people but also to all nations to the ends of the earth. The same divine plan continues today. As Christians, who know ourselves to be a people especially chosen by God, we cannot rest content with our own salvation in Christ. We are meant to be God's witnesses of this good news to others. Like God's servant in Isaiah (Isa 42:6); like Jesus, God's own Son (Luke 2:32); and like the apostles (Acts 13:47; 26:23), we also are called to be light to all nations. And we can have expectant faith that God will guide us in reaching out to unbelieving individuals, including members of other religions, just as he guided Peter and the early Christians.

Church Growth at Antioch; Peter's Escape

Acts 11:19–12:24

This section relates a major transition in Acts from its earlier focus on the witness of the apostles, and particularly Peter, to a focus on Paul and his companions. It also illustrates the rise of an important second home base, after Jerusalem, for Christian missionaries: the church at Antioch in Syria. It introduces the last of the roughly four phases in the spread of the Word from Jerusalem to the ends of the earth (Acts 1:8). The first phase focuses on the Twelve (Acts 2:1–6:7), the second on †Hellenists (6:8–8:40), the third on Peter (9:32–11:18), and the last on the Pauline missions (13:1–28:31).

However, the sections are interwoven to overlap each other, so that the transition from Peter to Paul in Acts 12–13 has already been partially anticipated. Luke recounts Saul's conversion and initial preaching (9:1–31), then Peter's ministry in Judea and to Cornelius (9:32–11:18). After describing Barnabas and Saul, that is, Paul, at Antioch (11:19–30), he reports Herod's persecution of the apostles James and Peter, Peter's rescue from prison, and Herod's death (12:1–24). Finally Luke completes the transition to Paul and his companions in 12:25–13:52.

The Church at Antioch (11:19–26)

---

¹⁹**Now those who had been scattered by the persecution that arose because of Stephen went as far as Phoenicia, Cyprus, and Antioch, preaching the word to no one but Jews.** ²⁰**There were some Cypriots and Cyrenians**

among them, however, who came to Antioch and began to speak to the
Greeks as well, proclaiming the Lord Jesus. [21]The hand of the Lord was
with them and a great number who believed turned to the Lord. [22]The
news about them reached the ears of the church in Jerusalem, and they
sent Barnabas [to go] to Antioch. [23]When he arrived and saw the grace of
God, he rejoiced and encouraged them all to remain faithful to the Lord
in firmness of heart, [24]for he was a good man, filled with the holy Spirit
and faith. And a large number of people was added to the Lord. [25]Then he
went to Tarsus to look for Saul, [26]and when he had found him he brought
him to Antioch. For a whole year they met with the church and taught a
large number of people, and it was in Antioch that the disciples were first
called Christians.

OT: Josh 23:8
NT: Matt 8:11; Acts 8:1; 1 Cor 15:58; Eph 2:11–13; Col 3:11
Catechism: the gospel first announced to Jews, 543; significance of the name Christian, 1289
Lectionary: Acts 11:21b–26; 13:1–3: St. Barnabas

Luke recalls the **persecution** on account of **Stephen** that had **scattered** the   **11:19**
disciples from **Jerusalem** (Acts 8:1–4). These fugitives, most of whom seem to
be †Hellenistic Jews, **went as far as Phoenicia, Cyprus, and Antioch** of Syria,
that is, well beyond the borders of Judea. Phoenicia, on the Mediterranean coast,
included Tyre and Sidon in present-day Lebanon, not far north of Caesarea, the
city in which Peter evangelized Cornelius (Acts 10–11). The island of Cyprus
in the Mediterranean Sea was the home of Barnabas (introduced in Acts 4:36).
The majority of those scattered were **preaching the word to no one but Jews.**

Most of the current action takes place at **Antioch.** Luke reports that there   **11:20–21**
**Cypriots and Cyrenians . . . began to speak to the Greeks as well, proclaiming
the Lord Jesus.**[1] Thus at Antioch was an outreach not only to Greek-speaking
Jews but also to Gentile Greeks, a mixed pattern that would be later seen in the
ministry of Paul and his companions on their missionary journeys throughout
most of Acts 13–28.

Luke does not indicate whether this preaching to Gentiles at Antioch pre-
ceded or followed the conversion of Cornelius's Gentile household and the
arrival of news about it in Antioch (Luke promised to write his narrative in
an "orderly" but not necessarily chronological sequence; Luke 1:3). However,
because Acts 10 reported the Cornelius event, it has prepared readers for this

---

1. The Greek text of Acts 11:20 has *Hellēnistas*, "Hellenists," which in Acts 6 means Greek-speaking
Jews; but here Luke clearly refers to a new outreach to *non-Jewish* ethnic or cultural Greeks, in contrast
to the previous preaching "to no one but Jews" (11:19).

new development. As noticed above, the preaching to Jews emphasized that Jesus was Israel's Messiah, but the preaching to Gentiles proclaimed Jesus in religious language more understandable to them, as the Lord who will judge all people (see Acts 17:31).

Luke emphasizes the outstanding success of the preaching to Greeks at Antioch, first by using an Old Testament expression, **the hand of the Lord was with them**, to indicate that the Lord Jesus himself had guided and blessed this outreach;[2] and second, by reporting **a great number** of Greek converts, as earlier he had mentioned large numbers of Jewish believers (2:41; 4:4; 6:7). There are two aspects to their conversion: the listeners **believed** and they **turned to the Lord** Jesus. To "believe" means to accept in faith the message of the gospel. The verb for "turned" here signifies repentance: turning away from sin and toward God. These are the two necessary human responses called for by the proclamation of the gospel. The same two are mentioned in Jesus' preaching at the beginning of his public ministry: "Repent, and believe in the gospel" (Mark 1:15).[3]

11:22–24   Earlier Luke had reported that the mother **church in Jerusalem** confirmed and authenticated the conversion of Samaritans by sending the apostles Peter and John to Samaria (Acts 8:14). Here the apostles are no longer mentioned, but the Jerusalem church **sent Barnabas** to **Antioch**. The reaction of Barnabas, as representative of the Jerusalem church, to the situation in Antioch is described in very positive terms: he **saw the grace of God**. He recognizes this conversion of Greeks as resulting from God's grace (*charis*) or free gift (see also Acts 5:31; 11:18). In reaction **he rejoiced** (*chairō*, a play on the similar sounding *charis*). True to his nickname "son of encouragement" (Acts 4:36), Barnabas **encouraged them all to remain faithful to the Lord in firmness of heart.**

Luke goes on to describe Barnabas as **a good man, filled with the holy Spirit and faith.** Earlier Stephen was described quite similarly as "a man filled with faith and the holy Spirit" (Acts 6:5).[4] During Barnabas's ministry at Antioch, **a large number of people was added to the Lord** in that church. The repeated mention of a large number converting to the Lord (vv. 21, 24, and 26) illustrates how the Church grows in stages. First, in verse 21 many Greeks were converted

2. This expression is especially common in Ezekiel, where it introduces visions (1:3; 8:1; 37:1; 40:1), expresses God's power physically moving the prophet (3:14), and enables Ezekiel to prophesy (33:22). New Testament examples are primarily from Luke, who uses it to express God's favor on the Baptist as a baby (Luke 1:66) and divine punishment in Paul's curse of Elymas (Acts 13:11).

3. However, Mark uses a different Greek word for "repent," *metanoeō*, meaning to change one's mind, feel remorse, be converted.

4. Those who are "filled with the holy Spirit" in Luke-Acts include John the Baptist (Luke 1:15), Elizabeth (1:41), Zechariah (1:67), Jesus (4:1); the 120 disciples (Acts 2:4), Peter (4:8), the gathered Jerusalem church (4:31), Stephen (7:55), Paul (9:17; 13:9).

Barnabas, "Son of Encouragement"

According to Acts, Barnabas played a key role in the growth of the early Church. His original name was Joseph, and he was "a Levite, a Cypriot by birth" (Acts 4:36). In the same verse Luke reports that the apostles renamed him "son of encouragement" ("son of X" is a common biblical idiom to name a person's dominant quality or characteristic). Barnabas introduced Saul to the members of the Jerusalem church who were hesitant to accept him (Acts 9:27). Later he was sent by the Jerusalem church as their delegate to Antioch (Acts 11:22), where he again lived up to his new name by encouraging "them all to remain faithful to the Lord in firmness of heart" (11:23). Barnabas then recruited Saul to teach and minister in the Antioch church (11:25–26). If Barnabas had not done so, Paul might have remained an insignificant figure, and the history of Christianity would have been very different.

Barnabas and Saul worked together in the Antioch church, which later authorized the two of them to bring a famine relief collection to the church in Jerusalem (11:30). Sometime after that, the church at Antioch commissioned Barnabas and Saul for their first missionary journey (13:2–4). Beginning in Acts 13:43, Luke reverses the order in which the pair are named, putting Paul first, which implies that Paul had now become the lead partner. Galatians 2:9 reports an agreement among the apostles that Paul and Barnabas would go especially to Gentiles, while James, Peter, and John would focus on ministry to Jews. Paul and Barnabas continued to work together both on missionary journeys and also back at Antioch until after the †Jerusalem Council, when they formed separate teams as a result of a disagreement (Acts 15:39–40).

by those who had been scattered by the persecution after Stephen's martyrdom. A second number were converted through the ministry of Barnabas (v. 24). Third, these new converts grew in faith as they were catechized by Barnabas and Paul together (v. 26). A similar growth in waves was seen in Acts 2:41 (three thousand souls) and 4:4 (five thousand men).

The last mention of **Saul** was his escape from persecution in Jerusalem and return home to **Tarsus** (Acts 9:30). Now Barnabas, recognizing Paul's gifts for preaching and teaching, goes there to seek him and bring him **to Antioch** to help him minister to the growing church in that city. Together **they met with the church** and catechized **a large number of people**. Luke's repeated references to large numbers (11:21, 24, and 26) accentuate the effectiveness and growth of the church's ministry in Antioch, especially to the Greeks.

11:25–26

Verse 26 is the first mention of the new name given to believers in Jesus: here **the disciples were first called Christians**, that is, followers of the Christ, or Messiah. They were probably called this by outsiders to distinguish them from other Jews, perhaps because **in Antioch** there was a significant influx of Greeks as well as Jews into the church. This name first given by outsiders may have been intended as derogatory,[5] but Christians soon recognized it as a perfectly apt description of who they are.

The Prophecy of Agabus (11:27–30)

---

[27]**At that time some prophets came down from Jerusalem to Antioch,** [28]**and one of them named Agabus stood up and predicted by the Spirit that there would be a severe famine all over the world, and it happened under Claudius.** [29]**So the disciples determined that, according to ability, each should send relief to the brothers who lived in Judea.** [30]**This they did, sending it to the presbyters in care of Barnabas and Saul.**

OT: Gen 41:30–31; 2 Kings 8:1; Joel 3:1
NT: Luke 11:49; Acts 2:17; Rom 15:26; Gal 2:10
Catechism: gifts of the Holy Spirit, 1830–32; care for the poor, 2443–49

11:27–28   The continuing communication between mother and daughter churches is illustrated when some prophets **came down from Jerusalem to Antioch**. This is the first mention of **prophets** functioning as a distinct ministry group among the followers of Christ, although Jesus' saying in Luke 11:49 seems to anticipate them: "The wisdom of God said, 'I will send to them prophets and apostles; some of them they will kill and persecute'" (see also Matt 7:22). Luke mentions **Agabus** as prominent among these Jerusalem prophets, as he will continue to be later (Acts 21:10–14). Agabus **predicted by the Spirit that there would be a severe famine all over the world.**[6] The added statement, **and it happened under Claudius,** is Luke's aside to readers, indicating that this prophecy was later fulfilled during the reign of Emperor Claudius (AD 41–54).

---

5. For example, Joseph A. Fitzmyer, *The Acts of the Apostles*, Anchor Bible 31 (New York: Doubleday, 1998), 478, quotes the Roman author Tacitus, *Annals* 15.44: "Those people, loathed for (their) vices, whom the rabble used to call Christians" (see also Fitzmyer, *Acts*, 477–78, and Luke Timothy Johnson, *The Acts of the Apostles*, Sacra pagina 5 [Collegeville, MN: Liturgical Press, 1992], 204–5).
6. The Greek is *oikoumenē*, "inhabited earth," which often signifies the Greek world or the Roman Empire, excluding "barbarian" places outside of it. The statement is an example of literary hyperbole in referring to the known Roman world or even simply to the surrounding region.

New Testament Prophets

**BIBLICAL
BACKGROUND**

In his Pentecost sermon, Peter explained what was happening to the disciples in the upper room by quoting the prophet Joel:

> "It will come to pass in the last days," God says,
> "that I will pour out a portion of my spirit upon all flesh.
> Your sons and your daughters shall prophesy,
> your young men shall see visions,
> your old men shall dream dreams.
> Indeed, upon my servants and my handmaids
> I will pour out a portion of my spirit in those days,
> and they shall prophesy." (Acts 2:17–18)

Peter indicates that the first effect of the Holy Spirit's coming is a universal dissemination of the gift of prophecy. Prophecy, the ability to speak God's word under the inspiration of the Holy Spirit, will no longer be limited to certain individuals with a special mission, but will belong to all God's people—men and women, young and old, slave and free.

Throughout Acts, Luke shows this gift of prophecy being exercised as part of the normal functioning of the Church. He mentions new converts who speak in tongues and prophesy (Acts 19:6) and Philip's "four virgin daughters gifted with prophecy" (21:9). Paul and Barnabas's mission is initiated by prophecy (13:1–3). Through their gift of prophecy, Judas and Silas are able to exhort and strengthen communities in Asia Minor to accept the decisions of the Jerusalem Council (Acts 15:31–32). The prophet Agabus predicts both a famine (11:28) and Paul's impending suffering (21:10–11). Prophecy in the form of visions and dreams is also frequent. These passages highlight the importance that Luke attributes to Christian prophecy as a gift empowered by the Holy Spirit, by which God speaks to and builds up his Church (see 1 Cor 14:1–5, 31).

Christian prophets held a position of honor and authority in the early Church second only to that of apostles (see 1 Cor 12:28; Eph 2:20). Like Luke, Paul in his letters places special value on prophecy as a charism that has exceptional power to build up the Church: "one who prophesies does speak to human beings, for their building up, encouragement, and solace" and "builds up the church" (1 Cor 14:3–4). Paul counsels Christians to "strive eagerly for the spiritual gifts, above all that you may prophesy. . . . Strive eagerly to prophesy" (1 Cor 14:1, 39). The book of Revelation makes numerous references to Christian prophets (10:7; 16:6; 18:20). The New Testament also warns against false prophets (Matt 24:11, 24; 1 John 4:1; Rev 2:20) and teaches that prophecies should be discerned (1 Cor 14:29; 1 Thess 5:19–22) and that prophets should be evaluated by their fruit (Matt 7:15–23).

11:29   The response of the **disciples** was most generous. They **determined that, according to ability, each should send relief to the brothers who lived in Judea.** In the Antioch community, it was not only the wealthy who became benefactors of the disciples suffering from the famine in Jerusalem. They all gave "according to ability" to the mother church in Jerusalem and to those disciples living near that city (see Rom 15:26; Gal 2:10).

11:30   The Christians of Antioch sent their contributions to the Jerusalem †**presbyters**, a Church leadership group mentioned for the first time here, who play a regular role throughout the rest of Acts. The Greek term *presbyteros* literally means "elder," and this term for Christian leaders gradually came to be understood as signifying a share in Christ's priestly ministry (hence it is the origin of the English word "priest"). In Acts 14:23 Paul and Barnabas place local presbyters in charge of the communities they found, after the pattern of the mother church in Jerusalem, which is now led by apostles and presbyters.

The Antioch collection for famine relief in Jerusalem was put **in care of Barnabas and Saul.** This famine relief collection for a sister church sets a precedent for interchurch sharing that will play an important part in Paul's own letters, especially to the Corinthians, Galatians, and Romans. In Acts the collection was from Antioch only and was sent to Jerusalem via Barnabas and Saul, before the pair embarked on their missionary journeys. The later famine collection that Paul mentions in his letters came from the churches that he founded, with no mention of Antioch, and was delivered by Paul himself to Jerusalem much later, after his Letter to the Romans (1 Cor 16:1–3; Rom 15:25–29; see Gal 2:10).

Herod's Persecution of the Church (12:1–19)

[1]About that time King Herod laid hands upon some members of the church to harm them. [2]He had James, the brother of John, killed by the sword, [3]and when he saw that this was pleasing to the Jews he proceeded to arrest Peter also. (It was [the] feast of Unleavened Bread.) [4]He had him taken into custody and put in prison under the guard of four squads of four soldiers each. He intended to bring him before the people after Passover. [5]Peter thus was being kept in prison, but prayer by the church was fervently being made to God on his behalf.

[6]On the very night before Herod was to bring him to trial, Peter, secured by double chains, was sleeping between two soldiers, while outside the door guards kept watch on the prison. [7]Suddenly the angel of the Lord stood by him and a light shone in the cell. He tapped Peter on the

side and awakened him, saying, "Get up quickly." The chains fell from his wrists. [8]The angel said to him, "Put on your belt and your sandals." He did so. Then he said to him, "Put on your cloak and follow me." [9]So he followed him out, not realizing that what was happening through the angel was real; he thought he was seeing a vision. [10]They passed the first guard, then the second, and came to the iron gate leading out to the city, which opened for them by itself. They emerged and made their way down an alley, and suddenly the angel left him. [11]Then Peter recovered his senses and said, "Now I know for certain that [the] Lord sent his angel and rescued me from the hand of Herod and from all that the Jewish people had been expecting." [12]When he realized this, he went to the house of Mary, the mother of John who is called Mark, where there were many people gathered in prayer. [13]When he knocked on the gateway door, a maid named Rhoda came to answer it. [14]She was so overjoyed when she recognized Peter's voice that, instead of opening the gate, she ran in and announced that Peter was standing at the gate. [15]They told her, "You are out of your mind," but she insisted that it was so. But they kept saying, "It is his angel." [16]But Peter continued to knock, and when they opened it, they saw him and were astounded. [17]He motioned to them with his hand to be quiet and explained [to them] how the Lord had led him out of the prison, and said, "Report this to James and the brothers." Then he left and went to another place. [18]At daybreak there was no small commotion among the soldiers over what had become of Peter. [19]Herod, after instituting a search but not finding him, ordered the guards tried and executed. Then he left Judea to spend some time in Caesarea.

OT: Exod 12:11–12; Isa 42:6–7
NT: Luke 22:1–2; 24:4–11; Acts 4:3; 5:18–19; 1 Pet 5:13
Catechism: intercessory prayer, 2634–36; help of angels, 334–36
Lectionary: Acts 12:1–11: Feast of Saints Peter and Paul (June 29)

Acts 11 ended with Barnabas and Saul working in the church at Antioch; now **12:1–3** Acts 12 somewhat abruptly shifts focus back to the persecution of the apostles in Jerusalem by **King Herod**. With a vague time reference, **about that time,** Luke simply says that Herod **laid hands upon some members of the church to harm them.** Herod's first victim, whom he had **killed by the sword,** was one of the Twelve, **James, the brother of John** and son of Zebedee. In the Gospel, James was one of Jesus' three closest disciples, with Peter and John, present with him at key moments: the raising of Jairus's daughter, the transfiguration, and the agony in the garden. With John, James expressed his willingness to "drink the cup" of Jesus and to be baptized with his baptism, that is, his passion (Mark

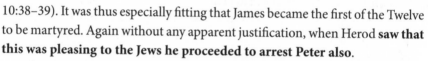

The Witness of Martyrdom

LIVING TRADITION

As Saint Pope John Paul II stated, to be Christian is to be prepared to suffer for our witness to Christ:

> The martyr, especially in our own days, is a sign of that greater love which sums up all other values. The martyr's life reflects the extraordinary words uttered by Christ on the Cross: "Father, forgive them, for they know not what they do" (Luke 23:34). The believer who has seriously pondered his Christian vocation, including what Revelation has to say about the possibility of martyrdom, cannot exclude it from his own life's horizon. The two thousand years since the birth of Christ are marked by the ever-present witness of the martyrs. . . . From the psychological point of view, martyrdom is the most eloquent proof of the truth of the faith, for faith can give a human face even to the most violent of deaths and show its beauty even in the midst of the most atrocious persecutions.[a]

a. John Paul II, *Incarnationis Mysterium*, 13.

10:38–39). It was thus especially fitting that James became the first of the Twelve to be martyred. Again without any apparent justification, when Herod **saw that this was pleasing to the Jews he proceeded to arrest Peter also**.

Luke inserts a brief aside to readers, explaining that this was during the **feast of Unleavened Bread**, which by the first century was regarded as a weeklong setting for the celebration of Passover, like our liturgical octaves.[7] Peter was thus following in the footsteps of Jesus, who was also arrested during the Passover.

12:4   Herod took Peter **into custody** and had him **put in prison**, placing an enormous **guard** of soldiers over him, **four squads of four soldiers each**. Just as the Jewish leaders had been concerned about arresting Jesus openly during the feast days,[8] Herod held **Peter** in prison until he could **bring him before the people after Passover**.

12:5   While Peter was a prisoner, **prayer by the church was fervently being made to God on his behalf**. Luke has set the stage for the miraculous events to follow, which illustrate the power of united and fervent intercession. On the opponent's side, Luke has emphasized the extraordinary lengths to which Herod went to keep Peter securely under guard in prison until he could be tried. Humanly speaking, Peter's situation was hopeless. On the Christian side, Luke stresses

---

7. The Passover was the first day in a weeklong celebration of the Feast of Unleavened Bread (see Exod 12:3–20; 34:18; Lev 23:4–8; Num 9:2–14; 28:16–17; Deut 16:1–8). Luke 22:1 treats them as synonymous.

8. "They said, 'Not during the festival, for fear that there may be a riot among the people'" (Mark 14:2; the parallel text in Luke 22:2 omits this detail).

the church's fervent prayer to God for Peter. God's power is now poised to bring to naught all human efforts to destroy Peter and prevent the further spread of the gospel.

The miraculous nature of Peter's rescue is heightened by the timing of the   12:6–9
rescue—**on the very night before Herod was to bring him to trial**—by the **double chains** with which the prisoner was **secured**, by the fact that he **was sleeping between two soldiers**, and by the presence of the **door guards** who **kept watch on the prison**. Despite these apparently insurmountable obstacles, **suddenly the angel of the Lord** appeared by him, **and a light shone in the cell**. The angel **awakened** Peter by tapping him and ordered, **"Get up quickly."** Immediately the **chains fell from his wrists**. The angel instructed Peter to get dressed and **follow** him, which Peter did. In this dramatic scene, Luke adds a touch of humor, which will continue through the account of Peter's meeting with the church: even as he was being rescued, Peter did not realize **that what was happening through the angel was real; he thought he was seeing a vision** or dream.

Luke narrates the scene of Peter's rescue with strong echoes of both God's deliverance of his people from slavery in Egypt and Jesus' death and resurrection. The community prays "fervently" (*ektenōs*) for Peter's release (Acts 12:5), as Jesus had prayed "so fervently" (*ektenesteron*) as he was suffering in the garden of Gethsemane (Luke 22:44). Peter is awakened, literally, "raised," from sleep (a common biblical metaphor for death) and commanded to "get up," literally, "arise," by an angel appearing in light, which recalls the dazzling clothes of the angels at Jesus' tomb (Luke 24:4). Peter's liberation anticipates our own resurrection, our rescue from death on the last day.

Like the exodus from Egypt (Exod 12:12), Peter's rescue occurs "on the very night," and Peter, like the Israelites, is to move quickly and be clothed for departure (Exod 12:11).[9] As God delivered his people from the wrath of Pharaoh, he now delivers a member of his new covenant people from government persecution. Stephen's speech asserted that the purpose of the exodus was not only to free God's people from bondage but also to enable them to worship God (Acts 7:7; see Exod 3:12). Here Peter is rescued from bondage to be able to rejoin the worshiping community (Acts 12:12).[10]

---

9. See David T. N. Parry, "Release of Captives: Reflections on Acts 12," in *Luke's Literary Achievement: Collected Essays*, ed. Christopher M. Tuckett, Journal for the Study of the New Testament: Supplement Series 116 (Sheffield: Sheffield Academic Press, 1995), 156–64, especially 160–61.

10. See Susan R. Garrett, "Exodus from Bondage: Luke 9:31 and Acts 12:1–24," *Catholic Biblical Quarterly* 52 (1990): 656–80, especially 660–64.

From Isaiah, Luke draws many allusions to freedom from bondage in darkness. For instance, Paul's mission to the Gentiles, "that they may turn from darkness to light and from the power of Satan to God" (Acts 26:18), alludes to the mission of the Servant of the Lord, "to lead out . . . from their fetters those who are bound, and out of the prison house . . . those who sit in darkness" (Isa 42:7 LXX).[11] Here Peter's release from prison is an image of God's rescue of all his people from the power of sin, Satan, and death.

12:10–11   Peter and the angel **passed** both the **first guard** and **the second**, arriving at the **iron gate leading out to the city, which opened for them by itself**. Once they were free and **down an alley**, the **angel** disappeared. Only at this point did Peter recover **his senses** and realize that the **Lord sent his angel** to deliver him from the Gentile and Jewish persecutors who had planned his execution. As the Lord God had liberated his people by his angel from the hand of Pharaoh (Num 20:16), so the Lord Jesus liberated Peter by his angel **from the hand of Herod**.

12:12–14   After narrating Peter's miraculous escape, Luke focuses again on the community that was praying for him at the **house of Mary, the mother of John who is called Mark**. Mary must have been a well-to-do Christian who had a house large enough for the Jerusalem Christians to gather in. When Peter **realized** that God had rescued him from prison, he went there and **knocked on the gateway door**. The servant girl **Rhoda came to answer it**. To emphasize the community's shock and joy at Peter's rescue, Luke relates the humorous behavior of Rhoda, who recognized **Peter's voice** but left him **standing** outside the locked gate, while she, **overjoyed**, ran in to announce to the praying Christians that Peter was outside.

12:15   Just as the church had earlier refused to believe the women who witnessed Jesus' empty tomb, for "their story seemed like nonsense" (Luke 24:11), here the church in disbelief accused Rhoda, **"You are out of your mind."** When **she insisted that it was so**, they countered, **"It is his angel."** This idea may stem from a belief that sometimes a person's guardian angel can stand in for the individual or act on that one's behalf.[12]

12:16–17   Meanwhile, during this debate about whether Peter could be at the door, Luke comically shows that **Peter continued to knock**, followed by the disciples' astonishment at seeing him after they finally unlock the door. Peter

11. Ibid., her translation on 662.

12. See Fitzmyer, *Acts*, 489. The reference to "his angel" is to Peter's guardian angel, an example of the biblical notion of angels who guard and help humans. Thus Israel praises "the angel who rescues me from all evil" (Gen 48:16 LXX, my translation). Tobit assures his wife regarding their son that "a good angel will go with him, his journey will be successful, and he will return in good health" (Tob 5:22). Jesus refers to the guardian angels of children: "I say to you that their angels in heaven always look upon the face of my heavenly Father" (Matt 18:10).

John Mark, Paul, and Peter

BIBLICAL BACKGROUND

Acts 12 introduces John Mark, who is identified in Col 4:10 as a cousin of Barnabas. Mark traveled with Barnabas and Saul on their first missionary journey (Acts 13:5), but for unknown reasons left their team at Pamphylia (13:13). Paul and Barnabas's subsequent quarrel about whether to take Mark on their next mission led to a parting of ways, with Mark traveling with Barnabas to Cyprus, while Silas accompanied Paul "through Syria and Cilicia" (Acts 15:37–41). Although Luke provides no indication of the outcome of this dispute, positive references to Mark in several later Pauline letters suggest that they eventually reconciled. Mark is listed among Paul's coworkers in Col 4:10 (see 2 Tim 4:11).

Ancient tradition holds that Mark later became Peter's interpreter in Rome and wrote his Gospel based on Peter's preaching (see 1 Pet 5:13, where Peter sends greetings from "Mark, my son"). Reflection on Acts 12 suggests a way in which Mark and Peter may have met, since the Jerusalem Christians gathered in the home of Mark's mother, where Peter went after his release from prison.

signaled them **with his hand** to listen quietly while he **explained** how **the Lord** Jesus had saved him from **prison**. He instructed them, **"Report this to James"**—not James the son of Zebedee, who had been martyred (12:2), but James the relative of Jesus who became the second leader of the Jerusalem church—**"and to the brothers."** The last group seems to refer to the whole Jerusalem community.

Then he left and went to another place, apparently leaving town and getting away from Herod. Neither the church at Mary's house nor the readers of Acts needed to know where Peter went. What the church did not know, they could not be forced to tell Herod, whose ruthlessness Luke will illustrate vividly by his treatment of the guards from whom Peter escaped (Acts 12:19). Where Peter went was less significant than the fact that he left Jerusalem with James in charge of the church.[13] Peter appears in Acts and other New Testament texts as spreading the gospel in other parts of the Roman Empire, and he was eventually martyred in Rome. By the time of the †Jerusalem Council (Acts 15), James had apparently become the leader of the Jerusalem church.

13. See Robert W. Wall, "Successors to 'the Twelve' according to Acts 12:1–17," *Catholic Biblical Quarterly* 53, no. 4 (October 1991): 628–43. One transition Wall accentuates in this passage is the transition of authority in Jerusalem from Peter to James, from the original Twelve to postapostolic leadership (641–43).

12:18–19   At daybreak the **soldiers** were alarmed **over what had become of Peter,** for whose captivity they were responsible. Their fears were fully justified, for **Herod,** after a fruitless **search** for Peter, tyrannically **ordered the guards tried and executed.** Then Herod returned to **Caesarea,** his home base, where he is at the center of the next events to be narrated (vv. 20–24).

Herod's Death (12:20–24)

²⁰He had long been very angry with the people of Tyre and Sidon, who now came to him in a body. After winning over Blastus, the king's chamberlain, they sued for peace because their country was supplied with food from the king's territory. ²¹On an appointed day, Herod, attired in royal robes, [and] seated on the rostrum, addressed them publicly. ²²The assembled crowd cried out, "This is the voice of a god, not of a man." ²³At once the angel of the Lord struck him down because he did not ascribe the honor to God, and he was eaten by worms and breathed his last. ²⁴But the word of God continued to spread and grow.

OT: 2 Macc 9:4–12; Ezek 28:2–10; Dan 4:27–30
NT: Acts 12:1

12:20–23   This story about Herod's anger with **the people of Tyre and Sidon** seems a digression from the story of Peter's rescue. Its function in Acts is to bring closure to the story of Herod by relating his later death and thus taking him off the stage. However, this story also has significant biblical and theological meaning.

The petition for **peace** by the people of those cities, because they were dependent on **food from the king's territory,** led to Herod's blasphemy and then to his death. The apparently desperate **crowd** resort to flattery in their efforts to win over Herod: **"This is the voice of a god, not of a man,"** as the Jewish historian Flavius Josephus similarly reports.[14] In response to these blasphemous accolades, Herod does **not ascribe the honor to God** (in contrast to what Paul and Barnabas will do in similar circumstances; 14:11–18). Because of this blasphemy, **the angel of the Lord struck him down** immediately, **and he was eaten by worms and breathed his last.** God cast down Herod from his arrogant acceptance of divine acclamation, as he had cast down the blasphemous king of Tyre from his pretensions to divine glory, when that king said "I am a god!" (Ezek 28:2–10). The death of this impious tyrant Herod, who had ordered the

14. *Antiquities of the Jews* 19.8.2, §345.

execution of James, is also portrayed in a fashion similar to the death of the earlier sacrilegious despot and persecutor, Antiochus IV Epiphanes (2 Macc 9:5–28).

After the tyrant was disposed of, **the word of God continued to spread and grow.** Once again Luke brings closure and transition from one focus to another—here from Peter in Acts 12 to Paul's ministries from Acts 13 onward—by repeating his thematic refrain about the spread of the word of God (Acts 6:7; 12:24; 19:20). The marvelous spread of the word of God is one of the main themes in Acts. The word has its own intrinsic dynamism and power to convince the hearts of those who hear it. In all circumstances and against

12:24

Death of Herod Agrippa I, according to Josephus

BIBLICAL BACKGROUND

Flavius Josephus, a Jewish historian from about the same time as Luke, gives his own description of Herod's death:

> Now, when [Herod] Agrippa had reigned three years over all Judea, he came to the city Caesarea, . . . and there he exhibited shows in honor of Caesar. . . . At this festival, a great multitude was gathered together of the principal persons of dignity throughout his province. On the second day of these shows, he put on a garment made wholly of silver, of a texture truly wonderful, and came into the theatre early in the morning, at which time the silver of his garment, being illuminated by the fresh reflection of the sun's rays upon it, shone out in a surprising manner, and was so resplendent as to spread awe over those who looked intently at him; and presently his flatterers cried out, one from one place, and another from another (though not for his good), that he was a god. And they added, "Be merciful to us; for although up to now we have reverenced you only as a man, from now on we will own you as superior to mortal nature." Upon this the king neither rebuked them nor rejected their impious flattery. But as he shortly afterward looked up, he saw an owl sitting on a certain rope over his head, and immediately understood that this bird was the messenger of ill tidings, as it had once been the messenger of good tidings to him; and he fell into the deepest sorrow. A severe pain arose in his belly, and began in a most violent manner. He therefore looked at his friends, and said, "I whom you call a god, am commanded presently to depart this life, while Providence thus reproves the lying words you just now said to me. And I, who was called immortal by you, am immediately to be hurried away by death." . . . And when he had been quite worn out by the pain in his belly for five days, he departed this life.[a]

a. *Antiquities of the Jews* 19.343–47, trans. William Whiston, in *The Works of Josephus: Complete and Unabridged* (Peabody, MA: Hendrickson, 1987, 1996), 523, translation modified.

all opposition, through various human instruments, the word of God spreads unstoppably from Jerusalem "to the ends of the earth" (1:8).

Reflection and Application (12:20–24)

Despite Luke's lightly humorous telling of these incidents, they retain a theological depth grounded in the biblical pattern of the all-powerful God bringing to naught the seemingly invincible efforts of tyrants against his people. Today, martyrdom for one's Christian faith is a real possibility in various places around the world. Even in democracies Christians find themselves subject to political and social pressures against the public exercise of our faith. When God wills, however, he can rescue us even from humanly impossible predicaments just as he freed Peter from prison. James and Peter are models of trusting in God's providence, whatever the personal outcome may be. No matter how bleak our situation may look, God is infinitely more powerful than any human or demonic adversary. With confidence in God, no one can stop us from witnessing to the message of God's love and the lordship of Jesus Christ.

The Mission of Barnabas and Saul

Acts 12:25–13:52

The beginning of the mission of Barnabas and Saul, as Luke recounts it, parallels the beginning of Jesus' mission. As Jesus was chosen by the Father and filled with the Holy Spirit for his public ministry (Luke 3:21–22), so also Barnabas and Saul are chosen by the Holy Spirit through prophecy and sent on their mission by the Spirit and the church (Acts 13:2–4). Jesus, filled with the Spirit, had his calling immediately tested by Satan, whom he decisively resisted (Luke 4:1–13). During their initial ministry in Cyprus, Barnabas and Paul, filled with the Spirit, are opposed by a magician named Bar-Jesus, whom Paul rebukes as a "son of the devil" (Acts 13:10). Jesus taught in synagogues and was acclaimed by the people, leading up to his first major sermon at Nazareth (Luke 4:15). The apostolic pair teach in synagogues on Cyprus (Acts 13:5), and Paul delivers his first major sermon at the invitation of the synagogue leaders in Antioch of Pisidia. Jesus' sermon at Nazareth was at first well received, but mixed reactions followed: "Isn't this the son of Joseph?" (Luke 4:22). When Jesus spoke of the prophets' ministry to Gentiles, his hearers reacted violently and expelled him from the city (4:24–29). Likewise, Paul's sermon in Pisidia is initially well received, but then he is rejected by jealous Jews when "almost the whole city gathered to hear the word of the Lord" (Acts 13:44–45). When Paul announces that he and Barnabas will "turn to the Gentiles" (13:46–47), they are evicted from the territory at Jewish instigation (13:50). After Jesus was expelled from the synagogue, "he passed through the midst of them and went away" (Luke 4:30). After their expulsion, Paul and Barnabas continued their journey and "went to Iconium" (Acts 13:51).

By calling attention to these parallels, Luke reinforces his theme that the Church's mission is a continuation and share in the mission of Jesus. Like the Servant of the Lord in Isaiah, both Jesus and Paul have been sent by God, not only to the chosen people but also to the Gentiles, "to the ends of the earth" (Isa 49:6). Even today, the Church continues Jesus' servant mission of bearing witness to all nations, just as Paul did.

Mission of Barnabas and Saul (12:25–13:3)

²⁵After Barnabas and Saul completed their relief mission, they returned to Jerusalem, taking with them John, who is called Mark.
¹Now there were in the church at Antioch prophets and teachers: Barnabas, Symeon who was called Niger, Lucius of Cyrene, Manaen who was a close friend of Herod the tetrarch, and Saul. ²While they were worshiping the Lord and fasting, the holy Spirit said, "Set apart for me Barnabas and Saul for the work to which I have called them." ³Then, completing their fasting and prayer, they laid hands on them and sent them off.

NT: Acts 11:30; 12:12; 13:9; 1 Cor 12:28
Catechism: the Holy Spirit and charisms, 798–800; Holy Orders and the laying on of hands, 1538, 1597; fasting and prayer, 1434, 1438, 1969, 2043
Lectionary: Acts 11:21b–26; 13:1–3: St. Barnabas

12:25 **Barnabas and Saul** were last mentioned as being sent on a **relief mission** to Jerusalem (Acts 11:30), which they have now **completed**. It is hard to envisage how, if they were already in Jerusalem, they could return **to Jerusalem**, especially since the next passage (Acts 13:1–3) finds them back in Antioch. A better translation of verse 25 would be, "After Paul and Barnabas completed their relief mission to Jerusalem, they returned [to Antioch]."[1] They bring as an assistant **John, who is called Mark**, last mentioned when Peter went to the church gathered at his mother's house in Jerusalem (Acts 12:12).

13:1 This new **church at Antioch** in Syria, north of Judea, has among its leadership **prophets and teachers**, two of the ecclesial ministries often listed by Paul.[2]

1. Luke Timothy Johnson, *The Acts of the Apostles*, Sacra pagina 5 (Collegeville, MN: Liturgical Press, 1992), 216. Joseph A. Fitzmyer, *The Acts of the Apostles*, Anchor Bible 31 (New York: Doubleday, 1998), 493, also argues for a similar translation and suggests taking the "phrase *eis Ierousalēm*" (Jerusalem) not with the verb "to return," but with the following participle "having completed," and using an alternate meaning of "in" for *eis*, thus: "having completed their ministry in Jerusalem," they returned to Antioch with John Mark.
2. Rom 12:6–8; 1 Cor 12:28; Eph 4:11; see also *Didache* 15.1: "Therefore appoint for yourselves bishops and deacons worthy of the Lord, . . . for they too carry out for you the ministry of the prophets

When speaking of the Jerusalem church, Luke mentions offices such as apostles, †presbyters, and the Seven (probably deacons, see 6:3);[3] but in describing church leadership in Antioch, he focuses more on ministries that arise from charisms: prophecy and teaching.

This list of five men is framed by **Barnabas** first and **Saul** last. **Symeon who was called Niger** has both a given name and an added name, like Joseph renamed Barnabas (4:36), "John, who is called Mark" (12:25), and "Saul, also known as Paul" (13:9). **Lucius of Cyrene** may have been among the Cyrenians who originally reached out to Greeks at Antioch (11:20). The mention of a connection between **Manaen** and **Herod the tetrarch** (as with "Joanna, the wife of Herod's steward Chuza," in Luke 8:3) might hint at the sources of Luke's information about Herod Antipas, tetrarch of Galilee during Jesus' ministry, and not to be confused with Herod Agrippa I, who persecuted James and Peter in Acts 12.[4]

The leaders' zeal to be under the constant guidance of the Holy Spirit is shown in their **worshiping the Lord and fasting**. The Greek verb for worship, *leitourgeō* (from which "liturgy" is derived), is often used in the †Septuagint for priestly ministry in the temple (see Exod 28:35; 1 Sam 2:11) and may imply liturgical celebration, including the Eucharist. Throughout Scripture, fasting is a way of humbling oneself before God (sometimes in repentance, as in 1 Sam 7:6), or asking for his help. For example, the Israelites fasted when they desperately needed God's guidance at a time of civil war (Judg 20:26).The elderly widow Anna worships God with prayer and fasting as she seeks the fulfillment of God's plan (Luke 2:36–38). The leaders of the Antioch church are fasting as they fervently seek God's will for their community and its mission. As they worship, **the holy Spirit** gives the leaders a prophetic directive: **"Set apart for me Barnabas and Saul."** Though the nature of **the work to which** the Spirit has **called them** is not explained here, the story that follows makes clear that it is an evangelizing mission.

13:2

After responding to this directive with further **fasting and prayer**, the leaders lay **hands** on Barnabas and Saul to express the community's setting them apart and commending them to God for this mission.[5] Barnabas and Paul are

13:3

---

and teachers." From *The Apostolic Fathers: Greek Texts and English Translations*, ed. and rev. Michael W. Holmes (Grand Rapids: Baker Books, 1999), 266–67.

    3. Acts mentions apostles in 2:42–43; 4:33–5:12; presbyters in 11:30. Both will act as leaders in Acts 15.

    4. Fitzmyer, *Acts*, 496–97.

    5. It is unlikely that this gesture refers to ordination here, since Barnabas was previously sent by the Jerusalem church to pastor the community in Antioch (Acts 11:22) and Paul attributes his apostolic authority to a direct commissioning by the risen Lord (Gal 1:1, 15–16).

The Laying On of Hands

BIBLICAL BACKGROUND

Laying on hands is a significant biblical gesture with a variety of purposes. In the Old Testament, fathers lay hands on their children for blessing (Gen 48:14); the people lay hands on the Levites to dedicate them to the Lord's service (Num 8:9–10); and Moses lays hands on Joshua to empower him as his successor (Num 27:18–23; Deut 34:9).

The laying on of hands can signify either an invocation of God's power or a consecration to him, although the two cannot always be distinguished. In the Gospels, parents ask Jesus to lay hands on their children and pray for them (Matt 19:13–15). Jesus lays hands on the sick, such as Jairus's daughter, to heal them (Mark 5:23, 41; see 6:5; 7:32). Later the apostles and other Christians do the same (Mark 16:18; Acts 9:12, 17). The apostles lay hands on new believers to confer the Holy Spirit (Acts 8:17–19; 19:6). Finally, laying on of hands is a way of ordaining those called to an office in the church (Acts 6:6; 14:23; 1 Tim 4:14).

then **sent** off on their missionary journey. At its completion, they will return and report its results to the community (14:26–27).

Reflection and Application (13:1–3)

The example of the church leaders of Antioch worshiping together and fasting to seek the guidance of the Holy Spirit remains relevant today. The Spirit still desires to guide and empower the mission activity of the Church, whether on a parish, diocesan, or international level. It is crucial that in our contemporary planning for our mission, we likewise seek and listen to the Spirit.

The following portion of Acts, describing Paul and Barnabas's mission, illustrates the confidence and blessing that comes when missionaries have a mandate from the Holy Spirit. Mission that proceeds from prayer and fasting, follows the Spirit's guidance, and enjoys the endorsement of the community will bear fruit.

Do we have as much zeal as the early Christians to seek God's guidance for mission through prayer and fasting? A common temptation in pastoral ministry is to first plan everything and then ask God's blessing on our plans, instead of letting the Holy Spirit take the lead. The testimony of Acts can build our confidence in what God is willing to do with those who open themselves to the Spirit's initiative and power.

First Mission Begins in Cyprus (13:4–12)

⁴So they, sent forth by the holy Spirit, went down to Seleucia and from there sailed to Cyprus. ⁵When they arrived in Salamis, they proclaimed the word of God in the Jewish synagogues. They had John also as their assistant. ⁶When they had traveled through the whole island as far as Paphos, they met a magician named Bar-Jesus who was a Jewish false prophet. ⁷He was with the proconsul Sergius Paulus, a man of intelligence, who had summoned Barnabas and Saul and wanted to hear the word of God. ⁸But Elymas the magician (for that is what his name means) opposed them in an attempt to turn the proconsul away from the faith. ⁹But Saul, also known as Paul, filled with the holy Spirit, looked intently at him ¹⁰and said, "You son of the devil, you enemy of all that is right, full of every sort of deceit and fraud. Will you not stop twisting the straight paths of [the] Lord? ¹¹Even now the hand of the Lord is upon you. You will be blind, and unable to see the sun for a time." Immediately a dark mist fell upon him, and he went about seeking people to lead him by the hand. ¹²When the proconsul saw what had happened, he came to believe, for he was astonished by the teaching about the Lord.

OT: Isa 6:9–10; 40:2–5
NT: Mark 1:27; Luke 3:4–6; 4:1–13; Acts 5:3; 19:13–20
Catechism: divination and magic, 2115–17; baptismal name, 2156, 2158; action through the Spirit, 1704, 1813; charisms, 799, 951

Verse 3 reported the church's human role in commissioning Barnabas and Saul for their journey. Now verse 4 focuses on the divine role: they are **sent forth by the holy Spirit**, who had singled them out for this mission through prophecy (v. 2).   **13:4–5**

Gun Powder Ma/Wikimedia Commons

Fig. 10. A small Roman sailing vessel, from a third-century sarcophagus.

205

Fig. 11. Paul's first missionary journey (Acts 13–14).

Several ancient cities were named **Seleucia** after the Hellenistic dynasty that had ruled the northern section of the Greek Empire left by Alexander the Great. This Seleucia was the Mediterranean port city for nearby Antioch. From here the missionary team sails to the island of **Cyprus**. They land at its eastern port of **Salamis** and immediately begin their ministry, proclaiming **the word of God in the Jewish synagogues**.

Barnabas and Saul had brought John Mark back from Jerusalem (12:25); now they include him **as their assistant** on mission. Although the community had commissioned only Barnabas and Saul, they added John Mark probably to help with practical details such as arrangements for travel and accommodation. Thus far there is no explicit mention of outreach to Gentiles, but only of preaching to Jews, and probably †God-fearing Gentiles, in the synagogues of Cyprus.

13:6   They travel without incident **through the whole island** until they arrive at the city of **Paphos**, on the west side of Cyprus. There they encounter their first conflict, with **Bar-Jesus**, meaning "son of Jesus." Jesus is the Greek form of Joshua (spelled the same as Joshua in Acts 7:45; Luke 3:29). Bar-Jesus was a Jew who is both a **magician** (*magos*), like the Samaritan Simon in Acts 8:9, and a **false prophet**. It may seem strange for a Jew to be a magician, which involved the occult, not entertainment by sleight of hand as today, since the Old Testament strictly forbids all forms of magic and dealings with the occult (Deut 18:10–12). But there is evidence that some first-century Jews dabbled in magic. This false prophet is contrasted with Paul and Barnabas, true prophets filled with and sent by the Spirit (vv. 1–4, 9).

13:7   Bar-Jesus is some kind of consultant for the Roman governor of the island, the **proconsul Sergius Paulus**, whom Luke calls **a man of intelligence**, perhaps because he **summoned Barnabas and Saul and wanted to hear the word of**

God. The proconsul's request leads to the missionaries' first proclamation of the gospel to a Gentile.

Luke now mentions another name for Bar-Jesus, **Elymas the magician**, claim-   **13:8** ing **that is what his name means**. Elymas does not appear in Greek dictionaries except as a proper name, so Luke's meaning is unclear. This false prophet opposes Barnabas and Saul's preaching **in an attempt to turn the proconsul away from the faith**. Here "faith" refers not to the act of believing but to the content of Christian faith. The word translated "turn away" means to pervert or mislead people (it is translated "twisting" in v. 10), as false prophets did (see Ezek 13:18, 22—the NABRE translates the Hebrew with "ensnare" and "discourage"). Elymas's opposition to Paul's mission parallels the role of Satan, who opposed Jesus from the beginning of his ministry (Luke 4:1–13).

The conflict between Bar-Jesus and Paul recalls biblical contests between   **13:9** true and false prophets, like those between Elijah and the prophets of Baal (1 Kings 18:19–40), and between Jeremiah and Hananiah (Jer 28). At issue is who is speaking God's truth and who is misleading the hearers. In each case, the conflict requires discernment about which spirit is inspiring each prophet. Paul's justified anger at Elymas's opposition to the word of God is similar to the anger of prophets and of God himself at his people's idolatry (Exod 32:8–10, 19; Num 25:3–8; Jer 7:13–20).

Luke uses the name "Paul" instead of "Saul" for the first time in verse 9, making the transition by simply writing **Saul, also known as Paul**. The most common explanation for the two names is that Saul is his Jewish name (after King Saul, the first Israelite king); Paul (meaning "little") is his Roman name. Paul is **filled with the holy Spirit**, as were some of the Old Testament judges, kings, and prophets (as in Judg 14:6, 19; 1 Sam 16:13; Ezek 11:5) and Peter and Stephen before they spoke or acted in power (Acts 2:4; 6:5; 7:55). Paul **looked intently** at the magician, an expression for giving penetrating attention.[6]

Paul's excoriation of Bar-Jesus—as **son of the devil, . . . enemy of all that is**   **13:10** **right, full of every sort of deceit and fraud**—is not merely rhetorical bluster. It is grounded in the biblical identification of the occult as the work of the devil.[7] This denunciation sharpens the contrast between Paul as a true prophet filled with the Holy Spirit and Bar-Jesus as a false prophet guided by Satan. As such he is more properly called "son of the devil" than "son of Jesus" (playing on his name Bar-Jesus). Paul accuses him of **twisting the straight paths of [the]**

---

6. See Luke 4:20; 22:56; Acts 1:10; 3:4, 12; 6:15; 7:55; 10:4; 11:6; 14:9; 23:1.
7. Peter, similarly, had accused the magician Simon: "I see that you are filled with bitter gall and are in the bonds of iniquity" (Acts 8:23).

Lord, in exact contrast to Isaiah's prophecy about making straight the paths of the Lord, fulfilled by John the Baptist (Isa 40:3–5 in Luke 3:4–6). The expression aptly describes Elymas's perverted opposition to God's plan by trying to hinder the proconsul from believing.

13:11   This incident is an ironic reminder of Saul's own blindness after he was confronted by the risen Jesus for persecuting Christians in Acts 9. As Saul himself had been temporarily blinded when Christ confronted him for trying to impede the gospel, so now his opponent is temporarily blinded for attempting to hinder the gospel. Willful unbelief leads to spiritual blindness, as in John 9:39 (see also Isa 6:10). The expression **the hand of the Lord is upon you** is a biblical expression for God's acting in power (as in Isa 40:2, Jerusalem "has received from the hand of the LORD double for all her sins"). The result of Paul's pronouncement, **"You will be blind . . . for a time,"** is instantaneous—**a dark mist** overtakes Elymas so that he goes about **seeking people to lead him by the hand**.

13:12   The sight of this miracle brings the proconsul to faith, ironically, from the darkness of paganism to the light of Christ. He is the highest-ranking Gentile to become a Christian in Acts. The **proconsul** is **astonished by the teaching about the Lord**, but his amazement appears occasioned especially by the miracle that accompanied that teaching. Works of power are a kind of teaching, as reflected in Mark 1:27: "What is this? A new teaching with authority. He commands even the unclean spirits and they obey him."

Paul's Arrival at Antioch in Pisidia (13:13–15)

[13]From Paphos, Paul and his companions set sail and arrived at Perga in Pamphylia. But John left them and returned to Jerusalem. [14]They continued on from Perga and reached Antioch in Pisidia. On the sabbath they entered [into] the synagogue and took their seats. [15]After the reading of the law and the prophets, the synagogue officials sent word to them, "My brothers, if one of you has a word of exhortation for the people, please speak."

NT: Acts 15:36–41; Luke 4:16–21; Heb 13:22

13:13–14   After the confrontation in **Paphos**, **Paul and his companions set sail** to the northwest for **Perga in Pamphylia**, a Roman province on the southern coast of Asia Minor, present-day Turkey, where they will begin their evangelizing on the mainland. **But John left them and returned to Jerusalem**. No reason is given for John Mark's departure, only this abrupt notice. Later it will become clear that Paul found Mark's abandonment of the mission unacceptable (Acts 15:36–41). For now Paul and Barnabas simply continue on from **Perga** to **Antioch in Pisidia**, farther north in Asia Minor, not to be confused with Antioch in Syria, where the missionaries began. **On the sabbath** they enter **the synagogue**, following Paul's standard practice of preaching first to Jews in synagogues (as at Iconium in Acts 14:1, at Corinth in 18:4, and at Ephesus in 18:19), then to Gentiles. Paul explicitly teaches the same pattern in Rom 1:16; see also 2:9–10.

The usual synagogue service included **the reading of the law and the prophets**. After this, **the synagogue officials** invite Paul and Barnabas to address the assembly. The officials apparently consider them important Jewish visitors, for they invite them to speak **a word of exhortation for the people**, that is, a scriptural homily. The Letter to the Hebrews describes itself as a "word of exhortation" (Heb 13:22 RSV), using the same Greek phrase. The synagogue officials surely do not expect what Paul will deliver: a radical reinterpretation of biblical history, culminating in an invitation to faith in Jesus.

13:15

Paul's Synagogue Sermon in Pisidian Antioch, Part I (13:16–25)

[16]So Paul got up, motioned with his hand, and said, "Fellow Israelites and you others who are God-fearing, listen. [17]The God of this people Israel chose our ancestors and exalted the people during their sojourn in the land of Egypt. With uplifted arm he led them out of it [18]and for about forty years he put up with them in the desert. [19]When he had destroyed seven nations in the land of Canaan, he gave them their land as an inheritance [20]at the end of about four hundred and fifty years. After these things he provided judges up to Samuel [the] prophet. [21]Then they asked for a king. God gave them Saul, son of Kish, a man from the tribe of Benjamin, for forty years. [22]Then he removed him and raised up David as their king; of him he testified, 'I have found David, son of Jesse, a man after my own heart; he will carry out my every wish.' [23]From this man's descendants God, according to his promise, has brought to Israel a savior, Jesus. [24]John heralded his coming by proclaiming a baptism of repentance to all the people of Israel; [25]and as John was completing his course, he would say, 'What do you suppose that I am? I am not he. Behold, one is coming after me; I am not worthy to unfasten the sandals of his feet.'"

OT: 1 Sam 8:12–16; 10:18–19; 1 Chron 17:7–14, 23–27; Ps 89:2–5
NT: Mark 1:4, 9; Luke 3:1–18

Catechism: prophecy of the Messiah, 522, 555, 702; God's promise to Israel, 60, 1611–12
Lectionary: Christmas Vigil Mass; Acts 13:22–26: Nativity of St. John the Baptist

This passage is the third retelling of Israel's history in a sermon in Acts, after Peter's in Acts 2 and Stephen's in Acts 7. Though these three summaries overlap in some details, each speech emphasizes different biblical figures and events, and each has distinct focuses. Taken together, they provide readers with Luke's overview of salvation history.

This sermon in Antioch in Pisidia, in Asia Minor, is the most complete statement of Paul's message to Jewish audiences. Paul's typical preaching to *Gentile* audiences will be presented in his sermons at Lystra (Acts 14:15–17) and Athens (Acts 17:22–31).

13:16   Paul begins his speech with the usual rhetorical flourishes: he rises, motions **with his hand** (beckoning for silence, as in Acts 12:17; 21:40), and charges them to **listen**. He addresses two groups among them, "**Fellow Israelites** and **you others** who are †**God-fearing**," that is, non-Jews who believe in the one God of Israel but have not become full converts. This sermon can be divided into three sections by Paul's three direct addresses to his listeners: "Fellow Israelites" (v. 16), "My brothers, children of the family of Abraham" (v. 26), and "my brothers" (v. 38).[8]

13:17–18   Paul identifies himself fully with his listeners. He refers to **the God of this people Israel**, as he had initially addressed them as "Fellow Israelites." That God **chose our ancestors** is a remarkably brief digest of God's call to Abraham and his descendants (Gen 12:1–8; 17:1–22). Paul omits the rest of Genesis to move immediately to Exodus.

God enabled the Israelites to flourish even in a foreign land: he **exalted the people** while they were living in **Egypt**. They multiplied so rapidly that the Egyptians became afraid of their power and enslaved them (Exod 1:7–14). **With uplifted arm** (a biblical expression for divine power), God **led them out of** Egypt. Focusing totally on God's action, Paul makes no mention of the human role of Moses in leading the people. Paul briefly summarizes the time between the exodus and the entrance into the promised land of Canaan: **for about forty years he put up with them in the desert** (Num 32:13). The negative tone of "put up with" epitomizes all the people's grumbling and rebellion against God and Moses, and God's forbearance, disciplining but not destroying them in the wilderness of Sinai.

8. See Fitzmyer, *Acts*, 507–8.

The conquest of the promised land is recapped in a single sentence, and **13:19–21** this event too is attributed entirely to the work of God. Omitting mention of Joshua, through whom God worked, Paul emphasizes that Israel's possession of their land is entirely God's gift. God first **destroyed seven nations in the land of Canaan.** Then **he gave them their land as an inheritance,** fulfilling his promises to Abraham, Isaac, and Jacob. As often in Acts, there is an approximate computation of time for these events: **at the end of about four hundred and fifty years.**[9]

Paul briefly touches on the period in which God **provided judges up to Samuel [the] prophet.** Samuel was the last of the judges—charismatic leaders whom God raised up from time to time to rescue Israel from oppression by their enemies. Paul's overview, like the book of Samuel, allows some ambivalence about the transition from judges to kings. God alone was Israel's king, yet he yielded to the people's request for a human king like those of other nations. Paul simply reports that at the time of Samuel, the people **asked for a king.** He passes over Samuel's objections to kingship (1 Sam 10:18–19) to state only that **God gave them Saul, son of Kish,** as their first king.[10]

God's removal of Saul and the following reign of **David** are also mentioned **13:22** only in passing. Paul emphasizes but one important attribute of David, which differs sharply from Saul's behavior: God **testified, "I have found David, son of Jesse, a man after my own heart; he will carry out my every wish."**[11] Unlike Saul, who disobeyed God's explicit orders (1 Sam 15:24; 1 Chron 10:13), David fulfilled God's will, despite the grave sins for which he repented (2 Sam 11–12 and 24). How much more perfectly, then, does David's sinless descendent, Jesus, fulfill God's will.

Passing over biblical history after the time of David, Paul cuts to the chase: **13:23** **"From this man's descendants God . . . has brought to Israel a savior, Jesus."** This took place according to God's **promise,** that is, the oracle to David that his dynasty and throne would last forever (2 Sam 7:12–16; 1 Chron 17:11–14, 23–27; Ps 89:2–5). This promise seemed to be broken when the last of the Davidic kings was deposed and exiled by the Babylonians, but Jews came to understand the oracle as promising a future messiah, a descendant of David

---

9. The 450 years refer to some 400 years in Egypt (Gen 15:13; Acts 7:6), forty years in the desert (Num 14:33–34), and about ten years for the conquest of Canaan. See Fitzmyer, *Acts*, 511.

10. Paul/Saul, who belonged to the tribe of Benjamin (see Rom 11:1; Phil 3:5), was probably named after King Saul, the most famous Benjamite.

11. See 1 Sam 13:14; 16:7. First and Second Kings hold up David as the standard by which the other kings of Judah are measured, particularly because of his avoidance of idolatry (see 1 Kings 15:3, 11; 2 Kings 14:3).

who would restore the kingdom to Israel (as the disciples expect in Acts 1:6). Paul proclaims the fulfillment of these promises in Jesus, Messiah and Savior.

13:24 Paul's Epistles do not mention John the Baptist, but here Paul's overview of salvation history puts significant emphasis on John's role, as do the Gospels. **John** is the final prophet who **heralded** Jesus' **coming** and thus provided the transition from the old covenant to the new. John prepared for the work of salvation that God was about to accomplish by making the people aware of their need for a savior: he proclaimed **a baptism of repentance to all the people of Israel** (see Luke 3:3).

13:25 Paul stresses the superiority of Jesus' identity and role over that of John. As the Baptist **was completing his course**, he explicitly denied a messianic role for himself: **"I am not he."** Between the lines is also a deeper self-effacement: the Greek phrase is, literally, "I am not" (*ouk eimi egō*), the negative of God's name as revealed in Exod 3:14 LXX, "I am" (*egō eimi*). Only God is I AM and Savior. As Catherine of Siena prayed, "I am she who is not, and you are He who is." John insists that he is only the Messiah's forerunner: **"One is coming after me."** So exalted is the coming one that John is **not worthy** to do the task of a slave for him: **to unfasten the sandals of his feet** (see Luke 3:16).

Paul's Sermon at Pisidian Antioch, Part II (13:26–43)

[26]**"My brothers, children of the family of Abraham, and those others among you who are God-fearing, to us this word of salvation has been sent.** [27]**The inhabitants of Jerusalem and their leaders failed to recognize him, and by condemning him they fulfilled the oracles of the prophets that are read sabbath after sabbath.** [28]**For even though they found no grounds for a death sentence, they asked Pilate to have him put to death,** [29]**and when they had accomplished all that was written about him, they took him down from the tree and placed him in a tomb.** [30]**But God raised him from the dead,** [31]**and for many days he appeared to those who had come up with him from Galilee to Jerusalem. These are [now] his witnesses before the people.** [32]**We ourselves are proclaiming this good news to you that what God promised our ancestors** [33]**he has brought to fulfillment for us, [their] children, by raising up Jesus, as it is written in the second psalm, 'You are my son; this day I have begotten you.'** [34]**And that he raised him from the dead never to return to corruption he declared in this way, 'I shall give you the benefits assured to David.'** [35]**That is why he also says in another psalm, 'You will not suffer your holy one to see corruption.'** [36]**Now David, after he had served the will of God in his lifetime, fell asleep,**

was gathered to his ancestors, and did see corruption. ³⁷But the one whom God raised up did not see corruption. ³⁸You must know, my brothers, that through him forgiveness of sins is being proclaimed to you, [and] in regard to everything from which you could not be justified under the law of Moses, ³⁹in him every believer is justified. ⁴⁰Be careful, then, that what was said in the prophets not come about:

⁴¹"Look on, you scoffers,
be amazed and disappear.
For I am doing a work in your days,
a work that you will never believe even if someone tells you.'"

⁴²As they were leaving, they invited them to speak on these subjects the following sabbath. ⁴³After the congregation had dispersed, many Jews and worshipers who were converts to Judaism followed Paul and Barnabas, who spoke to them and urged them to remain faithful to the grace of God.

OT: Ps 16:10; Hab 1:5; Isa 55:3
NT: Luke 4:16–21; 19:44; Acts 2
Catechism: apostles as witnesses to the resurrection, 642, 664, 858, 1124
Lectionary: Acts 13:14, 43–52: Fourth Sunday of Easter (Year C); Acts 13:22–26: Nativity of St. John the Baptist; Acts 13:32–39: Anointing of the Sick during Easter (optional)

Paul begins the second part of his sermon with another direct address to his listeners, as in verse 16: "**My brothers, children of the family of Abraham** [fellow Jews] **and those others among you** who are †**God-fearing** [non-Jews who believe in God]." In proclaiming that **to us this word of salvation has been sent**, Paul includes his God-fearing listeners with the Jews, the first recipients of the fulfillment of God's promises. Peter had said at Pentecost, "The promise is made to you and to your children and to all those far off, whomever the Lord our God will call" (2:39). Those far off include both †Diaspora Jews and Gentiles whom God would call. **13:26**

The failure of **the inhabitants of Jerusalem and their leaders to recognize** Jesus as Messiah is a common theme in Luke. Jesus wept over Jerusalem because "you did not recognize the time of your visitation" (Luke 19:44). The ignorance of those who condemned Jesus enables the Scriptures to be fulfilled and provides Jesus with a basis for interceding for their forgiveness from the cross: "Father, forgive them, they know not what they do" (Luke 23:34). Peter's repentant Jewish listeners at Pentecost received this forgiveness (Acts 2:37–41). **13:27**

By **condemning him they fulfilled the oracles of the prophets that are read sabbath after sabbath.** The irony of their fulfilling messianic prophecies by condemning the Messiah resembles Greek dramatic irony, which would have been familiar to many of Luke's Hellenistic readers. In dramatic irony, the actions of characters unknowingly bring about the opposite of what they desire, as in the tragedy *Oedipus Rex* by Sophocles. King Oedipus's flight from home to avoid the prophecy that he would kill his father and marry his mother results in his fulfilling the prediction by unwittingly doing both. Here God uses the very execution of Jesus to bring about his divine plan of salvation through him.

13:28–30   Paul emphasizes the injustice of Jesus' condemnation: **"Even though they found no grounds for a death sentence, they asked Pilate to have him put to death."** In God's plan, this execution of the innocent Jesus ironically brought to fulfillment **all that was written about him** in the Scriptures. The use of **tree** to refer to the cross (Acts 5:30; 10:39) recalls the curse in Deuteronomy: "Anyone hung on a tree is under God's curse" (Deut 21:23 NRSV). As Paul explains in Galatians, Christ ransomed us from the curse of the law by "becoming a curse for us" (Gal 3:13). God's reversal of wicked human deeds is most evident in what follows: they **placed him in a tomb. But God raised him from the dead**. This divine reversal of human tyranny recalls Mary's song: "He has thrown down the rulers from their thrones but lifted up the lowly" (Luke 1:52).

13:31   Because Paul knew Jesus only after his resurrection, he does not claim to be one of the original eyewitnesses who could testify that the risen Jesus was the same as the earthly Jesus. Jesus **appeared** to those disciples **who had come up with him from Galilee to Jerusalem** over a period of **many days** (Acts 1:3 uses the round number forty days). In Acts 1, the apostle Peter specified the requirement for this witness: "It is necessary that one of the men who accompanied us the whole time the Lord Jesus came and went among us, beginning from the baptism of John until the day on which he was taken up from us, become with us a witness to his resurrection" (1:21–22).

The original group of Galilean disciples are Jesus' **witnesses before the people** because they can vouch for the continuity between what he did and taught during his public ministry and what his followers have been saying about him since his resurrection. In the Church's teaching to this day, belief in what Jesus did and said, and in his resurrection from the dead, depends on the testimony especially of the twelve apostles.[12]

13:32–33   Paul includes himself among a second group of witnesses who are extending the testimony to Jesus throughout the world. **We ourselves**, in continuity with Jesus' early Galilean followers, **are proclaiming this good news to you**, the listeners in Antioch of Pisidia. This good news is that **what God promised our ancestors**, literally, "fathers," he has accomplished **for us**, their **children, by**

12. Catechism 642, 664, 858, 1124.

raising up Jesus. Jesus' resurrection fulfilled the promise to David mentioned in verse 23 above, that God would raise up a savior for Israel from David's descendants. Because the risen Jesus is an eternally living son of David whose reign will never end, he unconditionally fulfills the promise that David's throne will stand forever (2 Sam 7:13). Jesus' resurrection is the center and key to God's plan of salvation.

Jesus' resurrection also fulfills God's oracle in **the second psalm, "You are my son; this day I have begotten you."** That psalm originally referred to the new king in the lineage of David who was declared God's adopted son at the moment of his enthronement. As God's adopted son, the newly enthroned king was to rule God's people with God's authority and under his direction. Now this royal psalm is fulfilled in Jesus the Messiah, risen and enthroned in heaven so as to share God's dominion over the whole world. Psalm 2 is a reminder that Jesus' unending reign makes salvation available to all people in all times.

Paul alludes to God's promise to his people through Isaiah—**"I shall give you the benefits assured to David"** (Isa 55:3)—and connects it with David's expression of trust in Ps 16:10 (in its Greek translation): **"You will not suffer your holy one to see corruption."** This implies that Ps 16 is in some way a promise not only for David but also for all God's people. **13:34–35**

David **served the will of God in his lifetime**, literally, "in his own generation," but he **did see corruption**: he died and remains dead. Therefore Ps 16 must be a prophecy that looks beyond David to his descendant, Jesus, who **did not see corruption** because **God raised** him **up**. Jesus "served the will of God" in a preeminent way. Now, risen and eternally living, Jesus is able to serve the will of God by saving and ruling not only his own generation but also all people until the end of time. Peter's Pentecost speech made a similar argument based on Ps 16 (Acts 2:24–32, 36). **13:36–37**

The conclusion to the speech, signaled by the direct address, **"You must know, my brothers,"** is that through this obedient son of David and servant of God, Jesus, **forgiveness of sins is being proclaimed to you**. God's promise to David is fulfilled in the resurrection of Jesus and the forgiveness of sins that is now available **through him**. That forgiveness of sins is made possible by Jesus' death and resurrection is at the heart of the preaching of the gospel, as in Peter's speech in Acts 5:30–31: God raised Jesus and exalted him "at his right hand as leader and savior to grant Israel repentance and forgiveness of sins." **13:38–40**

Whereas Paul's Letters often speak of "justification," Luke usually prefers to speak of "forgiveness of sins," often related to repentance.[13] Here the two

---

13. Luke 3:3; 24:47; Acts 10:43; 26:18.

God's Covenant with David, "A Man after My Own Heart"

BIBLICAL BACKGROUND

Paul contrasts King David, whom God called "a man after my own heart" who "will carry out my every wish," with King Saul, who disobeyed God and was deposed from kingship (Acts 13:22). God's promise of a never-ending reign for David's offspring was first announced in Nathan's oracle to David in 2 Sam 7:12–16. Later biblical tradition interpreted this promise as God's covenant with David (Ps 89:2–5; 1 Chron 17:7–27). This promise became the basis for Jewish expectation of a Davidic Messiah.

In Nathan's oracle, God promised David, "I will raise up your offspring after you, sprung from your loins, and I will establish his kingdom. . . . I will establish his royal throne firm forever" (2 Sam 7:12–13). God further promised, "I will be a father to him, and he shall be a son to me" (7:14). As God's son, the descendant of David would exercise authority in God's name over the people. This promise was partially fulfilled in David's son Solomon, who became king and built God's temple in Jerusalem.

Obedience is pivotal for the covenant with David. Nathan's oracle states that if David's son does wrong, God will chastise him, though he will not totally remove him from his presence as he had removed Saul (2 Sam 7:14–15). Still, the oracle culminates with God's promise: "Your house and your kingdom are firm forever before me; your throne shall be firmly established forever" (7:16). The later reflections on this promise in 1 Chron 17 and Ps 89 do not mention that it is conditional on obedience. It is not surprising, therefore, that Jewish tradition came to consider the Davidic covenant to be unconditional.

It was a traumatic shock for Israel when a series of evil Davidic kings was finally followed by the people's exile to Babylon and the apparent end of David's dynasty. But later tradition came to understand God's covenant with David as promising an anointed descendant of his, a messiah, who would establish an everlasting Davidic kingdom. This expectation looked to a new age, the final times, when God would bring the present created order to an end and replace it with a new and perfect creation, as hinted in Isa 65:17–25.

Luke, however, does not lose sight of the key provision in the Davidic covenant: the son of David must be obedient to God his Father. In his Acts 13 sermon at Antioch in Pisidia, Paul sees God's promise to David and Isaiah's prophecies of an obedient Servant of the Lord[a] as converging in Jesus. Jesus is both son of David and completely obedient Servant of the Lord.

a. See Isa 42:1–4; 49:1–7; 50:4–11; 52:13–53:12.

notions are linked: forgiveness pertains to **everything from which you could not be justified under the law of Moses**. What observance of the law could not accomplish, Christ accomplished: **in him every believer is justified**, that is, brought into right relationship with God. This is the closest Luke-Acts comes to the language of Paul's Letters, which insist that justification comes not by doing works of the law but through faith in Jesus (Rom 3:20–22, 28; Gal 2:16).[14] Paul concludes his summary of the biblical history of salvation and ends with a caution for his audience to heed this message, so that the warnings of **the prophets not come about** against them.

Paul cites the prophet Habakkuk's warning that God would bring a tyrannical   **13:41** enemy nation, Chaldea (Babylon), against Judah (Hab 1:5–11). He quotes the †Septuagint paraphrase rather than the Hebrew, which makes it easier to apply Habakkuk's warning to his own listeners:[15] **Look on, you scoffers** who disbelieve the word proclaimed to you, and face the threat that you will **be amazed and disappear**. The warning no longer concerns a foreign threat against Israel in the time of Habakkuk. It admonishes Paul's current listeners not to scoff at his message, lest they perish. The listeners must believe that God is **doing a work in your days**, namely, forgiveness of sins and justification through the risen son of David, Jesus. Habakkuk's prophecy concludes with a warning that this is **a work that you will never believe even if someone tells you**, as Paul is now doing. The ancient Israelites ignored Habakkuk's words, to their own destruction; Paul cautions his listeners not to do likewise.

The reaction to Paul's speech in the synagogue is positive enough that the   **13:42–43** listeners invite Paul and Barnabas to **speak** again **the following sabbath**. After **the congregation** disperses, many of them, including both **Jews** and †**worshipers who were converts to Judaism**, remain and follow **Paul and Barnabas**. The verb "follow" (*akoloutheō*) is the same as that used in the Gospels for those who became Jesus' disciples (Luke 5:11, 28; see also 9:23). Paul and Barnabas urge these incipient believers **to remain faithful to the grace of God**, that is, to the free offer of salvation they have just heard (see Acts 20:24).

Address to the Gentiles (13:44–52)

⁴⁴**On the following sabbath almost the whole city gathered to hear the word of the Lord. ⁴⁵When the Jews saw the crowds, they were filled with**

---

14. See also Acts 10:43; 26:18.

15. The Hebrew of Hab 1:5 says, "Look over the nations and see! Be utterly amazed!" The †Septuagint reads, "Behold, you scoffers, and look, and be greatly amazed, and vanish."

jealousy and with violent abuse contradicted what Paul said. ⁴⁶Both Paul and Barnabas spoke out boldly and said, "It was necessary that the word of God be spoken to you first, but since you reject it and condemn yourselves as unworthy of eternal life, we now turn to the Gentiles. ⁴⁷For so the Lord has commanded us, 'I have made you a light to the Gentiles, that you may be an instrument of salvation to the ends of the earth.'"

⁴⁸The Gentiles were delighted when they heard this and glorified the word of the Lord. All who were destined for eternal life came to believe, ⁴⁹and the word of the Lord continued to spread through the whole region. ⁵⁰The Jews, however, incited the women of prominence who were worshipers and the leading men of the city, stirred up a persecution against Paul and Barnabas, and expelled them from their territory. ⁵¹So they shook the dust from their feet in protest against them and went to Iconium. ⁵²The disciples were filled with joy and the holy Spirit.

OT: Isa 49:6
NT: Luke 2:30–32; 9:5; Acts 1:1; 28:28, 31; Rom 1:16; 2:9–10
Catechism: joy, 736, 1832, 2015
Lectionary: Acts 13:14, 43–52: Fourth Sunday of Easter (Year C); Acts 13:46–49: Saints Cyril and Methodius

13:44–45   The excitement over Paul's speech is such that on **the following sabbath**, when he returns to the synagogue, **almost the whole city** gathers, which naturally would include large numbers of Gentiles. People come **to hear the word of the Lord**—the good news about Jesus' death, resurrection, and exaltation as Lord of all. At the sight of these huge **crowds, Jews** from the synagogue are **filled with jealousy** at the disciples' success, a motive that Luke sometimes identifies as causing persecution of Jesus' followers (Acts 5:17–18; 17:5; see also 7:9). These jealous Jews contradict Paul's message **with violent abuse**. The Greek word for their violent abuse is *blasphēmeō*, to revile or defame, or in reference to something divine, to blaspheme. Luke hints that their manner of speaking against the gospel is tantamount to blasphemy.

13:46   The response of **Paul and Barnabas** is to speak out **boldly**, openly and fearlessly—as Paul will continue to do until the very last sentence of Acts (28:31): **"It was necessary that the word of God be spoken to you first."** The gospel is addressed to Jews first because they are the chosen people to whom God's promises were first made (see Rom 9:4–5). Paul and Barnabas will now turn to the Gentiles because their Jewish listeners **reject** the message and thereby **condemn** themselves **as unworthy** of the **eternal life** that is being offered. Paul understands such rejection of the gospel as an exercise of human freedom.

Eternal life is what is at stake in people's response to the proclamation about Jesus, both then and now.[16]

Paul's turn to the Gentiles does not imply the abandonment of his mission to Jews (see Acts 9:15). Rather, it applies only to the locale in which he is preaching. In the next episode he will again begin in the synagogue (14:1). Throughout Acts, Paul continues his pattern of preaching the gospel first to Jews, then to Gentiles because of Jewish rejection (see 18:6; 28:28).

The reason for proclaiming the good news to the Gentiles is quite fun-   **13:47**
damental: **"For so the Lord has commanded us."** That command is from a prophecy in Isaiah: **"I have made you a light to the Gentiles, that you may be an instrument of salvation to the ends of the earth"** (Isa 49:6). Already in Isaiah it is clear that Israel has a universal mission far beyond its own borders: to enlighten the Gentiles by spreading knowledge of the one true God over the whole earth. In Luke's Gospel, the prophet Simeon applied this universal mission to Jesus: he is God's "salvation . . . in sight of all the peoples, a light for revelation to the Gentiles, and glory for your people Israel" (Luke 2:30–32). Now Paul and Barnabas claim the same mission for themselves. Once again, the Spirit-filled ministry of Jesus' disciples is a continuation of what "Jesus began to do and teach" during his public ministry (Acts 1:1, literal translation).

The Gospel itself did not show how Simeon's prophecy was fulfilled or how Jesus' mission actually affected Gentiles beyond Israel. It is in Acts that Jesus' mission to Gentiles is accomplished in what he does and teaches through his Spirit-filled disciples.

The response of the **Gentiles** on hearing this is most enthusiastic. They are   **13:48–49**
delighted and glorify **the word of the Lord**. In contrast to some Jews who had just rejected the word of God and therefore showed themselves unworthy of eternal life (v. 46), the joy and praise of these Gentiles are signs that they belong among those who are **destined for eternal life**.

The Greek for "destined" literally means appointed or assigned, as in military ranks. The passive form here is the †divine passive, implying that God is the acting subject: *God* has appointed these Gentiles for eternal life. This does not contradict free will, for we have just seen others who rejected the message and thus showed themselves unworthy of the eternal life offered to them. These Gentiles, in contrast, **came to believe**, or simply "believed." Luke shows the result with another summary of progress of the gospel: the **word of the Lord,**

---

16. Eternal life is repeatedly mentioned in Luke and Acts, although with less emphasis than in the Gospel of John. In Luke's Gospel the term refers to unending life after death (Luke 10:25; 18:18); in Acts it is mentioned only here in 13:46 and 48.

the good news about Christ (as in Acts 6:7; 12:24; 19:20), continues **to spread through the whole region**.

13:50   In reaction against Paul and Barnabas's missionary success, the **Jews . . . incited the women of prominence . . . and leading men of the city**. Through these influential people, they **stirred up a persecution**, the culmination of which was that Paul and Barnabas were **expelled . . . from their territory**.

13:51   Paul and Barnabas are reliving the same pattern established in response to Jesus' proclamation at Nazareth (Luke 4): an initial positive reaction followed by a mixed response and finally by violent expulsion. The missionaries here follow Jesus' instructions to his disciples for occasions when their preaching is rejected: **they shook the dust from their feet** (Luke 9:5; 10:11) as a gesture of **protest against them**. Undeterred by rejection in one city, they simply proceed onward to the next, **to Iconium**.

13:52   Meanwhile, back in Antioch of Pisidia, the new **disciples** are **filled with joy and the holy Spirit**, signs of genuine conversion and Christian community, undiscouraged by the expulsion of Paul and Barnabas from their city.

Reflection and Application (13:44–52)

As Paul and Barnabas begin their mission, they follow in the footsteps of their Lord, Jesus, and embark on the same mission that God had already revealed to the prophet Isaiah some half a millennium before Christ. Like the Servant of the Lord in Isaiah, and like Jesus himself, Paul and Barnabas are commissioned not only "to raise up the tribes of Jacob, and restore the survivors of Israel," but also to be "a light to the nations, that my salvation may reach to the ends of the earth" (Isa 49:6). Already in the Old Testament, it is clear that God's saving plan is not just for the chosen people but also for the reconciliation and salvation of the whole human race. The New Testament reveals how this universal saving plan is fulfilled as the Church carries out its mission to the world.

Nor does God's plan end with the ministry of the apostles. Like Jesus' early followers, we Christians today are called to witness to Christ wherever we are. God calls us to be his servants both to his chosen people, which now includes the Church, and also to people of all nations, ethnic groups, religions, and cultures, no matter how "primitive" or "advanced." As Peter proclaims, the mediator and savior whom God chose for the whole human race is his Son Jesus: "There is no salvation through anyone else, nor is there any other name under heaven given to the human race by which we are to be saved" (Acts 4:12).

Just as Jesus himself and his first witnesses met opposition, persecution, and even death, so his witnesses today are promised no more than similar opposition, perhaps even to death. As God could use the suffering of Jesus (Luke 22–23; see Isa 52:13–53:12) to reconcile people to himself, he can also use any persecution we undergo for our witness to Jesus to help in the salvation even of our very persecutors. Like Jesus and his follower Stephen, we too may be called upon to pray, "Father, forgive them, they know not what they do."

Paul in Asia Minor:
Iconium, Lystra, Derbe

Acts 14:1–28

Paul and Barnabas extend their missionary journey farther in Asia Minor, where they continue to meet with success with many Gentiles and some Jews and hostility from those Gentiles and Jews who disbelieve their message, with some of the latter pursuing them from one city to another. Back in Acts 8, persecution of Jesus' disciples in Jerusalem had prompted some, like Philip, to move beyond Jerusalem into Samaria and other areas. Here Jewish persecution in the †Diaspora likewise impels the Christian mission onward to new cities. The irony about this pattern is that in the first instance, Paul was the persecutor; now he and his fellow missionary Barnabas are the ones persecuted.

An important new development in this journey is their encounter with rustic audiences, whom Greeks and Romans tended to refer to as "barbarian" (see Col 3:11). This encounter underlines the difficulties of the Church's outreach in less-developed cultures, such as in Lystra, where the people try to worship Paul and Barnabas. The pagan misunderstandings that the apostles encounter are early lessons in the need for cultural awareness in presenting the gospel message.

Paul and Barnabas's return and report to the church that commissioned them provides a model for relationships between missionaries and the churches that send them forth. Paul was no solitary maverick; he worked as a member of a missionary team and returned and reported regularly to his home church in Antioch of Syria.

Paul and Barnabas at Iconium (14:1–7)

---

¹In Iconium they entered the Jewish synagogue together and spoke in such a way that a great number of both Jews and Greeks came to believe, ²although the disbelieving Jews stirred up and poisoned the minds of the Gentiles against the brothers. ³So they stayed for a considerable period, speaking out boldly for the Lord, who confirmed the word about his grace by granting signs and wonders to occur through their hands. ⁴The people of the city were divided: some were with the Jews; others, with the apostles. ⁵When there was an attempt by both the Gentiles and the Jews, together with their leaders, to attack and stone them, ⁶they realized it and fled to the Lycaonian cities of Lystra and Derbe and to the surrounding countryside, ⁷where they continued to proclaim the good news.

NT: Acts 4:30; 13:46; 14:14; 20:24
Lectionary: Acts 14:21–27: Fifth Sunday of Easter (Year C)

Paul and Barnabas continue their established missionary pattern at **Iconium**, a city in Asia Minor between Antioch of Pisidia, which they just left, and Lystra. Paul later writes that he endured great persecutions in all three of these cities (2 Tim 3:11). In Iconium they enter **the Jewish synagogue together**.[1] Their presentation is so persuasive **that a great number of both Jews and Greeks** come to believe in Christ. Here "Greeks" seems to be synonymous with "Gentiles" (as in Rom 1:16; Gal 3:28).

14:1

As previously at Antioch in Pisidia, **Jews** who were not persuaded **stirred up and poisoned the minds of the Gentiles against the brothers**. In evangelistic speeches, like Paul's at Antioch in Pisidia, Jews customarily are the ones addressed as "brothers." Here Luke calls Christians "the brothers" (including both men and women). The kinship bond of the Jewish people, based on ethnic ties, has now been extended to include all those who enter the family of God through faith in Jesus (see Luke 8:21).

14:2

This time Paul and Barnabas remain and face off against their opposition rather than moving on to the next town. They stay **for a considerable period, speaking out boldly for the Lord**. "Boldly" is Luke's favored expression for the courageous, confident preaching of the gospel. They refuse to be intimidated by negative counterpropaganda but argue vigorously for Jesus as Lord.

14:3

---

1. The Greek *kata to auto* can mean either "together" or "in the same way"; NRSV has "The same thing occurred" and NIV "as usual." The context seems to favor "in the same way" to indicate that they did not change their standard approach of entering synagogues first in each location.

The Lord in turn **confirmed**, or bore witness to, **the word about his grace**. The gospel is the word about God's "grace," as in Acts 20:24, because it concerns the *free gift* of salvation that God gives to those who believe in Jesus (see Rom 3:24; 5:15). The risen Jesus corroborates the truth of the gospel **by granting signs and wonders to occur through their hands** (see Mark 16:20; Heb 2:4). Such signs demonstrate that Jesus is indeed alive, that he has compassion on those who suffer, and that he is truly victorious over sin and its consequences.

Earlier the disciples prayed that God would do signs and wonders "through the name of your holy servant Jesus" (Acts 4:30), but here Jesus himself takes the initiative, granting on his own divine authority that the disciples work such miracles.

14:4

As is often the result of Christian witness in Acts, **people of the city** of Iconium are **divided** between those who side with **Jews** who opposed them and **others** (both Jews and Gentiles) who accept the message of **the apostles**. This is the first time Luke refers to Paul and Barnabas—or anyone other than the Twelve—as apostles, "those who are sent" (see also v. 14). Luke usually equates "apostles" with the original Twelve (Luke 6:13). But like the Twelve, Paul and Barnabas have been sent by the risen Lord.

14:5–7

The people's antagonism leads to **an attempt** to **attack and stone** Paul and Barnabas. When they become aware of this attempt, the missionaries flee **to the Lycaonian cities of Lystra and Derbe and to the surrounding countryside**. They are now in what Greeks considered "barbarian" territory, where they continue to **proclaim the good news**. Persecution does not stop the preaching of the gospel, but simply propels it onward to a new audience.

Paul and Barnabas at Lystra (14:8–20)

---

[8]At Lystra there was a crippled man, lame from birth, who had never walked. [9]He listened to Paul speaking, who looked intently at him, saw that he had the faith to be healed, [10]and called out in a loud voice, "Stand up straight on your feet." He jumped up and began to walk about. [11]When the crowds saw what Paul had done, they cried out in Lycaonian, "The gods have come down to us in human form." [12]They called Barnabas "Zeus" and Paul "Hermes," because he was the chief speaker. [13]And the priest of Zeus, whose temple was at the entrance to the city, brought oxen and garlands to the gates, for he together with the people intended to offer sacrifice.

[14]The apostles Barnabas and Paul tore their garments when they heard this and rushed out into the crowd, shouting, [15]"Men, why are you doing

this? We are of the same nature as you, human beings. We proclaim to you good news that you should turn from these idols to the living God, 'who made heaven and earth and sea and all that is in them.' ¹⁶In past generations he allowed all Gentiles to go their own ways; ¹⁷yet, in bestowing his goodness, he did not leave himself without witness, for he gave you rains from heaven and fruitful seasons, and filled you with nourishment and gladness for your hearts." ¹⁸Even with these words, they scarcely restrained the crowds from offering sacrifice to them.

¹⁹However, some Jews from Antioch and Iconium arrived and won over the crowds. They stoned Paul and dragged him out of the city, supposing that he was dead. ²⁰But when the disciples gathered around him, he got up and entered the city. On the following day he left with Barnabas for Derbe.

OT: Ps 104:14–15; Isa 44:9–20
NT: Luke 23:34; Acts 2:37–39; 3:1–13; 17:30–31; 2 Cor 11:25
Catechism: healing of sick, 1506–13; proclaiming Christ to all nations, 74, 751; turning from idols, 2097, 2112–14; natural revelation, 32, 1147

At Lystra in Lycaonia, Paul heals a **crippled man**. Readers may note similarities between this healing and Peter's healing of the lame man in Acts 3:1–13. Both healed men were crippled **from birth** and had **never walked**. Both Peter and Paul **looked intently** at the lame man. Both apostles offered a healing that the man did not expect (as Jesus had done in John 5). In addition, Paul sees that he has **the faith to be healed**. As he preaches, Paul observes the work of the Spirit in his listener and recognizes that he is welcoming the truth of the good news and is thus disposed to receive healing. As Jesus had seen the Canaanite woman's faith and healed her daughter (Matt 15:28), so Paul heals this Lycaonian man after seeing his faith.

14:8–9

Both Peter and Paul commanded the lame man to get up. Though Peter made his command "in the name of Jesus Christ the Nazorean," Paul simply orders the man: **"Stand up straight on your feet."** Paul calls out **in a loud voice**, perhaps with a tone of authority to increase the man's faith. Like the Jew in Acts 3:8, this Gentile man is instantaneously healed, jumps up, and begins to walk.

14:10

Both sets of onlookers who witnessed the healings misunderstood them and had to be corrected. Peter chided the Jerusalem Jews, "Why are you amazed at this, and why do you look so intently at us as if we had made him walk by our own power or piety?" (Acts 3:12). It was God who healed the man through faith in Jesus' name.

14:11–12

The pagan **crowds** of Lystra are even more misguided about the healing done by **Paul**. They cry out in **Lycaonian**, their native tongue, **"The gods have come down to us in human form."** Because Paul is **the chief speaker**, they call him

Fig. 12. Relief of
a garlanded bull,
from the temple
of Augustus in
Antioch of Pisidia
(see Acts 14:13).

Hermes, the messenger god, and **Barnabas** they dub **Zeus**, the chief god. This odd reaction may be based on a legend recounted by the poet Ovid, in which Zeus and Hermes visited this region in disguise, seeking hospitality but finding it only in one devout elderly couple, whom they later richly rewarded.

14:13   Whatever the reason for the crowd's conclusion, **the priest of Zeus, whose temple was at the entrance to the city**, wastes no time. Immediately he prepares **to offer sacrifice** to Paul and Barnabas, bringing **oxen and garlands to the gates**. Whether these were gates to the city or to the temple of Zeus is not clear, but Luke may be recalling another similarity to Peter's healing of the lame man at a gate of the temple.

14:14   **Barnabas and Paul** vehemently reject not only the Lycaonians' assumption that they are gods, but along with it their entire pagan belief system. Peter had to correct Jewish misunderstandings after the healing of the lame man (3:12), but Barnabas and Paul have a bigger problem on their hands. Because of the language barrier, they may not immediately realize what is going on. Once they become aware of the egregious error, they tear **their garments**, a sign of extreme distress in response to evil tidings (Gen 37:34; 2 Sam 13:31), blasphemy (Mark 14:63–64), or other serious sin. The apostles' reaction to this blasphemy is quite agitated: they rush out **into the crowd**, **shouting** to get the people's attention and interrupt their actions.

14:15   Paul and Barnabas upbraid the people for their foolish behavior: **"Men, why are you doing this? We are of the same nature as you, human beings"** (see Peter's similar correction in Acts 10:25–26). The miraculous healing they just witnessed has a totally different explanation: it confirms the **good news that you should turn from these idols to the living God**. The missionaries challenge their listeners to abandon their pagan beliefs and accept the truth that there is one **creator** God. They appeal to the testimony of creation, God's revelation of himself in nature, which prepares for the supernatural revelation of the gospel (see Rom 1:19–23).

14:16   A common theme in Luke-Acts is that God's saving plan allows for a time of divine tolerance of religious errors. For example, Jesus prayed on the cross, "Father, forgive them, they know not what they do" (Luke 23:34). Paul makes

Mocking Pagan Behavior

BIBLICAL BACKGROUND

There is some obvious humor in Luke's portrayal of the Lycaonians' bizarre behavior. From a biblical perspective, it appears ridiculous that pagans think Barnabas and Paul are gods in human form, and name one Zeus and the other Hermes because he did most of the talking. The picture of the priest of Zeus bringing garlands and preparing to sacrifice to human beings is equally ludicrous. But the humor has both a biblical precedent and a serious theological purpose.

Elijah taunts the prophets of Baal (1 Kings 18:27). The book of Isaiah repeatedly mocks the folly of idolatrous beliefs and practices in contrast to faith in the living God. A classic example of anti-idol mockery that has a serious theological message is Isa 44:9–20. The idol maker goes into the forest and finds a piece of wood. The absurdity of his behavior becomes apparent in what he does with it:

> Half of it he burns in the fire,
> and on its embers he roasts meat;
> he eats the roast and is full.
> He warms himself and says, "Ah!
> I am warm! I see the flames!"
> The rest he makes into a god,
> An image to worship and adore.
> He prays to it and says,
> "Help me! You are my god!"
> They do not know, do not understand;
> their eyes are too clouded to see,
> their minds, to perceive. (44:16–18)

Finally the prophet drives home his lesson:

> He does not think clearly;
> he lacks the wit and knowledge to say,
> "Half the wood I burned in the fire,
> on its embers I baked bread,
> I roasted meat and ate.
> Shall I turn the rest into an abomination?
> Shall I worship a block of wood?"
> He is chasing ashes!
> A deluded mind has led him astray;
> He cannot save himself, does not say,
> "This thing in my right hand—is it not a fraud?" (44:19–20)

For all its humor, the mockery of idolatry in Acts serves a similar purpose as in Isaiah: to draw people away from the worship of false gods to knowledge of the one true God, the creator of all.

a similar reference to an earlier time of divine forbearance of ignorance, this time for non-Jews: **"In past generations he allowed all Gentiles to go their own ways."** This implies that in the present generation, now that the good news of Christ is being announced, God is changing how he relates to the Gentile world. Paul will say more about this in his next speech to Gentiles, at Athens (Acts 17:30–31).

14:17　　Paul explains that the living God has left evidence of himself in the created world, using what is today called an argument from natural theology (as in Rom 1:19–20). **In bestowing his goodness**, God gave **witness** to his existence and providence. He provided lavishly for the creatures he made by giving **rains from heaven and fruitful seasons**, as well as **nourishment and gladness for your hearts** (an echo of Ps 104:14–15). Paul is appealing to evidence not only for God's existence but also for God's abundant goodness. He thus implicitly invites his listeners not only to believe in God but also to give God the thanksgiving they owe him (see Rom 1:21).

14:18　　With this plea the apostles **scarcely** restrain **the crowds from offering sacrifice to them**. Some first-century philosophers were known to exploit pagan credulity for their own profit. In contrast, Paul and Barnabas refuse gifts and veneration from these unbelievers.

14:19　　In contrast to Paul and Barnabas's honesty and humility, another group takes advantage of the credulity of the Lycaonians: **some Jews** arrive **from Antioch and Iconium**, the cities from which the apostles have just fled. These hostile outsiders manipulate the same gullible **crowds** whom Paul and Barnabas have refused to exploit. Perhaps they take advantage of the crowd's natural resentment at having their belief system so vehemently denied, or perhaps they accuse Paul and Barnabas of trickery. This might help explain the irony that the same crowds who had just tried to offer sacrifice to Paul now **stoned** him, **dragged him out of the city**, and left him for **dead**.

14:20　　Luke does not tell us whether the disciples prayed for Paul's resuscitation **after they gathered around him**, or whether he was actually dead. Paul simply **got up** and returned to **the city**. That Paul survived being stoned is confirmed by his own testimony in 2 Cor 11:25: "Three times I was beaten with rods, once I was stoned, three times I was shipwrecked." Quite matter-of-factly, Luke remarks that the **following day** Paul **left with Barnabas for Derbe**. Misunderstanding, slander, rejection, the trauma of stoning, and even the threat of death—these do not stop the apostles' mission. They simply move on to the next city. One might expect people to change their conduct in the face of such extreme negative reinforcement. Luke leaves readers free to draw their own conclusions about the faith, courage, and determination of these Christian missionaries and their source in the resurrection of Jesus and the gift of the Spirit.

The End of the First Mission (14:21–28)

²¹After they had proclaimed the good news to that city and made a considerable number of disciples, they returned to Lystra and to Iconium and to Antioch. ²²They strengthened the spirits of the disciples and exhorted them to persevere in the faith, saying, "It is necessary for us to undergo many hardships to enter the kingdom of God." ²³They appointed presbyters for them in each church and, with prayer and fasting, commended them to the Lord in whom they had put their faith. ²⁴Then they traveled through Pisidia and reached Pamphylia. ²⁵After proclaiming the word at Perga they went down to Attalia. ²⁶From there they sailed to Antioch, where they had been commended to the grace of God for the work they had now accomplished. ²⁷And when they arrived, they called the church together and reported what God had done with them and how he had opened the door of faith to the Gentiles. ²⁸Then they spent no little time with the disciples.

OT: Pss 22:26; 40:10–11
NT: Luke 24:46; Acts 13:3
Catechism: ordained ministry, 1546–51
Lectionary: Fifth Sunday of Easter (Year C); Rite of Ordination

Luke provides further glimpses into the missionary method of Paul and Barnabas. First they **proclaimed the good news** in Derbe, leading to positive results: they **made . . . disciples** (as Jesus had commanded in Matt 28:19). Then they retraced their steps, returning **to Lystra and to Iconium and to Antioch**, to check on and strengthen the churches they had founded. Readers may wonder how Paul can return to the same cities from which he was just expelled (13:50–51) or fled in fear for his life (14:5–6), or in which he was stoned (14:19). One reason is that he and Barnabas were persecuted for publicly preaching to unbelievers, but now they are ministering privately to believers. **They strengthened the spirits of the disciples and exhorted them to persevere in the faith**. Without follow-up, new converts can easily return to previous beliefs and patterns of conduct. They need reinforcement for their new faith, extensive instruction, and encouragement to remain constant in the difficulties they can expect to face.

14:21–22

The missionaries' trials occasion a new emphasis in their teaching: **"It is necessary for us to undergo many hardships to enter the kingdom of God."** Paul and Barnabas repeat the sober warnings that Jesus had given his followers: following him is a narrow and difficult way (Matt 7:14; 11:12). This inevitability of suffering and hardship characterizes God's plan of salvation as reported in Luke-Acts. The risen Jesus teaches, "Was it not necessary that the Messiah should suffer these things and enter into his glory?" (Luke 24:26). At the time of Paul's conversion, the Lord tells Ananias, "I will show him what he will have to suffer for my name" (Acts 9:16).

14:23   Providing permanent local leadership to guide the new churches after the founders moved on was essential to Paul's missionary task. Thus he and Barnabas **appointed presbyters for them in each church**. The word †presbyter means "elder," which implies that new church leaders were chosen from among the more mature and reliable converts, as later recommended in 1 Tim 3:1–9 and Titus 1:5–9. At the beginning these leaders were likely found among Jewish believers, whose knowledge of Scripture and adherence to biblical morality would have been a major advantage.

Paul and Barnabas seek the Spirit's guidance in commissioning the new leaders through **prayer and fasting**, following the example of Jesus, who fasted before he began his ministry and prayed before choosing his apostles (see Luke 4:2; 6:12). The church at Antioch in Syria had commissioned their own evangelizing mission in the same way (Acts 13:3, see sidebar, p. 204). They commend these new leaders **to the Lord**, since the successful ministry of church leaders ultimately depends on the risen Jesus.

14:24–25   Paul and Barnabas continue their Asian missionary journey **through Pisidia** to **Pamphylia**. The last city where they proclaim **the word** is **Perga**. From there they proceed to **Attalia**, the Mediterranean port from which they sail back to the church that sent them.

14:26   Their return **to Antioch** in Syria shows the close relationship between missionaries and the churches that commission them. It was the Antioch church that had **commended**, literally, "handed over," Barnabas and Paul to **the grace of God** in their missionary journey. The church at Jerusalem had provided impetus for the initial outreach to Jews and Samaritans; now, at the initiative of the Spirit (13:1–2), the church at Antioch took the lead in the mission to Gentiles.

14:27–28   Now that Paul and Barnabas have completed their appointed work, they exercise accountability for it. On arriving, they report to the church **what God had done with them**, glorifying God and building up the community by relating God's mighty works (see Pss 22:26; 40:10–11; 1 Pet 2:9). Their focus is on what God has achieved through them rather than on their own successes. They particularly report how God **opened the door of faith to the Gentiles**, a significant new development in the spread of God's word. Both Acts and Paul's Letters credit the evangelization of the Gentiles to God's initiative and grace (Gal 1:15–16; 2:7–9; Eph 3:7–10).

Following their return, Paul and Barnabas spend **no little time with the disciples** at their Antioch base. Even the greatest missionaries are refreshed by resting and spending time with fellow believers, receiving as well as giving, so they can be recharged for their next mission.

The Jerusalem Council

Acts 15:1–35

The Council of Jerusalem is unquestionably a climactic moment in the history of the Church, for in it the Church's message is decisively extended to all nations. The council reaches conclusions on two related concerns: first, how Gentiles can be saved by Christ; second, how they are to relate to their Jewish-Christian brothers and sisters. The meeting provides today's Church with a helpful model for resolving controversies and discerning God's will as new questions arise.

The need to consult the mother church of Jerusalem arises because of some Judean Christians' heated arguments with Paul and Barnabas about whether Gentile converts needed to submit to circumcision and the Mosaic law. The church of Antioch appeals to the authority of the Jerusalem apostles and elders. When the council convenes (v. 6), Peter responds to the vigorous opening debate by recounting the conversion of the Gentile Cornelius. Then he presents his conclusion from that experience: salvation is by faith in Jesus rather than through the law (v. 11). Paul and Barnabas then confirm Peter's theological explanation by witnessing to God's extraordinary blessing on their ministry to Gentiles.

The argument is settled when James, who by then has become the head of the Jewish-Christian Jerusalem community,[1] accepts Peter's argument and confirms it with the authority of Scripture: the conversion of Gentiles in God's saving plan is already foretold in the Old Testament. James then decrees a pastoral application of the principle enunciated by Peter: Gentiles should not be required to be circumcised but should only be asked to abide by the elements of the law

---

1. James, the relative of Jesus, probably assumed the leadership after Peter left Jerusalem (Acts 12:17).

necessary to preserve harmonious community life between Jewish and Gentile Christians, including common meals and intermarriage.

The Council of Jerusalem (15:1–12)

---

¹Some who had come down from Judea were instructing the brothers, "Unless you are circumcised according to the Mosaic practice, you cannot be saved." ²Because there arose no little dissension and debate by Paul and Barnabas with them, it was decided that Paul, Barnabas, and some of the others should go up to Jerusalem to the apostles and presbyters about this question. ³They were sent on their journey by the church, and passed through Phoenicia and Samaria telling of the conversion of the Gentiles, and brought great joy to all the brothers. ⁴When they arrived in Jerusalem, they were welcomed by the church, as well as by the apostles and the presbyters, and they reported what God had done with them. ⁵But some from the party of the Pharisees who had become believers stood up and said, "It is necessary to circumcise them and direct them to observe the Mosaic law."

⁶The apostles and the presbyters met together to see about this matter. ⁷After much debate had taken place, Peter got up and said to them, "My brothers, you are well aware that from early days God made his choice among you that through my mouth the Gentiles would hear the word of the gospel and believe. ⁸And God, who knows the heart, bore witness by granting them the holy Spirit just as he did us. ⁹He made no distinction between us and them, for by faith he purified their hearts. ¹⁰Why, then, are you now putting God to the test by placing on the shoulders of the disciples a yoke that neither our ancestors nor we have been able to bear? ¹¹On the contrary, we believe that we are saved through the grace of the Lord Jesus, in the same way as they." ¹²The whole assembly fell silent, and they listened while Paul and Barnabas described the signs and wonders God had worked among the Gentiles through them.

OT: Isa 42:24; Jer 6:19; Deut 6:16; Ps 95:10–11
NT: Acts 10, especially v. 28; 15:23–29; Rom 2:25–27
Catechism: magisterium, 888–92, 2034; authority of Peter, 880–83
Lectionary: Acts 15:1–2, 22–29: Sixth Sunday of Easter (Year C)

After Paul and Barnabas return to Antioch, some Jewish Christians **from**   15:1
Judea arrive there and begin teaching that Gentile converts must be **circumcised according to the Mosaic practice**; otherwise they **cannot be saved** (see

Acts 15:24; Gal 1:7). Since in the Old Testament Gentiles became part of God's people through circumcision, this assertion by the Judeans is not surprising. But these †Judaizing demands threaten the very foundations of the mission to the Gentiles (see Gal 5:1–4; Phil 3:2–3).

15:2   Because so much is at stake, the Judeans' claim causes **no little dissension and debate**. The local church at Antioch tries unsuccessfully to resolve the dispute. Ultimately it decides that **Paul, Barnabas**, and some **others** should **go up to Jerusalem** to consult the leaders of the mother church, **the apostles** and †**presbyters**, to settle **this question**. Since Jerusalem has confirmed the founding of the Antioch church (Acts 11:19–24), and since the people causing doubts are from Judea, the daughter church appeals to Jerusalem concerning this conflict that threatens the very basis of their doctrine and communal life.

15:3   Those in the delegation are **sent on their journey by the church**. On their way to Jerusalem **through Phoenicia and Samaria**, regions that have been evangelized earlier (Acts 8–9), they report to Christians **the conversion of the Gentiles**, causing **great joy**.

15:4   Their enthusiastic reception continues all the way into **Jerusalem**, where they are **welcomed by the church** and its leaders. First they report **what God had done with them**. Paul and Barnabas continue to focus on God's action through them, not on their own successes. Thus far their point of view about God's gathering Gentiles into his people seems to be received favorably.

15:5   In Jerusalem, however, their view is quickly challenged. The same objection that has been raised in Antioch is presented by some **Pharisees who had become believers**. Ironically, they belong to the same Jewish party of which Paul himself is a member (23:6). They insist that **it is necessary to circumcise** converts; in effect, one must become a Jew in order to become a Christian. In Luke-Acts, the term for "necessary" (Greek *dei*) often refers to God's will, so the implication is that circumcision is necessary for salvation in God's plan. They also argue that these new converts need to be directed **to observe the Mosaic law**, because circumcision implies acceptance of the entire law (see Gal 5:3).

15:6–7   Because this controversy is so critical to the future of the Church, the **apostles and the presbyters** gather in council to discuss it. The council begins with **much debate**, in which all participants are able to air their opposing viewpoints. Finally **Peter**, the head of the apostles (see Matt 16:18; Luke 22:31–32; Acts 1:15), intervenes. He reminds the community that **God** first chose him, Peter, as his instrument through whom **the Gentiles would hear the word of the gospel and believe**. This refers to his role in what had been a surprising

The Judaizing Problem in the Early Church

BIBLICAL BACKGROUND

It may seem strange today that some early Christians thought new believers had to be circumcised and keep the law of Moses in order to be saved. But in a biblical context, this viewpoint is understandable. In the Old Testament, God instituted circumcision as the sign of belonging to his covenant people (Gen 17:10–14), and later he mandated observance of the Mosaic law (Deut 28). Jesus, the Jewish Messiah, came to fulfill the law and renew the covenant (see Matt 5:17; Luke 22:20). However, he did so in a surprising and unexpected way. By his death and resurrection, Jesus fulfilled the law by perfectly accomplishing all that it symbolized and pointed to. His paschal mystery has brought about a new era in which Jews and Gentiles alike are saved through faith in him, and by baptism all these believers are incorporated into his body, the Church.

Both Acts and Paul's Letters vehemently counteract the †Judaizing claim that circumcision and the Mosaic law are still necessary for belonging to God's people. They regard this claim as an abandonment of the basic truth that we are saved by the grace of Christ (Acts 4:12). In the Letter to the Galatians, Paul even scolds his readers, "O stupid Galatians!" (Gal 3:1), because they have let themselves fall into the error of relying on works of the law.

Already in the Old Testament, God revealed that his plan was to send a savior not only for Israel but also for all people throughout the world (see Gen 12:3; Isa 2:3; 49:6). Both Acts and Galatians make clear, however, that it took a formidable transformation of mind-sets before some of the early Christians could appreciate the sufficiency of faith in Christ apart from circumcision and the law. Even Peter needed to hear a heavenly voice three times before he began to understand (Acts 10:10–16).

---

new development for the Church, the evangelization of the Gentile Cornelius and his household (Acts 10:1–11:18).

Peter further reminds his listeners that only God **knows the heart**, and that God **bore witness** that Gentiles could be full members of his people **by granting them the holy Spirit just as he did us**. God himself bypassed the need for circumcision by pouring out the Holy Spirit on Cornelius and his friends, just as had happened to the Jewish believers at Pentecost.

15:8–9

This demonstrates that God **made no distinction between us and them**, for both Jews and Gentiles receive the same divine gift **by faith**, and not through circumcision or the law. The perceptible outpouring of the Spirit made it evident that God had **purified** the **hearts** of these Gentiles from sin. In the Old

Covenant, the temple sacrifices had cleansed God's people from ritual defilement, enabling them to come before him in worship. But now in Christ both Jews and Gentiles are cleansed inwardly by the Holy Spirit and thus are given the ability to worship God as his daughters and sons. As Peter had recognized after his vision, the uncircumcised must no longer be considered unclean (Acts 10:28), or in modern terms, second-class citizens.

15:10   Peter gives a remarkably negative assessment of the demand that Gentiles be circumcised. He calls it **putting God to the test**—what Satan had tried to get Jesus to do (Luke 4:9–12) and had gotten Ananias and Sapphira to do (Acts 5:1–11), and which the Israelites had done in the desert (Deut 6:16; Ps 95:9). In effect, the †Judaizers were challenging God's authority and clear guidance, for they were ignoring how God himself was treating the Gentiles and were demanding circumcision, from which God had obviously exempted the Gentiles by giving them his Holy Spirit.

Peter further interprets their demands as **placing on the shoulders of** Gentile **disciples a yoke** that neither ancient Israelites nor first-century Jews were **able to bear.** The "yoke of the law" is an expression in both ancient and modern Judaism for the law of Moses, a whole way of life in covenant relationship with God.[2] But this does not mean they were fully able to keep the law, as Paul argues in Rom 3:9–23. Peter's statement about God's people not keeping the law has precedents in the Old Testament prophets, who denounced Israel for disobeying the law (see Isa 42:24; Jer 6:19), and is reinforced by Paul's teaching in Rom 2:25–27.

15:11   Peter concludes with the assertion that is at the core of the good news: **"We believe that we are saved through the grace of the Lord Jesus, in the same way as they."** Both Jews and Gentiles are saved by pure, unmerited grace, the grace won by Jesus' death and resurrection and God's free gift of his Holy Spirit.

15:12   Peter's theological demonstration subdues the arguments of the **whole assembly.** Then **Paul and Barnabas** further confirm what Peter has declared by reporting **the signs and wonders God had worked among the Gentiles**, keeping the focus on God's actions, not their own.

James on Dietary Law (15:13–21)

[13]**After they had fallen silent, James responded, "My brothers, listen to me. [14]Symeon has described how God first concerned himself with acquiring**

2. See Exod 19:5; 34:10; Joseph A. Fitzmyer, *The Acts of the Apostles*, Anchor Bible 31 (New York: Doubleday, 1998), 548.

from among the Gentiles a people for his name. [15]The words of the
prophets agree with this, as is written:

> [16]'After this I shall return
> and rebuild the fallen hut of David;
> from its ruins I shall rebuild it
> and raise it up again,
> [17]so that the rest of humanity may seek out the Lord,
> even all the Gentiles on whom my name is invoked.
> Thus says the Lord who accomplishes these things,
> [18]known from of old.'

[19]It is my judgment, therefore, that we ought to stop troubling the Gentiles
who turn to God, [20]but tell them by letter to avoid pollution from idols,
unlawful marriage, the meat of strangled animals, and blood. [21]For Moses,
for generations now, has had those who proclaim him in every town, as he
has been read in the synagogues every sabbath."

OT: Lev 17–18; Deut 14:2; Isa 45:21; Jer 12:15; 13:11; Amos 9:11–12
NT: Acts 13:30–37
Catechism: the old law and the new, 1963–64, 1967–68; magisterium 85–88, 890–92, 2034

When Paul and Barnabas finish their testimony, **James** responds by reinforc-   **15:13**
ing Peter's argument with a citation from the Old Testament. Like many speeches
in Acts, James's speech begins with a customary rhetorical introduction: **"My
brothers, listen to me."**

James uses Peter's original name in its more Semitic form, **Symeon**.[3] As   **15:14**
James summarizes the Cornelius story, he focuses solely on God's action: **"God
first concerned himself with acquiring from among the Gentiles a people
for his name."** The same biblical language that described God's formation of
the Israelites as his chosen people (Deut 14:2) is now used for Gentiles. God is
granting the privileged status of being his people not only to Jews but also to
believers from among the nations. They, too, can now belong to a "people for
his name."[4] As the Israelites had represented and honored God's name before
unbelieving peoples, so now converted Gentiles can also give witness to God's
holy name before unbelievers.

James argues that the **words of the prophets agree with this**. That is, the   **15:15**
Scriptures confirm that God had always intended to gather the Gentiles into his

---

3. The Hebrew form of the name, after Jacob's second son (Gen 29:33), is Shim'on.
4. The wording is similar to Jer 13:11 LXX, "to be for me a people of name," or "of my name."

people. The words he cites are mostly from Amos 9:11–12, but with elements from Jer 12:15 and Isa 45:21.

15:16   In its original context, **after this I shall return** (Jer 12:15)[5] meant that God would have mercy on his people after punishing them. The next line, from Amos, foretold that God would **rebuild the fallen hut of David**, that is, God would restore the Davidic dynasty, which was defunct since the Babylonian exile. God would **raise it up again**. Though the word here refers to restoring a fallen building, readers are meant to recall Paul's earlier argument that it was David's descendant, Jesus, who was literally raised up from the dead to rule without end (13:30–37).

15:17–18   God's intended result for Jesus' resurrection is **so that the rest of humanity may seek out the Lord**. In the Old Testament "the LORD" refers to God, but here "the Lord" seems to apply to Jesus, now risen and exalted as Lord. "The rest of humanity" are **all the Gentiles on whom** God's **name is invoked**. Such Gentiles include Cornelius and the converts at Antioch who were baptized in the name of the Lord Jesus (see Acts 11:20–21). The ancient prophecy takes on new meaning as it is now interpreted in light of Christ: **Thus says the Lord Jesus, who accomplishes these things**, that is, the inclusion of Gentiles into God's people that had been foretold **from of old** (Isa 45:21).

15:19   Based on Peter's testimony and its biblical confirmation, James, the leading spokesperson of the Jerusalem church, expresses agreement with Peter: **"It is my judgment, therefore, that we ought to stop troubling the Gentiles who turn to God."** The essential question, whether Gentile converts need to submit to circumcision and the Mosaic law in order to become members of God's people, has been decisively answered.

15:20   However, there is a second, pastoral concern that James now addresses. Devout Jews did not associate with Gentiles, especially at table, because of what Jewish law regarded as their unclean practices (see Acts 10:28). If uncircumcised Gentiles can now join Jewish believers as fellow members of the Church, how can the two groups relate to each other, especially in table fellowship, which is central to Christian life (Acts 2:42)? James provides a way by stipulating that Gentile converts must **avoid** four sources of defilement: **pollution from idols, unlawful marriage, the meat of strangled animals, and blood**.[6]

These four conditions have biblical precedent. They are drawn from those stipulations in the law of Moses that applied not only to Israelites but also to the

5. NABRE translates this as "bring them back."

6. The relationship between Galatians and what Acts reports about the decree of the Jerusalem Council is debated among scholars; see the overview by Charles B. Cousar, "Jerusalem, Council of," in *Anchor Bible Dictionary*, ed. David N. Freedman (New York: Doubleday, 1992), 3:766–68.

Gentile resident aliens who lived among them (Lev 17:8–18:30). **Pollution from idols** refers to eating meat that had been sacrificed to pagan gods—a common affair in the ancient pagan world, even for meat sold in the marketplace, and something that remained a temptation even for Christian converts (see 1 Cor 8:1–13; 10:18–33; Rom 14). It may also allude to immoral practices in pagan temple worship. **Blood** refers to consuming anything with blood in it (such as blood sausage), strictly forbidden in the law of Moses because blood, as the seat of life, is sacred (Gen 9:4; Lev 17:13–14; 19:26). The **meat of strangled animals** refers, similarly, to meat from animals not properly drained of blood (Lev 17:13–14).

The NAB translates the fourth item as **unlawful marriage**, interpreting the Greek *porneia* as referring to intermarriage within closer degrees of kinship than was allowed by the law of Moses (see Lev 18:6–18). But *porneia*, literally, sexual immorality, can also refer more broadly to the various forms of sexual immorality mentioned in Lev 18:6–23.

If Gentile Christians break from their pagan past by avoiding these four kinds of defilement, Jews and Gentiles together will be able to enjoy fellowship in one community and share in a single Eucharist.[7]

James appeals to the precedent that **for generations now** the law of **Moses** has been preached **in every city** throughout the Greco-Roman world, having been **read every sabbath in the synagogues**. For a long time, Gentile †God-fearers who have attended synagogues have been asked to avoid these practices, which violate the law of their Jewish hosts. James is simply requesting the same conditions of Gentile Christians. The key theological point is that these requests do not concern how Gentiles are to be saved, which was the original argument (Acts 15:1), but only how to facilitate Gentiles and Jews' living peacefully together in Christian community. Whereas Peter's pronouncement in verse 11 about how Gentiles are saved is a doctrinal matter, James's pronouncement in verse 20 is a disciplinary matter.

15:21

Letter of the Apostles (15:22–29)

[22]Then the apostles and presbyters, in agreement with the whole church, decided to choose representatives and to send them to Antioch with Paul and Barnabas. The ones chosen were Judas, who was called Barsabbas, and

---

7. Eventually the Council of Florence in 1442 pronounced that this decree was a temporary measure and no longer applied (see sidebar, p. 243).

Silas, leaders among the brothers. ²³This is the letter delivered by them: "The apostles and the presbyters, your brothers, to the brothers in Antioch, Syria, and Cilicia of Gentile origin: greetings. ²⁴Since we have heard that some of our number [who went out] without any mandate from us have upset you with their teachings and disturbed your peace of mind, ²⁵we have with one accord decided to choose representatives and to send them to you along with our beloved Barnabas and Paul, ²⁶who have dedicated their lives to the name of our Lord Jesus Christ. ²⁷So we are sending Judas and Silas who will also convey this same message by word of mouth: ²⁸'It is the decision of the holy Spirit and of us not to place on you any burden beyond these necessities, ²⁹namely, to abstain from meat sacrificed to idols, from blood, from meats of strangled animals, and from unlawful marriage. If you keep free of these, you will be doing what is right. Farewell.'"

OT: Lev 17–18

NT: 1 Cor 8–10; 1 Thess 1:1; 2 Thess 1:1; 1 Pet 5:12; Rev 2:14, 20

Catechism: Holy Spirit guides the Church, 768, 890–92; Jews and Gentiles made one, 781; handing down faith in formulas, 186

Lectionary: Acts 15:1–2, 22–29: Sixth Sunday of Easter (Year C)

15:22 Following James's speech, **the apostles and presbyters** arrive at a consensus decision **in agreement with the whole church**: they will **choose representatives** and **send them to Antioch with Paul and Barnabas**, who are representing the Antioch church at Jerusalem (v. 2). The chosen delegates are **Judas, who was called Barsabbas**, possibly a brother of "Joseph called Barsabbas," who had been a candidate to replace the fallen-away Judas Iscariot (Acts 1:23); and **Silas**, who will later replace Barnabas as Paul's missionary companion (15:40).[8] These two men are **leaders among the brothers** in the Jerusalem church, although their precise leadership role is not indicated; later they are identified as Christian prophets (Acts 15:32).

15:23 The **letter** that the delegation is to deliver follows standard Hellenistic letter-writing patterns. It begins by identifying the senders, the Jerusalem **apostles and the presbyters**. It then specifies the letter recipients, the Gentile Christians of **Antioch**, where the problem was acute, and the entire provinces of **Syria** (where Antioch was located) and **Cilicia**. The identification of both senders and recipients of the letter as **brothers** emphasizes their common identity as children of God the Father. By first stressing their unity in the family of God, the Council seeks to win over Gentile readers, before the letter

---

8. Outside of Acts, Silas is usually called by his Roman name, Silvanus (2 Cor 1:19; 1 Thess 1:1; 2 Thess 1:1; 1 Pet 5:12).

goes on to request that they make a few concessions, abandoning some of their previous practices.

The letter states that **some of our number**, Jewish Christians from Judea, had no authority to teach what they did but were acting on their own **without any mandate** from the mother church of Jerusalem. It acknowledges that these individuals have **upset** the Gentile converts of Antioch and **disturbed** their **peace of mind** by teaching that they cannot be saved without circumcision (15:1). Paul uses similar strong language in Gal 1:7.   **15:24**

The Jerusalem leaders emphasize that their decision was made **with one accord**, an expression Luke often uses for unity of heart and mind in the Church. They have decided to correct the error by choosing **representatives** to accompany **Barnabas** and **Paul** back to Antioch. Calling these men "**beloved**" conveys Jerusalem's solidarity with them. They are honored as men who have **dedicated their lives to**, or "risked their lives for," **the name of our Lord Jesus Christ**.   **15:25–26**

Judas and Silas will carry the letter and also **convey this same message by word of mouth**. It was common for the bearer of a letter to authenticate it by repeating orally at least the substance of its contents. Judas and Silas, evidently esteemed leaders among the early Christians, will unambiguously corroborate the council's decision concerning the controversy, in which Paul and Barnabas had represented only one side.   **15:27**

Ecumenical Councils

LIVING TRADITION

The †Jerusalem Council in Acts 15 is the earliest example of church leadership gathered in council to discern important questions of doctrine and pastoral practice. The solemn decision of the apostles and elders, guided by the Holy Spirit, established a precedent for councils throughout church history. The council deliberated over arguments from theology, Scripture, and pastoral experience, and the Holy Spirit guided all this human activity to a conclusion willed by God.

This practice has continued in the ecumenical councils, that is, councils of bishops representing the whole Church, beginning with the First Council of Nicaea in 325 and continuing, in the Western Church, to the Second Vatican Council in the 1960s. The Church accepts the solemn doctrinal definitions of the councils as binding and infallible, since the risen Lord Jesus continues to guide the Church and its leadership through the Holy Spirit (see the Catechism, 890–91).

15:28–29   Strikingly, the apostles and elders describe the conclusion of their delibera-
tions as **the decision of the holy Spirit and of us**: they are confident that their
decision was guided by the Holy Spirit, as Jesus had promised (John 16:13; see
Matt 18:18). This union of divine guidance and human discernment is similar
to the decision by the Antioch church to set apart Barnabas and Saul for mission in Acts 13:1–3.

The letter repeats the council's judgment not to impose on Gentiles **any
burden**, particularly circumcision and the Mosaic law, beyond what is necessary for communal life shared by Gentile and Jewish Christians. The essential
requirements are, with slight variations, the four conditions already mentioned
by James (v. 20).

The first, **to abstain from meat sacrificed to idols**, which James had referred
to as "pollution from idols" (v. 20), persisted as a serious concern among mixed
Jewish-Gentile Christian communities and is addressed at length by Paul in
1 Cor 8–10.[9] Even though sacrificed meat was sometimes the readiest source
of meat for poor people, the fact that it had first been offered to idols made it
problematic not only for Jews but particularly also for Christians who understood that what is offered to idols is really offered to demons (1 Cor 10:20–21).
Eating such meat was also liable to mislead new Christians into relapsing into
their previous idolatrous practices. The other three stipulations, to refrain **from
blood, from meats of strangled animals, and from unlawful marriage**, are
explained in the commentary on verse 20 above.

The letter makes it easier for the recipients to accept these requirements by
addressing a gracious exhortation to their free will: **"If you keep free of these,
you will be doing what is right."** Finally, the letter ends with a typical closing
salutation, **"Farewell."**

Delegates at Antioch (15:30–35)

**[30]And so they were sent on their journey. Upon their arrival in Antioch
they called the assembly together and delivered the letter. [31]When the
people read it, they were delighted with the exhortation. [32]Judas and
Silas, who were themselves prophets, exhorted and strengthened the
brothers with many words. [33]After they had spent some time there,
they were sent off with greetings of peace from the brothers to those
who had commissioned them. [34] [35]But Paul and Barnabas remained in**

---

9. Paul treats this matter with delicate pastoral sensitivity. See George T. Montague, *First Corinthians*,
Catholic Commentary on Sacred Scripture (Grand Rapids: Baker Academic, 2011), 140–82.

The Council of Florence on the Decree of Acts 15

In 1442 the ecumenical Council of Florence addressed the question of whether the apostolic decree of Acts 15:22–29 remains valid. The Council cited 1 Tim 4:4, "Everything created by God is good, and nothing is to be rejected when received with thanksgiving." After repeating the Jerusalem Council's decision that the ceremonial laws of Moses no longer oblige Christians, it went on to declare:

> The apostolic prohibition, to abstain *from what has been sacrificed to idols and from blood and from what is strangled* [Acts 15:29], was suited to that time when a single church was rising from Jews and gentiles, who previously lived with different ceremonies and customs. This was so that the gentiles should have some observances in common with Jews, and occasion would be offered of coming together in one worship and faith of God, and a cause of dissension might be removed, since by ancient custom blood and strangled things seemed abominable to Jews, and gentiles could be thought to be returning to idolatry if they ate sacrificial food.

The Council then stated that where Jews are no longer a significant part of the church, "since the cause of that apostolic prohibition has ceased, so its effect has ceased."[a]

a. "Bull of Union with the Copts," February 4, 1442, in *Decrees of the Ecumenical Councils*, vol. 1, *Nicaea I to Lateran V*, ed. Norman P. Tanner (Washington, DC: Georgetown University Press, 1990), 577.

Antioch, teaching and proclaiming with many others the word of the Lord.

OT: 1 Kings 13:32; Jer 11:6
NT: Acts 13:15
Catechism: handing down the faith in formulas, 186

The response of the church **in Antioch** to **the letter** is quite positive. By emphasizing that the people are **delighted with the exhortation**, Luke signals both acceptance of the decision and a strengthened bond of unity between the churches of Jerusalem and Antioch. The Greek word for exhortation, *paraklēsis*, can also mean consolation or comfort. The context suggests both meanings: the letter was an *exhortation* to keep the requirements of verse 29 and a *consolation* in its clear affirmation that uncircumcised believers are full members of the Church.

15:30–32

The Jerusalem delegates, **Judas and Silas**, remained for some time in Antioch, where they **exhorted and strengthened** the believers to fidelity to Christ. These men were **prophets**, that is, they were endowed by the Holy Spirit with the charism of prophecy so that their words had a divine power to encourage and strengthen the believers (see Paul's description of prophecy in 1 Cor 14:3).

15:33   Their mission completed, the delegates are **sent off with greetings of peace** to the leaders in Jerusalem who had sent them. Luke emphasizes the **peace** and harmony between the churches at Antioch and Jerusalem.

15:34–35   Some ancient manuscripts and translations of Acts add, in various wordings, verse 34: "But Silas decided to remain there." This statement prepares for verse 40, where Paul departs from Antioch with Silas on a missionary journey. Meanwhile **Paul and Barnabas** remain **in Antioch**, the home church that commissions their missionary journeys. Not unexpectedly, they are **teaching and proclaiming**, along with other teachers, **the word of the Lord**, the good news about Jesus and practical instruction about how to live as his disciples.

Reflection and Application (15:1–35)

The controversy over circumcising Gentiles and its resolution in the Jerusalem Council is a paradigm for settling later controversies in the Church. First, it illustrates the importance of not being afraid honestly to express one's opinions on questions that are not yet settled. Both sides need to be willing to listen respectfully and evaluate the opposing arguments. The issues need to be adequately discussed to arrive at as much clarity and consensus as possible. People from varied backgrounds may well have complementary perspectives, although sometimes, as in Acts 15, one position will be found to be true and the other mistaken.

Those responsible to decide on ecclesial questions are not self-selected individuals seeking to promote a particular agenda, but properly appointed church leaders who are accountable to Christ. Nor can the resulting decrees contradict previous doctrine on faith or morals. Ultimately, God's revelation, handed down in Scripture and tradition, provides the foundation for all discernment.

Acts 15 illustrates the importance of divine guidance as well as human reasoning for resolving even the deepest differences. From the first, the matter needs to be submitted prayerfully to the Holy Spirit. Earnest prayer together provides the setting for a sound and peaceful resolution.

When the apostolic example of Acts 15 is not followed, arguments can easily lead to polarization. Sometimes they result in actual schisms, as in the many

Protestant denominations that have split from one another over competing interpretations of Scripture. At other times they lead to dissenting subgroups that reject Church authority in regard to liturgical or moral questions. Dissent from what has been solemnly decided by the universal Church undermines Christian unity.

The Separation of Paul and Barnabas

Acts 15:36–16:15

After the decree of the council in Jerusalem regarding what is expected of Gentile members of the Church, Paul begins a new mission that takes him farther toward the "ends of the earth" (see Acts 1:8). He proposes to Barnabas that they begin by checking on the churches they recently founded in Asia Minor. But an unhappy split between the two men results in Paul's setting off with a new mission partner, Silas. On the way, he picks up another coworker, Timothy.

Paul's further travel plans in Asia Minor are thwarted by the Holy Spirit, but he receives a vision in which a man begs him to come help the people of Macedonia, precipitating a new stage of the Christian mission. At this point Luke presents himself as a member of Paul's team for the first time by beginning to use the first-person "we" (Acts 16:10). Thus with a new missionary team, Paul begins preaching in Macedonia, bringing the gospel into Europe for the first time.

Paul and Barnabas Separate (15:36–41)

[36]After some time, Paul said to Barnabas, "Come, let us make a return visit to see how the brothers are getting on in all the cities where we proclaimed the word of the Lord." [37]Barnabas wanted to take with them also John, who was called Mark, [38]but Paul insisted that they should not take with them someone who had deserted them at Pamphylia and who had

not continued with them in their work. [39]So sharp was their disagreement that they separated. Barnabas took Mark and sailed to Cyprus. [40]But Paul chose Silas and departed after being commended by the brothers to the grace of the Lord. [41]He traveled through Syria and Cilicia bringing strength to the churches.

NT: Acts 12:25–13:5; 13:13; Col 4:10; 1 Thess 2:11
Catechism: unity of the body of Christ, 791, 873

Now **Paul** proposes **to Barnabas** that they **make a return visit** to check on   **15:36**
the fledgling churches in the **cities** they have evangelized. This passage provides
a glimpse into the responsibility that Paul as a traveling missionary took for the
well-being of the churches he founded. His good example is in sharp contrast
to some contemporary evangelists who fail to follow up and provide for their
converts' continued spiritual growth.

Perhaps because John Mark was his cousin (Col 4:10), **Barnabas** wants him   **15:37–39**
to be reinstated on their team (Mark served with them on their first mission
in Acts 12:25–13:5). However, **Paul** is adamant that they should not bring
someone who had previously **deserted** the mission (Acts 13:13). **So sharp** is
the **disagreement** that they go their separate ways. Here Luke, without excuses,

Fig. 13. Paul's second missionary journey (Acts 15:36–18:22).

247

St. John Chrysostom on the Parting of Paul and Barnabas

Chrysostom understands this parting as due to complementary differences in personality and as resulting in a greater good:

Luke has already described the apostles' character to us, showing that one [Barnabas] was more tender and forgiving and the other [Paul] more strict and severe. For the gifts bestowed on them were different. That this is itself a gift is clear. . . . Likewise in the prophets we find different opinions and different characters. Elijah, for example, is severe, while Moses is meek. So here Paul is more vehement. But even so, notice his gentleness. "He thought best," it says, "not to take with them one who had withdrawn from them in Pamphylia." . . . Although there appears to be a sharp contention, in fact it was part of the divine plan that each man should receive his proper place. . . . The point is not that they differed in their opinions but that they accommodated themselves to each other. Thus a greater good resulted from their parting. . . . What then? Did they withdraw in enmity? God forbid! Recall how after this Barnabas received much praise from Paul in his epistles."[a]

a. John Chrysostom, *Homilies on the Acts of the Apostles* 34, in ACCS 193.

reports this painful breakup of the apostolic team of Paul and Barnabas. Yet the issues that divide them are matters of team discipline and loyalties, not doctrine.

This unhappy split had at least one providential result: there are now two apostolic teams instead of one. In the first, **Barnabas** sails with **Mark** to his native island of **Cyprus**, south of modern Turkey.

15:40–41   In the second team, **Paul** recruits **Silas** to accompany him overland in visiting the churches in Syria and Cilicia. Silas, a member of the Jerusalem delegation to Antioch (15:27), had apparently impressed Paul as they ministered together in Antioch. The two of them are **commended by the brothers to the grace of the Lord** (similar to Paul's blessings in 1 Cor 16:23; 2 Cor 13:13; Phil 4:23), a note conspicuously absent in the departure of Barnabas and Mark. The church of Antioch petitions Jesus' help and guidance for the new mission, as it had earlier for the mission of Paul and Barnabas (Acts 13:1–3).

The narrative focuses on Paul, the central character in the events that follow, even though Silas is along as his partner. Traveling through the Roman provinces of **Syria and Cilicia**, Paul brings **strength to the churches**. Paul shows fatherly pastoral concern for the churches he has founded, the same paternal care that is manifested so strongly in his letters: "As you know, we treated each one of you as a father treats his children, exhorting and encouraging you and insisting that you conduct yourselves as worthy of the God who calls you into his kingdom and glory" (1 Thess 2:11–12).

Timothy Joins the Team (16:1–5)

¹He reached [also] Derbe and Lystra where there was a disciple named Timothy, the son of a Jewish woman who was a believer, but his father was a Greek. ²The brothers in Lystra and Iconium spoke highly of him, ³and Paul wanted him to come along with him. On account of the Jews of that region, Paul had him circumcised, for they all knew that his father was a Greek. ⁴As they traveled from city to city, they handed on to the people for observance the decisions reached by the apostles and presbyters in Jerusalem. ⁵Day after day the churches grew stronger in faith and increased in number.

NT: Acts 14:8–21; Gal 2:3
Catechism: unity of the body of Christ, 791, 873

Paul returns to **Derbe** and **Lystra**, despite the traumatic memories Lystra **16:1** held for him. After he had healed a cripple, the pagan crowds had acclaimed him as a god but soon changed their minds and stoned him (Acts 14:8–20). But this region holds an unexpected benefit in a young recruit named **Timothy**, who will become an important member of Paul's team. Timothy is of mixed parentage, a **Jewish**-Christian **mother** (see 2 Tim 1:5) and a **Greek father**.

Because Timothy has a good reputation among the Christians of **Lystra and** **16:2–3** **Iconium, Paul** wants him to join the mission team, perhaps to substitute for Mark. However, the mixed religious background of Timothy's parents raises concerns about his acceptability to the **Jews of that region**. Timothy's religious identity was probably traced through his Jewish mother.[1] But because **his father was a Greek**, many Jews would realize that Timothy, though a Jew, had never been circumcised. They would therefore regard him with disapproval, creating a stumbling block to Paul's effectiveness in ministering to Jews. This situation leads **Paul** to have Timothy **circumcised**. Yet this act does not contradict the decision of the †Jerusalem Council that *Gentiles* need not be circumcised (Acts

---

1. Jewish descent is traditionally traced through the mother. The first written evidence to this custom is in the Mishnah, which is dated after Luke-Acts, but Acts 16 gives the impression that Luke considered this to be Timothy's case (Luke Timothy Johnson, *The Acts of the Apostles*, Sacra pagina 5 [Collegeville, MN: Liturgical Press, 1992], 284). Moreover, Timothy's mother and grandmother seem to have raised him as a Jew (2 Tim 1:5; 3:14–15).

15). Timothy's ethnic status is an interesting contrast to that of another Pauline companion, Titus, who is of wholly Gentile origin and therefore remains uncircumcised (Gal 2:3).

16:4   On their journey **from city to city**, the mission team promulgates **the decisions reached by the apostles and presbyters in Jerusalem**, namely, that Gentiles need not be circumcised to become Christian, but that they should follow four prescriptions that facilitate Jewish-Gentile life together in community (Acts 15:28–29).

16:5   The team's apostolic visitation, their promulgation of the Jerusalem decree, and its acceptance by the young Gentile communities—all result in the churches' growing **stronger in faith**. They also grow **in number**, a sign of God's favor.[2]

Reflection and Application (16:1–5)

Paul's invitation to Timothy to join the mission was clearly inspired, for it bore much fruit in the years to come. As Paul's protégé, his delegate to various churches, and the coauthor of several of his letters, Timothy became a major leader in the apostolic church. Paul's training of Timothy arose from one of his fundamental principles, perhaps arrived at through reflection on Jesus' ministry: "What you heard from me through many witnesses entrust to faithful people who will have the ability to teach others as well" (2 Tim 2:2). Those who have major roles of leadership in the Church are not called to do the ministry by themselves; rather, their role involves equipping others "for the work of ministry, for building up the body of Christ" (Eph 4:12). Paul's extensive collaboration with coworkers shows that this was a principle he took seriously, which contributed greatly to the immense fruitfulness of his life (see sidebar, p. 378).

"They" Becomes "We" (16:6–10)

[6]They traveled through the Phrygian and Galatian territory because they had been prevented by the holy Spirit from preaching the message in the province of Asia. [7]When they came to Mysia, they tried to go on into Bithynia, but the Spirit of Jesus did not allow them, [8]so they crossed through Mysia and came down to Troas. [9]During [the] night Paul had a vision. A Macedonian stood before him and implored him with these words, "Come over to Macedonia and help us." [10]When he had seen the

2. Luke frequently points out such growth, as in Acts 2:41; 4:4; 6:1, 7; 12:24; 13:49; 19:20.

vision, we sought passage to Macedonia at once, concluding that God had
called us to proclaim the good news to them.

Catechism: obedience of the baptized to their calling, 1269

As with Philip's ministry earlier in Acts, Paul's team experiences direct guid-   **16:6–8**
ance by **the holy Spirit** (8:26, 29, 39), who prevents them **from preaching**
the gospel in **the province of Asia**, the western part of what today is Turkey.
This divine control of the team's itinerary makes evident that the route they
took was God's will. Luke does not explain why the Spirit diverted them from
entering Asia; later Paul will enjoy significant missionary success in Ephesus,
the capital of Asia. Likewise, Luke leaves unsaid *how* the Holy Spirit prevented
them: was it through adverse circumstances, through prophecy (see 13:2), or
possibly an interior sense?

Instead, the team travels through **Phrygian and Galatian territory**.[3] When
they arrive in **Mysia**, they attempt to continue north into **Bithynia**, a Roman
province on the southern coast of the Black Sea, but again **the Spirit of Jesus**
does **not allow them**. This is the only occurrence of the phrase "the Spirit of
Jesus" in Acts.[4] It seems to be a way of indicating that the Spirit is intimately
united with the risen Jesus and is the means by which Jesus continues to be present and act through believers. Having been prevented from heading southwest
and forbidden to go north, Paul and his companions cross **through Mysia** in
a northwest direction and reach **Troas**, a port city on the Aegean Sea opposite
Macedonia.

While at Troas, in the **night** Paul sees a **vision** of a **Macedonian** man who   **16:9–10**
begs him, **"Come over to Macedonia and help us."** Accordingly, Luke says,
we sought passage to Macedonia at once. Paul and his companions discern
in this vision a call to evangelize in Macedonia. For the first time in history,
a Christian missionary enters Europe, an inconspicuous event that will have
incalculable influence on the history of the continent and of the world.

Commentators have long noted an obvious shift in the narrative perspective between verses 6–9 and verse 10. Aside from his prologues, up to now
Luke has reported all events in third-person perspective ("they" did this or
that). Suddenly at verse 10, there is a change to a first-person narrator who is
within the story: "We sought passage, . . . concluding that God had called us."

3. Since a previous section (15:41–16:5) showed Paul already active in towns of southern Galatia
(Iconium, Derbe, and Lystra), this mention of passing through Galatian territory must refer not to the
Roman province of Galatia, but to North Galatia, whose main towns were Ancyra, Pessinus, and Tavium
(Joseph A. Fitzmyer, *The Acts of the Apostles*, Anchor Bible 31 [New York: Doubleday, 1998], 578).
4. Its only other biblical occurrence is "the Spirit of Jesus Christ" in Phil 1:19; see also Rom 8:9; Gal 4:6.

This implies that Luke himself joined Paul's mission at Troas. From this point onward, Luke's further participation in the events he narrates will continue to be signaled by the presence or absence of "we."

Reflection and Application (16:5–10)

These six verses offer a fascinating glimpse into how human planning and divine guidance interact in the missionary activity of the apostle Paul. Unlike Paul's first mission trip, which came at the direct initiative of the Spirit (13:1–3), the second missionary journey arose from Paul's pastoral desire to visit and care for the new Christians (15:36). But the Spirit then intervenes in Paul's travels. We see Paul actively making reasonable plans, which God blesses. At the same time, we see him recognizing and submitting to the guidance of the Spirit when the Spirit says no, indicating a change of plans that requires a prayerful and obedient disposition. The experience suggests that God works through human initiative and planning but reserves the right to redirect our efforts and bring us to a different destination than we had in mind—in this case, the first Christian mission to Europe.

The Team Travels into Europe (16:11–15)

[11]We set sail from Troas, making a straight run for Samothrace, and on the next day to Neapolis, [12]and from there to Philippi, a leading city in that district of Macedonia and a Roman colony. We spent some time in that city. [13]On the sabbath we went outside the city gate along the river where we thought there would be a place of prayer. We sat and spoke with the women who had gathered there. [14]One of them, a woman named Lydia, a dealer in purple cloth, from the city of Thyatira, a worshiper of God, listened, and the Lord opened her heart to pay attention to what Paul was saying. [15]After she and her household had been baptized, she offered us an invitation, "If you consider me a believer in the Lord, come and stay at my home," and she prevailed on us.

OT: Lev 23:3; Tob 2:2
NT: Acts 5:14; 9:42; 11:17; 18:8; 1 Cor 1:16
Catechism: baptism of household, 1655

16:11–12   The first event in Luke's "we" narrative is a sea journey. The team sails from **Troas** across the Aegean Sea to the island of **Samothrace** and then to **Neapolis**, port city for nearby **Philippi**. Philippi was **a leading city** in **Macedonia and a Roman colony** founded by retired Roman army veterans. This meant that the elite of the city were Roman settlers, mostly military, who spoke Latin rather than the local language, Greek, and whose primary allegiance was to Rome.

The mission team begins by going **outside the city gate along the river** 16:13–15
where they **thought there would be a place of prayer**. What is meant by "place of prayer" is not clear; the Greek term was sometimes used for a synagogue, which they may have been hoping to find (see v. 16). In any case, they begin to evangelize some women who have gathered there. **Lydia** from **Thyatira** in Asia Minor (city of one of the seven churches addressed in the book of Revelation: Rev 2:18–26) is singled out as a †**worshiper of God**, that is, a Gentile who believed in the God of Israel but without becoming a Jewish convert. Lydia's trade as **a dealer in purple cloth** and her heading a household ample enough to host Paul's team indicate that she was rather well-to-do. Purple cloth was made with a dye produced from the shells of murex snails that live in the Mediterranean. Because of its great expense and quality (it grows darker with age rather than fading), murex purple was associated with royalty.

Luke attributes her receptiveness to **the Lord** Jesus, who **opened her heart** to **what Paul was saying**. Grace precedes and prepares for faith. As happened in the case of Cornelius (Acts 10:42–48), she and her entire **household** were **baptized**. Since households included infants and small children, these instances of whole households being baptized seem to be early evidence for Christian baptism of infants. That Lydia, as a woman, was head of her household suggests that she was a widow. She **prevailed** on Paul's team to stay at her home. The same verb is used to describe the two disciples' urging Jesus to stay with them at Emmaus (Luke 24:29).

Imprisonment and Release at Philippi

Acts 16:16–40

Paul and Silas are not looking for trouble in Philippi. But their expulsion of a fortune-telling spirit from a slave girl provokes her owners to incite a mob, which results in their being humiliated, beaten, and imprisoned. The further result is that they save their jailer from suicide and convert him to Christ. Thus Paul and Silas's missionary journey into Macedonia includes an abundant measure of both apostolic suffering and fruitfulness. Paul is already fulfilling the risen Jesus' prophecy to Ananias: "This man is a chosen instrument of mine to carry my name before Gentiles, kings, and Israelites, and I will show him what he will have to suffer for my name" (Acts 9:15–16).

Imprisonment at Philippi (16:16–24)

[16]As we were going to the place of prayer, we met a slave girl with an oracular spirit, who used to bring a large profit to her owners through her fortune-telling. [17]She began to follow Paul and us, shouting, "These people are slaves of the Most High God, who proclaim to you a way of salvation." [18]She did this for many days. Paul became annoyed, turned, and said to the spirit, "I command you in the name of Jesus Christ to come out of her." Then it came out at that moment.

[19]When her owners saw that their hope of profit was gone, they seized Paul and Silas and dragged them to the public square before the local authorities. [20]They brought them before the magistrates and said, "These people are Jews and are disturbing our city [21]and are advocating customs

that are not lawful for us Romans to adopt or practice." ²²The crowd joined
in the attack on them, and the magistrates had them stripped and ordered
them to be beaten with rods. ²³After inflicting many blows on them, they
threw them into prison and instructed the jailer to guard them securely.
²⁴When he received these instructions, he put them in the innermost cell
and secured their feet to a stake.

NT: 1 Thess 2:2
Catechism: exorcism, 1673; exorcism in baptism, 1237

16:16
On their way again toward **the place of prayer** by the riverside (see v. 13),
Paul's team is confronted by a **slave girl with an oracular spirit**, an evil spirit
that could tell fortunes. Literally, the Greek says that she had a *python spirit*,
named for Python, the mythical serpent killed by the god Apollo, which Greeks
considered as the guardian of the oracle at Delphi, a pagan shrine associated
with oracles and divination. This **fortune-telling** girl is a source of handsome
profit to her **owners**, who are exploiting her to make money for themselves.

16:17
The girl begins **to follow Paul and us**. By using "us," Luke again indicates
that he is a participant and eyewitness to the events. As she follows Paul's party,
she keeps crying out, **"These people are slaves of the Most High God"**—expressing the actual facts about the mission team in language understandable
to non-Jews. The term "Most High God" is also used in the Gospels by a man
possessed by demons (Mark 5:7; Luke 8:28). There is something paradoxical
in the acknowledgment by the demonic spirit that Paul's team serves the God
who is higher and more powerful than it. That they **proclaim to you a way of
salvation** is also true. The same phenomenon appears in the Gospels, where the
demons correctly identify Jesus. In both cases, correct doctrine proclaimed in
the wrong way is a hindrance rather than a help to the spread of the gospel—in
this case, by causing distraction or uneasiness to those who might otherwise
be inclined to listen to the preaching of the gospel.

16:18
Paul delays responding for **many days**, perhaps to prayerfully discern the
spiritual source of this unwanted publicity and the appropriate response. But
finally becoming **annoyed**, or "troubled" (NIV), he responds decisively by exorcising the spirit with a word: **"I command you in the name of Jesus Christ
to come out of her."** The power of Jesus exercised by Paul so exceeds the power
of the oracular spirit that the simple command drives it out immediately. This is
another example of the deeds Jesus did in his earthly ministry, such as exorcisms
by a word of command (Luke 4:33–36; 9:38–42), being continued through his
Spirit-filled disciples in Acts.

Fig. 14. Site of the
jail where Paul
and Silas were
held in Philippi
(Acts 16:23).

16:19–20   The immediate and predictable consequence of this exorcism is that the slave's owners, seeing **their hope of profit** collapse, take revenge against **Paul and Silas**. They haul them **before the local authorities** and charge them with being **Jews** who are **disturbing** the **city** by seeking to convert people from Roman to Jewish ways.

16:21   Apparently relying on local hostility to Jews, the slave owners accuse Paul's team with charges customarily brought against Jews: **"advocating customs that are not lawful for us Romans to adopt or practice."** Such anti-Judaism at Philippi might also explain why Paul's team had looked outside the city for a place of prayer where Jews were likely to meet (v. 13).

16:22   Anti-Jewish prejudice is confirmed by the **crowd** who join in the **attack** and the rash action of **the magistrates** (or "rulers")[1] who order, without trial, the humiliating punishment of being **stripped** and then **beaten with rods**. Paul refers to this treatment in his letters: "Three times I was beaten with rods" (2 Cor 11:25) and "We had suffered and been insolently treated, as you know, in Philippi" (1 Thess 2:2).

16:23–24   **After inflicting many blows**, the magistrates throw them **into prison** and order **the jailer to guard them securely**, perhaps indicating how powerful Paul was thought to be after the successful exorcism of the slave girl. The jailer follows **these instructions** by putting Paul and Silas **in the innermost cell** and securing **their feet to a stake**, literally, "to the wood"; other translations say

---

1. The term literally means "military leaders" and is used here because Philippi was a Roman colony founded by retired Roman army veterans.

"in the stocks." Thus shamefully and painfully treated, they are prevented from continuing their missionary activities.

Deliverance from Prison (16:25–40)

[25]About midnight, while Paul and Silas were praying and singing hymns to God as the prisoners listened, [26]there was suddenly such a severe earthquake that the foundations of the jail shook; all the doors flew open, and the chains of all were pulled loose. [27]When the jailer woke up and saw the prison doors wide open, he drew [his] sword and was about to kill himself, thinking that the prisoners had escaped. [28]But Paul shouted out in a loud voice, "Do no harm to yourself; we are all here." [29]He asked for a light and rushed in and, trembling with fear, he fell down before Paul and Silas. [30]Then he brought them out and said, "Sirs, what must I do to be saved?" [31]And they said, "Believe in the Lord Jesus and you and your household will be saved." [32]So they spoke the word of the Lord to him and to everyone in his house. [33]He took them in at that hour of the night and bathed their wounds; then he and all his family were baptized at once. [34]He brought them up into his house and provided a meal and with his household rejoiced at having come to faith in God.

[35]But when it was day, the magistrates sent the lictors with the order, "Release those men." [36]The jailer reported the[se] words to Paul, "The magistrates have sent orders that you be released. Now, then, come out and go in peace." [37]But Paul said to them, "They have beaten us publicly, even though we are Roman citizens and have not been tried, and have thrown us into prison. And now, are they going to release us secretly? By no means. Let them come themselves and lead us out." [38]The lictors reported these words to the magistrates, and they became alarmed when they heard that they were Roman citizens. [39]So they came and placated them, and led them out and asked that they leave the city. [40]When they had come out of the prison, they went to Lydia's house where they saw and encouraged the brothers, and then they left.

OT: Dan 3:23–45; Exod 14:30–31; 20:18–21; Judg 6:22–24; Tob 12:15–17
NT: Luke 13:3, 5; Acts 12:19; 22:25–29
Catechism: Christ freeing the captives, 714; people of God, 782; transformative power of baptism, 1226

Paul and Silas show extraordinary faith and fortitude: after being publicly   16:25–26
stripped, beaten, and imprisoned, they spend the night **praying and singing
hymns to God**. Readers who know the Old Testament will immediately recall

The Christian Response to Suffering

LIVING TRADITION

The Venerable Bede (672–735) admired the spirit of Paul and Silas:

The devotion of the apostles' hearts and the power of prayer are expressed [here] together, since in the depths of the prison they sang hymns, and their praise moved the earth of the prison, shook the foundation, opened the doors, and finally loosened the very chains of those who had been bound. In other words, anyone of the faithful "considers it all joy when he falls into various trials" (James 1:2) and gladly glories in his infirmities, so that the power of Christ may dwell in him (2 Cor 12:9). Such a one undoubtedly sings hymns with Paul and Silas within the darkness of the prison, and with the psalmist he recites to the Lord, "You are my refuge from the distress which surrounds me, my exaltation" (Ps 32:7).[a]

a. *Commentary on the Acts of the Apostles* 16:25, in ACCS 206.

the song of the three young men in the fiery furnace (Dan 3) and perhaps the martyrs at the time of the Maccabees (2 Macc 7). Gentile readers familiar with philosophical tradition might recall the death of Socrates or others who showed courage in prison. Their joyful response impresses the other **prisoners** who **listened** to them.

God's intervention to rescue Paul and Silas recalls the earlier rescues of Peter from prison (Acts 5:19–20; 12:6–11). But whereas Peter's escapes were surreptitious, here God frees his servants by means of **a severe earthquake** that rattles **the foundations of the jail**, opens the **doors**, and releases **the chains of all**.

16:27–29   The **jailer** abruptly awakens and sees **the prison doors wide open**. Thinking himself disgraced and facing a terrible reprisal for his failure to keep prisoners secure (as Herod executed Peter's guards after his escape; Acts 12:19), he prepares **to kill himself** by falling on his **sword**. But to his astonishment he finds that Paul has not only remained in the jail but has apparently influenced the other prisoners to remain, despite their loosened chains and the open doors. This startling event has the jailer **trembling with fear**, so that he falls **down before Paul and Silas** in religious awe. Fear and trembling is the typical human reaction to a †theophany, a manifestation of the presence and power of God (see Exod 14:30–31; 20:18–21; Judg 6:22–24; Tob 12:15–16).

16:30–32   No longer concerned about reprisals, the jailer himself brings Paul and Silas out of jail and begs them to answer the question now burning in his heart: **"What must I do to be saved?"** Both his question and their answer speak of what is essential with clarity and simplicity: **"Believe in the Lord Jesus and**

you and your household will be saved." Despite the midnight hour and their painful wounds, Paul and Silas seize the opportunity and evangelize the jailer and **everyone in his house.**

Only after hearing the gospel does the jailer, **at that hour of the night,**   16:33–34
take them in and bathe their **wounds.** Perhaps with the same source of water, **he and all his family** are **baptized.** Fittingly, these new Christians celebrate with **a meal,** filled with joy at **having come to faith in God** (as Levi had in Luke 5:27–29). Because the jailer was a pagan with no previous exposure even to Judaism, Luke describes his conversion as coming to belief in God, rather than in Jesus, although the necessity of faith in Jesus is explicitly indicated in verse 32. For a pagan to believe in Messiah Jesus is to enter into relationship with the God of Israel.

Luke does not explain why the next **day, the magistrates** ordered **the lic-**   16:35
tors, literally, "carriers of the rods" (NRSV "police"), by whom the missionaries had been beaten, to release Paul and Silas. One manuscript fills this gap in the narrative by explaining that it was because the earthquake made them afraid.[2]

When the **jailer** reports this decision **to Paul** and asks them to **go in peace,**   16:36–37
Paul refuses, insisting that the magistrates repair the damage to his and Silas's honor. Because the magistrates had acted so precipitously in **beating** them **publicly** and throwing them into **prison** without a trial, only now is Paul able to inform them that those they have treated so shamefully are **Roman citizens.**[3] Roman law protected citizens from beatings without being first tried in court (compare Acts 22:25). Paul refuses to allow these bungling officials to avoid the consequences of their illegal actions and **release** the missionary pair **secretly. By no means** is a very strong negative response. He insists that they **come themselves** and escort the missionaries out publicly, to restore their honor after unjustly disgracing them. This action would be important for the reputation of the incipient Christian community as well as for the missionaries' prospects for returning to Philippi.

Hearing this, **the magistrates** are **alarmed** to learn that Paul and Silas are   16:38–40
Roman citizens. Now on the defensive, they **placated** (RSV "apologized," NJB "urged") Paul and Silas, publicly escorting them out and asking **that they leave the city.** Paul and Silas accede to their request, but only after going to **Lydia's**

---

2. Bruce M. Metzger, *A Textual Commentary on the Greek New Testament*, 2nd ed. (Stuttgart: Deutsche Bibelgesellschaft, 1994), 398.
3. Partly due to a twentieth-century tendency to disbelieve claims about Paul in Acts that are not explicitly substantiated in Paul's own letters, some scholars have questioned whether Paul actually was a Roman citizen, but his Roman name (Paul) supports that claim, which will be insisted on even more in Acts 22:25–29. See Joseph A. Fitzmyer, *The Acts of the Apostles*, Anchor Bible 31 (New York: Doubleday, 1998), 590.

house to strengthen, console, and **encourage** the new Christians after this traumatic event.

Reflection and Application (16:25–40)

Even when we are trying to do the tasks that God gives us without calling attention to ourselves, we may be unfairly accosted. When Paul tried to quiet the possessed girl who was causing a disturbance by exorcising the demon from her, he brought severe maltreatment upon himself and Silas. However, Paul's handling of the situation shows us that we do not have to surrender all our rights when we are unjustly persecuted. Sometimes it is necessary to stand up for our rights as citizens. For example, bishops, preachers, and Christian institutions must defend their rights to the free exercise of religion in the face of pressures to conform to secular values. This applies to the Church's right to proclaim the gospel as well as to teach and practice her faith in regard to the whole range of moral issues. The outcome of resistance to external pressures and the defense of the Church's rights is not in our power to control, however, and ultimately we must entrust ourselves to God's providence. Even if we, like Paul and Silas, suffer at the hands of government authorities because of our testimony to the truth, we must continue to "obey God rather than men" (Acts 5:29).

Paul in Thessalonica, Beroea, and Athens

Acts 17:1–34

Paul and his missionary team continue to proclaim the word of God throughout Macedonia and Greece despite persecution and a mixed reception from Jews and Gentiles. In Athens, Paul encounters a new challenge to evangelization in the widespread idolatry and faulty philosophical worldviews prevalent there. Paul's major speech to the Athenians takes an approach different from his earlier speeches to Jews. Without initially mentioning Jesus, he focuses on the living God, who created and will judge the world. His mission as "a light to the Gentiles" (Acts 13:47) requires that he speak in terms familiar to the philosophically minded pagans in Athens. When he finally mentions Jesus as a man whom God raised from the dead and through whom God will judge the whole world, Paul runs into resistance from his Greek listeners, who refuse to accept the notion of resurrection.

Paul in Thessalonica (17:1–9)

¹When they took the road through Amphipolis and Apollonia, they reached Thessalonica, where there was a synagogue of the Jews. ²Following his usual custom, Paul joined them, and for three sabbaths he entered into discussions with them from the scriptures, ³expounding and demonstrating that the Messiah had to suffer and rise from the dead, and that "This is the Messiah, Jesus, whom I proclaim to you." ⁴Some of them were convinced and joined Paul and Silas; so, too, a great

number of Greeks who were worshipers, and not a few of the prominent women. ⁵But the Jews became jealous and recruited some worthless men loitering in the public square, formed a mob, and set the city in turmoil. They marched on the house of Jason, intending to bring them before the people's assembly. ⁶When they could not find them, they dragged Jason and some of the brothers before the city magistrates, shouting, "These people who have been creating a disturbance all over the world have now come here, ⁷and Jason has welcomed them. They all act in opposition to the decrees of Caesar and claim instead that there is another king, Jesus." ⁸They stirred up the crowd and the city magistrates who, upon hearing these charges, ⁹took a surety payment from Jason and the others before releasing them.

NT: Luke 4:16; 23:2; 24:25–27, 44–47; Acts 18–19

17:1 The main east-west road in the Roman Empire was the Via Egnatia, which ran from Byzantium (later Constantinople, now Istanbul in Turkey) to the Adriatic Sea. Paul and his team apparently follow this **road** westward from Philippi to **Thessalonica**, another Macedonian city. Although Luke used "we" in the account of the slave girl who harassed Paul in Philippi (Acts 16:17), he makes no claim to be with Paul and Silas after their arrest or during their departure from Philippi. In his account of events in Thessalonica, Luke continues the third-person "they," possibly to signal that he remained behind in Philippi. The next appearance of "we" will again be in Philippi (20:6), after Paul's ministry in Corinth and Ephesus.

There was no mention of a synagogue in Philippi, and most of Paul's activity there was with Gentiles. But Thessalonica does possess **a synagogue of the Jews**, and Jews will be the initial focus of his attention in this city.

17:2 Luke reminds us that Paul's **usual custom** in each new city was to begin his mission in a **synagogue**. Indeed Luke highlights Paul's similarity to Jesus, who also "went according to his custom into the synagogue on the sabbath day" (Luke 4:16).[1] In Thessalonica **for three sabbaths**, Paul makes persuasive arguments (as in 18:4, where he attempts "to convince both Jews and Greeks") based on **the scriptures**. Luke does not tell us which Old Testament passages Paul uses, but other evangelistic speeches in Acts refer to psalms of David, such as Ps 16 and 110 (see Acts 2:34–35; 13:35), and to Isaiah's Suffering Servant passages (Isa 42; 53; Acts 8:28–35; 26:23).

1. The Greek is almost identical: "according to his custom" (Luke 4:16) and, literally, "according to Paul's custom" (Acts 17:2).

As Jesus himself does in Luke 24:26–27, Paul expounds on Scripture to show that according to God's plan, **the Messiah had to suffer and rise from the dead**. The Messiah was to triumph not by military might but by taking on himself all human sin and evil, humbling himself even to "death on a cross" (Phil 2:8), thus reconciling to God the human race that had been alienated from him since Adam's disobedience (see Rom 5:12–19).

17:3

Paul's argument follows a form in Greek †rhetoric that Aristotle called an "enthymeme," a logical argument in which one of the three steps (major term, middle term, conclusion) is implied rather than stated. Paul's starting point (the major term) is that the Messiah had to suffer and rise from the dead. The implied middle term is that Jesus *did* suffer and rise from the dead, an event that was confirmed by Jesus' apostolic eyewitnesses. Paul's conclusion, then, is direct: **"This is the Messiah, Jesus, whom I proclaim to you."**[2]

As usual, many but not all of Paul's Jewish listeners are **convinced** by his proclamation. These join **Paul and Silas** and, presumably, begin preparing for baptism. Other converts include **a great number of Greeks who were worshipers** of the God of Israel and numerous **prominent women**, like the convert Lydia in Philippi.

17:4

In contrast to the "prominent women" who open their hearts to the gospel are the **worthless men loitering in the public square** who are **recruited** by some of the Jews to form a **mob** and **set the city in turmoil**. Luke attributes the opposition of these **Jews** to their jealousy at Paul's success in winning converts. The mob tries to find **Paul and Silas** at **the house of Jason**, an otherwise unknown Christian convert (possibly the same Jason mentioned in Rom 16:21). The intention is to drag them to be tried before **the people's assembly**. In Thessalonica the whole body of citizens carried out judicial functions.

17:5

Not finding Paul and Silas, the mob drags **Jason** and some of the other Christians before the authorities. Luke uses the correct term for Thessalonica's civic authorities: **city magistrates** (Greek *politarchēs*, literally, "ruler of the city"). He is consistently well-informed about the political background of the events he is relating.

17:6–7

The mob accuses the Christians of **creating a disturbance all over the world** or "undermining the civilized world" (or having "turned the world upside down," RSV). The irony in this charge is that the gospel does indeed turn the world and its values on its head (see Luke 1:52–53). The mob makes the further political

---

2. See William S. Kurz, "Hellenistic Rhetoric in the Christological Proof of Luke-Acts," *Catholic Biblical Quarterly* 42 (1980): 171–95.

accusation that the Christians **all act in opposition to the decrees of Caesar**. Both Jews and Christians' loyalty to the state was called into question because of their unwillingness to participate in emperor worship and other civic pagan religious ceremonies.

Their particular charge is that the Christians **claim instead that there is another king, Jesus**. As the Jewish authorities had accused Jesus before Pilate (Luke 23:2; see John 19:12), the Thessalonian mob misrepresents the Christian claim that Jesus is the Messiah-king as meaning **king** in a worldly sense. This charge accuses the Christians of constituting a political threat to the authority of the Roman emperor.

17:8–9   Although the accusers **stirred up** both **the crowd and the city magistrates**, these authorities do not overreact, as did those at Philippi (16:22–23). Rather, they follow Roman legal procedure: **upon hearing these charges**, they demand **a surety payment**, or bail, **from Jason and the others before releasing them**. If the Christians provoke any further trouble, they will forfeit this money; but they are not beaten or imprisoned without cause.

Reflection and Application (17:1–9)

The Christian claim that Jesus is Lord and King, to whom we owe absolute allegiance, was perceived by many people in the first century as a threat to the established Roman civil order. This perception was partly correct and partly incorrect. Christians are obliged to be good citizens, and to cooperate with civil authority as long as it does not overstep its bounds, but they do not accept the contention that the state has absolute power, as Caesar claimed. Jesus directed his listeners to "repay to Caesar what belongs to Caesar, and to God what belongs to God" (Luke 20:25). Jesus was accused of opposing taxes to Caesar (false in light of 20:25) and of maintaining "that he is the Messiah, a king" (23:2). But he insisted that his kingdom was not of this world, which is why his followers did not resist his arrest (John 18:36).

Paul teaches that Christians are to respect government authority but also to recognize that all authority, including that of the state, is established by God and therefore subject to and limited by God's authority (Rom 13:1–7). State authority has the good purpose of maintaining the public order, which is necessary for individuals and peoples to flourish. Therefore Christians are to pay taxes and to honor civil authorities (Rom 13:7). But there will be times when they must "obey God rather than men" (Acts 5:29).

Paul in Beroea (17:10–15)

¹⁰The brothers immediately sent Paul and Silas to Beroea during the
night. Upon arrival they went to the synagogue of the Jews. ¹¹These Jews
were more fair-minded than those in Thessalonica, for they received the
word with all willingness and examined the scriptures daily to determine
whether these things were so. ¹²Many of them became believers, as did
not a few of the influential Greek women and men. ¹³But when the Jews of
Thessalonica learned that the word of God had now been proclaimed by
Paul in Beroea also, they came there too to cause a commotion and stir up
the crowds. ¹⁴So the brothers at once sent Paul on his way to the seacoast,
while Silas and Timothy remained behind. ¹⁵After Paul's escorts had taken
him to Athens, they came away with instructions for Silas and Timothy to
join him as soon as possible.

NT: Acts 9:24–25

To avoid further trouble, the Thessalonian community **immediately** sends   **17:10**
Paul and Silas to Beroea, about fifty miles to the west. The decision to transfer
the two missionaries **during the night**, under cover of darkness (as in Acts
9:24–25), shows how serious they consider the opposition in Thessalonica. At

Paul's First Epistle

**BIBLICAL
BACKGROUND**

A few weeks or months after being driven out of Thessalonica Paul
wrote what most scholars believe is his first letter and the earliest
document in the New Testament, 1 Thessalonians. Being forced
to leave the city abruptly after a short stay, Paul was concerned
about the welfare of the Thessalonian Christians. Once Timothy
rejoined him, Paul sent Timothy back to Thessalonica to gather
a report on the church there. Timothy's report contained good
news: the new Christians were holding steadfastly to faith in the
Lord Jesus. Paul wrote to confirm his pastoral relationship with the
Thessalonians and to strengthen them in their faith. Rather than focusing on
Jewish members of the community, who are at the center of Luke's attention
in Acts 17, Paul addresses himself mainly to Gentile converts, who perhaps
were more numerous (see 1 Thess 1:9), exhorting them about holiness and
sexual morality, mutual charity, the resurrection, relations between leaders
and members, and daily Christian attitudes (1 Thess 4:3–5:22).

Beroea, Paul and Silas first go to **the synagogue of the Jews,** as they have in every city where there was a synagogue.

17:11–12   In contrast to many of Paul's previous audiences, the Beroean Jews receive **the word** with great eagerness. Luke describes them as **more fair-minded,** literally, "more noble" (RSV), than the Jews of **Thessalonica.** Their nobility consists in their open-mindedness and the fact that they search **the scriptures daily** to see if the good news about Jesus is consistent with God's earlier revelation. By looking at what the Old Testament itself has to say, they test the central Christian claim that Christ fulfills the Scriptures in his life, death, and resurrection (see Luke 24:44–47; John 5:39). As a result of their biblical investigations **many** Beroeans, both Jews and Greeks, become **believers.**

17:13–15   The contrast between the receptive Jews of Beroea and the hostile **Jews of Thessalonica** becomes sharper when the latter, hearing about Paul's preaching in Beroea, travel the fifty miles **to cause a commotion and stir up the crowds** against him. In response, the Christians once again prudently send Paul packing, while **Silas and Timothy** remain to strengthen the fledgling church. Paul continues to be the lightning rod for Jewish hostility, perhaps because he is the most effective speaker. **Paul's escorts** bring him to **Athens,** but since his preference is always to minister as a team, he gives **instructions for Silas and Timothy to join him as soon as possible.**

Fig. 15. View of the Parthenon, a temple dedicated to the goddess Athena, from the Areopagus where Paul preached (Acts 17:19–34).

Reflection and Application (17:10–15)

Today many Jewish converts to the Catholic faith can identify with the experience of the Jews of Beroea, who "received the word with all willingness and examined the scriptures daily to determine whether these things were so" (Acts 17:11). Rosalind Moss, a Jew who came to faith in Christ in 1975 and later entered the Catholic Church, writes about the first time she heard the Scriptures explained in light of Christ:

> For five months they [some young Jewish Christians] took me through Old Testament prophecies that pointed, they believed, to the Messiah. I tried to remain solid in my unbelief, frightened at the thought of falling prey to their thinking. But my defenses were a poor shield against a few verses from Isaiah which pierced me through.

> For to us a child is born,
>   to us a son is given;
> and the government will be upon his shoulder,
>   and his name will be called
> Wonder Counselor, Mighty God,
>   Everlasting Father, Prince of Peace. (Isa 9:6)

> Surely he has borne our griefs
>   and carried our sorrows;
> yet we esteemed him stricken,
>   smitten by God, and afflicted.
> But he was wounded for our transgressions,
>   he was bruised for our iniquities;
> upon him was the chastisement that made us whole,
>   and with his stripes we are healed. (Isa 53:4–5)

> They walked me through the story of the Exodus, which I knew well. . . . The Israelites, according to the Law given Moses on the Mountain, would bring lambs to the altar as a sin offering. . . . Every sacrifice and all of them together were a sign, they told me, a sign that would point to the One who would come and take upon Himself, not the sin of one person for a time, but the sin of all men, of everyone who had ever lived and whoever would be born, for all time. . . .
> I was shattered. . . . I was speechless. And in shock. I knew it was true.[3]

3. Rosalind Moss, "All This and Heaven, Too," in *Honey from the Rock: Sixteen Jews Find the Sweetness of Christ*, ed. Roy Schoeman (San Francisco: Ignatius Press, 2007), 164–69.

Paul in Athens (17:16–21)

---

[16]While Paul was waiting for them in Athens, he grew exasperated at the sight of the city full of idols. [17]So he debated in the synagogue with the Jews and with the worshipers, and daily in the public square with whoever happened to be there. [18]Even some of the Epicurean and Stoic philosophers engaged him in discussion. Some asked, "What is this scavenger trying to say?" Others said, "He sounds like a promoter of foreign deities," because he was preaching about 'Jesus' and 'Resurrection.' [19]They took him and led him to the Areopagus and said, "May we learn what this new teaching is that you speak of? [20]For you bring some strange notions to our ears; we should like to know what these things mean." [21]Now all the Athenians as well as the foreigners residing there used their time for nothing else but telling or hearing something new.

OT: Sir 3:20–24
NT: Rom 1:19–32; 2 Tim 4:3–4

17:16   By the time Paul arrived there, **Athens** had lost much of the importance it had centuries earlier as Greece's leading city and the birthplace of Greek philosophy. Nevertheless, its reputation as an intellectual and religious center endured, and the monuments of its past glory in the form of statues and temples of the gods made a striking impression. Luke gives readers an inside glimpse into Paul's profoundly negative reaction to idol worship in Athens before he quotes Paul's more diplomatic public comments in his speech on the Areopagus. While **Paul** is **waiting** for Silas and Timothy, he grows **exasperated** ("deeply distressed," NRSV; "revolted," JB, NJB; "provoked," RSV) **at the sight of the city full of idols**. Idolatry dishonors the true God and leads people into degrading beliefs and practices (see Rom 1:19–32).

17:17   Because of his zealous reaction, and perhaps because he has time on his hands as he waits for his companions, Paul debates not only in his usual place and time, **in the synagogue** on the Sabbath (Acts 13:14, 44; 17:2; 18:4) with his usual listeners, **Jews** and [†]**worshipers** of the God of Israel, but also **daily in the public square** (or "marketplace") **with whoever happened to be there**. In the square, Paul's method would have looked a good deal like the philosophers of his day who challenged the behavior or beliefs of people passing by.

17:18   The two most popular Greek schools of thought in the first century were those of **the Epicurean and Stoic philosophers** (see sidebar). Paul engages them **in discussion** as a fellow philosopher, but they cannot make sense of his message. **Some** mockingly refer to him as a **scavenger**, literally, "seed-picker," applied to

Epicurean and Stoic Philosophers

BIBLICAL
BACKGROUND

Classical Greek philosophy developed in four main schools of thought in ancient Athens. The earliest schools were the Platonists, about 400 BC, and the Aristotelians, or Peripatetics, about 350 BC. The Epicureans and Stoics appeared around 300 BC and by the first century AD were the two most popular schools of thought in Athens. However, by this time all four schools had evolved, and some had borrowed elements from others.

Epicurus (341–270 BC) and his followers did not believe in an afterlife and held that the world was formed by the chance unions of atomic particles. Since they believed that even gods were formed from atoms and did not intervene at all in human lives, Epicureans declared that people could live free of the widespread pagan dread that the gods might arbitrarily victimize them. However, neither could people expect that the gods would help them. We are on our own in this universe and have to make the best of this present life, since there is no other. Some Epicureans considered pleasure a sign that one is living a good life, as enjoying one's job is an indication that one is doing it well. Although the Epicureans did not deny there were gods, their disbelief in divine intervention and their rejection of religion made them look to outsiders like atheists.

Zeno founded the Stoics about 320 BC. The school is named after a *stoa* or colonnade in Athens where Zeno taught. Stoics sought to live according to nature, which they perceived as divine and whose guiding principle was "reason" (*logos*). They taught that everything is subject to the laws of nature or "fate," which probably contributed to the ancient and modern stereotype of the Stoic as one who resignedly puts up with circumstances. Stoic ethics stressed self-sufficiency, self-control, and obedience to reason and duty. The Stoics were perceived as being more open to religious belief than Epicureans, and some later Stoics exhibited a genuine religious spirit. Some Stoic ideas on divine providence were used and adapted by ancient Jewish and Christian thinkers.[a]

a. See Joseph A. Fitzmyer, *The Acts of the Apostles*, Anchor Bible 31 (New York: Doubleday, 1998), 604–5; Luke Timothy Johnson, *The Acts of the Apostles*, Sacra pagina 5 (Collegeville, MN: Liturgical Press, 1992), 313.

idle babblers or empty talkers who pick up and pass on scraps of information. **Others** think he is introducing **foreign deities**. Perhaps they misinterpret Paul's **preaching about 'Jesus' and 'Resurrection'** (Greek *anastasis*, which sounds like a female name) as promotion of a pair of deities.

The philosophers lead Paul to the **Areopagus**, or Hill of Ares (from *Ares*, the Greek god of war, and *pagos*, "rocky hill"). Since Mars is the Roman name

17:19–20

for Ares, the place is sometimes referred to as Mars Hill. This was where the governing council of ancient Athens traditionally met.[4] The audience asks Paul to explain his **new teaching**, since they find some of his **notions** to be **strange** and want **to know what these things mean**. Their question underlines how foreign the biblical message is to the pagan worldview.

17:21   An ancient stereotype about **Athenians** was that they were preoccupied with **telling or hearing something new**. To a person always seeking novelty, serious reflection and the sincere quest for truth are equally alien. Yet the penchant for intellectual fads is not limited to those living in ancient Athens. Paul warns in 2 Tim 4:3–4, "The time will come when people will not tolerate sound doctrine but, following their own desires and insatiable curiosity [literally, "with itching ears"] will accumulate teachers and will stop listening to the truth and will be diverted to myths."

Paul's Speech in Athens (17:22–34)

[22]Then Paul stood up at the Areopagus and said:

"You Athenians, I see that in every respect you are very religious. [23]For as I walked around looking carefully at your shrines, I even discovered an altar inscribed, 'To an Unknown God.' What therefore you unknowingly worship, I proclaim to you. [24]The God who made the world and all that is in it, the Lord of heaven and earth, does not dwell in sanctuaries made by human hands, [25]nor is he served by human hands because he needs anything. Rather it is he who gives to everyone life and breath and everything. [26]He made from one the whole human race to dwell on the entire surface of the earth, and he fixed the ordered seasons and the boundaries of their regions, [27]so that people might seek God, even perhaps grope for him and find him, though indeed he is not far from any one of us. [28]For 'In him we live and move and have our being,' as even some of your poets have said, 'For we too are his offspring.' [29]Since therefore we are the offspring of God, we ought not to think that the divinity is like an image fashioned from gold, silver, or stone by human art and imagination. [30]God has overlooked the times of ignorance, but now he demands that all people everywhere repent [31]because he has established a day on which he will 'judge the world with justice' through a man he has appointed, and he has provided confirmation for all by raising him from the dead."

---

4. The council itself came to be called "the Areopagus," even when it met in another location, so some scholars believe that Paul was brought to speak before the council rather than to the place called Mars Hill.

[32]When they heard about resurrection of the dead, some began to scoff, but others said, "We should like to hear you on this some other time." [33]And so Paul left them. [34]But some did join him, and became believers. Among them were Dionysius, a member of the Court of the Areopagus, a woman named Damaris, and others with them.

OT: Gen 1:26–28; 2 Chron 32:19; Isa 44:9–20; Jon 4:11

NT: Luke 12:47–48; 23:34; John 2:19–21; Acts 3:17; 7:47–50; 2 Cor 6:2; 1 Tim 1:13

Catechism: God creator of all, 287, 301; last judgment, 1038–41; resurrection, 992–1001; natural revelation, 32, 2566

Although Paul is repulsed by the sight of so many idols in the city (17:16), he begins his speech in the Areopagus diplomatically: **"I see that in every respect you are very religious,"** literally, "revering of divinities," but the Greek can also mean "very superstitious." Paul may be deliberately playing on this ambiguity. He is appealing to common ground with his listeners, describing them positively as very religious. However, some in the crowd might hear an implied critique of Athenian popular piety as being superstitious, a view that many philosophers would share.

17:22

Paul carefully seeks an opening for his presentation of the gospel. His reference to his **looking carefully at your shrines** would be understood by his listeners in a positive sense. He mentions that he noticed **an altar inscribed, "To an Unknown God."** Although this is the only record of an Athenian altar with this particular inscription, other ancient sources indicate the presence in Athens of altars that did not name any particular god.[5] The presence of such an altar, Paul asserts, shows that the Athenians **unknowingly worship** the only God there is, the God whom Paul will now **proclaim** to them. In this way, Paul is able to present the gospel as an extension and correction of what they already know, rather than as a total rejection of their previous religious understanding.

17:23

Paul begins his proclamation of the gospel by addressing the Athenians' mistaken religious ideas, just as he did when the people of Lystra attempted to worship him and Barnabas as gods (Acts 14:15–17). The key to his clarification is the doctrine of creation, the bedrock Judeo-Christian doctrine that is found in the first verse of the Bible and the first article of the creed: **"God . . . made the world and all that is in it."** As creator, God is **the Lord of heaven and earth**, absolute master over all that he has made. This biblical understanding of creation means that God is not one being among other beings in the world. Rather, he is absolutely transcendent over all he has made, and the entire universe depends on him at every moment for its existence. It follows that, in stark

17:24

---

5. See Johnson, *Acts*, 315; Fitzmyer, *Acts*, 607.

contrast to pagan ideas, God **does not dwell in sanctuaries made by human hands**. Stephen had made a similar point about God's temple in Jerusalem (Acts 7:48). The expression "made by human hands" recalls Old Testament diatribes against idols, which are human-made in contrast to the living God (2 Chron 32:19; see John 2:19–21). Paul's words also echo the heroic mother in 2 Macc 7:28: "Look at the heavens and the earth and see all that is in them; then you will know that God did not make them out of existing things; and in the same way the human race came into existence."

17:25   The transcendent God is not **served by human hands** as if **he needs anything**. This means that his creating and sustaining the world have no ulterior motive but are free acts of love and generosity. According to some pagan creation myths, the gods created human beings as their slaves, to serve them by growing food and sacrificing animals. On the contrary, Paul emphasizes, God needs nothing that humans could possibly provide, because **it is he who gives to everyone life and breath and everything** (see Ps 50:7–15). What could we possibly give to our creator, who gives us our very existence and everything else we have?

Vatican I: God Is Known by Reason and Revelation

LIVING TRADITION

The First Vatican Council (1869–70) taught that God can be known by reason through a consideration of the created world, but that he also has revealed himself in a supernatural way:

> The same holy mother church holds and teaches that God, the source and end of all things, can be known with certainty from the consideration of created things, by the natural power of human reason: *ever since the creation of the world, his invisible nature has been clearly perceived in the things that have been made* (Rom 1:20). It was, however, pleasing to his wisdom and goodness to reveal himself and the eternal laws of his will to the human race by another, and that a supernatural, way. This is how the Apostle puts it: *In many and various ways God spoke of old to our fathers by the prophets; but in these last days he has spoken to us by a Son* (Heb 1:1–2).
> It is indeed thanks to this divine revelation, that those matters concerning God which are not of themselves beyond the scope of human reason, can, even in the present state of the human race, be known by everyone without difficulty, with firm certitude, and with no intermingling of error.[a]

a. Vatican I, *Dogmatic Constitution on the Catholic Faith*, in *Decrees of the Ecumenical Councils*, vol. 2, *Trent to Vatican II*, ed. Norman P. Tanner (Washington, DC: Georgetown University Press, 1990), 806.

Paul further emphasizes the unity of **the whole human race**, which God **17:26**
made from one couple, Adam and Eve (Gen 1:26–28),[6] and is now spread over
the entire surface of the earth (Gen 1:28). The common ancestry of all human
beings is the foundation for Paul's teaching on original sin in Rom 5:12–19;
1 Cor 15:21–22.

God **fixed** both the **ordered seasons** of the year (see Gen 8:22) and the geographical **boundaries** of the **regions** in which various peoples dwell (see Gen
10). Thus God is master of both nature and human history. Paul is drawing
on the biblical teaching that God "set up the boundaries of the peoples" (Deut
32:8). This does not mean that international borders are established by God
but that the division of the human race into distinct peoples, languages, and
cultures is not by pure chance but is part of God's providence for human beings.

The beauty, complexity, and order of God's creation was intended to arouse **17:27**
human curiosity, with the result **that people might seek God, even perhaps**
grope for him and find him (see Wis 13:5; Rom 1:20). That human beings
ought to "seek the Lord" is a fundamental teaching of Scripture.[7] Without the
benefit of revelation, the search for God is like a blind person's groping. Yet
some Gentiles do succeed in discovering God, which is possible because **indeed**
he is not far from any one of us. Not being part of the world, God is able to
be present to everyone and everything in the world.

Paul's speeches in Acts are always adapted to the understanding of his au- **17:28**
dience. Whereas his preaching to Jews is based explicitly on Scripture, here
speaking to Gentiles he refers instead to their own writers and philosophers. The
statement **"In him we live and move and have our being"** may be a quotation
from the Greek poet Epimenides (sixth century BC), whom Paul also quotes
in Titus 1:12. It is not a statement of pantheism, which claims that everything
is God or a part of God. Rather, Paul proclaims that God is fully present to us
at every moment of our lives, and we are utterly dependent on him.

Paul next cites another Greek poet, Aratus (born about 310 BC), who wrote,
"We too are his offspring." Paul does not interpret Aratus as claiming that we
are physically descended from God, as, for example, in the myth that Hercules
was sexually begotten by Zeus. Rather, he means it to be understood in the
light of Gen 1:26, where God creates human beings in his image and likeness
(see Luke 3:38). In this sense God is the Father of all human beings. "Have
we not all one Father? Has not the one God created us?" (Mal 2:10). Yet, as
Paul affirms elsewhere, we become God's children in the fullest sense by being

---

6. See Catechism, 360; Pope Pius XII, *Humani Generis*, 37.
7. See Pss 27:8; 105:4; Prov 28:5; Wis 13:6; Isa 55:6.

reborn in Christ as adopted sons and daughters of God (Rom 8:15; Gal 4:5–6; see John 1:12–13).

17:29   Paul now mounts a full-scale attack on idolatry: **"We ought not to think that the divinity** [literally, "the divine"] **is like an image fashioned from gold, silver, or stone by human art and imagination."** The term for "image" here is not the word for humans created in God's image in Genesis (*eikōn*), but rather *charagma*, a crafted likeness such as an idol. The foolishness of worshiping products of **human art and imagination** is a common theme in Old Testament critiques of idolatry, as in Wis 13:10 (see also Isa 44:9–20):

> But wretched are they, and in dead things are their hopes,
> who termed gods things made by human hands:
> Gold and silver, the product of art, and images of beasts,
> or useless stone, the work of an ancient hand.

The Spoils of the Egyptians

LIVING TRADITION

For the Fathers of the Church, the insights attained by various schools of philosophy and the secular sciences were a marvelous gift, to be adapted by Christians and brought into the service of the gospel. The Fathers often spoke metaphorically of this secular wisdom as "the spoils of the Egyptians." As Origen explained to his friend Gregory:

> I wish to ask you to extract from the philosophy of the Greeks what may serve as a course of study or a preparation for Christianity, and from geometry and astronomy what will serve to explain the sacred Scriptures. . . .
> Perhaps something of this kind is shadowed forth in what is written in Exodus from the mouth of God, that the children of Israel were commanded to ask from their neighbors and those who dwelt with them vessels of silver and gold, and raiment, in order that, by spoiling the Egyptians, they might have material for the preparation of the things which pertained to the service of God.[a]

Just as God instructed the fleeing Israelites to take precious items from Egypt for the sake of liturgical worship (Exod 11:2; 35:5, 22), so too, Christians may adopt secular wisdom in order to explain the faith and build up the Church. This does not mean uncritically accepting all the ideas held by secular thinkers, but discerning what is true in them and purifying them in the light of the gospel.

a. *Letter to Gregory Thaumaturgus*, in *ANF* 4:393.

Some Greek philosophers made similar arguments against the worship of idols.

Paul makes a clear distinction between the **times of ignorance**, in which   17:30–31
God overlooked human errors concerning divine truths, and **now**, the time of fulfillment and complete revelation through his Son, the risen Messiah and Savior. God previously showed forbearance toward idol-worshiping Gentiles because of their excusable ignorance. Paul said the same to the pagans of Lystra: "In past generations he allowed all Gentiles to go their own ways" (Acts 14:16). God was similarly forbearing to Jews who did not accept Jesus before his resurrection (Luke 23:34; see Acts 3:17; 13:27). These affirmations are part of a broader biblical theme of God's patience with human ignorance (Jon 4:11; Luke 12:47–48; 1 Tim 1:13).

However, now that God has given the fullness of revelation in the risen Christ, he **demands**, or "commands" (RSV, NRSV), **that all people everywhere repent** of their erroneous views. The creator of the world has now **established a day on which he will "judge the world with justice"** to reward the good and punish the evil (see John 5:27–29; Rom 2:3–10; 2 Cor 5:10). Although all will be judged for their deeds, salvation is available as a free gift of God to be received in faith (Acts 15:11; Eph 2:4–8). God will judge human beings by **a man he has appointed**, one who shares our nature and thus understands our struggles and temptations (see Heb 2:18). God has confirmed Jesus' authority to judge **by raising him from the dead**. Jesus' exaltation to God's right hand enables him to share in God's role as judge of all people. Whereas the apostles' sermons to Jews stress Jesus as Messiah and Lord (Acts 2:29–36; 5:31), the sermons to Gentiles emphasize Jesus as judge, sharing in the authority of the creator God (Acts 10:42; 24:25).

The Athenians' attentive hearing of Paul's argument comes to a halt as soon   17:32
as he mentions **resurrection of the dead**. For the ancient Greeks, the idea of the body's being raised was considered both absurd and repugnant. Some Greek philosophers, such as Platonists, held that the soul is immortal. But they viewed the body, with its physical cravings, as a prison that impedes the soul's faculties of intellect and will. At death the soul finally attains freedom by being released from the body. The biblical view, in contrast, is that the human being is a union of soul and body, or better, an embodied soul (see Ps 16:9; Matt 10:28). To survive death merely as a soul is not to be a complete human being. Thus true salvation must be salvation of the whole human person, soul and body.

The audience's difficulty in grasping Paul's preaching of the resurrection leads to a divided response, as when he preached to Jews, though here expressed in a more typically Greek way: **some began to scoff**, but **others** expressed a mild interest: **"We should like to hear you on this some other time."**

17:33–34   Though **some** listeners **join** Paul and become **believers**, not many conversions result from his preaching in Athens. Two converts are singled out by name: **Dionysius, a member of the Court of the Areopagus**, and **a woman named Damaris**. The fourth-century church historian Eusebius reports that Dionysius became the first bishop of Athens.[8] Although nothing else is known of Damaris, she may also have been a prominent member of the church in Athens, like Lydia at Philippi, since some manuscripts describe her as "respectable" and "honorable."

Paul's preaching in Athens appears less successful than most of his other sermons in Acts. A common but doubtful theory holds that Paul's mixed results at Athens led him to drop the strategy of adapting his message to his audience and instead to preach only "Jesus Christ, and him crucified"; then 1 Cor 2:1–5 is cited in support of this view. However, Paul's sermon on the Areopagus, as recounted by Luke, is not based on the kind of rhetorical eloquence or human wisdom that he rejects in 1 Corinthians. Moreover, the point most rejected by the Athenians, the resurrection, is one on which Paul does not give ground in the least (see 1 Cor 15).

Reflection and Application (17:22–34)

Paul's proclamation of the gospel in Athens contains lessons for our evangelizing today. Paul openly discusses his faith with people in the public square. He does not wait for people to come to church, as we may be inclined to do, but rather goes out in search of the lost like the good shepherd (Luke 15:4–7). Convinced of the truth and necessity of the gospel, Paul is not afraid or ashamed to bring his faith into the conversation, despite the unfamiliarity and even strangeness of the Christian message to the people with whom he is talking (see Rom 1:16). Instead, he does his best to explain and defend his beliefs.

When Paul is invited to speak, he finds something positive to say about the sincere religious striving of those to whom he is speaking, although he knows their beliefs to be deeply erroneous. He looks for common ground, even affirming something true in their religion that he can use as a starting point for sharing the gospel. As he says in 1 Cor 9:22, "I have become all things to all, to save at

---

8. A well-known Christian mystical writer of the fifth century wrote under the pseudonym of Dionysius (or Denys) the Areopagite to indicate that he followed in the footsteps of this philosopher who found fulfillment in the Christian faith. See Frank E. Wheeler, "Dionysius," in *Anchor Bible Dictionary*, ed. David N. Freedman (New York: Doubleday, 1992), 2:201.

least some." The message is essentially the same as what he preaches to Jewish audiences—the proclamation of Jesus as Lord—but he tailors his approach to his pagan audience, which must first grasp the notion of a single all-powerful creator God before understanding his Son Jesus as Savior. Paul quotes pagan poets to support his argument, yet corrects his audience's mistaken ideas about divinity. He explains the necessity of repentance and tells them the sober truth about future judgment. He boldly asserts Jesus' resurrection, though he surely knows that this assertion will cause many Greeks to scoff. Finally, he is not discouraged when only a few receive his message. With evangelical fortitude, he sets out for his next mission, in the city of Corinth.

Paul's Mission in Corinth

Acts 18:1–28

Compared to Paul's mixed reception in Athens, his subsequent mission to Corinth is both more eventful and more successful. We see Paul preaching in synagogues every Sabbath and working closely with Priscilla and Aquila at their common trade, until the arrival of his assistants Silas and Timothy enables him to dedicate himself full time to evangelization. After Jewish rejection he turns to Corinthian Gentiles and is encouraged by Jesus in a vision. An attempt to have him condemned by the Roman proconsul fails.

After extended ministry in Corinth, Paul returns by sea to his home base in Antioch of Syria. This ends his second missionary journey. Soon afterward his third missionary journey begins with another visit to strengthen the churches he and Barnabas established in Asia Minor (18:23). The stage is set for Paul's extraordinarily fruitful ministry at Ephesus in Acts 19.

Paul in Corinth (18:1–11)

[1] After this he left Athens and went to Corinth. [2] There he met a Jew named Aquila, a native of Pontus, who had recently come from Italy with his wife Priscilla because Claudius had ordered all the Jews to leave Rome. He went to visit them [3] and, because he practiced the same trade, stayed with them and worked, for they were tentmakers by trade. [4] Every sabbath, he entered into discussions in the synagogue, attempting to convince both Jews and Greeks.

⁵When Silas and Timothy came down from Macedonia, Paul began to occupy himself totally with preaching the word, testifying to the Jews that the Messiah was Jesus. ⁶When they opposed him and reviled him, he shook out his garments and said to them, "Your blood be on your heads! I am clear of responsibility. From now on I will go to the Gentiles." ⁷So he left there and went to a house belonging to a man named Titus Justus, a worshiper of God; his house was next to a synagogue. ⁸Crispus, the synagogue official, came to believe in the Lord along with his entire household, and many of the Corinthians who heard believed and were baptized. ⁹One night in a vision the Lord said to Paul, "Do not be afraid. Go on speaking, and do not be silent, ¹⁰for I am with you. No one will attack and harm you, for I have many people in this city." ¹¹He settled there for a year and a half and taught the word of God among them.

OT: Gen 26:2–4; Num 21:34; Deut 3:2; Ezek 3:17–21; 33:7–9
NT: Luke 10:10–11; Acts 13:51; 15:14; 18:12
Catechism: strength and courage as gifts of Spirit, 1303, 1520

After leaving **Athens** Paul arrives at **Corinth**, the capital city and a commercial center of southern Greece. There he meets **a Jew named Aquila** from **Pontus**, a Roman province in northwest Asia Minor. Aquila and **his wife Priscilla** had lived in **Italy** but were forced to relocate by the expulsion of **all the Jews** from **Rome** by the emperor **Claudius**. The ancient historian Suetonius, who mentions this event, writes that the expulsion was occasioned by inter-Jewish strife over a certain "Chrestus," which is probably a misspelling of the Latin name for Christ, *Christus*.[1] Paul stays and works with this couple since they share the same **trade** as **tentmakers**, or leatherworkers and makers of tents and awnings. In his letters Paul emphasizes the fact that he supported himself by manual labor (1 Cor 4:12; 9:6–12; 1 Thess 2:9; 2 Thess 3:6–9), to set a good example and to distinguish himself from philosophical and religious teachers who charged a fee for their teaching and whose aim was personal gain. Aquila and Priscilla will become important coworkers with whom Paul will live, work, and communicate by letter—here in Corinth, in Ephesus, and later, probably after Claudius's death, back in Rome.[2]   **18:1–3**

Paul's initial missionary pattern in Corinth is to labor at tentmaking during the work week and preach the gospel on Saturdays.[3] According to his usual   **18:4**

---

1. Suetonius, *Life of Claudius* 25.
2. See Acts 18:18–19; Rom 16:3–5; 2 Tim 4:19; and comments on Acts 18:26.
3. Although Christians gathered to worship on Sunday, the Lord's day (Acts 20:7; Rev 1:10), Jewish Christians like Paul continued to observe the Jewish Sabbath. The transition to Sunday as the Christian day of rest was gradual.

The Las Vegas of the Ancient World

BIBLICAL BACKGROUND

In the ancient world, the city of Corinth was synonymous with moral depravity. Located on a narrow neck of land that connected the two parts of Greece (the Peloponnesian Peninsula and the mainland), Corinth was a major intersection for both sea and land traffic. As such, it was a wealthy commercial center that gathered traders, hucksters, sailors, slaves, and people of every stripe from all over the Roman Empire. The city was also the location for the Isthmian Games, held every two years and second only to the Olympics in popularity. The skyline of Corinth was dominated by the Acrocorinth, a steep, rocky hill atop which stood the temple of Aphrodite, Greek goddess of love.[a]

Given its cosmopolitan atmosphere, it is not surprising that Corinth had a reputation for drunkenness and debauchery. In ancient Greek the term "Corinthian girl" came to mean a prostitute, and the verb *korinthiazomai*, "to Corinthianize," meant to fornicate. Various pagan cults and mystery religions competed for adherents. The moral degradation and confusion in the culture of Corinth provides the backdrop for Paul's arrival with an astounding message: there is salvation and freedom from sin in Christ! Here some of his greatest evangelistic work was accomplished. As he later wrote in his First Letter to the Corinthians, "Jews demand signs and Greeks look for wisdom, but we proclaim Christ crucified, a stumbling block to Jews and foolishness to Gentiles, but to those who are called, Jews and Greeks alike, Christ the power of God and the wisdom of God" (1 Cor 1:22–24).

a. Strabo, *Geographica* 8.6, 20.

approach in every new city, **every sabbath** he engages in **discussions in the synagogue, attempting to convince both Jews and Greeks** of the truth of the gospel. "Greeks" here probably refers to †God-fearers, non-Jews who were attracted to Judaism and attended synagogue services.

18:5 Paul's pattern changes after **Silas and Timothy** arrive **from Macedonia**. Their presence and the financial support they apparently bring, probably from Philippi (see Phil 4:15), enable Paul **to occupy himself totally with preaching the word**, presumably all week long. Paul's witness **that the Messiah was Jesus** is the heart of Paul's preaching **to the Jews** who, like the Jews during Jesus' ministry, look forward to a Messiah who will restore Israel and inaugurate the kingdom of God. The idea of "messiah" would make little sense to Gentiles who do not know the Bible.

The Prophet's Role as Sentinel

BIBLICAL BACKGROUND

Paul portrays himself as fulfilling the prophetic role of sentinel described in Ezek 33:1–9. Prophets are called to warn the people of imminent judgment and the need to repent. If the prophet warns sinners and they repent, the sinners will be spared and the prophet honored. On the other hand, if God's sentinel fails to warn them, the unrepentant will die because of their sins, but the sentinel will also be held accountable for their deaths.

The sentinel image underlines the solemn duty of God's representatives, especially prophets and apostles, to communicate God's message of salvation. Later, in Paul's farewell to the Ephesian elders, he makes a similar claim: "I solemnly declare to you this day that I am not responsible for the blood of any of you, for I did not shrink from proclaiming to you the entire plan of God" (Acts 20:26–27).

These Jewish listeners, however, contradict and insult Paul. In response he shakes out **his garments**, in accord with Jesus' instructions: "Whatever town you enter and they do not receive you, go out into the streets and say, 'The dust of your town that clings to our feet, even that we shake off against you'" (Luke 10:10–11). Paul and Barnabas had performed a similar gesture after being rejected in Antioch of Pisidia (Acts 13:51). Paul accompanies this gesture with a declaration similar to that of the prophet Ezekiel (Ezek 3:17–21; 33:7–9): **"Your blood be on your heads! I am clear of responsibility."** He is telling his listeners that he bears no culpability for their failure to respond to God's word, for he has done all he could to deliver it to them. They, not Paul, are responsible for the judgment they will incur on account of rejecting the gospel. As on previous occasions (see Acts 13:46), Paul now turns his attention **to the Gentiles**. 18:6

Because of his rejection in the synagogue, Paul ceases preaching there and goes instead to the **house** of **Titus Justus.**[4] Like Lydia in Philippi (Acts 16:14), Titus Justus is a †**worshiper of God**, a Gentile who reveres the God of Israel but does not become a Jew. As before, Paul's turn to the Gentiles does not imply that he renounces his mission of witnessing to Jews. Rather, he turns to the Gentiles in a given city only after first preaching to Jews. Titus's house is conveniently located **next to a synagogue**, making it still accessible to Jewish listeners. 18:7

4. The more likely manuscript reading is *Titius* Justus. Although he could be the same person as Paul's coworker Titus, mentioned in Galatians and 2 Corinthians and to whom the Letter to Titus is addressed, no evidence besides the name supports this identification.

First and Second Corinthians

BIBLICAL BACKGROUND

First Corinthians, written from Ephesus in AD 56, provides invaluable information regarding the nitty-gritty problems of an early Christian community. Among other topics, Paul addresses problematic attitudes and factions (1:10–4:21), immorality (5:1–6:20), questions about marriage and celibacy (7:1–40), the Eucharist (10:14–22; 11:17–34), charisms and charity (1 Cor 12–14), and the resurrection (1 Cor 15).

Second Corinthians, written from Macedonia in AD 57, tells of Paul's apostolic sufferings and his response, and explains his understanding of ministry (2 Cor 3–5). At the same time this letter vividly portrays Paul's stormy, yet affectionate, relationship with the Corinthian church (1:12–2:17; 6:11–13; 7:2–16). It contains an inspired fundraising appeal for the poor of Jerusalem (2 Cor 8–9). Paul also defends his ministry and humble approach against criticisms of other evangelists to whom he ironically refers as "superapostles" (2 Cor 10–13).

18:8   A prominent Jew comes **to believe in the Lord** Jesus: **Crispus, the synagogue official**, whose baptism Paul himself mentions in 1 Cor 1:14. Like Lydia (Acts 16:15) and the Philippian jailer (Acts 16:31–33), Crispus is converted **along with his entire household** (see 1 Cor 1:14).

Crispus and Titus are the first among many **Corinthians** who **believed and were baptized**. Paul's ministry lays a strong foundation for the church in Corinth, to whom Paul himself will later write letters, two of which are preserved in the canon of Scripture.[5]

18:9–10   Paul receives a guiding **vision** at **night**, possibly in a dream, like his vision in Troas (Acts 16:9). In this case **the Lord** Jesus himself reassures Paul, **"Do not be afraid."** Having experienced repeated rejection by his own people, Paul needs encouragement to continue his witness. The Lord gave similar reassurances to Isaac (Gen 26:2–4), Moses (Num 21:34; Deut 3:2), and Joshua (Josh 8:1) in times of adversity. Jesus exhorts Paul to continue the mission he has begun: **"Go on speaking, and do not be silent, for I am with you."** "I am with you" is often God's response to the fear and trepidation of those to whom he has given a humanly impossible mission (see Exod 3:12; Judg 6:16; Luke 1:28).

The risen Lord adds the promise, **"No one will attack and harm you."** Although Jews will bring charges against Paul before the provincial governor

---

5. See 1 Cor 5:9 and 2 Cor 2:3–4 for mention of two letters that were not preserved for posterity.

(Acts 18:12), they will not succeed in harming him. Further, Jesus assures Paul, **"I have many people in this city"** who still need to hear the gospel message, whom God desires to add to the "people for his name" (Acts 15:14).

Paul therefore settles in Corinth **for a year and a half**, preaching and teaching **the word of God**, that is, the good news of salvation in Christ and the whole way of life that goes with it. This extended time is needed for attracting a significant number of new believers.

18:11

Accusations before Gallio (18:12–17)

¹²**But when Gallio was proconsul of Achaia, the Jews rose up together against Paul and brought him to the tribunal,** ¹³**saying, "This man is inducing people to worship God contrary to the law."** ¹⁴**When Paul was about to reply, Gallio spoke to the Jews, "If it were a matter of some crime or malicious fraud, I should with reason hear the complaint of you Jews;** ¹⁵**but since it is a question of arguments over doctrine and titles and your own law, see to it yourselves. I do not wish to be a judge of such matters."** ¹⁶**And he drove them away from the tribunal.** ¹⁷**They all seized Sosthenes, the synagogue official, and beat him in full view of the tribunal. But none of this was of concern to Gallio.**

NT: Acts 17:5–9; 18:8; 1 Cor 1

Fig. 16. Remains of the tribunal at Corinth where Paul was brought before the proconsul Gallio (Acts 18:12).

18:12–13   The public disturbance described in verses 12–17, which occurred **when Gallio was proconsul of Achaia**, provides important evidence for the dating of Paul's ministry. From an ancient Greek inscription that mentions Gallio's brief period as administrator of Achaia, the riot can be dated precisely to AD 51 or 52. **The Jews** organize a united attack on **Paul** and bring him before **the tribunal**, as Jewish leaders had brought Jesus before the Roman governor Pilate (Luke 23:1). They try to get the proconsul to take their side by accusing Paul of **inducing people to worship God contrary to the law**. The charge is intentionally worded in ambiguous language, for "contrary to the law" could mean not only against Jewish law but also against Roman law.

18:14–15   Gallio, however, sees through the subterfuge and declares that their complaint **is a question of arguments over** Jewish doctrine, and therefore irrelevant to his secular Roman court. Gallio is one of several Roman officials cited by Luke, including Pilate and the centurion at the cross, who attest to the innocence of Jesus or his disciples. Because the charge is a religious concern and not a matter of **crime or malicious fraud**, he tells them, **"See to it yourselves."** As a Roman official, he does **not wish to be a judge of such matters**.

18:16–17   Gallio's rejection of their case is forceful: he drives them **away from the tribunal**. Both the ensuing Jewish reaction and Gallio's nonresponse to it are puzzling. Jews seize **Sosthenes, the synagogue official**, and publicly beat him up. It is not clear whether this is the same Sosthenes whom Paul mentions as the cosender of 1 Corinthians (1 Cor 1:1); nor do we know the nature of his relationship to Crispus, the other Corinthian synagogue official converted by Paul (v. 8; see 1 Cor 1:14).

If Sosthenes was not a Christian convert, the Jewish motive for beating him may have been frustration with him as the leader of their failed attempt to have Paul convicted by Gallio. More likely, Sosthenes had become an influential Christian and the Jews turn on him when they cannot get at Paul. Either way, they interpret Gallio's laissez-faire attitude as license to beat Sosthenes since their concern is an intramural Jewish matter. Jews in Thessalonica had similarly turned on Jason when they could not find Paul (Acts 17:5–9).

But none of this was of concern to Gallio. Gallio's failure to respond to obvious lawbreaking in his presence might be a deliberate sign of his contempt for intra-Jewish squabbles. Or it might stem from a similar anti-Semitic prejudice that magistrates had demonstrated at Philippi, so that he does not care if a Jew is openly beaten in violation of Roman law.

Return to Syrian Antioch (18:18–23)

[18]Paul remained for quite some time, and after saying farewell to the brothers he sailed for Syria, together with Priscilla and Aquila. At Cenchreae he had his hair cut because he had taken a vow. [19]When they reached Ephesus, he left them there, while he entered the synagogue and held discussions with the Jews. [20]Although they asked him to stay for a longer time, he did not consent, [21]but as he said farewell he promised, "I shall come back to you again, God willing." Then he set sail from Ephesus. [22]Upon landing at Caesarea, he went up and greeted the church and then went down to Antioch. [23]After staying there some time, he left and traveled in orderly sequence through the Galatian country and Phrygia, bringing strength to all the disciples.

OT: Num 6:1–21
NT: Acts 15:40–41; 18:26; 21:23–24
Catechism: vows, 2102–3

18:18 After ministering in Corinth **for quite some time** (v. 11 said it was "a year and a half"), Paul bids **farewell** to the community and sails for the church at Antioch, from which he had begun his mission (15:40–41). **Priscilla and Aquila** accompany him on the first leg of his return (see 18:26), but Silas and Timothy seem not to do so.

Before sailing from Corinth's port of **Cenchreae**, Paul gets his **hair cut because he had taken a vow**. Luke does not make clear what kind of vow this is, but it is probably a †Nazirite vow, a form of consecration to God for Israelite laypeople that included abstention from alcohol and from cutting one's hair (Num 6:1–21). On completing the terms of the vow, a Nazirite would offer sacrifices in the temple and shave his head; verse 22 implies that after arriving in Caesarea, Paul did in fact go to the temple in Jerusalem. The mention of this detail shows that Paul is still an observant Jew. This will be further underlined by James's request that Paul join four men taking a vow and pay their expenses so as to silence those who accuse Paul of breaking the Mosaic law (Acts 21:23–24).[6]

18:19–21 In the first leg of his voyage, Paul sails to **Ephesus**, where he leaves his coworkers Priscilla and Aquila, probably with the plan that they will set up their tentmaking business and make acquaintances in preparation for his return for

6. See Mikeal C. Parsons, *Acts*, Paideia: Commentaries on the New Testament (Grand Rapids: Baker Academic, 2008), 261; Luke Timothy Johnson, *The Acts of the Apostles*, Sacra pagina 5 (Collegeville, MN: Liturgical Press, 1992), 329–30; and Joseph A. Fitzmyer, *The Acts of the Apostles*, Anchor Bible 31 (New York: Doubleday, 1998), 634.

The Nazirite Vow

The Nazirite vow, described in Num 6:1–21, was a voluntary commitment that Israelites could make to show special devotion to the Lord or to give thanks for a favor received. Although the Nazirite vow was usually temporary, it was in some respects a precedent for consecrated life in the Church. It was a way that laypeople, that is, nonpriests, could specially consecrate themselves to God. It involved abstaining from wine and strong drink, from contact with corpses, and from cutting one's hair (Num 6:4–6). The colorful story of Samson (Judg 13–16) is a famous instance of a lifelong Nazirite consecration: "No razor has touched my head, for I have been consecrated to God from my mother's womb. If I am shaved, my strength will leave me, and I shall be as weak as any other man" (Judg 16:17). After Delilah tricked him and cut his hair, Samson did lose his strength, leading to his imprisonment and blinding by the Philistines, until his hair grew and God gave him strength for a final triumph over Israel's enemies (Judg 16:28–30).

The ritual for a Nazirite who "completes the period of his dedication" included animal sacrifices that could involve considerable expense (Num 6:13–15), which may be the rite that Paul carries out in Acts 21:24).

---

a mission like the one he carried out with them in Corinth. Before departing from Ephesus, Paul enters **the synagogue** and engages in **discussions with the Jews**, according to his usual missionary pattern. His efforts are apparently well received, since they ask him to stay longer. Paul declines but promises, **"I shall come back to you again, God willing."** His return and prolonged mission in Ephesus will be reported in Acts 19.

18:22   Paul sails from Asia Minor to the port of **Caesarea** in Palestine; from there **he went up**, that is, he went to Jerusalem. Because of the special holiness of Jerusalem and the temple as a pilgrimage destination, travelers even today speak of going *up* to Jerusalem, regardless of the direction from which they approach the city. When travelers leave Jerusalem, they likewise go *down*. Thus, after Paul greets **the church** in Jerusalem, he goes **down to Antioch**, which is to the north in Syria.

18:23   **After staying** at his home base in Antioch for an unspecified length of **time**, Paul departs on his third missionary journey. This time he travels by land into Asia Minor, again visiting the churches. Paul travels **in orderly sequence** ("from place to place," NIV, RSV, NJB) through the **Galatian country and Phrygia**. His purpose is to bring **strength to all the disciples** he made in these

International Mapping

Fig. 17. Paul's third missionary journey (Acts 18:23–21:15).

areas—strengthening them, for instance, by answering their questions and giving them fuller instruction and exhortation.

Apollos (18:24–28)

[24]A Jew named Apollos, a native of Alexandria, an eloquent speaker, arrived in Ephesus. He was an authority on the scriptures. [25]He had been instructed in the Way of the Lord and, with ardent spirit, spoke and taught accurately about Jesus, although he knew only the baptism of John. [26]He began to speak boldly in the synagogue; but when Priscilla and Aquila heard him, they took him aside and explained to him the Way [of God] more accurately. [27]And when he wanted to cross to Achaia, the brothers encouraged him and wrote to the disciples there to welcome him. After his arrival he gave great assistance to those who had come to believe through

grace. [28]He vigorously refuted the Jews in public, establishing from the
scriptures that the Messiah is Jesus.

NT: Luke 1:4; 3:4; Acts 9:2; 19:1; 24:14; Rom 16:1; 1 Cor 3:5–6
Catechism: inspiration and truth of Scripture, 106–7; interpretation of Scripture, 109–14

18:24   During Paul's absence, **Apollos**, who will later play a major role in the church at Corinth (1 Cor 3:5–6), arrives **in Ephesus**. He is a **Jew** and **native of Alexandria**, capital of the Roman province of Egypt and, along with Rome, Ephesus, and Syrian Antioch, one of the most important cities in the Roman Empire. He is **an authority on the scriptures** and an **eloquent speaker**. The Greek for "eloquent" here, *logios*, can also mean "learned." Probably both apply to Apollos because of his knowledge of the Scriptures and ability to argue from them. Later, in the patristic era, Alexandria would become well known as a great center of Christian learning, especially of spiritual interpretation of the Scriptures.

18:25   Some of the information about Apollos here is confusing. On the one hand, Luke reports that he was **instructed in the Way of the Lord**, that is, Christianity (see Acts 9:2; 24:14), and that he **taught** about Jesus **accurately** and **with ardent spirit**. This is a positive assessment, though not as positive as saying he was "filled with the Holy Spirit," as were others, such as the apostles, Stephen, and Paul. On the other hand, Apollos **knew only the baptism of John**. If he has been instructed in the †Way (like Theophilus in Luke 1:4), how could he know "only the baptism of John"? One explanation is that Apollos knew *John's* teaching about "the way of the Lord," meaning "prepare the way of the Lord" (Luke 3:4). John also taught that a greater one would come after him, without knowing in detail how this prophecy would be fulfilled in Jesus. Apollos is apparently familiar with John's preaching and some of Jesus' deeds and sayings but not with the full truth of Jesus' identity and mission.

18:26   Unaware that his knowledge is incomplete, Apollos begins to preach **boldly in the synagogue**. When **Priscilla and Aquila** hear about him, they discreetly take him **aside** and fill in the gaps, namely, that the Lord proclaimed by John is the crucified and risen Lord Jesus and that "the Way of the Lord" is the path of discipleship that one enters through baptism into Christ. It is noteworthy that Priscilla's name appears before Aquila's, suggesting that she has the more active role in instructing Apollos. Four out of the six times Priscilla is mentioned in the New Testament, her name appears first.[7] Although both she and her husband, Aquila, were valued coworkers of Paul, Priscilla was more prominent, indicating that, despite the generally inferior position of women in the first century

---

7. Acts 18:2, 18, 26; Rom 16:3; 1 Cor 16:19; 2 Tim 4:19.

and limitations on their public teaching (1 Cor 14:34–35; 1 Tim 2:12–15), the early Church was able to appreciate the insight and abilities of gifted women.

After some ministry in Ephesus, Apollos wishes **to cross to Achaia**—southern Greece—where he will follow up Paul's ministry (see Acts 19:1; 1 Cor 3:5–6). Because of his ability to defend the Christian message from Scripture, the Ephesian Christians encourage him and write to the **disciples** in Achaia to welcome him. Introducing a traveling Christian missionary with a letter of recommendation was a common practice in the early Church. For example, Paul wrote to the Romans, "I commend to you Phoebe our sister, . . . a minister [Greek *diakonos*] of the church at Cenchreae" (Rom 16:1). In Achaia, Apollos gives **great assistance** to the Christians, **who had come to believe through grace**. Luke here reminds us that their conversion was primarily due to God's grace rather than to God's human instruments such as Paul.

18:27

A special contribution of Apollos to the Christians in Achaia is in apologetics. He **vigorously** refutes the Jews **in public**, defending the recently converted Christians from Jewish criticisms of their beliefs and **establishing from the scriptures that the Messiah is Jesus** (as in Luke 24:25–27, 44–47; Acts 2:22–36; 17:2–3). This Christian interpretation of the Old Testament also contributes to the catechesis of the community. Thus the learned biblical preacher Apollos furthers the faith of those Corinthians converted by Paul. This corresponds to Paul's statement in 1 Cor 3:6: "I planted, Apollos watered, but God caused the growth."

18:28

Reflection and Application (18:1–28)

Christian ministers always have to keep in mind that the ministry is God's work, not ours. As the master in charge of the work, God is responsible for the success of the ministry as well as the needs of those who serve him. In times of opposition or failure, the best antidote to a defeatist impulse is earnest prayer, seeking Jesus' reassurance that he is with us and will protect us. At the same time, Christian ministers have to realize that they are not indispensable in any particular mission or city. In his absence, Paul's efforts were furthered not only by his own trained assistants but also by other ministers such as Apollos. The same is true today. In the end, all Christian workers die and must be replaced in the Lord's vineyard.

Ephesus

Acts 19:1–41

Throughout Acts, Luke has been showing how the early Christians interacted with Jews, Gentiles sympathetic to Judaism, Greco-Roman pagans, uncivilized idol-worshipers, and even Greek philosophers. For such diverse audiences, the missionaries need to keep adjusting both their evangelizing approaches and their defense against attacks. Paul's ministry at Ephesus, a city famous for its involvement in magic as well as for its temple of the goddess Artemis, illustrates how the early Christians dealt with magical practices, which they encountered not only among pagans but even among some Jews. They also had to contend with the fact that the Christian message can have political and economic repercussions, leading to hostility and even persecution.

Paul in Ephesus (19:1–12)

[1]While Apollos was in Corinth, Paul traveled through the interior of the country and came [down] to Ephesus where he found some disciples. [2]He said to them, "Did you receive the holy Spirit when you became believers?" They answered him, "We have never even heard that there is a holy Spirit." [3]He said, "How were you baptized?" They replied, "With the baptism of John." [4]Paul then said, "John baptized with a baptism of repentance, telling the people to believe in the one who was to come after him, that is, in Jesus." [5]When they heard this, they were baptized in the name of the Lord Jesus. [6]And when Paul laid [his] hands on them, the holy Spirit

came upon them, and they spoke in tongues and prophesied. [7]Altogether there were about twelve men.

[8]He entered the synagogue, and for three months debated boldly with persuasive arguments about the kingdom of God. [9]But when some in their obstinacy and disbelief disparaged the Way before the assembly, he withdrew and took his disciples with him and began to hold daily discussions in the lecture hall of Tyrannus. [10]This continued for two years with the result that all the inhabitants of the province of Asia heard the word of the Lord, Jews and Greeks alike. [11]So extraordinary were the mighty deeds God accomplished at the hands of Paul [12]that when face cloths or aprons that touched his skin were applied to the sick, their diseases left them and the evil spirits came out of them.

OT: Isa 40:3; Mal 3:1
NT: Matt 28:19; Luke 3:4, 16; Acts 1:5; 11:15–16; 13:24–25
Catechism: Holy Spirit and baptism, 798, 1279, 2670
Lectionary: Acts 19:1b–6a: Confirmation Mass (optional)

When Paul arrives at **Ephesus**, he finds a group of **disciples**, but something   **19:1–3** seems to be missing. He pinpoints the problem by asking, **"Did you receive the holy Spirit when you became believers?"** Their surprising answer is that they **never even heard that there is a holy Spirit**. This rules out the possibility that they could be full-fledged Christians, since Christian initiation entails receiving the Spirit as Jesus' disciples did at Pentecost (Acts 2:1–4; 8:14–17; 10:44–48). They were baptized only **with the baptism of John.**

John's **baptism of repentance** only prepared the way for Jesus, as the Gospel   **19:4** explains (Luke 3:4). Here **Paul** reemphasizes the point: John himself had told **the people to believe in the one who was to come after him, that is, in Jesus,** who "will baptize you with the holy Spirit and with fire" (Luke 3:16).

In response, these disciples are **baptized in the name of the Lord Jesus**. Luke   **19:5** is not necessarily repeating the actual baptismal formula.[1] Rather, his intent is to emphasize their Christian baptism in distinction from the baptism of John. Being baptized into "the name of the Lord Jesus" means to come into a personal union with Jesus, to belong to him, to follow him as his disciple. The Church today, as throughout Christian tradition, baptizes new believers "in the name of the Father, and of the Son, and of the Holy Spirit," the Trinitarian formulation at the end of Matthew's Gospel (Matt 28:19).

---

1. See Joseph A. Fitzmyer, *The Acts of the Apostles*, Anchor Bible 31 (New York: Doubleday, 1998), 643–44.

19:6–7   The Greek text uses a single sentence for the entire sequence of their baptism (instead of the two in the NAB), implying that the rite of baptism, begun in verse 5, was only complete **when Paul laid [his] hands on them**. The immediate consequence is that **the holy Spirit** comes upon them, thus continuing to fulfill Jesus' promise: "John baptized with water, but . . . you will be baptized with the holy Spirit" (Acts 1:5; 11:16). The outward signs of the Spirit's coming on these disciples are the same as occurred at Pentecost: **they spoke in tongues and prophesied**. Another hint that the Pentecost event is being repeated is the detail that **there were about twelve men**, recalling the twelve tribes of Israel and the twelve apostles. In Scripture the number twelve often symbolizes the people of God (see sidebar).

19:8   In Ephesus as in other cities, Paul begins by preaching in the **synagogue**. **For three months** he debates skeptical Jews **boldly with persuasive arguments about the kingdom of God**. Presumably he is declaring that the centuries of Jewish longing for God's reign (see Isa 24:23; 52:7) have been fulfilled in the life, death, and resurrection of Jesus.

19:9   As often before, the Jewish reaction to Paul's message is mixed: **some in their obstinacy and disbelief** resist his teaching. They publicly contradict Paul and disparage **the Way**, the shorthand term for Christianity (Acts 9:2). Because he can no longer preach there without public opposition, Paul withdraws from the synagogue, taking his new **disciples** with him. But he quickly finds another venue, just as he did in Corinth (Acts 18:7). Through **daily discussions in the**

The Venerable Bede on the Twelve Baptized at Ephesus

LIVING TRADITION

The Venerable Bede explains the use of the number twelve in Acts:

> Behold Asia, which not long before was unworthy to be visited by the apostles [Acts 16:6], now consecrated by the apostolic number [twelve] and exalted by a prophetic gift! And it should be noted that the Holy Spirit showed signs of his coming, both here in the twelve disciples, and earlier in the hundred and twenty [Acts 1:15] (which is the number twelve multiplied ten times). I believe that the former [manifestation occurred] in Jerusalem, and this one in Ephesus, which is a Greek city, to show that whether the one who believes is from the Jews or the gentiles, [the Spirit] fills . . . those who share the unity of the catholic and apostolic church.[a]

a. *Commentary on the Acts of the Apostles*, Cistercian Studies Series 117 (Kalamazoo, MI: Cistercian Publications, 1989), 154.

Ephesus

Ephesus, the location of Paul's longest mission (nearly three years, Acts 20:31), was the fourth largest city in the Roman Empire, with a population of about two hundred thousand people, about 10 percent of whom may have been Jews. It was the capital of the Roman province of Asia (the western part of modern-day Turkey), a center of commerce, and quite wealthy. The city's boast was the magnificent temple to the goddess Artemis, considered one of the seven wonders of the ancient world. Ephesus also featured temples to the goddess Roma, to the divine Caesar, and to an assortment of other deities, and the city was known for the practice of magic (see Acts 19:18–19). Although little remains of the temple of Artemis, archaeological excavations have uncovered many other temples, magnificent apartments, and the theater where Demetrius and his fellow silversmiths rioted to protest Paul's preaching and its economic impact (Acts 19:23–40).

lecture hall of Tyrannus, he further instructs those who were persuaded by his teaching.

Paul continues his **discussions** in that lecture hall **for two years**, thus pro-longing his stay in Ephesus even longer than in Corinth. With some hyperbole, Luke reports the sweeping **result**: not only the people of Ephesus but also **all the inhabitants of the province of Asia heard the word of the Lord, Jews and Greeks alike**. Paul's strategy was to use major cities as a base from which new converts could fan out, bringing the gospel to the surrounding areas. Evidence for the influence of Paul's Ephesian mission upon other Asian cities is found in his references to Miletus, Hieropolis, and Laodicea (Acts 20:15–17; Col 4:13, 16; 2 Tim 4:20), in his Letter to the Colossians, and in the existence of seven churches of Asia to whom the book of Revelation was addressed near the end of the first century (Rev 1:4, 11). *[19:10]*

Luke emphasizes not only the remarkable success of Paul's preaching but also the astounding miracles that God worked through him. So **extraordinary** are these **mighty deeds** that they impressed even a city that was renowned for its magic practices. **When face cloths or aprons that touched his skin were applied to the sick**, a practice that could easily look like magic to Ephesians, **their diseases left them and the evil spirits came out of them**. In distinction from magic, however, Luke makes clear that it was not the cloths themselves but **God** who **accomplished** these healings. This remarkable period of evangeliza-tion in Ephesus, marked by an abundance of healings and exorcisms, parallels *[19:11–12]* similar seasons reported by Luke in the ministry of Jesus (Luke 4:40–41; 6:17–19; 7:21–22), of the Twelve (Acts 2:43; 4:29–33), and of Peter (Acts 5:15–16).

Reflection and Application (19:1–12)

If Paul were to visit a typical Catholic parish today, he might be inclined to ask the same question he posed to the disciples in Ephesus: "Did you receive the Holy Spirit when you believed?" In the Church of the New Testament, the presence and activity of the Holy Spirit were visible in charisms of prophecy and tongues (Acts 10:46; 19:6; 1 Cor 12; 14), in bold testimony to the gospel (Acts 4:13, 29–33; Eph 6:18–20), in Spirit-filled praise and worship (Eph 5:18–20), and through signs and wonders (Acts 2:43; 4:30; 5:12; Rom 15:19; Heb 2:4). We twenty-first-century Catholics likewise need to seek and open ourselves to the graces of Pentecost if we are to fulfill our calling to be faithful witnesses in a new evangelization.

Powerful preaching, conversions of large groups of people, and remarkable signs and wonders have been more frequent in Church history than many Catholics realize. We would do well to pray for such preaching, conversions, and signs and wonders in our time.

The use of "face cloths or aprons that touched [Paul's] skin" provides biblical precedent for what are traditionally called second-class relics—items of clothing or other objects used by a saint and venerated by the faithful, through which, on occasion, God works miraculously (see Catechism 1674–76).

Jewish Exorcists (19:13–20)

[13]Then some itinerant Jewish exorcists tried to invoke the name of the Lord Jesus over those with evil spirits, saying, "I adjure you by the Jesus whom Paul preaches." [14]When the seven sons of Sceva, a Jewish high priest, tried to do this, [15]the evil spirit said to them in reply, "Jesus I recognize, Paul I know, but who are you?" [16]The person with the evil spirit then sprang at them and subdued them all. He so overpowered them that they fled naked and wounded from that house. [17]When this became known to all the Jews and Greeks who lived in Ephesus, fear fell upon them all, and the name of the Lord Jesus was held in great esteem. [18]Many of those who had become believers came forward and openly acknowledged their former practices. [19]Moreover, a large number of those who had practiced magic collected their books and burned them in public. They calculated

their value and found it to be fifty thousand silver pieces. ²⁰Thus did the word of the Lord continue to spread with influence and power.

NT: Matt 27:9
Catechism: magic, 2117; exorcism, 1673

The following incidents further clarify the distinction between magic and divine signs and wonders. Seeing Paul's exorcisms, **some itinerant Jewish exorcists** decide to imitate his obviously effective methods by invoking **the name of the Lord Jesus over those with evil spirits**. They awkwardly emulate Paul's commands: **"I adjure you by the Jesus whom Paul preaches."** This illustrates the fact that to do something in Jesus' "name" (like the baptisms in v. 5 above) is not merely to recite a formula. It is also to act under his authority in faith and in a personal relationship to him. The commands of these exorcists, including the **seven sons of Sceva, a Jewish high priest**, are not grounded in such faith.   **19:13–14**

The result of their efforts is humorous but makes a point: **the evil spirit** answers them, **"Jesus I recognize, Paul I know, but who are you?"** The demonic spirit thus implicitly admits that it would have to obey commands given by Jesus or by those exercising Jesus' authority, such as Paul. However, because the sons of Sceva have no relationship to Jesus, they have no access to the power of his name. Rather, they are trying to use his name as a kind of magic formula.   **19:15**

In a dramatic turn of events, the single possessed **person with the evil spirit** leaps at all seven exorcists and so overpowers them that they flee **naked and wounded from that house**.   **19:16**

Reports of their humiliation become **known to all the Jews and Greeks** living in **Ephesus**. As a result **the name of the Lord Jesus** is **held in great esteem**, for it exhibits undeniable power. Even demons evidently hold that name in fear and respect. The sobering example of the misuse of Jesus' name in magical fashion prompts many of the new Christian converts to renounce the magical practices they had indulged in.   **19:17–18**

The awe aroused by the affair leads even non-Christians to carry out a voluntary **public** book burning. The number of these **books** is underscored by the calculation of **their value** at the enormous sum of **fifty thousand silver pieces**.[2] The number is vast in comparison to the thirty silver pieces paid to Judas for betraying Jesus (Matt 27:9).   **19:19**

This anecdote illustrates the powerful impact the gospel is beginning to have in Ephesus. The result of this victory of the name of Jesus over practices of magic is that **the word of the Lord** continues to **spread with influence and power**.   **19:20**

2. A silver piece—a drachma—was a day's wage for a manual laborer.

Magic versus Miracles

LIVING TRADITION

The Catechism explains the difference between magic and miracles, and why magic—in the form of occult involvement, not entertainment by sleight of hand—violates our relationship with God. Unlike miracles that God works in response to faith and prayer, magic is a self-seeking attempt to manipulate occult powers:

> All practices of *magic* or *sorcery,* by which one attempts to tame occult powers, so as to place them at one's service and have a supernatural power over others—even if this were for the sake of restoring their health—are gravely contrary to the virtue of religion. These practices are even more to be condemned when accompanied by the intention of harming someone, or when they have recourse to the intervention of demons. Wearing charms is also reprehensible. *Spiritism* often implies divination or magical practices; the Church for her part warns the faithful against it. Recourse to so-called traditional cures does not justify either the invocation of evil powers or the exploitation of another's credulity.[a]

"Charms" refers not to innocent jewelry like a charm bracelet but to magical amulets worn to protect against harm or bring good fortune. "Spiritism," often called spiritualism, refers to communication with the spirits of the dead, usually through a medium. Trying to communicate with the dead in this way is forcefully condemned in Scripture (Deut 18:10–12). "Traditional cures" refers not to natural remedies like herbal teas but to cures by witch doctors, which are thought to utilize power from evil spirits. All of these practices risk opening oneself to evil spirits and are therefore dangerous. Even if some of them do not directly involve evil spirits, they may be used to deceive and manipulate simple people.

a. Catechism, 2117; see Mark 1:25–26; 3:15; 6:7, 13; 16:17; *Code of Canon Law*, canon 1172.

Paul's Plans (19:21–22)

[21]When this was concluded, Paul made up his mind to travel through Macedonia and Achaia, and then to go on to Jerusalem, saying, "After I have been there, I must visit Rome also." [22]Then he sent to Macedonia two of his assistants, Timothy and Erastus, while he himself stayed for a while in the province of Asia.

NT: Luke 9:31; 10:1; Acts 20:22; Rom 16:23; 2 Tim 4:20

19:21   **When this was concluded**, literally, "as these things were fulfilled," with perhaps a hint of God's plan being accomplished, **Paul made up his mind** (or "resolved in the Spirit," NRSV) to leave Ephesus.

Paul decides to visit his newly founded churches on European soil, in **Macedonia and Achaia**, before proceeding back to the mother church in **Jerusalem**. His plan to go to Jerusalem parallels Jesus' decision to journey to Jerusalem (Luke 9:51), which was a turning point in the Gospel. In God's plan, arrest and suffering in the holy city is in store for Paul as it had been for Jesus.[3] Paul is imitating the Lord in his passion.

Paul feels constrained by God's will to **visit Rome also** (see Acts 23:11, where Jesus will call him to witness there). Acts will end with Paul in Rome under house arrest, but proclaiming Jesus and the kingdom of God "with complete assurance and without hindrance" (28:31).

In preparation for his return **to Macedonia**, Paul sends **two of his assistants, Timothy and Erastus**, ahead of him while he stays **for a while in the province of Asia**. As an effective team leader, Paul knows how to recruit and deploy capable people who are willing to share in his mission. Timothy was recruited by Paul in the region of Derbe and Lystra (Acts 16:1); with Silas he became one of Paul's main coworkers. Erastus is mentioned only here in Acts, but Rom 16:23 refers to an Erastus as the city treasurer of Corinth (see also 2 Tim 4:20).

19:22

The Riot of the Silversmiths (19:23–40)

[23]About that time a serious disturbance broke out concerning the Way. [24]There was a silversmith named Demetrius who made miniature silver shrines of Artemis and provided no little work for the craftsmen. [25]He called a meeting of these and other workers in related crafts and said, "Men, you know well that our prosperity derives from this work. [26]As you can now see and hear, not only in Ephesus but throughout most of the province of Asia this Paul has persuaded and misled a great number of people by saying that gods made by hands are not gods at all. [27]The danger grows, not only that our business will be discredited, but also that the temple of the great goddess Artemis will be of no account, and that she whom the whole province of Asia and all the world worship will be stripped of her magnificence."

[28]When they heard this, they were filled with fury and began to shout, "Great is Artemis of the Ephesians!" [29]The city was filled with confusion, and the people rushed with one accord into the theater, seizing Gaius and Aristarchus, the Macedonians, Paul's traveling companions. [30]Paul wanted to go before the crowd, but the disciples would not let him, [31]and

---

3. Luke 9:31; 13:33–34; 18:31; Acts 20:22–23; 21:11–13.

even some of the Asiarchs who were friends of his sent word to him advising him not to venture into the theater. [32]Meanwhile, some were shouting one thing, others something else; the assembly was in chaos, and most of the people had no idea why they had come together. [33]Some of the crowd prompted Alexander, as the Jews pushed him forward, and Alexander signaled with his hand that he wished to explain something to the gathering. [34]But when they recognized that he was a Jew, they all shouted in unison, for about two hours, "Great is Artemis of the Ephesians!"

[35]Finally the town clerk restrained the crowd and said, "You Ephesians, what person is there who does not know that the city of the Ephesians is the guardian of the temple of the great Artemis and of her image that fell from the sky? [36]Since these things are undeniable, you must calm yourselves and not do anything rash. [37]The men you brought here are not temple robbers, nor have they insulted our goddess. [38]If Demetrius and his fellow craftsmen have a complaint against anyone, courts are in session, and there are proconsuls. Let them bring charges against one another. [39]If you have anything further to investigate, let the matter be settled in the lawful assembly, [40]for, as it is, we are in danger of being charged with rioting because of today's conduct. There is no cause for it. We shall [not] be able to give a reason for this demonstration." With these words he dismissed the assembly.

NT: Acts 1:11, 16; 2:14; 9:2; 17:22; 18:25–26; 19:9; 24:22
Catechism: idolatry, 2112–14, 2138

In ancient times as today, people appreciate a historian who tells his story in an interesting manner. Luke does not disappoint in this regard. In recounting this event, he reports the advance of the gospel and the confusion of its opponents with style and a touch of humor.

19:23   Before Paul has a chance to leave Ephesus for Macedonia, **a serious disturbance** breaks out **concerning the Way**. Two typical marks of Lukan style appear in this sentence. The first is his characterization of the trouble as, literally, "not a little disturbance," an artful understatement. The second is his reference to Christianity as the †Way.[4]

19:24   The cause of the commotion is **a silversmith named Demetrius**, who makes **miniature silver shrines** of the goddess **Artemis**, the patroness of Ephesus. Artemis, known in Latin as Diana, was a huntress in Greco-Roman mythology,

4. See the commentary (above) on Acts 9:1–2.

and she is portrayed in some statues as a mother goddess with multiple breasts.[5] The city boasted a large and famous temple dedicated to her, considered one of the seven wonders of the ancient world. Luke again uses understatement in writing that Demetrius **provided no little work for the craftsmen**. The motive for Demetrius's objection to the gospel was more economic than religious.

Craftsmen were often organized in guilds. Demetrius calls a **meeting** of   **19:25** silversmiths and other craftsmen to find a way to eliminate the threat of Paul's monotheistic preaching. He appeals to the workers' economic anxieties, reminding them that their **prosperity derives from** making statues and other items in honor of the goddess Artemis. Luke often highlights economic concerns as a major impediment to following God's will (Luke 8:33–37; 18:24–25), even functioning as an incentive to persecute anyone who threatens one's earnings (Acts 16:19).

Demetrius warns the tradesmen of the damage to their livelihood that Paul   **19:26** has already done **in Ephesus** and throughout **the province of Asia**. There is a touch of irony in Demetrius's claim that **Paul has persuaded and misled a great number of people** with his message **that gods made by hands are not gods at all**. As the Servant of the Lord in Isaiah was called to do (Isa 43:10–12), Paul has been testifying to the Gentiles the truth that there is only one true God. It is the promoters of idolatry, rather than Paul, who mislead people.

Demetrius warns his fellow craftsmen of a twofold **danger**. The most im-   **19:27** mediate and personal is that the **business** of making idols **will be discredited**, and thus they will lose their livelihood. Second is a loss of credibility for **the temple of the great goddess Artemis**, Ephesus's claim to fame. From their pagan perspective, it is a grave matter if Artemis, **whom the whole province of Asia and all the world worship** (a common local exaggeration) is **stripped of her magnificence**.

In reaction to this menace, the listeners are **filled with fury** and begin to   **19:28–31** shout, **"Great is Artemis of the Ephesians!"** This provokes citywide **confusion** as a crowd rushes into **the theater** (which could seat about 25,000 people)[6] and seizes **Gaius and Aristarchus**, Macedonian **traveling companions** of Paul. The scene is one of total chaos. **Paul** hopes to calm **the crowd** with a speech, but his fellow disciples wisely refuse to **let him** enter the fray. Noting as he often does Paul's relationships with influential people, Luke adds that **even some of**

---

5. See F. W. Beare, "Artemis," in *The Interpreter's Dictionary of the Bible*, ed. George A. Buttrick (Nashville: Abingdon, 1962), 1:241–42; and Hubert M. Martin Jr., "Artemis," in *Anchor Bible Dictionary*, ed. David N. Freedman (New York: Doubleday, 1992), 1:464–65.

6. Luke Timothy Johnson, *The Acts of the Apostles*, Sacra pagina 5 (Collegeville, MN: Liturgical Press, 1992), 348; Fitzmyer, *Acts*, 659.

Fig. 18. Statue of Artemis of Ephesus, the principal goddess of Asia (Acts 19:24–28).

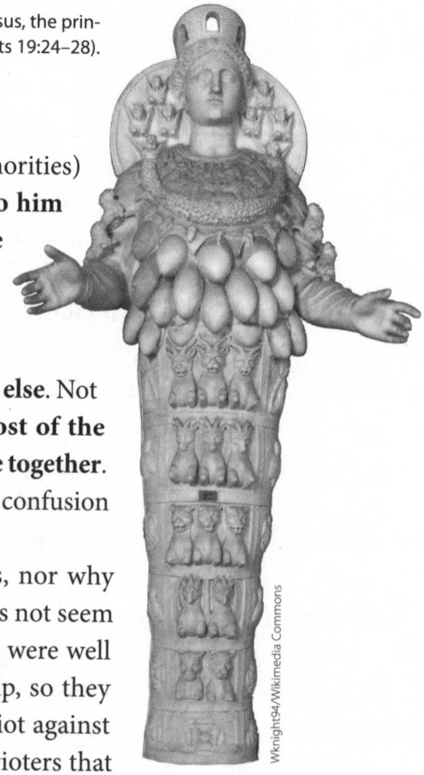

the Asiarchs (Ephesian provincial authorities) **who were friends of his sent word to him advising him not to venture into the theater.**

19:32   The mob scene that follows again contains a touch of humor: some are **shouting one thing, others something else.** Not only is the assembly **in chaos** but **most of the people** have **no idea why they had come together.** This pagan mob exhibits ignorance and confusion bordering on the farcical.

19:33–34   It is not clear who **Alexander** was, nor why **the Jews pushed him forward.** He does not seem to have been a Christian. But Jews too were well known for rejecting idolatrous worship, so they may also have felt threatened by this riot against Paul and wanted to make clear to the rioters that Paul did not belong to their Jewish community.[7]

Alexander signals for attention, but the crowd refuses to listen once they realize he is **a Jew**—an example of anti-Jewish sentiment similar to that expressed in Philippi and Corinth (Acts 16:20–21; 18:17). The mob drowns him out, and their fanaticism is revealed in their shouting **in unison, for about two hours,** "**Great is Artemis of the Ephesians!**"

19:35   Finally **the town clerk**[8] manages to calm **the crowd.** To win their favor, he begins by expressing his agreement with their concern: "**Who does not know** that Ephesus **is the guardian of the temple of the great Artemis and of her image that fell from the sky?**" Pagans venerated meteorites and images of the gods, including that of Artemis, which they claimed had fallen from above. The point of this rhetorical question may be to show how Paul's declaration that "gods made by hands" are no gods at all (v. 26) does not apply to this sacred stone, which allegedly was not made by hands but came from the sky.[9]

7. See Mikeal C. Parsons, *Acts*, Paideia: Commentaries on the New Testament (Grand Rapids: Baker Academic, 2008), 276; Fitzmyer, *Acts*, 660–61.
8. Greek *grammateus*, the word used in the Gospels for Jewish scribes.
9. See Parsons, *Acts*, 276.

Fig. 19. Ruins of the twenty-thousand seat theater at Ephesus, site of the riot in Acts 19:29–40.

The town clerk reassures the crowd that, of course, the importance of the cult **19:36–37**
and temple of Artemis **are undeniable**. Therefore, they **must calm** themselves
and avoid doing **anything rash**, lest they provoke a repressive reaction from
the Romans. Having won a hearing, the clerk goes on to mollify the crowd by
pointing out that Paul and his companions **are not temple robbers**. Nor have
they **insulted our goddess**, despite Demetrius's allegation that Paul said "gods
made by hands are not gods at all" (v. 26; see Acts 14:16–17 and 17:23–29 for
the nuanced way Paul addresses pagan idolatry).

The clerk insists that if the **craftsmen** have a **complaint** against Paul and his **19:38–40**
companions, they should use the legal means available, including bringing them
to trial. He urges that any further matters be **settled in the lawful assembly**,
not by mob action, and warns that their **conduct** puts them **in danger of being
charged** by the Romans **with rioting**. Thus he dismisses **the assembly**. Through
this narrative, Luke shows the Christians' innocence of any wrongdoing that
would justify the riot against them.

Reflection and Application (19:23–40)

Paul's struggles in Ephesus illustrate how easily Christian preaching and
teaching can provoke fierce reactions. Both then and now, speaking the truth

expressed in God's word sometimes has political or economic repercussions that lead to persecution. For example, a priest working with big-city gangs trafficking in drugs was tolerated as long as he did not interfere with the drug lords' profits. Once he became a threat to their business, they killed him. Sometimes Christians find protection from mistreatment in laws or fair-minded authorities, as Paul and his companions did in Ephesus. In other circumstances, corrupt authorities or unjust laws not only fail to protect Christian witness but are themselves the cause of oppression. Looking behind such conflicts, Paul explains that "our struggle is not with flesh and blood but with the principalities, with the powers, with the world rulers of this present darkness, with the evil spirits in the heavens" (Eph 6:12). The strategy he recommends is to "draw your strength from the Lord," to "put on the armor of God," and to "pray at every opportunity in the Spirit" (Eph 6:10, 13, 18).

Paul the Itinerant Pastor

Acts 20:1–16

This section briefly summarizes the Pauline mission team's itinerary after their harrowing experiences in Ephesus, leading up to Paul's farewell address to the Ephesian elders in Miletus (Acts 20:17–38). Paul and his companions, including Luke (the "we" narrator, as in vv. 5–6), travel from Ephesus to Macedonia and Greece, then back to Miletus near Ephesus. Full of place names and travels, this report illustrates how heavily Paul relied on teamwork and the collaboration of new Christians from the lands that he was evangelizing. Along the way, Paul raises a young man to life at Troas, as Jesus had raised the son of a widow of Nain on his travels (Luke 7:11–16).

Journey to Macedonia and Greece (20:1–3)

¹When the disturbance was over, Paul had the disciples summoned and, after encouraging them, he bade them farewell and set out on his journey to Macedonia. ²As he traveled throughout those regions, he provided many words of encouragement for them. Then he arrived in Greece, ³where he stayed for three months. But when a plot was made against him by the Jews as he was about to set sail for Syria, he decided to return by way of Macedonia.

OT: Esther 2:21–22; 1 Macc 9:60; Ps 21:12 (= 21:11 NRSV)
NT: Acts 9:24–25; 13:2–4; 16:6–7

20:1   Having narrowly escaped mob violence in Ephesus, **Paul** and his team continue their travels by sea and land. This section demonstrates Paul's pastoral concern for the well-being of the communities he founded. Before leaving Ephesus, he summons the **disciples** for a pep talk after the distressing ordeal recounted in 19:23–40, **encouraging** them to hold fast their newfound faith in Christ. Only then does he set out **on his journey to Macedonia**. On his return to Asia Minor, Paul will avoid Ephesus, possibly for safety reasons, but will stop at nearby Miletus, where he will deliver his major farewell address to the Ephesian elders (Acts 20:17–38).

20:2–3 On his trip through Macedonia, Paul continues to provide **many words of encouragement** to the churches he founded in Philippi, Thessalonica, and Beroea. Moving southward into Greece, Paul stays there for **three months**, presumably bolstering the churches of Athens and Corinth. It was probably during this period, from Corinth, that Paul wrote his Letter to the Romans, in which he shared his hopes to visit Rome soon on his way to preach the gospel in Spain (Rom 15:23–24, 29).

Intending to head toward Jerusalem, Paul is **about to set sail for Syria**, where his journey began, but discovers that some **Jews** have organized a conspiracy against him. To evade their **plot**, Paul changes his plans and decides to travel overland **by way of Macedonia**, rather than going more directly by sea (see map, p. 287). Paul's travel decisions stem not only from the Holy Spirit (see Acts 13:2–4; 16:6–7) but also from a prudential weighing of his circumstances.

Return to Troas (20:4–6)

[4]Sopater, the son of Pyrrhus, from Beroea, accompanied him, as did Aristarchus and Secundus from Thessalonica, Gaius from Derbe, Timothy, and Tychicus and Trophimus from Asia [5]who went on ahead and waited for us at Troas. [6]We sailed from Philippi after the feast of Unleavened Bread, and rejoined them five days later in Troas, where we spent a week.

OT: Lev 23:5–6; Num 28:16–17; 2 Chron 30:13–15
NT: Rom 16:21; Eph 6:21; Col 4:7; 2 Tim 4:12, 20; Titus 3:12

20:4   Luke names seven of Paul's travel companions, who come from many of the churches he recently founded. **Sopater** from **Beroea** is otherwise unknown, unless he is the Sosipater of Rom 16:21. **Aristarchus** was called a Macedonian in Acts 19:29; here he is more precisely identified as **from Thessalonica** in Macedonia, along with **Secundus**, who is otherwise unknown.

Luke earlier mentioned a Gaius and Aristarchus, who were Macedonians (Acts 19:29), so this **Gaius from Derbe** in Asia Minor is probably a different person; Gaius was a common name.

The last six names are in pairs. Gaius from Derbe is mentioned with **Timothy**, whom Paul first met at "Derbe and Lystra" (Acts 16:1). The last pair are **Tychicus and Trophimus from Asia**. Trophimus reappears in Acts 21:29 as "the Ephesian," and 2 Tim 4:20 mentions that he was left sick in Miletus. This is the only mention of Tychicus in Acts, but he appears in 2 Tim 4:12 as sent to Ephesus (also in Eph 6:21; Col 4:7; Titus 3:12).

Verse 5 begins another "we" section, which extends to 20:15. Luke reports that Paul and his seven companions **went on ahead** by land and **waited for us in Troas**. At this point, then, Luke is not with Paul but with a second group who travel by sea to meet Paul's party. This group sails **from Philippi**, or its port, Neapolis, **after the feast of Unleavened Bread**, a weeklong feast that begins at Passover. After **five days** at sea, Luke's group rejoins Paul and his party in the Asian port of **Troas**. The reunited companions spend **a week** together in Troas.

20:5–6

Eutychus Restored to Life (20:7–12)

> [7]On the first day of the week when we gathered to break bread, Paul spoke to them because he was going to leave on the next day, and he kept on speaking until midnight. [8]There were many lamps in the upstairs room where we were gathered, [9]and a young man named Eutychus who was sitting on the window sill was sinking into a deep sleep as Paul talked on and on. Once overcome by sleep, he fell down from the third story and when he was picked up, he was dead. [10]Paul went down, threw himself upon him, and said as he embraced him, "Don't be alarmed; there is life in him." [11]Then he returned upstairs, broke the bread, and ate; after a long conversation that lasted until daybreak, he departed. [12]And they took the boy away alive and were immeasurably comforted.

OT: 1 Kings 17:21–23; 2 Kings 4:32–36
NT: Luke 7:11–17
Catechism: risen with Christ, 1002–4; dying with Christ, 1005–14; the breaking of bread, 1329, 1343, 1396; Sunday, the Lord's day, 1166–67, 1193, 2191

This is the first mention of a Christian liturgy on Sunday, **the first day of the week**, which Christians celebrate as the Lord's Day (see Rev 1:10) because

20:7

The Lord's Day, the Day of Worship

LIVING TRADITION

The people of Israel celebrate the Sabbath, the seventh day of the week, as the day of rest and worship in communion with the Lord, a practice based on the Genesis account of six days of creation followed by God's day of rest (Gen 2:1–3; Exod 20:8–11). Christian tradition transferred the celebration of the Lord's Day to the first day of the week, Sunday, because of the Lord Jesus' resurrection on that day—the beginning of the *new* creation. According to the Catechism (1166),

> "By a tradition handed down from the apostles which took its origin from the very day of Christ's Resurrection, the Church celebrates the Paschal mystery every seventh day, which day is appropriately called the Lord's Day or Sunday." The day of Christ's Resurrection is both the first day of the week, the memorial of the first day of creation, and the "eighth day," on which Christ after his "rest" on the great sabbath inaugurates the "day that the Lord has made," the "day that knows no evening." The Lord's Supper is its center, for there the whole community of the faithful encounters the risen Lord who invites them to his banquet.[a]

a. See John 21:12; Luke 24:30.

it was the day Jesus was raised from the dead.[1] They gather **to break bread**, an expression the early Christians often used for the Eucharist. According to the biblical pattern established already in the Old Testament (Exod 24:3–11; Neh 8:8–10) and by the example of the risen Jesus at Emmaus (Luke 24:25–32), the Church celebrates the liturgy of the Word before the liturgy of the Eucharist[2]— first hearing the word of the Lord and then enjoying Eucharistic communion with him. So Paul first gives a prolonged homily, **speaking until midnight**, in view of the fact he is **going to leave on the next day**.

20:8–9   Luke relates the account of **Eutychus** with humor, even though his falling to his death must have been quite alarming. The text stresses the **many lamps in the upstairs room**: these oil-burning vessels generated both heat and smoke, which can make people drowsy. **Eutychus** was a **young man**—the Greek can refer to an older boy or young unmarried man—and his name means "Lucky." As a youth might do, he **was sitting on the window sill**, and as **Paul talked on and on** he **was sinking into a deep sleep**. (Many a high school or college

---

1. See Matt 28:1. Along with Rev 1:10 and 1 Cor 16:2, here Acts 20:7 is one of three New Testament texts that mention the Christian day of worship.
2. See Exod 24:3–11; Neh 8:8–10.

teacher can relate to this scene.) Finally, he was **overcome by sleep** and **fell down from the third story**. The not-surprising result was that **when he was picked up, he was dead**.

Paul's reaction recalls the prophets Elijah and Elisha, who each raised a boy 　　**20:10**
from the dead by lying on his dead body (1 Kings 17:21–23; 2 Kings 4:32–36). Paul **threw himself upon** the dead youth and **embraced him**, telling the group not to be **alarmed** because **there is life in him**. Whether the boy was really dead or only seemed to be dead is not clear from this statement alone. However, because it is very similar to what Jesus said about Jairus's dead daughter, "She is not dead, but sleeping" (Luke 8:52), Luke probably expects readers to realize that the boy really died and was restored to life when Paul embraced him.

Without explicitly saying so, Luke implies that Paul's actions included praying to God to revive the boy. This differs from Jesus' raising of the widow's son at Nain, in which Jesus acted directly on his own authority.

After Eutychus was revived, Paul **returned upstairs, broke the bread, and** 　　**20:11–12**
ate, resuming the liturgy that was interrupted by the boy's fall. Because miracles bear witness to the truthfulness and saving power of the gospel (Mark 16:20; Heb 2:4), the boy's resurrection provides an unforgettable testimony to the authenticity of Paul's preaching. Luke concludes the episode by saying that **they took the boy away alive**. The RSV translation of the next phrase better fits Luke's propensity for understatement: they "were not a little comforted."

Journey to Miletus (20:13–16)

¹³We went ahead to the ship and set sail for Assos where we were to take Paul on board, as he had arranged, since he was going overland. ¹⁴When he met us in Assos, we took him aboard and went on to Mitylene. ¹⁵We sailed away from there on the next day and reached a point off Chios, and a day later we reached Samos, and on the following day we arrived at Miletus. ¹⁶Paul had decided to sail past Ephesus in order not to lose time in the province of Asia, for he was hurrying to be in Jerusalem, if at all possible, for the day of Pentecost.

OT: Tob 2:1; 2 Macc 12:32
NT: Acts 2:1; 1 Cor 16:8

Luke continues to distinguish carefully between when he is present with Paul, 　　**20:13–15**
signaled by the first-person "we," and when he is not. Again, as in verses 4–6, Luke is with a group that departs by sea while Paul travels overland. At **Assos**

they take **Paul on board, as he had arranged**, and sail onward. From there to **Miletus** the whole group travels by sea, sailing from port to port in one-day trips.

20:16   To save time Paul decides **to sail past Ephesus** because he is **hurrying to be in Jerusalem, if at all possible, for the day of Pentecost**. Pentecost is fifty days after Passover, and already at least two weeks have passed since that feast (see v. 6), so they only have a few weeks to make it to Jerusalem. However, Paul will wait in **Miletus** for the Ephesian elders to come and meet him (v. 17). Paul may have feared that in Ephesus he would be swamped by people wanting to see him, like popular preachers today, or that he risked provoking another riot if he returned to the city so soon.

Reflection and Application (20:1–16)

In these incidents Paul models several practices that are useful for spreading the good news. First, he exhibits flexibility in his travel and mission plans. When he is rejected or unexpectedly finds doors either closed or opened for evangelization, he adjusts. The riot was his cue that it was time to leave Ephesus. But first he met with and encouraged the Christian disciples there, placing the needs of his flock ahead of his own safety.

Paul illustrates the importance of teamwork by recruiting coworkers wherever he evangelizes. Pope Benedict XVI, in an address at a Roman parish, called for a "change of mentality" regarding laypeople. The laity are not to be regarded merely as "collaborators with the clergy" but are truly "'co-responsible' for the being and action of the Church."[3] Paul is no lone ranger. His example is a salutary reminder of the value of cooperating with others.

Paul also sets an example of nourishing the people of God by both word and sacrament, first fortifying his converts with substantial teaching (no five-minute homily here!) and then celebrating the Eucharist with them. Then as now, the vitality of the Church requires that at Sunday Mass people receive substantive nourishment for the mind, heart, and will through the one table of God's word and Christ's body.

Although rejection or even persecution may be the result of our often-difficult efforts to bear witness to Jesus, we too can rely on God's power. If the dead can be raised, then surely hardened hearts can be moved and peoples' lives can be transformed by God's power working through us. Paul provides a wonderful example of letting nothing dismay us as we persistently pursue our God-given mission.

3. Address to a pastoral conference of the diocese of Rome, May 26, 2009.

Paul's Farewell Speech

Acts 20:17–38

Acts 20 relates Paul's solemn farewell address to the elders of the church at Ephesus. His itinerant evangelization and church-founding activity in Acts is drawing toward a close, and this farewell address provides a fitting conclusion.

A farewell address is a literary form that appears often in ancient Jewish and Greek writings. Several typical elements stand out in Paul's speech. First, he addresses people who are succeeding him in his leadership role, the †presbyters who provide pastoral oversight to the church. Paul reminds them of his own conduct among them, presenting himself as an example of Christian life and leadership. He declares that he has fulfilled his obligations and asserts his innocence of any wrongdoing toward them. Then he intimates that his death is near and prepares them for the future by warning about crises that they will need to face after his departure, especially threats from false teachers. Paul gives a final blessing and prays with them. Finally, he expresses his affection for them with a tearful good-bye. Paul's farewell speech illustrates his spiritual closeness to the churches he founded and to the leaders he commissioned to carry on his work.

Paul's Farewell Speech at Miletus (20:17–24)

¹⁷From Miletus he had the presbyters of the church at Ephesus summoned. ¹⁸When they came to him, he addressed them, "You know how I lived among you the whole time from the day I first came to the province

of Asia. ¹⁹I served the Lord with all humility and with the tears and trials that came to me because of the plots of the Jews, ²⁰and I did not at all shrink from telling you what was for your benefit, or from teaching you in public or in your homes. ²¹I earnestly bore witness for both Jews and Greeks to repentance before God and to faith in our Lord Jesus. ²²But now, compelled by the Spirit, I am going to Jerusalem. What will happen to me there I do not know, ²³except that in one city after another the holy Spirit has been warning me that imprisonment and hardships await me. ²⁴Yet I consider life of no importance to me, if only I may finish my course and the ministry that I received from the Lord Jesus, to bear witness to the gospel of God's grace."

OT: Deut 31–34; Josh 23–24; 1 Sam 12; 1 Chron 28–29; 1 Macc 2:49–70; Isa 49:5–6
NT: Mark 1:15; Luke 9:51; 18:31–33; 22:24–27; 2 Tim 4:2–4
Catechism: our weakness, God's strength, 853; priests called to holiness of life, 1589
Lectionary: Acts 20:17–18a, 28–32, 36: Rite of Ordination; Pope St. Gregory VII; Pope St. Damasus

20:17   Although Paul avoids Ephesus because of his haste to get to Jerusalem (see Acts 20:16), it is important to him to address that church's leaders for what he thinks may be the last time (Acts 20:25). Therefore, he summons **the presbyters** to meet him at Miletus, an important seaport thirty-five miles south of Ephesus. Before his death Moses had likewise summoned the elders of Israel for a farewell address and solemn warning (Deut 31:28). Paul's speech marks the transition from the apostles, the first-generation leaders of the Church who were directly appointed by Jesus, to their successors, the bishops.

20:18   Paul begins by referring to his own good example as a model for church leadership: **"You know how I lived among you."** Ancient teachers—including the biblical prophets, Greek philosophers, and Jesus himself—were well aware that they taught their disciples as much by the way they lived as by the content of their teachings. Paul insists that his way of life and pattern of ministry has been steadfast **from the day I first came to the province of Asia,** of which Ephesus was the capital city. He is implying that he consistently practiced what he preached, a claim his listeners would be able to verify from their own experience.

20:19   Paul **served the Lord** Jesus in his ministry to the Ephesian church. Paul's ministry, like that of the Suffering Servant in Isaiah (Isa 53) and the Lord Jesus, entailed personal sacrifice rather than self-aggrandizement. It was carried out **with all humility** and with **tears and trials . . . because of the plots of the Jews.** As Paul explains in Romans, these tears were not only because of persecution but also because of his anguish at seeing his fellow Jews miss out on Christ: "I

310

Farewell Addresses in Scripture

BIBLICAL
BACKGROUND

Farewell addresses fulfill an important sociocultural function, providing the transition from a venerable figure (in this case, Paul) to a younger generation that will follow in his steps (the Ephesian presbyters/elders). They enable the leader to express his love for his followers, ensure a smooth transition to new leadership, and summarize his most important lessons.

Paul's speech is within a biblical tradition of solemn farewell addresses, such as those of Moses (Deut 31–34), Joshua (Josh 23–24), Samuel (1 Sam 12), David (1 Chron 28–29), and Mattathias (1 Macc 2:49–70). In the New Testament, Jesus' farewell to his disciples before his passion is recounted in John 13–17.

Other biblical examples help us appreciate elements of Paul's farewell. Like Paul, the prophet Samuel insisted that he did not use his authority to enrich himself at the expense of his people (1 Sam 12:3–5). As Paul instructed his successors in their responsibilities, so too Mattathias selected two of his sons, Simeon and Judas Maccabeus, for special tasks after his death (1 Macc 2:65–66). Paul's exhortation to the elders recalls Moses' exhortation to Joshua (Deut 31:7–8) and David's exhortation to his son Solomon (1 Chron 28:20).[a]

In each case, farewell speeches demonstrate God's care for his people in providing them with leadership in every generation. Leaders are entrusted with the solemn task of faithfully shepherding God's people and handing on what they themselves have been taught.

a. See William S. Kurz, *Farewell Addresses in the New Testament*, Zacchaeus Studies: New Testament, A Michael Glazier Book (Collegeville, MN: Liturgical Press, 1990).

have great sorrow and constant anguish in my heart. For I could wish that I myself were accursed and separated from Christ for the sake of my brothers, my kin according to the flesh" (Rom 9:1–3).

The first example of his ministry that Paul mentions is his open, honest, and courageous transmission of the entire gospel message that he was commissioned to teach, including its less-popular components. He testifies that he **did not at all shrink from telling you what was for your benefit**. Preachers are always tempted to avoid touchy topics, such as repentance from sin. But Paul prized speaking the truth to his flock, not winning their approval by telling them what they want to hear.

Paul's Second Letter to Timothy is also a kind of farewell address, and in it Paul insists on teaching the truth consistently, regardless of what the audience prefers to hear:

20:20

Proclaim the word; be persistent whether it is convenient or inconvenient;[1] convince, reprimand, encourage through all patience and teaching. For the time will come when people will not tolerate sound doctrine but, following their own desires and insatiable curiosity, will accumulate teachers and will stop listening to the truth and will be diverted to myths. (2 Tim 4:2–4)

Paul taught the undiluted and unvarnished gospel message both **in public**, whether in the marketplace (Acts 17:17) or in lecture halls (19:9), or privately, as in the house of Titus Justus (18:7).

20:21   To both Jewish and Gentile audiences, Paul taught the same twofold response to the gospel: all must come **to repentance before God and to faith in our Lord Jesus**. Paul's message echoes that of Jesus in the Gospels: "Repent, and believe in the gospel" (Mark 1:15).

20:22–23   Next Paul foretells his sufferings. He asserts that he is **compelled** (the Greek literally means "bound") **by the Spirit** to return **to Jerusalem**. The Holy Spirit is guiding Paul's journey, as God's plan had similarly motivated Jesus' journey to Jerusalem (Luke 9:51). Paul explains his foreboding: **"In one city after another the holy Spirit has been warning me that imprisonment and hardships await me."** Luke has not yet recounted any such prophetic warnings, but he will give explicit examples in the next chapter (21:10–14).

20:24   Responding generously to the threat of suffering, Paul goes further: **"I consider life of no importance to me, if only I may finish my course."** His supreme priority is carrying out the mission Jesus has entrusted to him. Paul likes to use sports metaphors (1 Cor 9:24–27; 2 Tim 2:5), perhaps because he was an ardent fan or an athlete himself. He uses the same metaphor in his farewell message in 2 Tim 4:7–8: "I have competed well; I have finished the race."

Paul's advance knowledge and willingness to suffer in Jerusalem parallel Jesus' predictions of his passion: "He took the Twelve aside and said to them, 'Behold, we are going up to Jerusalem and everything written by the prophets about the Son of Man will be fulfilled. He will be handed over to the Gentiles and he will be mocked and insulted and spat upon; and after they have scourged him they will kill him, but on the third day he will rise'" (Luke 18:31–33).

It is instructive to see how Paul sums up **the ministry** he **received from the Lord Jesus**. His role is to give testimony: **"to bear witness to the gospel of God's grace."** Paul can testify to God's grace with conviction because he has experienced it himself (see 1 Cor 15:9–10; 1 Tim 1:15–16). Similarly, recovering

---

1. Greek *euchairōs, achairōs*, literally, "in season, out of season."

alcoholics are often particularly eloquent witnesses to God's mercy and grace because of their own experience of forgiveness.

Paul's Farewell Speech Continued (20:25–35)

²⁵"But now I know that none of you to whom I preached the kingdom during my travels will ever see my face again. ²⁶And so I solemnly declare to you this day that I am not responsible for the blood of any of you, ²⁷for I did not shrink from proclaiming to you the entire plan of God. ²⁸Keep watch over yourselves and over the whole flock of which the holy Spirit has appointed you overseers, in which you tend the church of God that he acquired with his own blood. ²⁹I know that after my departure savage wolves will come among you, and they will not spare the flock. ³⁰And from your own group, men will come forward perverting the truth to draw the disciples away after them. ³¹So be vigilant and remember that for three years, night and day, I unceasingly admonished each of you with tears. ³²And now I commend you to God and to that gracious word of his that can build you up and give you the inheritance among all who are consecrated. ³³I have never wanted anyone's silver or gold or clothing. ³⁴You know well that these very hands have served my needs and my companions. ³⁵In every way I have shown you that by hard work of that sort we must help the weak, and keep in mind the words of the Lord Jesus who himself said, 'It is more blessed to give than to receive.'"

OT: 1 Sam 12:3–5; Ezek 3:17–19
NT: 1 Cor 8:1; 9:18; 2 Cor 11:9; Gal 3:18; Eph 1:14
Catechism: living in the truth, 27, 2470, 2752; humility, 2546, 2559, 2713; bishops, 1560; priests, 1562; deacons, 1571

Believing that impending imprisonment or death in Jerusalem will prevent   20:25–27
his return to Ephesus, Paul solemnly tells the Ephesian elders, **"None of you
. . . will ever see my face again."**
    Paul emphasizes that he has fulfilled his obligations to the Ephesian church (see vv. 18–21). He **did not shrink from proclaiming . . . the entire plan of God**, that is, he did not avoid the hard teachings. By saying he is **not responsible** for their **blood**, Paul places himself in the role of a prophet as a sentinel, or watchman. In Ezekiel, God tells the prophet,

Son of man, I have appointed you a sentinel for the house of Israel. When you hear a word from my mouth, you shall warn them for me. If I say to the wicked, You shall surely die—and you do not warn them or speak out to dissuade the wicked from their evil conduct in order to save their lives—then they shall die for their sin, but I will hold you responsible for their blood. (Ezek 3:17–18)

20:28
If Paul is a sentinel, so are the elders, and he advises them where to begin their guard duty: **"Keep watch over yourselves."** Leaders can hardly help others if they are not living godly lives themselves. Jesus made a similar point about removing a beam from one's own eye to see clearly enough to remove a splinter from a neighbor's eye (Luke 6:41). The elders are to care for **the whole flock** of which they are **overseers** (Greek *episkopoi*, from which the word "bishops" is derived).[2] Luke seems to use the terms overseers and elders (v. 17) interchangeably (see sidebar, p. 111).

The overseers' leadership role is conferred not by human decisions but by **the holy Spirit**, who calls them to **tend the church of God**. The explanatory phrase, **that he acquired with his own blood**, may sound strange, as though implying that God the Father has blood. Therefore, some manuscripts instead have "church of the Lord," more obviously referring to Jesus, who acquired the church by shedding his blood on the cross.[3] But if "the church of God" is the original wording, it is a clear instance of asserting the divinity of Jesus.

20:29–30
A common feature of farewell addresses is warnings of future dangers. Thus, continuing the shepherd imagery, Paul warns that after his departure **savage wolves** will enter the church and **will not spare the flock**. False teachers from the outside will prey on vulnerable members for their own advantage. But Paul predicts a threat from the inside as well: **from your own group**, false teachers will emerge, **perverting the truth to draw the disciples away after them**. True teachers lead people to fidelity to Jesus' person and teaching, whereas false teachers reshape the message to enhance their own influence, undermining faith and unity. The New Testament contains numerous warnings about false teachers.[4]

20:31
Therefore, Paul warns them, **"Be vigilant,"** literally, "watch," and be ready for such false teachers from without and within. Paul explains how to be vigilant by recalling his own example: he **unceasingly admonished** each of them **with tears**. The Greek for "admonish" means warn, exhort, or instruct. As a pastor, Paul was deeply invested in the well-being of every member of his flock.

2. This is Luke's only use of this word, although he does use the cognate *episkopē*, "office" for the replacement of Judas (Acts 1:20). Both words denote "watching over."
3. Luke-Acts, like the rest of the New Testament, mostly uses the word "God" to refer to God the Father and "Lord" to refer to Jesus.
4. See Matt 7:15; 24:11, 24; Luke 21:8; Eph 4:14; 1 Tim 1:3–7; 4:1–3; 2 Tim 3:1–9, 13; 4:3–4; 2 Pet 2:1; 1 John 2:26; Rev 2:2, 14, 20.

Paul commends them, that is, entrusts them for safekeeping, **to God** and to that gracious word of his, literally, "to the word of his grace" (RSV). Paul recognizes that a dynamic power resides in the gospel (see Rom 1:16). It has power to **build** them **up**; the Greek verb, *oikodomeō*, means to build a house, in this case, the house of God that is the Christian community. The word of God's grace can also **give** them **the inheritance** that God has planned for them. In the Old Testament, the inheritance of God's people was the promised land of Canaan (Num 34:2); now in Christ it is eternal life (Heb 9:15; 1 Pet 1:4). This inheritance will be for **all who are consecrated**, that is, all who are made holy by baptism into Christ.

20:32

Now Paul echoes the solemn declaration of the prophet Samuel that while he was in authority over the people, he never cheated them or enriched himself at their expense (1 Sam 12:3–5). Similarly, Paul never took advantage of his authority or coveted **anyone's silver or gold or clothing**. Instead, he provided for himself and his **companions** with his own **hands**—probably referring to his tentmaking trade (see Acts 18:3). Paul must have been a highly skilled and industrious craftsman to have earned enough outside of ministry hours to provide materially for himself and others. For Paul, it was extremely important to the credibility of the gospel that he did not depend on the fledgling Christian communities for financial support (see 1 Cor 9:18; 2 Cor 11:9).

20:33–34

Paul's example was intended to teach **that by hard work of that sort we must help the weak**. Consistent with his Jewish heritage, Paul emphasizes the dignity and importance of work. The biblical teaching on work differs radically from many Greek philosophers, who tended to look down on manual labor as befitting only slaves. To reinforce the precept of using one's labor to benefit those less fortunate, Paul appeals to **words of the Lord Jesus himself**, a saying not recorded in the Gospels, which Paul must have learned from oral tradition: **"It is more blessed to give than to receive."**

20:35

Parting Gestures (20:36–38)

[36]When he had finished speaking he knelt down and prayed with them all. [37]They were all weeping loudly as they threw their arms around Paul and kissed him, [38]for they were deeply distressed that he had said that they would never see his face again. Then they escorted him to the ship.

OT: Gen 48:11; 1 Sam 20:41
NT: Luke 22:41; Acts 21:5; Rom 16:16; Eph 3:14; 2 Tim 1:4
Catechism: intense fellowship, 2636

20:36–38   Paul concludes his address with farewell gestures: **he knelt down and prayed with them all**. Although standing is also a common biblical posture for praying (see Dan 3:25 [= Prayer of Azariah 2 NRSV]; Luke 18:13), kneeling is a way of expressing humility and supplication before God (1 Kings 8:54; Luke 22:41; Acts 9:40; 21:5). Paul's departure evokes profound emotion, with the elders **weeping loudly as they threw their arms around Paul and kissed him** good-bye. Their sorrow is due to his statement **that they would never see his face again**, which seems to imply his impending death. The episode ends with their accompanying Paul **to the ship**.

Reflection and Application (20:36–38)

Paul's farewell to the Ephesian elders reveals the love he had for those to whom he ministered. It also demonstrates the nobility and generosity of his ministry, and it provides a salutary example for church leaders today. Throughout Church history Paul has been esteemed for the theological content of his teaching. But in this address, as in his Letters to the Corinthians (1 Cor 4:15–17; 9:15–27; 10:32–11:1), Philippians (1:21–26; 3:7–17; 4:11–13), and Timothy (2 Tim 1:13; 2:8–12; 3:10–11), Paul emphasizes the teaching conveyed through his *example*. He demonstrates an extraordinary consistency in sacrificial service, hard work, generosity, and patience in adversity. And he does not suffer from a false humility that can make people reluctant to point to their own example. He realizes that his flock needs to learn the Christian life not just by words but also by watching and imitating him, as he imitates Christ (1 Cor 11:1).

Like Jesus in his farewell to the Twelve at the Last Supper, Paul teaches the elders at Ephesus the true meaning of Church leadership. Their authority should be exercised in a spirit of service, not of self-promotion. As Jesus told his apostles, "The kings of the Gentiles lord it over them and those in authority over them are addressed as 'Benefactors'; but among you it shall not be so" (Luke 22:25–26). As Paul was about to leave, he and his followers wept and prayed together, expressing grief at their separation. We too can support one another in life's hardships by showing brotherly and sisterly Christian affection and by praying together and for each other.

Paul's Journey to Jerusalem

Acts 21:1–26

Paul now completes his journey to Jerusalem. Along the way he encounters warnings from Christian prophets that suffering awaits him there. In Luke's Gospel, Jesus set his face to go to Jerusalem even though he himself repeatedly foretold that he would encounter suffering and death there. Paul has a similar determination to fulfill his mission by going to Jerusalem, despite the trials that await him.

When Paul and his party arrive, James, the chief elder of the Jerusalem church, warns Paul of rumors that he discourages Jewish disciples in the †Diaspora from practicing their Jewish faith and circumcising their children. To counter this gossip, James encourages Paul to demonstrate his loyalty to Jewish devotional practices. Paul acts on James's suggestion, but while his gesture may be sufficient to allay the concerns of Jewish Christians, it does not prevent the attack of Jewish opponents from Asia who have also come to Jerusalem for the feast.

Arrival in Tyre (21:1–6)

[1]When we had taken leave of them we set sail, made a straight run for Cos, and on the next day for Rhodes, and from there to Patara. [2]Finding a ship crossing to Phoenicia, we went on board and put out to sea. [3]We caught sight of Cyprus but passed by it on our left and sailed on toward Syria and put in at Tyre where the ship was to unload cargo. [4]There we sought out the disciples and stayed for a week. They kept telling Paul through the Spirit not to embark for Jerusalem. [5]At the end of our stay we left and

resumed our journey. All of them, women and children included, escorted us out of the city, and after kneeling on the beach to pray, **⁶we bade farewell to one another. Then we boarded the ship, and they returned home.**

OT: Ps 95:6
NT: Luke 22:41; Acts 20:36; Eph 3:14
Catechism: Holy Spirit and prophecy, 243

21:1–3   As Paul boards ship at Miletus, Luke resumes narrating in the first-person "we" as one of Paul's companions. The ship arrives at **Patara**, a port on the coast of present-day Turkey. There they find what is probably a large merchant ship capable of **crossing** the four-hundred-mile expanse of the Mediterranean Sea to **Phoenicia**, present-day Lebanon, rather than following the coastline and making many stops, as smaller ships would do. A direct voyage assures Paul the possibility of reaching Jerusalem by Pentecost (Acts 20:16). They pass by the island of **Cyprus** and sail on to **Syria**, of which the Phoenician coast was a part, finally arriving at the port city of **Tyre**.

21:4   While the ship's cargo is being unloaded, and perhaps fresh cargo loaded, Paul and his companions find some **disciples** at Tyre and stay with them **for a week**. Paul's warm reception by Christians in Tyre and other cities may indicate that he already knew those communities from previous trips between Antioch and Jerusalem. Or it may simply reflect the Christian custom of hospitality to missionaries. Through prophecies, these disciples keep **telling Paul through the Spirit not to embark for Jerusalem**. In their affection for Paul, they try to persuade him to avoid imminent suffering. He rejects their urging because he is more concerned to fulfill his mission than to ensure his own safety. His determination to continue is not disobedience to the Spirit, since his decision to go to Jerusalem was itself motivated by the Spirit (Acts 19:21; 20:22).

21:5–6   After the week's **stay** the band of missionaries resume their **journey** southward by boat. **All** the local disciples, **women and children included** (indicating the entire community's love that Paul enjoyed), make the same reverent and affectionate gestures as the Ephesians at Miletus. They escort the team **out of the city** and, **kneeling on the beach to pray**, bid **farewell**. The community in Tyre remains an inspiring example of Christian hospitality and love.

Arrival at Caesarea (21:7–14)

⁷We continued the voyage and came from Tyre to Ptolemais, where we greeted the brothers and stayed a day with them. ⁸On the next day we

resumed the trip and came to Caesarea, where we went to the house of
Philip the evangelist, who was one of the Seven, and stayed with him.
⁹He had four virgin daughters gifted with prophecy. ¹⁰We had been there
several days when a prophet named Agabus came down from Judea. ¹¹He
came up to us, took Paul's belt, bound his own feet and hands with it,
and said, "Thus says the holy Spirit: This is the way the Jews will bind the
owner of this belt in Jerusalem, and they will hand him over to the Gentiles." ¹²When we heard this, we and the local residents begged him not
to go up to Jerusalem. ¹³Then Paul replied, "What are you doing, weeping
and breaking my heart? I am prepared not only to be bound but even to
die in Jerusalem for the name of the Lord Jesus." ¹⁴Since he would not be
dissuaded we let the matter rest, saying, "The Lord's will be done."

OT: Isa 20:2–4; Jer 13:1–9; 16:1–4; 19:1–13; Ezek 4:1–17
NT: Luke 22:42; Eph 4:11; 2 Tim 4:5
Catechism: Holy Spirit and prophecy, 243; prophecy as special grace, 2004; role of prophets in
   Israel, 2595; "Thy will be done," 2824–25

Paul and his team, including Luke, continue southward along the Mediter-   21:7–8
ranean coast, visiting the local Christian community at each port. Finally they
arrive in the Holy Land at **Caesarea**, the endpoint of their sea voyage. Caesarea
Maritima was a port city built by Herod the Great (today located halfway between Tel Aviv and Haifa).

Here they visit **Philip the evangelist**, last mentioned in chapter 8. This is
the only time Luke uses the title "evangelist," though it is quite appropriate for
Philip's ministry to the Samaritans and the Ethiopian eunuch. In Paul's Letters,
evangelists are included in a list of church ministries (Eph 4:11), and Timothy
is told to "perform the work of an evangelist" as part of his responsibility as
pastor (2 Tim 4:5). Philip is also **one of the Seven** ordained to ministry in Acts
6:1–6, whom later tradition identifies as deacons.

Luke goes out of his way to mention that Philip **had four virgin daugh-**   21:9
ters gifted with prophecy, perhaps to illustrate the literal fulfillment of Joel's
prophecy quoted by Peter at Pentecost: "Your sons and your daughters shall
prophesy" (Acts 2:17). Paul strongly promotes this gift in 1 Corinthians: "Strive
eagerly for the spiritual gifts, above all that you may prophesy" (1 Cor 14:1; see
also vv. 2–5).

The **prophet named Agabus** was introduced in Acts 11:27–28 as one of   21:10
the prophets who foretold a severe famine that later took place. A distinction
seems to exist between individuals like Agabus, who exercised a ministry or
office of prophet (11:27; 1 Cor 12:28–29; Eph 3:5; 4:11), and a wider number

of Christians who exercised the charism of prophecy on an occasional basis
(1 Cor 14:1–4, 31).

21:11   Like many of the Old Testament prophets, Agabus delivers his prophecy not
only in words but also with a symbolic gesture that drives home the message:
he **took Paul's belt** and **bound his own feet and hands with it**. According to
Agabus, **the holy Spirit** has revealed that Paul will likewise be bound in **Jerusalem**. There the Jews **will hand him over to the Gentiles**, echoing Jesus' prediction of his own passion (Mark 10:33; Luke 18:32).[1] This prophecy confirms
the messages Paul himself has been hearing on his way (Acts 20:23).

21:12–13   Understandably, in view of this warning, Paul's travel companions and the
Christians of Caesarea beg him **not to go up to Jerusalem**. However, their
human affection for Paul interferes with obedience to God's will for him. **Paul**
gently turns aside their emotional entreaties: "**What are you doing, weeping
and breaking my heart?**" Despite his love for them, his resolve remains un-
moved. He is **prepared** not only to become a prisoner but also, if need be, **to
die** a martyr's death **in Jerusalem for the name of the Lord Jesus**.

21:14   Seeing that Paul could not be **dissuaded**, they "remained silent" (NRSV,
a literal rendering). Their response, "**The Lord's will be done**," echoes Jesus'
response to the Father in Gethsemane (Luke 22:42). As much as they love Paul,
they recognize Christ's claim on his life.

Paul and James in Jerusalem (21:15–26)

[15]**After these days we made preparations for our journey, then went up to
Jerusalem.** [16]**Some of the disciples from Caesarea came along to lead us to
the house of Mnason, a Cypriot, a disciple of long standing, with whom
we were to stay.** [17]**When we reached Jerusalem the brothers welcomed us
warmly.** [18]**The next day, Paul accompanied us on a visit to James, and all
the presbyters were present.** [19]**He greeted them, then proceeded to tell
them in detail what God had accomplished among the Gentiles through
his ministry.** [20]**They praised God when they heard it but said to him,
"Brother, you see how many thousands of believers there are from among
the Jews, and they are all zealous observers of the law.** [21]**They have been
informed that you are teaching all the Jews who live among the Gentiles
to abandon Moses and that you are telling them not to circumcise their
children or to observe their customary practices.** [22]**What is to be done?**

1. What actually happens is that a Roman commander arrests Paul when a Jewish mob tries to kill
him (21:27–33). Later the Jewish leaders press charges against Paul to the Roman governor (24:1; 25:2).

They will surely hear that you have arrived. ²³So do what we tell you. We
have four men who have taken a vow. ²⁴Take these men and purify yourself
with them, and pay their expenses that they may have their heads shaved.
In this way everyone will know that there is nothing to the reports they
have been given about you but that you yourself live in observance of the
law. ²⁵As for the Gentiles who have come to believe, we sent them our decision that they abstain from meat sacrificed to idols, from blood, from the
meat of strangled animals, and from unlawful marriage." ²⁶So Paul took
the men, and on the next day after purifying himself together with them
entered the temple to give notice of the day when the purification would
be completed and the offering made for each of them.

OT: Num 6:1–21
NT: Acts 6:11–14; 7:58; 11:20; 15:1–41; 18:18; 24:17–18
Catechism: vows, 2102; purification of heart, 2517–19

Paul's group, now traveling by land, makes the final leg of the sixty-five-mile   **21:15**
journey **up to Jerusalem**, three or four days' journey on foot. People traveling from any direction are said to go "up" to Jerusalem, the holy city in which
God's temple was located.

Paul's group arrives at **the house of Mnason, a Cypriot, a disciple of long**   **21:16**
standing ("an early disciple," RSV), where arrangements have been made for
them to stay. The inclusion of Mnason's name suggests he was well known in
the Church, though he is mentioned only here in the New Testament. He has
both financial means and the willingness to host Paul and his mostly Gentile
Christian companions (20:4), overcoming the cultural barriers that had previously divided Jews and Gentiles (see Acts 10:28).

Luke continues to point out the esteem that the Jewish-Christian church of   **21:17**
Jerusalem, including James, had for Paul. The church offers the same reception
that Paul's earlier delegation from Antioch had received on arriving for the
†Jerusalem Council (Acts 15:4): they **welcomed us warmly**.

The group's first step is a **visit to James**, who is now clearly the leading †pres-   **21:18**
byter or elder in the church of Jerusalem. Although Luke does not call James a
bishop, the fourth-century church historian Eusebius refers to him as the "first
elected to the episcopal throne of the church in Jerusalem."² Peter had implicitly
recognized James's authority over the Jerusalem church when he left to bring
the gospel to other places (Acts 12:17). Luke stresses that Paul was meeting with
all the presbyters, the full council of elders who led the church at Jerusalem.

2. Eusebius, *Ecclesiastical History* 2.1.2.

21:19–22   As at the Jerusalem Council (Acts 15:4), Paul recounts **what God had accomplished among the Gentiles through his ministry**, that is, he proclaims the wondrous deeds of the Lord (see Pss 71:17; 40:10–11; Isa 12:4; 1 Pet 2:9). Their response is similar to the joy of those who heard his earlier testimony about the conversion of Gentiles (Acts 15:3). In both cases, Paul's testimony to God's action encourages and builds up the church, so that Christians **praised God**.

They also complement Paul's news of Gentile conversions with news of **many thousands of believers . . . from among the Jews**. These new Jewish converts remain **zealous observers of the law**. James takes this opportunity to inform Paul of a false rumor that has been spread among them, namely, that Paul is **teaching** †Diaspora Jews **to abandon Moses**, and **not to circumcise their children or to observe their customary practices**. These charges are similar to those that Jews—ironically, including Paul himself (Acts 7:58)—had raised against Stephen in Acts 6:11–14.

21:23–24   James warns Paul that these Jewish disciples will be suspicious of him. James, as leader of the mother church, therefore advises Paul to counteract the false report by means of a public act of Jewish piety. Paul is to take **four men who have taken a vow**, probably as †Nazirites (Num 6:1–21; see sidebar, p. 286), **and purify yourself with them**. What precisely Paul was expected to do is not quite clear. While Paul himself had previously taken a Nazirite vow (Acts 18:18), this temple purification was probably with water (Num 19:12) and may have been related to his returning to the holy city of Jerusalem after time spent in Gentile lands.[3]

James also advises Paul to pay the expenses that would enable these men to fulfill their vow. The costs associated with a Nazirite vow were considerable,[4] and it was considered an act of Jewish piety to associate oneself with the vow of Nazirites by paying their expenses. James assumes that Paul has financial resources at his disposal from his own earnings (see 20:34–35) or from the churches he established.

James's reason for asking Paul to do this is to demonstrate publicly that he himself continues to live **in observance of the law**, even though he does not require Gentile followers of Jesus to become Jews through circumcision and observance of the Mosaic law. Concerning this passage, St. Augustine explains that by performing ceremonies that he was rumored to condemn, Paul would

---

3. This could be the case if the later regulation in the Mishnah (*Oholot* 2:3) was in force at this time (see Joseph A. Fitzmyer, *The Acts of the Apostles*, Anchor Bible 31 [New York: Doubleday, 1998], 694). On the other hand, Palestinian Jews commonly engaged in ritual purification before entering the temple (John 11:55), and archaeologists have unearthed extensive purification facilities in Jerusalem.

4. Numbers 6:14–15 prescribes the offering of a lamb, a ewe lamb, a ram, and a basket of bran cakes mixed with oil, along with other grain offerings and libations.

Fig. 20. A first-century *mikvah* (ritual bath) located just south of the Temple Mount. Paul may have used this or one like it for purification rites (Acts 21:24).

affirm two things: "that the Jews were not to be prevented from observing these obligations as if they were wrong and that the Gentiles were not to be forced to observe them as if they were necessary."[5]

James reiterates the decision of the Jerusalem Council regarding Gentile believers (see Acts 15:19–20, 28–29). Luke restates this to reinforce this decision for readers of Acts, rather than from any need to inform Paul, who was himself part of the original decision and the delegation to promulgate it in Acts 15. The **decision** was that Gentile Christians should **abstain from meat sacrificed to idols, from blood, from the meat of strangled animals, and from unlawful marriage**. The three dietary regulations enable Gentile and Jewish Christians to share meals, including the Eucharist, by eliminating food forbidden by the law both to Israelites and to Gentile resident aliens living among them (see comment on Acts 15:20). The fourth item, which can be translated "fornication" or "unchastity" (NRSV, RSV), requires Gentile Christians to abide by standards of morality and marriage prescribed for both Israel and foreigners living among them, again facilitating harmony among Jewish and Gentile Christians.

Paul heeds James's advice. **After purifying himself** by the customary Jewish bathing rituals, he enters **the temple**. He notifies the authorities **of the day when the purification** of the four men will **be completed** and **the offering made for each of them**. Unfortunately, his action will be seriously misunderstood.

21:25

21:26

5. Augustine, *Letters* 82, in ACCS 264.

Paul's Arrest and Defense

Acts 21:27–23:35

The later chapters of Acts highlight the striking parallels between the passion of Jesus and the "passion of Paul." For Paul, as for Jesus, there is a triple prediction of his sufferings, and in each case, his friends try to prevent it. His arrival in Jerusalem is marked by a Jewish plot to kill him. He is brought before the high priest and the Sanhedrin, and then before the Roman governor and Herod, where Jews accuse Paul of actions against the Jewish people and Caesar. Jewish chief priests seek his death, while the governor declares him innocent three times and Herod treats him as innocent once. He submits to the Father's will. Although there are numerous differences in the details, Paul clearly is sharing in the sufferings of Jesus, the Suffering Servant (Isa 52:13–53:12), as Jesus foretold he would (Acts 9:15–16).

The transition from Paul's active ministry to his passion in the footsteps of his Lord enters its first major phase when Paul is seized and beaten by a Jewish mob in the temple courtyard. Though rescued by Roman soldiers, he will have to endure several years of Roman captivity and repeated trials under diverse authorities, including Roman provincial governors and, ultimately, the emperor in Rome.

While walking his way of the cross, Paul twice gives testimony of his conversion from being a persecutor of Jesus' disciples to becoming a disciple himself. Paul's own account emphasizes his continuing Jewish identity and zeal, now focused on serving the risen Jewish Messiah, Jesus of Nazareth.

Paul's Arrest (21:27–40)

[27]When the seven days were nearly completed, the Jews from the province of Asia noticed him in the temple, stirred up the whole crowd, and laid hands on him, [28]shouting, "Fellow Israelites, help us. This is the man who is teaching everyone everywhere against the people and the law and this place, and what is more, he has even brought Greeks into the temple and defiled this sacred place." [29]For they had previously seen Trophimus the Ephesian in the city with him and supposed that Paul had brought him into the temple. [30]The whole city was in turmoil with people rushing together. They seized Paul and dragged him out of the temple, and immediately the gates were closed. [31]While they were trying to kill him, a report reached the cohort commander that all Jerusalem was rioting. [32]He immediately took soldiers and centurions and charged down on them. When they saw the commander and the soldiers they stopped beating Paul. [33]The cohort commander came forward, arrested him, and ordered him to be secured with two chains; he tried to find out who he might be and what he had done. [34]Some in the mob shouted one thing, others something else; so, since he was unable to ascertain the truth because of the uproar, he ordered Paul to be brought into the compound. [35]When he reached the steps, he was carried by the soldiers because of the violence of the mob, [36]for a crowd of people followed and shouted, "Away with him!"

[37]Just as Paul was about to be taken into the compound, he said to the cohort commander, "May I say something to you?" He replied, "Do you speak Greek? [38]So then you are not the Egyptian who started a revolt some time ago and led the four thousand assassins into the desert?" [39]Paul answered, "I am a Jew, of Tarsus in Cilicia, a citizen of no mean city; I request you to permit me to speak to the people." [40]When he had given his permission, Paul stood on the steps and motioned with his hand to the people; and when all was quiet he addressed them in Hebrew.

OT: Num 6:13–21
NT: Luke 23:18; Acts 6:11–14; 21:11
Catechism: Jesus and the law of Moses, 577–82

This episode begins shortly before Paul could fulfill **the seven days** of his   21:27
purification, in association with the four men whose †Nazirite vow rituals he is
sponsoring.[1] **Jews from the province of Asia** (the western part of modern-day
Turkey), quite possibly from Ephesus, notice him **in the temple**. As earlier in

1. See the commentary on 21:23–26 and sidebar on Nazirite vows, p. 286.

Acts (6:9; 8:1), controversy regarding the Christian movement arises especially among Greek-speaking Jews, this time from the †Diaspora.

Already hostile to Paul when he was in Ephesus, these Jews now incite **the whole crowd** and seize Paul. Not only do they misrepresent what he preached in Asia, but they also mistakenly think he has brought an uncircumcised companion from Asia beyond the Court of the Gentiles into the sacrosanct inner courts of the temple, which Gentiles were strictly forbidden to enter.

21:28   Their accusations are that Paul is **teaching everyone everywhere against the people and the law and this place**, similar to the Sanhedrin's charges against Stephen (Acts 6:11–14). Worse, they charge that Paul has **brought Greeks into the temple**, a sacrilege that ritually **defiled** the temple and was recognized even by Rome as a capital offense. Archaeologists have recovered two of the signs posted on a barrier that surrounded the inner courts of the temple, signs bearing this message in Greek: "No foreigner may enter within the barricade which surrounds the temple and enclosure. Anyone who is caught trespassing will bear personal responsibility for his ensuing death."[2]

21:29–30   These Asian Jews had recognized **Trophimus the Ephesian** going about with Paul **in the city** and mistakenly **supposed that Paul had brought him into the temple**. Their charge incites a riot, which Luke describes, perhaps with some hyperbole, as the **whole city** being **in turmoil with people rushing together**. They drag Paul **out of the temple**. To keep the rioting outside the sacred temple grounds, they close **the gates**.

21:31–32   As the crowd is **trying to kill** Paul, news reaches **the cohort commander** or tribune (Greek *chiliarchos*, literally, "commander of a thousand") that **all Jerusalem** is **rioting**. The commander, probably located at Fortress Antonia next to the temple complex, brings a cohort of **soldiers** and **centurions** (commanders of a hundred) to charge the crowd and stop them from **beating Paul**.

21:33–36   The commander arrests Paul and has him **secured with two chains**, probably between two soldiers. This fulfills Agabus's prophecy about Paul's being bound in Acts 21:11, although it is not the Jews who actually carry it out. Amid the mob's chaotic shouting, the commander is **unable to ascertain the truth** regarding Paul's alleged crime. The Greek for "truth" here, *asphalēs*, emphasizes factual information rather than mere hearsay, which would be useless in court. It is related to the word that Luke used in his promise of "certainty" to Theophilus in Luke 1:4. So the commander moves **Paul** to the quieter area within **the compound** or fortress. Paul has to be **carried by the soldiers because of the**

2. F. F. Bruce, *The Book of Acts*, rev. ed., New International Commentary on the New Testament (Grand Rapids: Eerdmans, 1988), 409.

violence of the mob, which was shouting, **"Away with him!"** This shout echoes the cry of the Jerusalem mob against Jesus in Luke 23:18, "Away with this man!" The **cohort commander** assumes that Paul must be the **Egyptian** revolutionary who tried to capture Jerusalem with **four thousand assassins**, literally, "knife-wielders." But when **Paul** unexpectedly addresses him in **Greek**, the commander realizes that Paul is not that fugitive. According to the Jewish historian Josephus, in AD 54 (about three years before this incident in Acts 21) an Egyptian false prophet gathered an army on the Mount of Olives, telling them that at his command the walls of Jerusalem would fall flat. When the promised miracle did not happen, the Romans killed many of his followers, though the Egyptian escaped.[3]

21:37–38

Paul emphasizes that, though ethnically a **Jew**, he is a citizen of **Tarsus**, a respectable **city** and capital of the province of **Cilicia**. As such, Paul asks permission **to speak to the people**. Surprisingly, he manages to **quiet** the mob, then addresses them **in Hebrew**, or more precisely, the closely related †Aramaic, the language of first-century Palestine for which there was no separate term.

21:39–40

Paul's Defense before the Jerusalem Jews (22:1–21)

[1]"My brothers and fathers, listen to what I am about to say to you in my defense." [2]When they heard him addressing them in Hebrew they became all the more quiet. And he continued, [3]"I am a Jew, born in Tarsus in Cilicia, but brought up in this city. At the feet of Gamaliel I was educated strictly in our ancestral law and was zealous for God, just as all of you are today. [4]I persecuted this Way to death, binding both men and women and delivering them to prison. [5]Even the high priest and the whole council of elders can testify on my behalf. For from them I even received letters to the brothers and set out for Damascus to bring back to Jerusalem in chains for punishment those there as well.

[6]"On that journey as I drew near to Damascus, about noon a great light from the sky suddenly shone around me. [7]I fell to the ground and heard a voice saying to me, 'Saul, Saul, why are you persecuting me?' [8]I replied, 'Who are you, sir?' And he said to me, 'I am Jesus the Nazorean whom you are persecuting.' [9]My companions saw the light but did not hear the voice of the one who spoke to me. [10]I asked, 'What shall I do, sir?' The Lord answered me, 'Get up and go into Damascus, and there you will be told about everything appointed for you to do.' [11]Since I could see nothing

---

3. *Antiquities of the Jews* 20.8.6, §§169–72; *Jewish War* 2.13.5, §§261–63.

because of the brightness of that light, I was led by hand by my companions and entered Damascus.

[12]"A certain Ananias, a devout observer of the law, and highly spoken of by all the Jews who lived there, [13]came to me and stood there and said, 'Saul, my brother, regain your sight.' And at that very moment I regained my sight and saw him. [14]Then he said, 'The God of our ancestors designated you to know his will, to see the Righteous One, and to hear the sound of his voice; [15]for you will be his witness before all to what you have seen and heard. [16]Now, why delay? Get up and have yourself baptized and your sins washed away, calling upon his name.'

[17]"After I had returned to Jerusalem and while I was praying in the temple, I fell into a trance [18]and saw the Lord saying to me, 'Hurry, leave Jerusalem at once, because they will not accept your testimony about me.' [19]But I replied, 'Lord, they themselves know that from synagogue to synagogue I used to imprison and beat those who believed in you. [20]And when the blood of your witness Stephen was being shed, I myself stood by giving my approval and keeping guard over the cloaks of his murderers.' [21]Then he said to me, 'Go, I shall send you far away to the Gentiles.'"

OT: Isa 6:1–10
NT: Luke 4:23–29; Rom 12:5; 1 Cor 12:12, 27; 2 Cor 4:6; Gal 1:13–14
Catechism: bearing witness to truth, 2471–73; baptism and forgiveness of sins, 977–80, 1262–66
Lectionary: Acts 22:3–16: Feast of the Conversion of St. Paul

22:1–2   The story of Paul's conversion is told three times in Acts, not only because of its importance but also to present the event from three different perspectives—that of Luke as narrator in Acts 9, that of Paul in speaking to Jews here in Acts 22, and that of Paul in addressing a mixed audience including a Roman governor in Acts 26. In each telling Paul highlights the elements most important for each audience. Here he begins by deferentially addressing the Jews as one of them: **"My brothers and fathers."** His opening is typical for a defense speech: **"Listen to what I am about to say to you in my defense."** The crowd becomes **all the more quiet** because he is speaking in their own mother tongue, **Hebrew,** or probably in †Aramaic.

22:3   Because Paul's listeners are Jews, this version of his call story focuses especially on his Jewishness. Paul boldly proclaims, **"I am a Jew, born in Tarsus in Cilicia, but brought up in this city."** He thus identifies himself as a †Diaspora Jew but also maintains that he was educated, presumably in the Old Testament and Jewish oral traditions, in Jerusalem at **the feet of Gamaliel**, a prominent teacher and member of the †Sanhedrin. It was this same Gamaliel who in Acts 5:39 suggested that the Sanhedrin release the apostles to avoid possibly even "fighting against God." Paul's facility with Jewish modes of interpreting Scripture, as evidenced in his letters, is consistent with his having studied under a Jewish teacher of the law, and his openness toward Gentiles is consistent with the rabbinic school of Hillel, to which Gamaliel belonged.

Paul's Letters corroborate his claim that he was well **educated** in the **ancestral law** of Israel, and that he **was zealous for God**, ardently devoted to God's honor, holiness, and law (Phil 3:4–6). He makes a similar declaration in Galatians: "I . . . progressed in Judaism beyond many of my contemporaries among my race, since I was even more a zealot for my ancestral traditions" (Gal 1:13–14).

A conspicuous feature of Paul's zeal was that he **persecuted this Way**, a title   22:4–5 for Christianity (see Acts 9:2; 18:25–26; 19:9, 23). Paul persecuted Christians even **to death**, as at Stephen's execution (8:1). As described in Acts 9, Paul's harassment included **binding** Christian **men and women**, and here he adds **delivering them to prison**. Paul even invokes **the high priest and the whole council of elders** as witnesses to the fact that he had **letters** from them to Jewish leaders in **Damascus** and was on his way there to bring captured Christians **to Jerusalem**.

Paul reports that as he neared **Damascus**, he was halted by **a great light**   22:6–8 **from the sky**, so that he **fell to the ground**. A **voice** said, **"Saul, Saul, why are you persecuting me?"** Paul did not know to whom the voice belonged: **"Who are you, sir?"**[4]

The answer, **"I am Jesus the Nazorean whom you are persecuting,"** indicates that Jesus identifies his persecuted followers with himself: in persecuting Christians, Paul is persecuting *Jesus*. This union of Christians with Christ is the basis of Paul's theology of the Church as the body of Christ (see 1 Cor 12:27).

Paul's description of what his **companions** saw and heard—they **saw the**   22:9 **light but did not hear the voice**—differs slightly from the version narrated by Luke in Acts 9:7, which says they heard the voice but saw no one. In both cases they heard a sound or saw a light that indicated to them something was happening. But they did not see the speaker or hear the speaker's voice (or what he was saying).[5] The main point of both versions is that the companions are not witnesses of the resurrection as Paul is, because a witness both sees and hears, and only Paul both saw and heard the risen Jesus.

The Lord, now openly identified as such by Paul, answered him with the   22:10–11 instruction to **go into Damascus**, where he would be **told about** the mission

---

4. In Acts, the Greek *kyrios* usually means "Lord," which seems a more appropriate translation for a heavenly appearance, even when its identity is not known, than the more neutral "sir."

5. The Greek word *phonē*, used at Acts 9:7 and 22:9, can mean either "voice" or "sound."

Christ's Union with His Members

The Catechism (795) affirms Christ's profound union with his followers, using St. Augustine's term "the whole Christ" for Christ and his Church:

> Christ and his Church thus together make up the "whole Christ" [*Christus totus*]. The Church is one with Christ. The saints are acutely aware of this unity:
>> Let us rejoice then and give thanks that we have become not only Christians, but Christ himself. Do you understand and grasp, brethren, God's grace toward us? Marvel and rejoice: we have become Christ. For if he is the head, we are the members; he and we together are the whole man. . . . The fullness of Christ then is the head and the members. But what does "head and members" mean? Christ and the Church.[a]

a. St. Augustine, *In Johannis evangelium* 21.8 (PL 35.1568).

that God had for him. The reference to the **brightness** (*doxa*, literally, "glory") of **that light** which blinded Paul is strikingly similar to Paul's statement in 2 Cor 4:6: "God who said, 'Let light shine out of darkness,' has shone in our hearts to bring to light the knowledge of the glory of God on the face of [Jesus] Christ." The revelation of the risen Jesus shattered the darkness in which Paul had been living. Because he was blinded by the light, Paul had to be **led by hand** into **Damascus**.

22:12   Acts 9 identifies Ananias simply as a disciple, but here Paul emphasizes to his Jewish listeners that **Ananias** was **a devout observer of the law, and highly spoken of by all the Jews** of Damascus. Through Ananias, Paul's blindness was healed instantaneously.

22:13–14   Ananias highlighted the Judaism that he and Paul shared by solemnly attributing Paul's Damascus road experience to **the God of our ancestors**, who **designated** Paul (literally, "handpicked in advance") to receive divine revelation. God's revelation to Paul was threefold: **to know his will**, meaning God's plan of salvation (see Eph 1:9–10; 3:3–5; Col 1:9); **to see** Jesus **the Righteous One**, a Messianic title from Jer 23:5; 33:15;[6] and **to hear the sound of his voice**. God chose Paul to know the truth and to personally encounter the risen Messiah. Small wonder that Paul became a changed man!

6. Thus Peter refers to Jesus as "the Holy and Righteous One" (Acts 3:14) and Stephen calls him "the righteous one" (Acts 7:52). "Righteous" connotes faithfulness to God's law and innocence of wrongdoing (the same word is used by the centurion in Luke 23:47 and there is translated "innocent").

Although in verses 6–8 Paul mentions seeing only light, the context of the   22:15
account, plus Ananias's statement that Paul saw "the Righteous One" (v. 14),
especially in the light of Paul's testimony in his letters (1 Cor 9:1; 15:8; Gal
1:15–16), make it clear that Paul saw not only light but also the risen Christ.
Because Paul both saw and heard the risen Jesus, Ananias tells him that he
will be his witness before all, literally, "before all people." Paul considers this
encounter with the risen Lord to be his primary credential as an apostle: "Am I
not an apostle? Have I not seen Jesus our Lord?" (1 Cor 9:1). As an eyewitness,
Paul will testify to what he has **seen and heard**.

Ananias instructed Paul to immediately be **baptized** and have his **sins washed**   22:16
away. Paul himself will write powerfully about the power of baptism to wash
away sins (1 Cor 6:11; Eph 5:26; Titus 3:5). Baptism entails **calling upon** Jesus'
name for forgiveness and as one's Lord. This is a Christian adaptation of Joel
3:5 (= 2:32 NRSV; see Acts 2:21), "Everyone who calls on the name of the LORD
will escape harm," indicating that all who call upon *Jesus* as their Lord through
faith and baptism will be saved (see Rom 10:13).

The next event in Paul's story, his prayer experience in the Jerusalem temple,   22:17
was not mentioned in Acts 9. Paul reports that he **returned to Jerusalem**,
diplomatically omitting mention of his debates with Jews in Damascus, which
had led to his fleeing to Jerusalem (Acts 9:22–26). While he **was praying in the**
temple, he **saw the Lord** for the second time, this time in **a trance** or ecstasy,
like Peter's in Acts 10:10.

Paul's vision and commission by the Lord Jesus in the temple recall the   22:18
prophet Isaiah's vision and commission by the Lord God in the temple (Isa
6:1–10). Earlier, Paul had identified himself with the Servant of the Lord in
Isaiah (Acts 13:47, citing Isa 49:6). In this vision, Jesus gives directions to his
servant concerning his mission: **"Leave Jerusalem at once, because they will not**
accept your testimony about me." Jesus does not explain why Paul's testimony
would be unacceptable whereas that of other apostles like Peter was accepted by
many Jerusalem Jews (Acts 2:41). As we have seen, Paul, like Stephen (6:8–10),
would be especially effective in debating and refuting Jews (9:20–23) and would
evoke a similarly violent response.

Paul responds to Jesus with puzzlement, not understanding why some Jews   22:19–21
will reject his testimony. After all, he says, **"They** know how **from synagogue**
to synagogue I used to imprison and beat those who believed in you." Paul
acknowledges that he had been so much on the side of Jewish persecutors that
he participated in shedding **the blood** of **Stephen**. But Jesus' final command is

"Go, I shall send you far away to the Gentiles." Paul's mission would extend far beyond the Jewish people.

Reflection and Application (22:1–21)

Despite being mobbed by some of his Jewish coreligionists, Paul in his defense speech emphasizes how important his Jewish background and identity is to him. By extension, Paul's Jewish identity is equally important to his companion and disciple Luke—and to us, Luke's readers. God's plan to reconcile humanity was accomplished through Abraham and his descendants, the chosen people. When God's Son became man, he became a Jew, born in David's city of Bethlehem and raised in Nazareth. The early disciples of Jesus were Jews, not only from Galilee and Judea but also from other regions of the Roman world (Acts 2). Although Luke, a second-generation Christian, was apparently a Gentile, his esteem for Paul's vocation to his own people as well as to Gentiles comes through plainly in Acts.

As members of the body of Christ, the Jewish Messiah, Christians ought to value their roots in God's chosen people. Elements from Jewish worship and ethical teaching are still foundational in Christian prayer, preaching, and Church structures. We are grateful to our "elder" Jewish brothers and sisters,[7] without whom we ourselves would have remained pagans seeking and groping for God to find him, but without God's biblical guidance and saving plan (Acts 17:27). As Paul says, "To them belong the patriarchs, and from them, according to the flesh, comes the Messiah" (Rom 9:5 NRSV).

Paul Imprisoned (22:22–29)

[22]They listened to him until he said this, but then they raised their voices and shouted, "Take such a one as this away from the earth. It is not right that he should live." [23]And as they were yelling and throwing off their cloaks and flinging dust into the air, [24]the cohort commander ordered him to be brought into the compound and gave instruction that he be interrogated under the lash to determine the reason why they were making such an outcry against him. [25]But when they had stretched him out for the whips, Paul said to the centurion on duty, "Is it lawful for you to scourge a man who is a Roman citizen and has not been tried?" [26]When

---

7. In the first recorded papal visit to a synagogue on April 13, 1986, in Rome, Pope John Paul II addressed Jews as "our dearly beloved brothers, . . . our elder brothers."

the centurion heard this, he went to the cohort commander and reported it, saying, "What are you going to do? This man is a Roman citizen." [27]Then the commander came and said to him, "Tell me, are you a Roman citizen?" "Yes," he answered. [28]The commander replied, "I acquired this citizenship for a large sum of money." Paul said, "But I was born one." [29]At once those who were going to interrogate him backed away from him, and the commander became alarmed when he realized that he was a Roman citizen and that he had had him bound.

NT: Luke 4:22–29; Acts 16:36–39

Just as the citizens of Nazareth listened to Jesus until he spoke about the prophets Elijah and Elisha's ministering to Gentiles rather than Jews (Luke 4:22–29), the Jewish crowd here listens to Paul **until he said this**. At the mention of the risen Jesus' sending Paul to the Gentiles, they demand that he be taken **away from the earth** and even declare, **"It is not right that he should live."** Perhaps they interpret outreach to Gentiles who do not keep the Mosaic law as a sacrilegious repudiation of Israel's unique standing as God's chosen people. **22:22–24**

By now the crowd is so out of control that they begin **yelling and throwing off their cloaks and flinging dust**. The **cohort commander** has Paul brought inside to be **interrogated under the lash** so he might discover **the reason** for this **outcry**. Such interrogation under torture was illegal for Roman citizens, but the officer is unaware of Paul's status.

At the last moment, **Paul** challenges the **centurion on duty** about the legality of scourging **a Roman citizen** who **has not been tried**. Alarmed, **the centurion** reports this news to the **cohort commander**. Roman citizenship was highly prized and remained in a family by birth. Those who were not born citizens could purchase citizenship or obtain it as a reward for some service to the state. The law protected citizens from interrogation under torture or beatings and without trial (Acts 16:37–38) and gave them the right to appeal to the supreme tribunal at Rome (Acts 25:11–12).[8] **22:25–29**

After discovering that Paul is indeed a **Roman citizen**, the **commander** confides that his own **citizenship** cost him **a large sum of money**. Paul replies that his was by birth. Fearing punishment for mistreating a Roman citizen, the commander and cohort now treat Paul with kid gloves.

---

8. F. F. Bruce, "Citizenship," in *Anchor Bible Dictionary*, ed. David N. Freedman (New York: Double-day, 1992), 1:1048–49.

Why Did Paul Invoke His Citizenship?

LIVING TRADITION

Like some contemporary readers, the patristic author Theodoret of Cyr wondered why Paul would invoke his citizenship to avoid scourging after he had repeatedly refused to avoid a situation where he knew he would be arrested (Acts 20:22–24; 21:10–14). Theodoret responds that it is generally God's will that Christians take normal steps to avoid capture or suffering so that they can continue their ministry:

> Thus the apostle called himself at one time a Pharisee and at another a Roman, not because he was afraid of death but because it was fair to do so in a fight. Likewise he appealed to Caesar upon learning of the Jews' plot against him. . . . For our Master certainly does not wish us to throw ourselves into obvious peril. This [Jesus] taught us not only with words but also through action, for more than once he avoided the murderous violence of the Jews.[a]

The obvious exception is when Christians, like their Lord (Luke 9:51; 13:33), sense God's calling them to accept suffering or death in fulfillment of their mission (21:13).

a. Theodoret, *Letters* 3, in ACCS 274.

Paul before the Sanhedrin (22:30–23:11)

[30]The next day, wishing to determine the truth about why he was being accused by the Jews, he freed him and ordered the chief priests and the whole Sanhedrin to convene. Then he brought Paul down and made him stand before them.

[23:1]Paul looked intently at the Sanhedrin and said, "My brothers, I have conducted myself with a perfectly clear conscience before God to this day." [2]The high priest Ananias ordered his attendants to strike his mouth. [3]Then Paul said to him, "God will strike you, you whitewashed wall. Do you indeed sit in judgment upon me according to the law and yet in violation of the law order me to be struck?" [4]The attendants said, "Would you revile God's high priest?" [5]Paul answered, "Brothers, I did not realize he was the high priest. For it is written, 'You shall not curse a ruler of your people.'"

[6]Paul was aware that some were Sadducees and some Pharisees, so he called out before the Sanhedrin, "My brothers, I am a Pharisee, the son of Pharisees; [I] am on trial for hope in the resurrection of the dead." [7]When he said this, a dispute broke out between the Pharisees and Sadducees, and the group became divided. [8]For the Sadducees say that there is no resurrection or angels or spirits, while the Pharisees acknowledge all three.

⁹A great uproar occurred, and some scribes belonging to the Pharisee party stood up and sharply argued, "We find nothing wrong with this man. Suppose a spirit or an angel has spoken to him?" ¹⁰The dispute was so serious that the commander, afraid that Paul would be torn to pieces by them, ordered his troops to go down and rescue him from their midst and take him into the compound.

¹¹The following night the Lord stood by him and said, "Take courage. For just as you have borne witness to my cause in Jerusalem, so you must also bear witness in Rome."

OT: Exod 22:27 (= 22:28 NRSV)
NT: Luke 20:27; Acts 27:24
Catechism: conscience, 1776–1802; Pharisees, 576, 579, 595–96, 993

The next day the commander seeks to **determine the truth** sufficiently to make a decision about the case. Since it is still unclear why Paul is being **accused by the Jews,** he convenes **the chief priests and the whole Sanhedrin** and has Paul **stand before them,** hoping that a preliminary inquiry in his presence will uncover the real reason for the commotion.   **22:30**

Paul begins his defense with an expression of solidarity, addressing the **Sanhedrin** as **my brothers** and asserting that he has **conducted** himself **with a perfectly clear conscience.** Paul's writings confirm that he placed a high value on preserving a good conscience (1 Cor 8:7–12; 2 Cor 1:12; 1 Tim 1:5, 19; 3:9). Contrary to interpreters who imagine that Paul's gospel of grace arose in reaction to feelings of guilt, he insists on his innocence **before God to this day** (see 1 Cor 4:3–4; Phil 3:6).   **23:1**

When the **high priest Ananias,**[9] who occupied the office from AD 47 to 59, orders **his attendants to strike** Paul on the **mouth** without justification, Paul responds with a declaration of divine judgment: **"God will strike you, you whitewashed wall."** It is a biting protest against the hypocrisy of these proceedings that pretend to be carrying out Jewish law, similar to Jesus' indictment of Pharisees as hypocrites and whitewashed tombs (Matt 23:27). How can Ananias **sit in judgment** upon Paul, when his **order** to strike Paul is **a violation of the law?** Probably the precept Paul has in mind is Deut 1:16–17, which calls for judging with impartiality; the high priest treats Paul as a wrongdoer before he has been heard. Paul's response is like that of Jesus who, according to John   **23:2–3**

---

9. According to F. F. Bruce (*Acts*, 425), Ananias "brought no credit to the sacred office. Josephus tells how his servants went to the threshing floors to seize the tithes that ought to have gone to the common priests [*Antiquities of the Jews* 20.206], while the Talmud preserves a parody of Ps 24:7 in which his greed was lampooned. . . . He did not scruple to use violence and assassination to further his interests." Ananias was assassinated by fellow Jews at the beginning of the Jewish War in AD 66.

18:22–23, protested an unjust blow during his trial before the high priest. In the Sermon on the Plain, Jesus taught nonresistance to abuse, even to the point of offering the other cheek to one who strikes you (Luke 6:27–30). But this is a disposition of heart, not a law obliging literal conformity in every circumstance; here Paul deems prophetic rebuke to be the appropriate response. On other occasions Paul shows willingness to suffer abuse by enduring mistreatment and beatings without invoking divine judgment.[10]

23:4-5   When the **attendants** challenge him for reviling **God's high priest**, Paul responds that he **did not realize** Ananias **was the high priest**. This is certainly possible, since Paul had not resided in Jerusalem for many years, although some interpret Paul's words to imply an ironic observation that Ananias certainly had not acted like a high priest. In any case, Paul acknowledges that Scripture says not to **curse a ruler** of Israel (Exod 22:27 [= 22:28 NRSV]), implicitly apologizing.

23:6-7   Recognizing that he will not get a fair hearing in this forum, Paul cleverly turns the attention of the **Sanhedrin** away from himself by instigating a controversy between the rival parties of †**Sadducees** and **Pharisees**. He declares that he is a lifelong **Pharisee, the son of Pharisees** (see Phil 3:5). The Pharisees believed in **the resurrection of the dead**, based on Scripture (see Dan 12:2) as interpreted by Jewish tradition. Yet ironically Paul is **on trial for** this same **hope**. In contrast, the Sadducees denied the resurrection (see Luke 20:27; Acts 4:1–2) because it is not unambiguously taught in the Torah, the first five books of the Bible and the only books they acknowledged as Scripture. As Paul hoped, his tactic causes **a dispute** to break out **between the Pharisees and Sadducees**, which prevents the Sanhedrin from agreeing to condemn Paul.

23:8-9   The result of Paul's clever tactic is a **great uproar**, in which **scribes belonging to the Pharisee party** insist there is **nothing wrong** with Paul, although they fail to mention Paul's main contention, that *Jesus* has been raised from the dead. As part of his strategy to divide the Sanhedrin, Paul had referred to Jesus' resurrection only indirectly, asserting that he was "on trial for hope in the resurrection of the dead" (v. 6). The Pharisees acknowledge a possibility that the Sadducees would not accept: **"Suppose a spirit or an angel has spoken to him?"**

23:10-11   As the **dispute** threatens to get out of hand, the **commander** (or "tribune," RSV) uses his **troops** to **rescue** Paul again and bring him to safety in **the compound**. Though saved from physical harm, Paul remains under arrest, even if it is primarily protective custody without chains. The following night **the Lord** Jesus appears to Paul to reassure him, as he had at earlier moments of crisis (Acts 18:9; 22:17–18), saying, **"Take courage."**

10. Acts 14:19–22; 16:22–28; 20:22–24; 1 Cor 4:11–12; 2 Cor 4:7–11; 11:23–25; 12:10.

Pharisees and Sadducees

Although Paul was acting shrewdly when he proclaimed his agreement with the Pharisees in the Sanhedrin, there was truth to his claim. The Pharisees were closer to Christians in their views than were other Jewish groups of the time. They believed in divine providence, angels, resurrection from the dead, final judgment, and the practice of almsgiving, fasting, and prayer—all of which provided some common ground with Christian beliefs. The Gospels, especially Matthew, often focus on the Pharisees' opposition to Jesus, yet Jesus dines in their homes (Luke 7:36; 11:37). Some, like Nicodemus, were his secret disciples (John 3:1; 19:39).

The Sadducees, who belonged to the priestly aristocracy, were rivals of the Pharisees. They accepted only the Torah as authoritative, not later biblical books or oral traditions. They denied the resurrection of the body, reward or punishment after death, and the existence of angels and demons. They recognized no meaningful life after death.[a]

Some Pharisees became followers of Jesus (Acts 15:5), and it may be that Sadducees were among the priests who believed (6:7). After the destruction of Jerusalem and the temple in AD 70, the party of the Sadducees disappeared, whereas Pharisaic beliefs continued to undergird developments both in rabbinic Judaism and in Christianity.

a. Josephus, *Jewish War* 2.14.162–65.

Although in the hearing before the Sanhedrin, Paul mentioned only the notion of hope in the resurrection, before the Jewish mob he had witnessed directly to the resurrection of Jesus (Acts 22:6–21). The risen Lord thus credits Paul with having **borne witness to my cause in Jerusalem**. But the Lord has greater plans for Paul: he **must also bear witness** in the capital of the empire, **Rome**. This is both a commission and a prophecy, which encourages Paul as he endures circumstances completely beyond his control. Later, in a storm at sea, Paul will tell the sailors with him that an angel repeated this prophecy, as a promise that Paul and those in the ship with him would survive the storm (Acts 27:23–24).

Paul's Transfer to Caesarea (23:12–35)

[12]When day came, the Jews made a plot and bound themselves by oath not to eat or drink until they had killed Paul. [13]There were more than forty who formed this conspiracy. [14]They went to the chief priests and elders

and said, "We have bound ourselves by a solemn oath to taste nothing until we have killed Paul. [15]You, together with the Sanhedrin, must now make an official request to the commander to have him bring him down to you, as though you meant to investigate his case more thoroughly. We on our part are prepared to kill him before he arrives." [16]The son of Paul's sister, however, heard about the ambush; so he went and entered the compound and reported it to Paul. [17]Paul then called one of the centurions and requested, "Take this young man to the commander; he has something to report to him." [18]So he took him and brought him to the commander and explained, "The prisoner Paul called me and asked that I bring this young man to you; he has something to say to you." [19]The commander took him by the hand, drew him aside, and asked him privately, "What is it you have to report to me?" [20]He replied, "The Jews have conspired to ask you to bring Paul down to the Sanhedrin tomorrow, as though they meant to inquire about him more thoroughly, [21]but do not believe them. More than forty of them are lying in wait for him; they have bound themselves by oath not to eat or drink until they have killed him. They are now ready and only wait for your consent." [22]As the commander dismissed the young man he directed him, "Tell no one that you gave me this information."

[23]Then he summoned two of the centurions and said, "Get two hundred soldiers ready to go to Caesarea by nine o'clock tonight, along with seventy horsemen and two hundred auxiliaries. [24]Provide mounts for Paul to ride and give him safe conduct to Felix the governor." [25]Then he wrote a letter with this content: [26]"Claudius Lysias to his excellency the governor Felix, greetings. [27]This man, seized by the Jews and about to be murdered by them, I rescued after intervening with my troops when I learned that he was a Roman citizen. [28]I wanted to learn the reason for their accusations against him so I brought him down to their Sanhedrin. [29]I discovered that he was accused in matters of controversial questions of their law and not of any charge deserving death or imprisonment. [30]Since it was brought to my attention that there will be a plot against the man, I am sending him to you at once, and have also notified his accusers to state [their case] against him before you."

[31]So the soldiers, according to their orders, took Paul and escorted him by night to Antipatris. [32]The next day they returned to the compound, leaving the horsemen to complete the journey with him. [33]When they arrived in Caesarea they delivered the letter to the governor and presented Paul to him. [34]When he had read it and asked to what province he belonged, and learned that he was from Cilicia, [35]he said, "I shall hear your

case when your accusers arrive." Then he ordered that he be held in custody in Herod's praetorium.

OT: Esther 2:21–22; 1 Macc 9:60
NT: Luke 1:3; Acts 18:14–15

During Paul's Roman custody, **more than forty** fanatical **Jews** bind themselves   23:12–15
by **oath** (literally, "anathematize themselves," put themselves under a curse if
they break the oath) **not to eat or drink until they had killed Paul**. It is a kind
of antifasting, motivated by murderous rage, in contrast to the prayerful fasting
of the disciples as they seek to spread the gospel under the leading of the Spirit
(Acts 13:2–3; 14:23). Now under an extreme self-imposed urgency, the plotters
urge the Sanhedrin to **request** the **commander** to bring Paul to them under
the pretense that they would **investigate his case more thoroughly**. They plan
to ambush and **kill** him on the way. Their plan fails, though we are not told
whether they end up breaking the vow or dying of thirst.

The **son** of Paul's **sister**, who apparently lives in Jerusalem, somehow gets   23:16–22
wind of **the ambush**. One way the Lord protects his servants from harm is to
expose the plots of their enemies (Acts 9:23–25; see 1 Sam 19:1–2; Jer 11:18–19).
As happened to Jesus in his public ministry (Luke 4:29–30; 13:31–32), no harm
will come to Paul until he has completed the mission that God has entrusted to
him. Since Paul is in protective custody rather than imprisoned for a crime, his
family members have access to him, and the resourceful nephew is able to report
the plot **to Paul**, who in turn sees that his military custodians are informed.

The commander, who is responsible for the security of prisoners in his cus-   23:23–24
tody, responds by ordering an overwhelming force of **two hundred soldiers**
with **seventy horsemen and two hundred auxiliaries**. They are to assemble that
very night, put **Paul** on a horse, and conduct him safely **to Felix the governor**
at **Caesarea**, about 65 miles to the northwest. Though the use of 470 military
personnel to protect a man from 40 would-be assassins seems excessive, a show
of force can serve as a deterrent to those plotting violence.

Luke provides the gist of an official **letter** of explanation from the commander,   23:25–27
Claudius Lysias, to **the governor Felix**, who was in office from AD 52 to 59
(a successor of Pontius Pilate, who ruled from AD 26 to 36). Lysias addresses
Felix as **his excellency** (literally, "to the most excellent governor"), using the
same formal appellation by which Luke addressed his Gospel to "most excellent
Theophilus" (Luke 1:3). He begins with the simple salutation typical of Greek
letters: **greetings** (from Greek *chairō*, "rejoice"). The body of the letter recites the
basic facts about Paul, who was **seized by the Jews and about to be murdered**,

when the tribune **rescued** him by **intervening** with his **troops**. Lysias claims his intervention came when he **learned** Paul **was a Roman citizen**, which puts his action in a good light. However, his awareness of Paul's citizenship actually came later, when Paul protested as the commander was about to have him flogged—a detail that Lysias would hardly volunteer to the governor. Rescuing a Roman citizen from a mob was a commendable act that Lysias might have hoped would be remembered when he came up for promotion.

23:28–30   The rest of the account is straightforward. Lysias tried to discover **the reason for their accusations** by bringing Paul before **their Sanhedrin**. This phrase implicitly stresses that both accused and accusers were Jews. Just as the proconsul Gallio determined at Corinth (Acts 18:14–15), so Lysias found that the issues concerned merely **controversial questions of their law** and did **not** involve **any charge deserving death or imprisonment**. This declaration of Paul's innocence of any crime against Rome is similar to the repeated verdicts of Jesus' innocence by Pilate, culminating in the exclamation of the centurion at Jesus' death, "This man was innocent beyond doubt" (Luke 23:4, 14, 22, 47). The letter ends by explaining that on being informed of the **plot**, Lysias decided to send Paul to Felix **at once**, and he has also **notified his accusers** to bring their charges before the governor.

23:31–35   As ordered, the **soldiers** escort their prisoner **by night to Antipatris**, a town with a military post about halfway between Jerusalem and Caesarea. The **next day** the soldiers return to Jerusalem, **leaving** only the seventy **horsemen to complete the journey** with Paul, since the threat of ambush lessened the farther Paul was from Jerusalem. Once in **Caesarea**, they deliver **the letter to the governor** along with the prisoner. After reading the letter and learning that Paul is **from Cilicia**, which was under the authority of Felix's Roman superior, Felix promises to **hear** Paul's **case** when his **accusers** arrive from Jerusalem. Meanwhile, Paul is **held in custody** at Caesarea. The dispassionate and relatively impartial treatment Paul receives through the Roman legal system is in striking contrast to the ferocious hostility he meets from the leaders of his own people.

Reflection and Application (23:12–35)

Paul's recourse to the legal rights available to him sets a useful example for contemporary Christians who encounter discrimination, persecution, or even court trials, imprisonment, and martyrdom. Although Paul was aware of the possibility that eventually he would die a martyr's violent death, like St. Thomas More he utilized every available legal recourse to avoid that end to his earthly

Fig. 21. A Roman aqueduct in Caesarea Maritima, where Paul was held in prison for two years (Acts 24:27).

ministry as long as he was able. He used the rights of his Roman citizenship to ensure that witness to Jesus would reach as far as Rome, the center of the empire.

Citizens of democratic nations today also need to avail themselves of every political and legal remedy to fight for religious freedom and for the rights of those who cannot defend themselves: the unborn, disabled, sick, and elderly. They need to protect pastors, educators, and parents against laws that would limit the teaching of Catholic sexual morality. They have to resist government injustice against the powerless and coercive laws that mandate cooperation in evils like abortion and same-sex marriage. As Paul did not hesitate to use Roman law to protect his Christian mission, neither should we be reluctant to use the laws of our country to protect our freedom to spread the gospel and to defend the human rights of all.

Trials before Roman Governors

Acts 24:1–25:12

With Paul's capture in Jerusalem, his evangelizing missions have come to an end. In the final chapters of Acts, we observe Paul, innocent of wrongdoing, enduring multiple trials, imprisonments, and adversities after the example of Jesus his Lord. He suffers much not only from his original Jewish enemies but also at the hands of Roman officials, especially Felix but also Festus, both of whom are far from just in their treatment of him. Even Paul's appeal to his Roman citizenship, though it spares him an immediate flogging and assassination, does not prevent him from having to suffer long incarceration and aggravating legal trials.

Trial before Felix (24:1–23)

¹Five days later the high priest Ananias came down with some elders and an advocate, a certain Tertullus, and they presented formal charges against Paul to the governor. ²When he was called, Tertullus began to accuse him, saying, "Since we have attained much peace through you, and reforms have been accomplished in this nation through your provident care, ³we acknowledge this in every way and everywhere, most excellent Felix, with all gratitude. ⁴But in order not to detain you further, I ask you to give us a brief hearing with your customary graciousness. ⁵We found this man to be a pest; he creates dissension among Jews all over the world and is a ringleader of the sect of the Nazoreans. ⁶He even tried to desecrate our temple, but we arrested him. [7] ⁸If you examine him you will be able to learn from

him for yourself about everything of which we are accusing him." ⁹The Jews also joined in the attack and asserted that these things were so.

¹⁰Then the governor motioned to him to speak and Paul replied, "I know that you have been a judge over this nation for many years and so I am pleased to make my defense before you. ¹¹As you can verify, not more than twelve days have passed since I went up to Jerusalem to worship. ¹²Neither in the temple, nor in the synagogues, nor anywhere in the city did they find me arguing with anyone or instigating a riot among the people. ¹³Nor can they prove to you the accusations they are now making against me. ¹⁴But this I do admit to you, that according to the Way, which they call a sect, I worship the God of our ancestors and I believe everything that is in accordance with the law and written in the prophets. ¹⁵I have the same hope in God as they themselves have that there will be a resurrection of the righteous and the unrighteous. ¹⁶Because of this, I always strive to keep my conscience clear before God and man. ¹⁷After many years, I came to bring alms for my nation and offerings. ¹⁸While I was so engaged, they found me, after my purification, in the temple without a crowd or disturbance. ¹⁹But some Jews from the province of Asia, who should be here before you to make whatever accusation they might have against me— ²⁰or let these men themselves state what crime they discovered when I stood before the Sanhedrin, ²¹unless it was my one outcry as I stood among them, that 'I am on trial before you today for the resurrection of the dead.'"

²²Then Felix, who was accurately informed about the Way, postponed the trial, saying, "When Lysias the commander comes down, I shall decide your case." ²³He gave orders to the centurion that he should be kept in custody but have some liberty, and that he should not prevent any of his friends from caring for his needs.

OT: Dan 12:2; Num 19:11–12
NT: 1 Cor 16:1–3; 2 Cor 8–9; Phil 2:22–25; 4:18, Philem 13
Catechism: Christians and civil authority, 2255, 2266, 2498; clear conscience, 2471, 2776–82; resurrection and judgment, 1021–22, 1038–41

Luke provides a vivid picture of Paul's judicial trial before **the governor Felix**, with arguments by the attorney hired by the Jewish Sanhedrin, **a certain Tertullus**, followed by Paul's defense speech on his own behalf. The trial begins **five days** after Paul's arrival in Caesarea, when **the high priest Ananias** arrives **with some elders** who share his authority over Jews in Jerusalem. Their **advocate** (Greek *rhētōr*, an orator or lawyer) presents **formal charges against Paul to the governor**.   **24:1**

Tertullus begins his speech with a flattering attempt to win a positive hearing from **most excellent Felix**. Since Felix had a reputation for being a very   **24:2–4** poor administrator (see sidebar, p. 347), the compliment is not even believable. Tertullus claims that the Jews **have attained much peace through you**, although first-century Roman historians record precisely the opposite. The lawyer credits Felix with **reforms** achieved through his **provident care**, for which he expresses **all gratitude**. Having buttered up the governor as much as he dares, Tertullus asks for **a brief hearing with your customary graciousness**.

24:5   Then come Tertullus's actual charges against Paul: he is **a pest** or trouble-maker who creates **dissension** (Greek *stasis*, which can refer to quarrels, civil strife, or even riots) **among Jews all over the world**—an obvious exaggeration. Although Tertullus is trying to portray this dissension as a threat to Roman order, it comes across as an unconvincing accusation. Also unpersuasive is the charge that Paul is a menace as **a ringleader of the sect of the Nazoreans** (the only New Testament use of this term for followers of Jesus of Nazareth). The term "sect" (*hairesis*, from which "heresy" is derived) is often used by Luke and other ancient authors to indicate parties within Judaism. Thus the implication is that the conflict in question is primarily between two Jewish parties, which does not bolster Tertullus's effort to portray these problems as public matters undermining imperial order.

24:6–9   Tertullus's most serious charge is that Paul **even tried to desecrate our temple**, for that would indeed threaten civil order in Jerusalem, because such desecration was likely to provoke a disturbance. According to Tertullus that charge is the reason the Jews **arrested** Paul. He ends his opening argument with an invitation to Felix to **examine** Paul himself and verify the accusations. The Jewish leaders join **in the attack**, vouching for the truth of Tertullus's charges.

24:10   **The governor** gives Paul a chance to defend himself. Paul's courteous introductory words attempt to win a positive hearing, while steering clear of flattery. He acknowledges that Felix has **been a judge over this nation for many years**, implying that he is well informed about Jewish concerns, so Paul can describe himself as **pleased** to make his defense before him.

24:11–13   Paul summarizes his case, inviting Felix to **verify** the details for himself. Some **twelve days** ago, he **went up to Jerusalem** as a good Jew **to worship**, not to cause trouble. Paul does not consider his conversion to Christ a departure from Judaism; rather, he has continued his Jewish devotional practices. He flatly denies that the Jews found him **arguing with anyone or instigating a riot** anywhere. Paul also asserts that his opponents are unable to **prove** any of their **accusations** against him.

24:14–16   Paul explains to Felix that he worships **the God** of his Jewish **ancestors**, the same God who has now been revealed in his Son Jesus Christ. Paul emphasizes

The Judgment of the Just and Unjust

LIVING TRADITION

The Catechism teaches that every person will be judged by God in both a personal judgment immediately after death and a public judgment at the end of the world:

> Death puts an end to human life as the time open to either accepting or rejecting the divine grace manifested in Christ (see 2 Tim 1:9–10). The New Testament speaks of judgment primarily in its aspect of the final encounter with Christ in his second coming, but also repeatedly affirms that each will be rewarded immediately after death in accordance with his works and faith. (1021)

Quoting the last judgment scene in Matt 25:31–46, when the "sheep" will be separated from the "goats," the Catechism affirms that the just will have eternal life with Christ, but the unjust will go into eternal punishment (1038). "The Last Judgment will reveal that God's justice triumphs over all the injustices committed by his creatures and that God's love is stronger than death (see Song 8:6)" (1040).

the continuity between Judaism and his Christian faith. He practices Judaism **according to the Way**, that is, Christianity, the whole way of life that is entailed in being a disciple of Jesus. He continues to **believe everything** in the Jewish Scriptures, **the law** and **the prophets**, which he now recognizes as pointing forward to the Messiah Jesus. He also has **the same hope in God** as the Jews, that is, hope in a future **resurrection** of the dead, both **the righteous and the unrighteous**. Many Jews, including the Pharisees, believed in a resurrection on the basis of Dan 12:2: "Many of those who sleep / in the dust of the earth shall awake; / Some to everlasting life, / others to reproach and everlasting disgrace." Because Paul believes in God's future judgment, he strives to keep his **conscience clear before God and man.**

Paul says he **came to bring alms** for his **nation** and **offerings** to God in the temple. This offering should not be confused with the Antioch church's earlier collection for the Jerusalem church during a famine, which Barnabas and Paul carried to Jerusalem (Acts 11:27–30). During his later evangelizing missions, Paul collected funds from his Gentile churches for the poor of the church in Jerusalem (Rom 15:25–28; 1 Cor 16:1–3; 2 Cor 8–9). Paul's Letters put major emphasis on that collection, which may have included the alms he mentions here. That collection fulfilled a promise he made to the Jerusalem apostles when they blessed his apostolate to the Gentiles (Gal 2:10).

24:17

345

24:18   Paul completed his **purification**, probably with water (Acts 21:26; see Num 19:11–12), and was found **in the temple without a crowd or disturbance**. This is Paul's defense against Tertullus's charge that he had desecrated the temple (v. 6).

24:19   Those who found him in the temple were **some Jews from the province of Asia**. Paul complains that those eyewitnesses are not present to bring their **accusation** before Felix in person. Without their presence, the charges are mere hearsay, which is not valid evidence in a court trial. Roman jurisprudence took a dim view of accusers who did not come forward to bear witness to their charges.[1]

24:20–21   In the absence of eyewitnesses to his temple arrest, Paul insists that his accusers are not qualified to give any testimony about him, other than to **state what crime they discovered** at his earlier trial **before the Sanhedrin**. Based on what they witnessed then, the only charge they can validly support is, ironically, Paul's exclamation that he was **on trial** for **the resurrection of the dead**, which is no crime at all. Paul's defense demonstrates that his accusers have no evidence that he caused a civil disturbance or defiled the temple. The real issue, he suggests, is a theological disagreement.

24:22   **Felix**, either judging the evidence insufficient or not wanting to displease the Jewish leaders, postpones deliberation until **Lysias**, the officer who removed Paul from the mob in the temple, should arrive. Felix promises to **decide** Paul's case after he hears Lysias's testimony. Luke notes that Felix **was accurately informed** about the Christian movement. Perhaps this is one of Paul's reasons for welcoming a hearing before him (v. 10). During his time in office, Felix would have become familiar with the conflicts between the followers of Jesus and other Jews.

24:23   In the meantime Felix puts Paul **in custody** under **the centurion**. Paul is to be allowed **some liberty**, and his friends are permitted to care **for his needs**. It was Roman practice to allow an inmate's family or friends to supply his needs, which reduced the cost of feeding prisoners. In his letters Paul refers to help given him by fellow Christians such as Epaphroditus (Phil 2:22–25; 4:18) and Onesimus (Philem 13) during his imprisonments.

Captivity in Caesarea (24:24–27)

[24]**Several days later Felix came with his wife Drusilla, who was Jewish. He had Paul summoned and listened to him speak about faith in Christ Jesus. [25]But as he spoke about righteousness and self-restraint and the coming**

1. Charles H. Talbert, *Reading Acts: A Literary and Theological Commentary on the Acts of the Apostles*, Reading the New Testament series (New York: Crossroad, 1997), 202.

346

judgment, Felix became frightened and said, "You may go for now; when I find an opportunity I shall summon you again." [26]At the same time he hoped that a bribe would be offered him by Paul, and so he sent for him very often and conversed with him. [27]Two years passed and Felix was succeeded by Porcius Festus. Wishing to ingratiate himself with the Jews, Felix left Paul in prison.

OT: Deut 16:19; Eccles 7:7
NT: Rom 2:16; 14:12; 1 Cor 4:5; 2 Cor 5:10; 1 Tim 2:15; 2 Tim 1:7; Heb 9:27
Catechism: righteousness, 1987–95; self-control, 1832; the coming judgment, 1021–22, 1038–41

Felix does not keep his promise to decide Paul's case when Lysias arrives. **24:24–25** Instead, he has Paul brought before him for a conversation with his Jewish **wife Drusilla**, who might help him understand some of the Jewish issues in Paul's case. As Herod Antipas had listened to the preaching of John the Baptist (Mark 6:18, 20), Felix listens to Paul **speak about faith in Christ Jesus**, a message that includes teaching about the kind of conduct God requires and the accountability of every person before God. At Paul's mention of **righteousness and**

Felix the Governor

BIBLICAL BACKGROUND

Felix, the Roman procurator of Samaria and Judea, did not have a stellar reputation. He had been a slave and was freed by the mother of the emperor Claudius. According to the Roman historian Tacitus, Felix "with all cruelty and lust wielded the power of king, with the mentality of a slave."[a] Opinions about Felix's rule are almost universally negative, stressing his harshness and notoriously incompetent administration, which led to violent unrest. Several uprisings occurred during his term, including riots in Caesarea that led to the killing and plundering of many Jews by Felix's troops. A delegation of Jews traveled to Rome to bring charges against him for this fiasco and other injustices, but Felix escaped punishment due to the powerful influence of his brother Pallas, who served as secretary of the treasury.

Felix's wife Drusilla was the beautiful daughter of Herod Agrippa I. The Jewish historian Josephus writes that Felix went to great efforts to seduce her away from her first husband, Azizus, king of Emesa in Syria.[b] Drusilla was one of three queens that Felix married, one of whom was the granddaughter of Antony and Cleopatra.[c]

a. Tacitus, *Histories* 5.9; see Tacitus, *Annals* 12.54.
b. Josephus, *Jewish War* 2.253–70.
c. Joseph A. Fitzmyer, *The Acts of the Apostles*, Anchor Bible 31 (New York: Doubleday, 1998), 739.

self-restraint and the coming judgment, Felix becomes frightened, probably because these points hit close to home regarding his adulterous relationship with Drusilla and other vices (see sidebar, p. 347). He dismisses Paul for the time being.

24:26–27   Felix allowed Paul to languish in prison for **two years**. Luke suggests that the main reason he listened to Paul **very often** was his hope for **a bribe**. Bribing officials was common in the Roman Empire, and Felix may have thought that Paul's network of Christian friends would pay for his release. Eventually, however, **Porcius Festus** took over the governorship. Felix further showed his lack of concern for justice by leaving **Paul in prison** in order to **ingratiate himself with the Jews**.

Reflection and Application (24:24–27)

The repeated conversations between a corrupt Roman governor and his Christian prisoner were most unusual. Besides the hope for a bribe, something else may have induced Felix to keep summoning Paul. As the adulterous King Herod had been both intrigued and disturbed by John the Baptist's preaching (Mark 6:18, 20), the truth of Paul's gospel message may have simultaneously attracted and frightened Felix.

Paul was a gifted evangelist. He knew how to talk winningly to all kinds of people (1 Cor 9:22). He did not shrink from speaking about moral issues and final judgment, but he did so skillfully, without causing unnecessary offense to his listener. Despite Paul's efforts, Felix did not repent but left the man he liked to talk to in prison. Like Paul, we are called to "proclaim the word; be persistent whether it is convenient or inconvenient; convince, reprimand, encourage through all patience and teaching" (2 Tim 4:2).

Appeal to Caesar (25:1–12)

[1]Three days after his arrival in the province, Festus went up from Caesarea to Jerusalem [2]where the chief priests and Jewish leaders presented him their formal charges against Paul. They asked him [3]as a favor to have him sent to Jerusalem, for they were plotting to kill him along the way. [4]Festus replied that Paul was being held in custody in Caesarea and that he himself would be returning there shortly. [5]He said, "Let your authorities come down with me, and if this man has done something improper, let them accuse him."

⁶After spending no more than eight or ten days with them, he went down to Caesarea, and on the following day took his seat on the tribunal and ordered that Paul be brought in. ⁷When he appeared, the Jews who had come down from Jerusalem surrounded him and brought many serious charges against him, which they were unable to prove. ⁸In defending himself Paul said, "I have committed no crime either against the Jewish law or against the temple or against Caesar." ⁹Then Festus, wishing to ingratiate himself with the Jews, said to Paul in reply, "Are you willing to go up to Jerusalem and there stand trial before me on these charges?" ¹⁰Paul answered, "I am standing before the tribunal of Caesar; this is where I should be tried. I have committed no crime against the Jews, as you very well know. ¹¹If I have committed a crime or done anything deserving death, I do not seek to escape the death penalty; but if there is no substance to the charges they are bringing against me, then no one has the right to hand me over to them. I appeal to Caesar." ¹²Then Festus, after conferring with his council, replied, "You have appealed to Caesar. To Caesar you will go."

OT: Num 35:31
NT: Matt 22:21; Acts 18:12–17; 1 Cor 4:3
Catechism: Christians and civil authority, 2255, 2266, 2498

After arriving in **the province** about AD 59, Festus went **up from Caesarea to Jerusalem**. Not even Paul's two-year imprisonment had calmed the anger of the Jewish authorities, who immediately press **their formal charges against Paul** before the new governor. They even attempt the same plot that some unsuccessfully tried two years before under Felix (Acts 23:12–21), asking Festus to send Paul to **Jerusalem** so they can ambush him en route. Festus, perhaps knowing of the previous conspiracy, wisely replies that Paul will remain in the governor's headquarters in Caesarea. He invites the Jewish **authorities** to bring their charges against Paul there.

25:1–5

On his return to **Caesarea**, Festus takes his seat **on the tribunal**, an elevated platform for judges, for a second trial of Paul. Luke summarizes this hearing briefly. The **Jews who had come down from Jerusalem** again bring **many serious charges** against Paul, this time not bothering to hire a prosecutor like Tertullus. However, just as in Paul's earlier trial, they are **unable to prove** any of the accusations.

25:6–7

Again **defending himself**, Paul denies all their charges, insisting that he has **committed no crime** against either the Jewish leaders or the Roman government, nor has he desecrated **the temple**.

25:8

25:9–10   **Festus** proves little better than the corrupt Felix, for he too tries **to ingrati-ate himself with the Jews** by asking Paul if he is **willing** to accept a change of forum, to stand trial before the Jewish authorities in **Jerusalem**. Festus is less interested in justice for Paul than in avoiding the conflicts with the Jewish leadership that characterized his predecessor's tenure (see sidebar, p. 347). Realizing this, **Paul** insists that he should be tried by the Romans, since he stands before **the tribunal of Caesar**, that is, in a Roman court. In palpable irony, Paul realizes he has a better chance of obtaining justice from the pagan Romans than from his fellow Jews.

25:11–12   In a striking expression of both a clear conscience and freedom from fear of death, Paul declares that he does **not seek to escape the death penalty** if he deserves it. Nevertheless, he insists that the **charges** against him have **no substance**. Since he is a Roman citizen, **no one has the right** to hand him over to a Jewish court in Jerusalem, where the outcome would certainly be negative. Paul therefore exercises his right as a citizen and makes an **appeal to Caesar**, to be tried in Rome before the emperor or his delegate. According to Talbert, "An appeal to Caesar was a costly business. The appellant would personally have to undertake the costs of travel to Rome, the living costs while there, and perhaps the costs of actually litigating the case, including securing witnesses."[2] But in Paul's case, it is better than the alternative. After conferring with his **council**, Festus declares, **"You have appealed to Caesar. To Caesar you will go."** No doubt he is relieved to get this controversial prisoner off his hands.

Fig. 22. The Roman emperor Nero, before whom Paul probably stood for trial (see Acts 25:11–12).

2. Ibid., 205.

Paul before Agrippa

Acts 25:13–26:32

Jesus prophesied that his followers would be taken "before synagogues and before rulers and authorities" (Luke 12:11). Paul now appears before rulers—Herod Agrippa, a Jewish king, and Festus, a Roman governor—as he had previously appeared before synagogues (Acts 13:15–41). These events also fulfill the prophecy of Ananias after Paul's conversion on the road to Damascus (9:15–16).

As part of his defense, Paul provides an account of his conversion from persecutor to proclaimer of Christianity, which was already narrated in Acts 9 and in Paul's speech to the Jewish crowd in Jerusalem in Acts 22. This third version focuses more on the *mission* conferred on Paul by the risen Christ and thus comes closest to Paul's own description of his conversion in Gal 1:11–17.

When Paul shifts from explaining his own behavior to evangelizing the king, Agrippa avoids directly answering him and terminates the proceedings. Though Agrippa and Festus later admit that Paul is innocent of anything deserving death, his appeal to the emperor removes him from their jurisdiction, so they cannot legally free him. Like his Lord Jesus, Paul is repeatedly declared innocent yet is not spared further suffering.

Paul before King Agrippa (25:13–27)

¹³When a few days had passed, King Agrippa and Bernice arrived in Caesarea on a visit to Festus. ¹⁴Since they spent several days there, Festus referred Paul's case to the king, saying, "There is a man here left in custody

by Felix. [15]When I was in Jerusalem the chief priests and the elders of the Jews brought charges against him and demanded his condemnation. [16]I answered them that it was not Roman practice to hand over an accused person before he has faced his accusers and had the opportunity to defend himself against their charge. [17]So when [they] came together here, I made no delay; the next day I took my seat on the tribunal and ordered the man to be brought in. [18]His accusers stood around him, but did not charge him with any of the crimes I suspected. [19]Instead they had some issues with him about their own religion and about a certain Jesus who had died but who Paul claimed was alive. [20]Since I was at a loss how to investigate this controversy, I asked if he were willing to go to Jerusalem and there stand trial on these charges. [21]And when Paul appealed that he be held in custody for the Emperor's decision, I ordered him held until I could send him to Caesar." [22]Agrippa said to Festus, "I too should like to hear this man." He replied, "Tomorrow you will hear him."

[23]The next day Agrippa and Bernice came with great ceremony and entered the audience hall in the company of cohort commanders and the prominent men of the city and, by command of Festus, Paul was brought in. [24]And Festus said, "King Agrippa and all you here present with us, look at this man about whom the whole Jewish populace petitioned me here and in Jerusalem, clamoring that he should live no longer. [25]I found, however, that he had done nothing deserving death, and so when he appealed to the Emperor, I decided to send him. [26]But I have nothing definite to write about him to our sovereign; therefore I have brought him before all of you, and particularly before you, King Agrippa, so that I may have something to write as a result of this investigation. [27]For it seems senseless to me to send up a prisoner without indicating the charges against him."

NT: Luke 23:6–12; Acts 12
Catechism: Church of Gentiles and Jews, 781

25:13   Sometime after the judicial session in which the Jewish authorities brought accusations against Paul, **King Agrippa and Bernice** arrive **in Caesarea** for a state **visit to Festus**, the new governor. Agrippa, Bernice, and Festus's wife Drusilla (Acts 24:24) were all siblings, children of Herod Agrippa I, who had James the apostle killed (12:1–2) and whose own death was recounted in Acts 12:23. Agrippa II was the last of Herod's line to rule in Palestine; he died about the year 92. After Bernice was widowed, she came to live at her brother's court, and there was widespread gossip about an incestuous relationship between them.[1]

1. Josephus, *Antiquities of the Jews* 20.7.3, §§145–46.

During their visit, **Festus** consults with **the king** about Paul, who was left **in**   25:14–15
custody by Felix, the preceding governor. As recounted in verse 2, the Jewish
authorities **brought charges against** Paul and demanded his **condemnation.**

Festus says he reminded the Jewish leaders that it was against **Roman** custom   25:16–18
to hand over anyone **before he has faced his accusers and had the opportu-**
nity to defend himself. Thus Festus paints a positive picture of Roman justice,
which Luke's readers know it does not entirely deserve. When Paul's **accusers**
arrived in Caesarea to present their charges in person, Festus was surprised that
they **did not charge him with any of the crimes** he assumed they would, such
as disturbing the Roman peace or advocating illegal practices (see 16:20–21).

Rather, their complaints had to do with **issues** about **their own religion**—an   25:19
intramural religious dispute of no interest to the Roman justice system. The
word used here for "religion" means, literally, "fearing a demon or divinity,"
which may carry a positive sense of reverence toward the gods or a negative
sense of superstition. Festus's way of describing the conflict represents an out-
sider's perspective. His reference to **a certain Jesus who had died but who Paul**
claimed was alive reveals his befuddlement over the controversy.

Festus relates that he asked Paul whether he was willing to **stand trial** before   25:20–22
the Sanhedrin in **Jerusalem.** But because **Paul appealed** to **the Emperor's**
decision, Festus has held him in custody until he **could send him to Caesar.**
Though Paul has thus evaded execution in Jerusalem, he will not be able to
circumvent a long confinement by the Romans.

Agrippa tells **Festus** that he **should like to hear this man,** echoing a similar
desire by his great-uncle Herod Antipas to see Jesus (Luke 9:9; 23:8). Festus
promises that he will do so the next day. Like Jesus before him, Paul has aroused
the curiosity of secular political leaders.

Agrippa and Bernice arrive **with great ceremony** at the **audience hall.** As   25:23–24
a king and queen, they are entitled to wear royal purple robes and gold crowns;
Festus, as a Roman governor, might be wearing the scarlet robe appropriate to
his rank. They are joined by **cohort commanders** and **prominent men of the**
city. The many notable observers turn the hearing into an elite social event.
Addressing **King Agrippa** and the whole audience, Festus presents Paul as the
man whose immediate death was petitioned by the **Jewish populace.** Luke uses
the Greek word for "crowd" or "multitude" to suggest the people's acting more
as a mob than as God's chosen people.

Festus repeats his finding that Paul has **done nothing deserving death.**   25:25
The four declarations of Paul's innocence by a Roman governor and Herod
Agrippa II in Acts (25:18, 25; 26:31, 32) parallel the four expressions of Jesus'

innocence by a Roman governor and Herod Antipas in the Gospel (Luke 23:4, 8–12, 14–15, 22). As Jesus was law-abiding and innocent, so is his apostle Paul. Festus concludes by stating that because Paul **appealed to the Emperor**, he **decided to send him** to Rome.

25:26–27   Festus offers an explanation for this public hearing: he seeks counsel from King Agrippa, as someone knowledgeable about Jewish matters, in order to compose a report to **our sovereign**, literally, "the lord," *kyrios*, Caesar. Up to this point, Festus has **nothing definite**, "firm," or "certain," with which to charge Paul. In another parallel with Jesus' passion, the Roman governor Festus enlists Herod Agrippa's input concerning Paul, just as Pilate had sought Herod Antipas's opinion regarding Jesus (Luke 23:6–12).

Both Roman governors, Pilate and Festus, faced a similar problem. A prisoner had been handed over to them that the local Jewish authorities wanted them to execute but who was innocent of any capital crime according to Roman law. In the end, Pilate acceded to political pressure and crucified Jesus, whereas Festus found a way out. Paul's appeal to Caesar enabled Festus to send his problematic prisoner far away to Rome for the emperor's decision.

King Herod Agrippa Hears Paul (26:1–23)

[1]Then Agrippa said to Paul, "You may now speak on your own behalf." So Paul stretched out his hand and began his defense. [2]"I count myself fortunate, King Agrippa, that I am to defend myself before you today against all the charges made against me by the Jews, [3]especially since you are an expert in all the Jewish customs and controversies. And therefore I beg you to listen patiently. [4]My manner of living from my youth, a life spent from the beginning among my people and in Jerusalem, all [the] Jews know. [5]They have known about me from the start, if they are willing to testify, that I have lived my life as a Pharisee, the strictest party of our religion. [6]But now I am standing trial because of my hope in the promise made by God to our ancestors. [7]Our twelve tribes hope to attain to that promise as they fervently worship God day and night; and on account of this hope I am accused by Jews, O king. [8]Why is it thought unbelievable among you that God raises the dead? [9]I myself once thought that I had to do many things against the name of Jesus the Nazorean, [10]and I did so in Jerusalem. I imprisoned many of the holy ones with the authorization I received from the chief priests, and when they were to be put to death I cast my vote against them. [11]Many times, in synagogue after synagogue, I

punished them in an attempt to force them to blaspheme; I was so enraged against them that I pursued them even to foreign cities.

[12]"On one such occasion I was traveling to Damascus with the authorization and commission of the chief priests. [13]At midday, along the way, O king, I saw a light from the sky, brighter than the sun, shining around me and my traveling companions. [14]We all fell to the ground and I heard a voice saying to me in Hebrew, 'Saul, Saul, why are you persecuting me? It is hard for you to kick against the goad.' [15]And I said, 'Who are you, sir?' And the Lord replied, 'I am Jesus whom you are persecuting. [16]Get up now, and stand on your feet. I have appeared to you for this purpose, to appoint you as a servant and witness of what you have seen [of me] and what you will be shown. [17]I shall deliver you from this people and from the Gentiles to whom I send you, [18]to open their eyes that they may turn from darkness to light and from the power of Satan to God, so that they may obtain forgiveness of sins and an inheritance among those who have been consecrated by faith in me.'

[19]"And so, King Agrippa, I was not disobedient to the heavenly vision. [20]On the contrary, first to those in Damascus and in Jerusalem and throughout the whole country of Judea, and then to the Gentiles, I preached the need to repent and turn to God, and to do works giving evidence of repentance. [21]That is why the Jews seized me [when I was] in the temple and tried to kill me. [22]But I have enjoyed God's help to this very day, and so I stand here testifying to small and great alike, saying nothing different from what the prophets and Moses foretold, [23]that the Messiah must suffer and that, as the first to rise from the dead, he would proclaim light both to our people and to the Gentiles."

OT: 1 Sam 3:10; Isa 49:6
NT: Luke 1:2; 2:37–38; 4:6–7; 6:46; 22:30; 24:26–27, 45–46; 2 Cor 11:24; Gal 1:15–17; 5:6; Phil 3:5–6
Catechism: the Messiah must suffer, 601; resurrection of the dead, 988–1004
Lectionary: Acts 26:19–23: St. Boniface

Agrippa invites **Paul** to **speak** for himself, as he had in all his previous trials.   26:1–3
Despite his chains (see v. 29), Paul gestures in the usual rhetorical manner. He begins his **defense** (Greek *apologia*, from which we get the term "apologetics" for defense of the faith) with a standard request for attention. He professes that he is **fortunate** to be able to **defend** himself in the king's presence, for Agrippa is **an expert in all the Jewish customs and controversies** and is therefore able to understand his argument.

Paul begins his case history by describing his **manner of living** as a Jew from   26:4–5
his **youth**. He lived among his people, first in the †Diaspora Jewish community

in Tarsus and then **in Jerusalem**. He has always been a **Pharisee**, belonging to **the strictest party** or sect of the Jewish **religion**. Paul's word for religion here, meaning religious worship or observance, is more positive than the term for religion or superstition used earlier by Festus (Acts 25:19). As both Acts and Paul's own letters repeatedly insist, Paul lived as a most zealous Pharisaic Jew.

26:6–8   Paul argues that the only genuine reason for his **trial** is his **hope** in God's **promise** to the **ancestors** of both Paul and his accusers, namely, that life does not end at death but "there will be a resurrection of the righteous and the unrighteous" (Acts 24:15; see 23:6; 25:19). This hope originates as far back as God's promise to Abraham (see Gal 3:14; Heb 11:17–19). Paul speaks of **twelve tribes**, referring to Israel in its totality, even though few remained from the ten northern tribes exiled by the Assyrians in the eighth century BC (see sidebar). God's people **hope** for the fulfillment of **that promise** as they **fervently worship God day and night**. An earlier representative of such Jewish hope is the prophetess Anna (of the northern tribe of Asher), who "worshiped night and day" in the temple and spoke about Jesus to "all who were awaiting the redemption of Jerusalem" (Luke 2:37–38). Paul insists, **"On account of this hope I**

The Hope of Israel

BIBLICAL
BACKGROUND

From New Testament times till today, Christians have tried to imagine what God's promised restoration of his people might be like. Even the apostles asked Jesus about this before he ascended to heaven (Acts 1:6). Their expectation was based on numerous Old Testament promises, such as Amos's prophecy that God would "rebuild the fallen hut of David" (Amos 9:11, quoted by James in Acts 15:16), and Ezekiel's oracle that the twelve tribes would be raised from their graves and reunited (Ezek 37:11–22; see Isa 11:11; Jer 16:15). Isaiah 49:6, which Paul applies to his own mission (Acts 13:47), explicitly includes Gentiles among the restored people of God.

Jesus referred to God's people at the end of history as the twelve tribes, promising that his apostles "will sit on thrones judging the twelve tribes of Israel" (Luke 22:29–30; see Matt 19:28). Acts shows the beginning of the fulfillment of these prophecies as the good news of the Messiah Jesus spreads first among the Jews; then among the Samaritans, descended in part from the ten northern tribes; then among the Gentiles (see Acts 1:8). The complete restoration will come at the resurrection of the dead, when God's people will be restored to life in the fullest sense and the risen Lord will visibly reign over all creation.

am accused by Jews, O king" (as he had declared in Acts 23:6). Whatever the Jewish hope of national restoration may have been, Paul focuses its fulfillment entirely on resurrection from the dead, of which Jesus' resurrection is the first instance. Thus he asks the king and court, **"Why is it thought unbelievable among you that God raises the dead?"**

Paul's defense continues with his depiction of himself as a fellow Jew who, like his opponents, formerly rejected the claims of Christians. So extreme was his antipathy that he was convinced he **had to** act decisively **against the name of Jesus the Nazorean.** The phrase "had to" is the same Greek word, *dei,* that appears throughout Luke-Acts to express the necessity of the will and plan of God. Paul previously thought it was God's will for him to oppose Christians, as his Jewish accusers are still doing.

26:9

Thus Paul persecuted and imprisoned **the holy ones,** or "saints," a term for God's faithful people found in the Psalms (30:4; 31:23; 34:9 RSV) and Daniel (7:18, 21–27 RSV). His **authorization** for these raids came **from the chief priests.** Paul admits that he even **cast** his **vote** for their execution. In **synagogue after synagogue** he **punished them,** possibly by flogging, which Paul himself later endured in synagogues, as he says in 2 Cor 11:24: "Five times at the hands of the Jews I received forty lashes minus one." All this was done in **an attempt to force them to blaspheme** against the name of Jesus. Paul stresses that he **was so enraged** at Christians, whom he considered renegade, heretical Jews, that he persecuted them **even to foreign cities,** although only Damascus is mentioned in Acts.

26:10–11

Paul now recounts his own conversion as he was **traveling to Damascus.** This is the third narration of Paul's encounter with the risen Jesus: the first two were by Luke as narrator (Acts 9) and by Paul to the Jewish mob who had captured him (Acts 22). There are minor variations in the three accounts, depending on who is narrating and who is listening.

26:12

Here for the first time we are told that the event took place at **midday.** Paul describes the **light from the sky** in fuller detail: it was **brighter than the sun** and shone around Paul and his **traveling companions.** Whereas the earlier versions mentioned only Paul's falling down (9:4; 22:7), here he says, **"We all fell to the ground."** Paul **heard a voice** speaking in **Hebrew,** probably meaning the colloquial †Aramaic. Jesus called Paul by his Jewish name: **"Saul, Saul, why are you persecuting me?"** Calling a person by name twice signifies a particular intensity, as in "Abraham, Abraham!" (Gen 22:11), "Moses, Moses!" (Exod 3:4). With the phrase "persecuting *me,*" Jesus identifies his followers with himself. Only this account adds a Greek proverb, with which Agrippa and Festus would

26:13–14

presumably be familiar: **"It is hard for you to kick against the goad."** A goad is a farmer's pointed stick used to round up cattle. Fitzmyer explains: "In Greek literature the proverb expresses as idle or useless any resistance to divine influence in future conduct."[2]

26:15–16   In response to Paul's question, **"Who are you, sir?,"** the Lord identified himself: **"I am Jesus whom you are persecuting."** He ordered Paul to **stand** and explained the **purpose** for which he **appeared** to him. This account of Paul's story omits Ananias's role. Here it is Jesus himself who commissions Paul, as stated in Gal 1:15–17. This difference too can be explained by varying emphases for differing audiences. Ananias's Jewish credentials and his role in bringing Saul into the Church are very important in the overall narrative of Acts and therefore for Paul's primary conversion account in Acts 9. This detail was also significant to the Jewish audience in Acts 22, but it is irrelevant to Felix and Agrippa in Acts 26.

Jesus' **purpose** is to **appoint** Paul **as a servant and witness**. The word for "servant" is the same term that described John Mark as "assistant" to Paul and Barnabas (13:5). It also appears in the Gospel prologue for the "ministers of the word" who handed down the events Luke records (Luke 1:2): Paul is one such minister of the word from whom Luke learned. Paul is to be a witness of what he has **seen** concerning the risen Jesus and what he **will be shown** when he is instructed (by Ananias, Acts 9:10–19; 22:12–16) about Jesus, baptism, and the Christian mission.

26:17–18   Jesus also promises to **deliver** Paul **from this people** (the Jews) **and from the Gentiles** to whom he sends him. This assurance enables Paul henceforward to face insurmountable obstacles without fear. Paul will be protected in his mission **to open their eyes** in order **that they may turn from darkness to light**. Those without Christ are in the darkness of ignorance and false doctrine until they come to the light of Christian faith, as in the hymn "Amazing Grace": "I once was blind, but now I see." Acts 9 recounts that Paul was temporarily blinded after his encounter with the risen Lord. Here there is no mention of his blindness; rather, blindness describes the spiritual condition of the Gentiles to whom he is sent.

Conversion to Christ also means turning **from the power of Satan to God**, which implies a rescue from the domain of the devil and a transfer to the influence and protection of God. Since the world is under Satan's power (see Luke 4:6; John 12:31; Eph 2:1–2; 1 John 5:19), to believe in Christ is to change one's allegiance "from the power of darkness . . . to the kingdom of [God's] beloved

2. Joseph A. Fitzmyer, *The Acts of the Apostles*, Anchor Bible 31 (New York: Doubleday, 1998), 758–59.

Son" (Col 1:13). Even though nonbelievers would not recognize that they are somehow subject to Satan, Christian faith reveals that their worldly value systems are more influenced by Satan's values, such as fame, wealth, pleasure, and power, than by God's.

Paul's call also includes the promises, found repeatedly in the Gospel and Acts, that those who believe will receive **forgiveness of sins** (Luke 24:47; Acts 2:38; 5:31; 10:43; 13:38). For the first time an additional promise is mentioned, that they will receive **an inheritance**, or "lot." Israel's hope entailed entering into its "inheritance," a word that originally referred to a portion of the promised land of Canaan but came to refer to eternal life with God. What is striking here is that Gentile converts are **among those who** share in this blessing, and the means by which they are **consecrated**, or made holy, is **faith** in Jesus.

Paul reports, **"King Agrippa, I was not disobedient to the heavenly vi-**   26:19–20
sion," an indirect way of saying that his mission was God's will. Paul briefly recaps his subsequent evangelizing activity. He preached first **in Jerusalem**, followed by **the whole country of Judea**. Heretofore Acts has not mentioned any missionary activity in Judea by Paul, only by Peter (9:32–43). However, the pattern corresponds to what Jesus prophesied for his followers: "You will be my witnesses in Jerusalem, throughout Judea and Samaria, and to the ends of the earth" (1:8). After preaching in Jewish territory, Paul turned **to the Gentiles**.

Paul has woven the content of the gospel into his personal story. Now he describes the response that the gospel requires. Using language reminiscent of Jesus' parting instruction (Luke 24:47), Paul says he **preached the need to repent and turn to God**. Conversion requires renouncing one's sins and erroneous beliefs, and turning to God in faith and obedience. After turning to God, converts must change their behavior as evidence that their faith is genuine (see Luke 3:8), not relying on mere words such as "Lord, Lord" (Luke 6:46).

Paul contends that his preaching mission is the real reason **why the Jews . . .**   26:21–23
tried to kill him. Despite their hostility, with **God's help** he has been able to continue his testimony. In fact, what he preaches is **nothing different** from the prophecies of salvation found in the **prophets and Moses** in the Jewish Bible. As the risen Jesus stated on the road to Emmaus, the entire Old Testament bears witness **that the Messiah must suffer** and be **the first to rise from the dead** (Luke 24:26–27, 45–46; see Acts 4:2; 17:3). As preached earlier, several psalms refer to the sufferings and vindication of David's descendant, Jesus (Acts 2:25–35). Scripture also foretells that through his Spirit-filled disciples the risen Christ **would proclaim light both to our people** (the Jews) and **the Gentiles**. Thus Christ fulfills the mission of the Servant of the Lord in Isa 49:6.

As Paul describes the risen Lord's commission to him, to bring unbelievers from darkness to light, he aims to do just that in this very speech. What begins as his legal defense becomes his testimony of faith and proclamation of the gospel, as King Agrippa soon recognizes (v. 28). This reflects Paul's zeal to evangelize (see 2 Tim 4:2) and fulfills a prophecy of Jesus: You will be led "before kings and governors because of my name. It will lead to your giving testimony" (Luke 21:12–13).

Reactions to Paul's Speech (26:24–32)

[24]While Paul was so speaking in his defense, Festus said in a loud voice, "You are mad, Paul; much learning is driving you mad." [25]But Paul replied, "I am not mad, most excellent Festus; I am speaking words of truth and reason. [26]The king knows about these matters and to him I speak boldly, for I cannot believe that [any] of this has escaped his notice; this was not done in a corner. [27]King Agrippa, do you believe the prophets? I know you believe." [28]Then Agrippa said to Paul, "You will soon persuade me to play the Christian." [29]Paul replied, "I would pray to God that sooner or later not only you but all who listen to me today might become as I am except for these chains."

[30]Then the king rose, and with him the governor and Bernice and the others who sat with them. [31]And after they had withdrawn they said to one another, "This man is doing nothing [at all] that deserves death or imprisonment." [32]And Agrippa said to Festus, "This man could have been set free if he had not appealed to Caesar."

NT: Luke 1:4
Catechism: evangelization, 429, 848, 852, 1122

26:24–25   Paul's speech elicits two quite different responses from the Roman governor **Festus** and the Jewish king **Agrippa**. Because **Festus** does not know Israel's Scriptures to which Paul refers, he loudly calls Paul **mad** from **much learning**. Paul calmly denies he is insane, insisting that he speaks **words of truth and reason** ("the sober truth," NRSV), terms that express Greek ideals of discretion, soundness of mind, and moderation.

26:26   Paul then directs his appeal to Agrippa, better informed about both Scripture and recent events in Judea. **"The king knows about these matters."** Paul therefore addresses Agrippa **boldly**, a favorite Lukan expression for forthright, fearless speech. Paul is convinced that none **of this**—the Christian witness to

Jesus and the mixed responses of Jews and Gentiles—**has escaped** Agrippa's **notice**. The events regarding Jesus and the spread of Christianity were **not done in a corner**; they are quite public and accessible to investigation. This assertion of the public nature of the origins of Christianity, in fact, contributes to Luke's goal in writing Luke-Acts: so that Theophilus "may realize the certainty of the teachings you have received" (Luke 1:4).

Rather abruptly, Paul's defense becomes an evangelizing appeal to **King Agrippa**. Paul asks him, **"Do you believe the prophets?"** Before the king can respond, Paul adds, **"I know you believe."** Since Paul has just identified Christian belief with the fulfillment of biblical prophecy (vv. 22–23), he is pushing the king to acknowledge the truths he is proclaiming. As a good evangelist, Paul is calling for a response to his message.

26:27

Agrippa dodges a direct answer with his somewhat ironic response, **"You will soon persuade me to play the Christian."** The RSV translates it: "In a short time you think to make me a Christian!" The wording indicates that the king is aware that Paul is evangelizing him, and he is not prepared to embrace Christianity. Paul's response is to **pray to God** that eventually Agrippa and everyone hearing Paul might become as he is, a Christian believer. Although in an earthly sense Paul is the underdog, a chained prisoner standing before a king and his imposing retinue, he boldly claims that he has something infinitely more valuable than the king's wealth and power (see Matt 13:44–46). He concludes with a humorous touch: **except for these chains**.

26:28–29

This exchange ends the proceedings. The **king** rises, along with **the governor and Bernice and the others**, signaling that the hearing is over. There is no mention of Festus's original purpose, to seek Agrippa's help in preparing an explanation of why he is sending Paul to Caesar (Acts 25:14–22, 24–27). Instead, the rulers admit among themselves that Paul **is doing nothing** that **deserves death or imprisonment**—another of the several "not guilty" verdicts in Acts concerning Paul (see 23:29; 25:25). Agrippa's statement to Festus further confirms Paul's innocence: **"This man could have been set free if he had not appealed to Caesar"**—which takes the matter out of their jurisdiction.

26:30–32

Reflection and Application (26:24–32)

Paul's defense before the Jewish king Agrippa and Roman governor Festus demonstrates that he does not have a naive or overly spiritual view of what it means to rely on grace in defending himself before civil authorities (see Luke 21:15). While entrusting himself to the Spirit, Paul deploys his rhetorical, legal, and practical savvy, both to demonstrate his innocence and to bear witness to Jesus. Paul testifies respectfully, wisely, and boldly to the truths of the faith before these powerful rulers, despite Festus's ignorance and Agrippa's lack of true receptivity.

When God summons us to witness to our faith, he expects us to use the resources he has given us, but ultimately to rely on the Spirit. God has endowed us with natural talents, life experience, and various kinds of training that we are to use to promote the gospel and to persuade people about the truth. But in the end God alone can convince the hearts of our hearers.

Shipwreck en Route to Rome

Acts 27:1–44

In this last of the "we" passages in Acts, Luke indicates that he accompanies Paul on his sea voyage to Rome. The account has the vividness of an eyewitness report, with many details regarding places, nautical terms, and storms at sea. The story shows Paul's calm practicality in the midst of a crisis. His confidence, despite the danger of imminent death, was based on his faith in the Lord's promise that he would live to testify about Jesus in Rome.

Paul's example through a terrifying storm at sea reminds Christians to keep their eyes fixed on Jesus and on the Father's providence rather than on whatever danger they encounter. Paul acts to promote the well-being and safety of all, even when the decision making is outside his control. When at last the vessel runs aground, not only Paul but also everyone on board makes it safely to shore, just as Paul has foretold.

Departure for Rome (27:1–5)

¹When it was decided that we should sail to Italy, they handed Paul and some other prisoners over to a centurion named Julius of the Cohort Augusta. ²We went on board a ship from Adramyttium bound for ports in the province of Asia and set sail. Aristarchus, a Macedonian from Thessalonica, was with us. ³On the following day we put in at Sidon where Julius was kind enough to allow Paul to visit his friends who took care of him. ⁴From there we put out to sea and sailed around the sheltered side of

363

Fig. 23. Paul's voyage to Rome and shipwreck (Acts 27–28).

Cyprus because of the headwinds, ⁵and crossing the open sea off the coast
of Cilicia and Pamphylia we came to Myra in Lycia.

NT: Acts 19:29; 20:4; 21:1–8; Philem 13

27:1   Luke again signals his presence with Paul on this climactic sea voyage **to
Italy** by using "we." **Paul and some other prisoners** are put under the authority
of **Julius**, a **centurion of the Cohort Augusta**, a unit of up to 1,000 troops that
was stationed in Syria. "Augusta," a title of honor indicating a special association
with the emperor, was given to several cohorts. Julius may have been an officer
appointed to supervise the transport of grain to Rome.[1]

27:2   Paul's journey to Rome uses three ships, the first sailing from Caesarea to
Myra, on the southern coast of Asia (27:1–5); the second from Myra, blown off
course by a storm and ending at Malta (27:6–44); the third, after wintering in
Malta, to Puteoli, in southern Italy (28:11–13). The journey begins at Caesarea,
where the guards and prisoners boarded **a ship from Adramyttium**, a port at
the northwest corner of **Asia** (the western part of modern Turkey), which was
headed back to ports in Asia.

The group with Paul includes **Aristarchus**, a companion **from Thessalonica**
who had been briefly seized by the Ephesian mob (Acts 19:29) and later joined
Paul's mission team (20:4). Paul's Letters mention Aristarchus as his "fellow

---

1. F. F. Bruce, *The Book of Acts*, rev. ed., New International Commentary on the New Testament
(Grand Rapids: Eerdmans, 1988), 477.

prisoner," possibly a metaphor for constant companion in his imprisonment
(Col 4:10), and one of his coworkers sharing in sending greetings to Philemon
(Philem 24).

Ships avoided the open sea when possible, preferring to follow shorelines,   27:3
especially when heading west against prevailing westerly winds. This ship made
the same kind of short hops between coastal ports as on Paul's voyage to Caesarea (Acts 21:1, 7–8). After a one-day trip north to **Sidon**, the centurion **Julius
was kind enough to allow Paul to visit his friends.** Paul's Letters confirm that
fellow Christians ministered to his needs as a prisoner (see Philem 13).

The ship puts out again, hugging **the sheltered** east **side of Cyprus.** It then   27:4–5
heads north, across **the open sea** to the port of **Myra** in southern Asia Minor.
There they will change ships.

Hazards of Winter Sailing (27:6–12)

⁶There the centurion found an Alexandrian ship that was sailing to Italy
and put us on board. ⁷For many days we made little headway, arriving at
Cnidus only with difficulty, and because the wind would not permit us to
continue our course we sailed for the sheltered side of Crete off Salmone.
⁸We sailed past it with difficulty and reached a place called Fair Havens,
near which was the city of Lasea.

⁹Much time had now passed and sailing had become hazardous because
the time of the fast had already gone by, so Paul warned them, ¹⁰"Men, I
can see that this voyage will result in severe damage and heavy loss not
only to the cargo and the ship, but also to our lives." ¹¹The centurion, however, paid more attention to the pilot and to the owner of the ship than to
what Paul said. ¹²Since the harbor was unfavorably situated for spending
the winter, the majority planned to put out to sea from there in the hope
of reaching Phoenix, a port in Crete facing west-northwest, there to spend
the winter.

OT: Lev 23:27
NT: 1 Cor 16:6; Titus 3:12

The next ship on which **the centurion** Julius transports the prisoners is an   27:6–8
Alexandrian ship bound for **Italy.** Alexandria, a major city in Egypt, exported
much of the food needed by Italy and the city of Rome. The long passage to
Italy gets off to an unfavorable start, for they make **little headway** sailing west
against the wind, until finally reaching the port of **Cnidus**, on the southwest

tip of Asia Minor. Because the contrary **wind** prevents them from continuing straight west toward Italy, they sail for **the sheltered** southern **side of Crete,** sailing even there **with difficulty,** until arriving at the harbor of **Fair Havens.**

27:9–10   Already it has taken them so long that **sailing** has become **hazardous,** for it is now autumn, after **the time of the fast** for the Day of Atonement (Lev 23:27) in late September, and heading toward the stormy winter season. Paul's warning that sailing at that time would result in **severe damage and heavy loss** of cargo, ship, and human life is not just the advice of an experienced traveler. His natural knowledge is enhanced by a prophetic intuition. Later Paul will revise this prediction when he receives the assurance of an angel that no one on the ship will be lost, only the ship (see vv. 21–24).

27:11–12   Not surprisingly, the **centurion** does not heed Paul but pays **more attention to the pilot and to the owner of the ship.** The great apostle Paul, like the rest of us, had to deal with circumstances in which his insight is not recognized and his advice is not heeded. Because the **harbor** at Fair Havens was unsuitable **for spending the winter,** the decision makers decided to continue on toward **Phoenix, a port in Crete.**

The Storm Hits, but Paul Offers Encouragement (27:13–26)

[13]A south wind blew gently, and thinking they had attained their objective, they weighed anchor and sailed along close to the coast of Crete. [14]Before long an offshore wind of hurricane force called a "Northeaster" struck. [15]Since the ship was caught up in it and could not head into the wind we gave way and let ourselves be driven. [16]We passed along the sheltered side of an island named Cauda and managed only with difficulty to get the dinghy under control. [17]They hoisted it aboard, then used cables to undergird the ship. Because of their fear that they would run aground on the shoal of Syrtis, they lowered the drift anchor and were carried along in this way. [18]We were being pounded by the storm so violently that the next day they jettisoned some cargo, [19]and on the third day with their own hands they threw even the ship's tackle overboard. [20]Neither the sun nor the stars were visible for many days, and no small storm raged. Finally, all hope of our surviving was taken away.

[21]When many would no longer eat, Paul stood among them and said, "Men, you should have taken my advice and not have set sail from Crete and you would have avoided this disastrous loss. [22]I urge you now to keep up your courage; not one of you will be lost, only the ship. [23]For last night an angel of the God to whom [I] belong and whom I serve stood by me

²⁴and said, 'Do not be afraid, Paul. You are destined to stand before Caesar; and behold, for your sake, God has granted safety to all who are sailing with you.' ²⁵Therefore, keep up your courage, men; I trust in God that
it will turn out as I have been told. ²⁶We are destined to run aground on
some island.'"

OT: Ps 18:5–17; Jon 1:2–16
NT: Matt 8:24–27
Catechism: perseverance in faith, 162, 2742; help of angels, 334–36

Hoping that the presence of a gentle **south wind** would take them to their   27:13–14
desired winter harbor, the crew cautiously sails westward along the southern
coast of Crete toward the port of Phoenix. Unexpectedly, the wind changes
violently: **an offshore wind of hurricane force struck.**

Unable to make headway against the fierce wind, the sailors give way and   27:15–17
let the ship **be driven** off course. The ship finds temporary shelter off **an island
named Cauda**, near Crete. Before reemerging onto the open sea, **with difficulty** the sailors hoist the lifeboat aboard and reinforce the **ship** with **cables.**
They fear shipwreck on **the shoal of Syrtis**, off the North African coast, which
was a dreaded hazard to ships. So they lower **the drift anchor** in an attempt to
slow the ship's movement but are driven unrelentingly westward by the wind,
across the open sea.

The ship is **pounded by the storm so violently** that on the second day, to   27:18–20
lighten the ship, the sailors jettison **some cargo**, possibly grain to be sold in Italy,
and **on the third day** they even cast overboard **the ship's tackle**, gear needed
to control the ship. There follow **many days** of stormy darkness. **Finally** they
lose **all hope** of **surviving.**

Although the NAB translates, **When many would no longer eat**, the Greek   27:21–24
may simply mean that the men had been a long time without food. At a time
when the ship's company are hopeless and weak from hunger, **Paul** stands and
addresses them with surprising good news. After reminding them of his earlier
warning not to sail from Crete (27:9–10), perhaps to give his present words
greater weight, he now exhorts them to take **courage** because **not one** of them
will be lost, only the ship. The basis of Paul's assurance is a visit by **an angel
of the God to whom [I] belong and whom I serve**, literally, "worship." To his
pagan fellow passengers who worship many gods, Paul describes himself as the
servant and adorer of the God who is truly in control. The angel, the messenger
of this God, has told Paul not to fear because he is **destined to stand before**

Caesar in Rome.[2] Two years earlier, when Paul's life was in danger from the Jews in Jerusalem, Jesus himself had appeared to him with essentially the same message: "Just as you have borne witness to my cause in Jerusalem, so you must also bear witness in Rome" (23:11). But now the angel of God adds that for Paul's sake, **"God has granted safety to all"** who are sailing with him. How can this message of the angel be reconciled with Paul's earlier prophecy that lives would be lost if the ship set sail from Fair Havens so late in the season (27:10)? Prophecies are sometimes conditional, and their predicted outcomes can be modified by prayer, like the prophecy of Hezekiah's death (Isa 38:1–6), or by repentance, like Jonah's prophecy of the destruction of Nineveh (Jon 3:4–10). Apparently Paul's prayer during the storm has not been only for himself and his mission but also for the safety of all (see 1 Tim 2:4), and God has granted his prayer. Now his pagan shipmates can also rely on God's promise that they will survive and suffer only material loss.

27:25–26   Many Romans of Paul's time were aware of Stoic philosophical teaching about fate and destiny. They could thus appreciate Paul's claim that he is destined to stand before Caesar. Although they might think that fate predetermined this, Paul (and Luke as author) clearly indicates that it was rather God's personal plan for Paul's life. Therefore Paul again encourages them, **"I trust in God that it will turn out as I have been told."** His prophecy is even more specific: **"We are destined to run aground on some island."** There at least their lives will be saved.

Fear of Running Aground, Then Shipwreck (27:27–44)

[27]**On the fourteenth night, as we were still being driven about on the Adriatic Sea, toward midnight the sailors began to suspect that they were nearing land.** [28]**They took soundings and found twenty fathoms; a little farther on, they again took soundings and found fifteen fathoms.** [29]**Fearing that we would run aground on a rocky coast, they dropped four anchors from the stern and prayed for day to come.** [30]**The sailors then tried to abandon ship; they lowered the dinghy to the sea on the pretext of going to lay out anchors from the bow.** [31]**But Paul said to the centurion and the soldiers, "Unless these men stay with the ship, you cannot be saved."** [32]**So the soldiers cut the ropes of the dinghy and set it adrift.**

2. Both here in 27:24 and in v. 26, the NAB uses "destined" to translate the Greek *dei*, which literally means, "it is necessary." This is a word that Luke often uses to indicate that something must happen for God's will to be fulfilled.

The Venerable Bede on Paul's Prophecy

In his commentary on Acts, The Venerable Bede brings out some theological implications of this account, explaining that Paul mentions the angel in order to call his listeners to faith:

"For last night an angel of God stood by me." [Paul] was not building himself up in saying this, but he was summoning them to faith. For this reason the sea was permitted to be stirred up, that both through that which was not heard and through that which was heard, the spiritual grace in Paul might be revealed."[a]

a. *Commentary on the Acts of the Apostles* (Kalamazoo, MI: Cistercian Publications, 1989), 188.

³³Until the day began to dawn, Paul kept urging all to take some food. He said, "Today is the fourteenth day that you have been waiting, going hungry and eating nothing. ³⁴I urge you, therefore, to take some food; it will help you survive. Not a hair of the head of anyone of you will be lost." ³⁵When he said this, he took bread, gave thanks to God in front of them all, broke it, and began to eat. ³⁶They were all encouraged, and took some food themselves. ³⁷In all, there were two hundred seventy-six of us on the ship. ³⁸After they had eaten enough, they lightened the ship by throwing the wheat into the sea.

³⁹When day came they did not recognize the land, but made out a bay with a beach. They planned to run the ship ashore on it, if they could. ⁴⁰So they cast off the anchors and abandoned them to the sea, and at the same time they unfastened the lines of the rudders, and hoisting the foresail into the wind, they made for the beach. ⁴¹But they struck a sandbar and ran the ship aground. The bow was wedged in and could not be moved, but the stern began to break up under the pounding [of the waves]. ⁴²The soldiers planned to kill the prisoners so that none might swim away and escape, ⁴³but the centurion wanted to save Paul and so kept them from carrying out their plan. He ordered those who could swim to jump overboard first and get to the shore, ⁴⁴and then the rest, some on planks, others on debris from the ship. In this way, all reached shore safely.

OT: Ps 107:23–31
NT: Luke 21:18, 22; Acts 12:19; 2 Cor 11:25

The travelers' misery on the stormy **Adriatic Sea** lasts two weeks. Finally,   27:27–29
around **midnight** of the fourteenth day, **the sailors** begin to sense they are

nearing land. As their repeated **soundings** indicate progressively shallower depths, they fear they might **run aground on a rocky coast**, so they drop **four anchors** and pray **for day to come**. Paul's words about running "aground on some island" (27:26) are coming to pass.

27:30–31   To escape what appears to be inevitable shipwreck, the **sailors** try to **abandon ship** by lowering the lifeboat to save themselves, pretending to **lay out anchors**. But not only is Paul a man of prayer and a scholar; he also is an experienced and perceptive traveler. He notices the actions of the sailors, understands what they are attempting, and warns **the centurion and the soldiers**. Although he has received a divine promise that God is giving him the lives of those traveling with him, he does not presume that promise is unconditional. Rather, God often uses human means. In this case the ship's company **cannot be saved** unless the sailors, the only ones who can steer the vessel, **stay with the ship**.

27:32   This time the **soldiers** listen to Paul, who with God's help has finally earned the centurion's trust. They **cut the ropes** of the lifeboat and **set it adrift**. The sailors now have to remain on board until the ship actually reaches shore.

27:33–34   As dawn nears, Paul repeatedly urges his shipmates **to take some food**. This is practical advice since they will need physical and psychological strength to get to land. He reminds them that they have **eaten nothing** for fourteen days in their anxiety over the storm. Paul reassures them about the outcome of their situation with words that echo Jesus' promise to his disciples about God's protection amid persecution (Luke 21:17–18): **"Not a hair of the head of anyone of you will be lost."**

27:35–36   Paul reinforces his exhortation by his own example of eating **in front of them all**. Luke describes Paul's actions in terms that closely resemble the institution of the Eucharist (Luke 22:19). Luke's purpose is to hint at the salvific

Paul the True Pilot

LIVING TRADITION

St. John Chrysostom reflects on the remarkable fact that the Roman centurion heeded his prisoner Paul:

> With the ship in danger and shipwreck awaiting, the prisoners were saved through Paul.... The centurion who was free needed his prisoner who was in chains, the skillful pilot needed him who was not a pilot, or rather, who was the true pilot. For it is not a vessel such as this that he steers but the church of the whole world (for he had learned from him who was also the master of the sea), and [Paul] does this not by the art of humankind but by the wisdom of the Spirit.[a]

a. *Homilies on the Acts of the Apostles* 53, in ACCS 307.

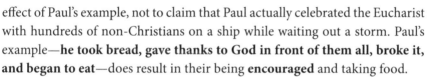

Eucharistic Allusions in Paul's Blessing

LIVING TRADITION

The third-century patristic author Ammonius of Alexandria explains Paul's purpose in blessing and breaking bread in Acts 27:35–36:

> "He took bread, and giving thanks to God in the presence of all, he broke it and began to eat." Since Paul saw that they had believed out of necessity and that the time was not opportune to announce Christ to them, as they were broken in spirit and uncertain, he teaches them some piety, namely, not to break bread before giving thanks to the one God, and then to eat. And he teaches us the same, and the way of celebrating Eucharist appears to be this: "We give thanks to you, God, because you deigned to allow us to live until now, without eating bread. Therefore giving glory to you, we break bread for sustenance."[a]

a. *Catena on the Acts of the Apostles* 27:35–36, in ACCS 308.

effect of Paul's example, not to claim that Paul actually celebrated the Eucharist with hundreds of non-Christians on a ship while waiting out a storm. Paul's example—**he took bread, gave thanks to God in front of them all, broke it, and began to eat**—does result in their being **encouraged** and taking food.

The Alexandrian grain **ship** was large enough to hold **two hundred seventy-six of us**. The inclusive use of the first person indicates Luke's feeling of solidarity   **27:37–38**

Fig. 24. St. Paul's Bay, Malta, where according to tradition the shipwreck of Acts 27 occurred.

not only with Paul but also with all on the ship, who together were undergoing the same dramatic trial. After eating, they lighten the ship, to make it easier to get it to land, **by throwing the wheat into the sea.**

27:39–41　　When day finally comes, they do **not recognize the land**. They plan **to run the ship ashore** as high as possible on a sandy **beach**, landing with the least possible damage to the ship. Therefore, they **cast off the anchors** into the sea and unfasten the restraints on **the rudders** that steadied them when they were being so badly buffeted by wind. This enables them to steer. Then they use the **foresail**, a smaller sail on the foremost mast that can catch the wind from behind without using the large main sails, to propel the ship cautiously toward the **beach**. Before they reach shore, however, they strike **a sandbar** and run **aground**. With the **bow** immobile, **the stern**, or rear of the ship, begins **to break up under the pounding** of the waves.

27:42–44　　Acts 12 shows that guards were liable to execution if their prisoners escaped.[3] After Peter escaped from prison, "Herod . . . ordered the guards tried and executed" (12:19). To avoid a similar fate, as the ship is breaking apart, the soldiers plan **to kill the prisoners** to ensure that **none might swim away and escape**.

However, because **the centurion** has grown attached to his unusual prisoner and wants **to save Paul**, he prevents the soldiers from carrying out their plan. Instead, he orders those who can do so to **swim** to shore, and **the rest** to make it to shore on **planks** or **debris from the ship**. It is not a glorious arrival—they are saved by the skin of their teeth—but the important thing is that all reach shore **safely**, just as Paul has assured them during the storm (27:22–26).

Reflection and Application (27:27–44)

One of the greatest threats to survival in perilous circumstances is a paralyzing fear that clouds our ability to respond appropriately. Thus Paul's fellow travelers began to despair after being battered for two weeks by a violent storm at sea, even to the point of no longer eating. Paul was able both to encourage them, to give a good example of eating to regain strength, and to give alert and helpful advice because he, unlike them, was not afraid of dying.

Paul's lack of fear of death was grounded in his steadfast faith in God's assurance to him that he would survive to bear witness to Jesus in Rome. As a young priest, I once experienced something similar, though less dramatic. When some people whom I trusted were praying for me to be empowered by the Holy Spirit,

3. For the same reason, the Philippian jailer was tempted to suicide when he thought his prisoners had escaped (Acts 16:27).

Paul's Own Description of His Shipwrecks

BIBLICAL BACKGROUND

Paul himself refers to his numerous sufferings and narrow escapes from death in 2 Cor 11:23–27. He even mentions that he had been shipwrecked more than once: "Three times I was shipwrecked, I passed a night and a day on the deep." What is amazing about this is that most people did not survive shipwreck in the ancient world. Although God allowed Paul to suffer in his service, his providence kept Paul alive for the mission that God had in mind for him.

Although Acts 27:24 indicates that God saved the crew and other passengers in answer to Paul's prayers, the rescue is not in the form of a miracle, although God does give prophetic assurances to Paul. Here God saves Paul and his shipmates by the ordinary means of causing their ship to run aground on an inhabited island. Their safety depends on human cooperation, including sensible and skilled responses to challenging navigational circumstances.

one of them pronounced a vivid prophecy about how God would work through my priesthood in the future. I was so convinced that that prophecy was true that I lost most of my anxieties and fears, even about death, because I would have to live for some time if the prophecy was to be fulfilled. My ongoing memory of that prophecy was quite effective in dramatically lessening in me even the normal human fear of death. The event has enabled me to appreciate Paul's fearlessness in facing the most threatening perils because he was convinced he would survive anything until he got to Rome.

Though not everyone receives the kinds of prophetic assurances that Paul experienced, Paul's case can inspire hope in God's providence over us and those for whom we care, even when we do not sense it. Such hope can overcome fears even in extremely threatening circumstances.

We can increase our faith and hope by persistent prayer, like the desperate father in Mark 9:24: "I do believe, help my unbelief!" If we form a habit of surrendering every fear that arises in our lives to God, especially through the intercession of Mary, we can arrive at a peace about our concern. This peace calms our emotions and enables us to think clearly enough to respond to the crisis in the most effective manner.

From Malta to Rome

Acts 28:1–16

On the island of Malta, the residents are quite hospitable to Paul and his ship-mates, although their reactions to his being bitten by a poisonous snake are rather humorous. First, they jump to the conclusion that he is a murderer being punished by the goddess Justice. Then, after waiting in vain for him to drop dead, they conclude that he must be a god.

Malta's most prominent inhabitant, a man named Publius, generously hosts the survivors of the shipwreck for three days. After Paul heals Publius's father of a fever, the islanders bring all their sick to Paul, and they are healed. The surprising result is that the natives of Malta treat Paul the prisoner and his party—the Roman guards, the ship's captain and crew, and his fellow passengers—with great courtesy and honor, and they provide provisions when they resume their sea voyage toward Rome. Thus the final stage of Paul's journey as a bound prisoner manifests quite a striking reversal: God has "lifted up the lowly" (Luke 1:52).

Winter in Malta (28:1–10)

[1]Once we had reached safety we learned that the island was called Malta. [2]The natives showed us extraordinary hospitality; they lit a fire and welcomed all of us because it had begun to rain and was cold. [3]Paul had gathered a bundle of brushwood and was putting it on the fire when a viper, escaping from the heat, fastened on his hand. [4]When the natives saw the snake hanging from his hand, they said to one another, "This man must certainly be a murderer; though he escaped the sea, Justice has not let

him remain alive." ⁵But he shook the snake off into the fire and suffered no harm. ⁶They were expecting him to swell up or suddenly to fall down dead but, after waiting a long time and seeing nothing unusual happen to him, they changed their minds and began to say that he was a god. ⁷In the vicinity of that place were lands belonging to a man named Publius, the chief of the island. He welcomed us and received us cordially as his guests for three days. ⁸It so happened that the father of Publius was sick with a fever and dysentery. Paul visited him and, after praying, laid his hands on him and healed him. ⁹After this had taken place, the rest of the sick on the island came to Paul and were cured. ¹⁰They paid us great honor and when we eventually set sail they brought us the provisions we needed.

NT: Mark 16:18; Luke 16:19–25; 19:2–10, 41–44; 24:29–32; Acts 14:8–20
Catechism: communion of faith, 185, 949, 1102
Lectionary: Acts 28:7–10: Mass for the Sick

Once we had reached safety can be more literally translated as "having   28:1
been saved," implicitly by God. This reading hints that the travelers' reaching land in one piece is a sign and anticipation of the ultimate salvation that God gives to all who trust him. The travelers learn that they have landed on **Malta**, a small island south of Sicily.

The word for **natives** is *barbaros*, the Greek term for all people who do not   28:2
speak Greek. It can have the sense of "foreigner." The Maltese natives show the shipwrecked travelers **extraordinary hospitality**. Because of the **rain** and the **cold**, they light a **fire**, around which they welcome all those who have just swum ashore.

The striking hospitality of the islanders continues a theme from the Gospel of Luke, where hospitality is a sign of welcoming the visitation and action of God (16:19–25; 19:2–10; 24:29–32). Jesus wept over the lack of hospitality of the inhabitants of Jerusalem who refused to believe in him, and who will be punished "because you did not recognize the time of your visitation" (19:44). Hospitality for shipwrecked travelers was highly valued in ancient Mediterranean cultures. Here in Acts the friendliness of rustic strangers on Malta provides a stark contrast to the rejection Paul had experienced from his own Jewish compatriots in Pisidian Antioch, Thessalonica, and Jerusalem (13:50; 17:1–10; Acts 22–23).

The islanders' change of mind after Paul is bitten by a poisonous snake recalls   28:3–6
the reaction of the inhabitants of Lystra after Paul and Barnabas healed a lame man (14:8–20). At first they called them "gods"; then they stoned Paul.

Here on Malta the sequence flows in the opposite direction. When they see the poisonous snake on Paul's **hand**, they conclude that he must be a murderer and that even though **he escaped the sea, Justice**, the goddess who enforces justice among humans, has finally caught up with him and is punishing him with death. This is analogous to biblical teaching that no grave sin will escape God's notice or punishment.

After waiting for Paul to drop dead but observing that he has **suffered no harm**, the natives change their minds and call him **a god.** For Luke, this incident fulfills Jesus' prophecy to his disciples, "Behold, I have given you the power 'to tread upon serpents' and scorpions and upon the full force of the enemy and nothing will harm you" (Luke 10:19; see Mark 16:18).

28:7–8   **Publius, the chief of the island,** welcomes the travelers and shows them hospitality **for three days**. When Paul learns that Publius's **father** is **sick with a fever** (perhaps what was later called Malta fever, caused by the Brucella bacteria) **and dysentery**, he ministers to his host by visiting the father. Through prayer and the laying on of **hands**, Paul heals him—an act reminiscent of Jesus' healing Peter's mother-in-law from fever (Luke 4:38–39). Paul is sharing in Jesus' power to heal the sick, as Jesus had enabled his followers to do (Luke 4:40; 9:1–2; 10:8–9). This healing illustrates how Jesus' disciples in Acts continue "all that Jesus did and taught" (Acts 1:1). It nevertheless reveals a difference: whereas Paul and others heal in the name of Jesus or through prayer (such as Peter in 3:6; 9:40), Jesus healed simply on his own authority.

28:9–10   Jesus' healings led to crowds of the sick coming to be healed (Luke 4:38–40); similarly, after Paul's healing of Publius's father, **the rest of the sick on the island came to Paul and were cured**. Although nothing is said explicitly, there is no reason to doubt that Paul took the occasion to evangelize them. Malta today is a deeply Catholic country, and its inhabitants trace the origin of their faith to this visit of Paul.

These healings have the further result that the islanders pay Paul and his companions **great honor**. Luke skips over the remaining months of the winter layover to mention that when the new sailing season began, the people of the island supplied all the needed **provisions**, and the travelers finally **set sail** for Rome. Like Jacob in Laban's house and Joseph in Egypt, God is with Paul, blessing him and blessing those around him because of him.

Arrival in Rome (28:11–16)

[11]**Three months later we set sail on a ship that had wintered at the island. It was an Alexandrian ship with the Dioscuri as its figurehead.** [12]**We put in at Syracuse and stayed there three days,** [13]**and from there we sailed round**

the coast and arrived at Rhegium. After a day, a south wind came up and in two days we reached Puteoli. ¹⁴There we found some brothers and were urged to stay with them for seven days. And thus we came to Rome. ¹⁵The brothers from there heard about us and came as far as the Forum of Appius and Three Taverns to meet us. On seeing them, Paul gave thanks to God and took courage. ¹⁶When he entered Rome, Paul was allowed to live by himself, with the soldier who was guarding him.

NT: Acts 21
Lectionary: Acts 28:11–16, 30–31: Dedication of the Basilica of Saints Peter and Paul, Apostles (Nov. 17)

Three months later, when the sailing season reopens, the Roman guards and their prisoners **set sail** on another **Alexandrian ship**. The ship's **figurehead** is the **Dioscuri**, or Castor and Pollux, twin gods who were revered by pagans for protection at sea. Ironically, that ship bears to Rome one who brings the good news of the *true* protectors, God and his Son Jesus Christ, which will have an incalculable impact on the future of Rome and all Europe. The first stop is the port of **Syracuse** in Sicily, where they stay **three days**. They then sail to **Rhegium** in Calabria, on the toe of Italy, and finally to **Puteoli**, on the western side of Italy, the principal port of the Bay of Naples, where their sea journey ends. *(28:11–13)*

At Puteoli, Paul and his companions find some fellow Christians and stay with them a week, presumably with permission from Paul's guards. The statement, **thus we came to Rome**, is probably anticipatory, introducing what follows: "This is how we came to Rome." Word of the apostle's arrival must have reached **Rome** during Paul's weeklong stay with the church in Puteoli, since Roman Christians come **as far as the Forum of Appius** (about 43 miles from Rome) and **Three Taverns** (about 33 miles) **to meet** the party.[1] Their hiking such a distance, presumably on foot, to meet him and his companions renews Paul's **courage** and inspires him to give **thanks to God**. It is hard to overstate the value of such expressions of hospitality and esteem toward fellow Christians, especially those working hard or suffering for the gospel. *(28:14–15)*

Once Paul reaches **Rome**, the "we" narrative ends, and Luke relates the final part of Acts, regarding Paul's house arrest in Rome, in the third person (28:17–31). Luke thus suggests another subtle parallel between Paul's sufferings and the passion of Jesus. Paul, like Jesus, was accompanied by disciples on his way to his trials and possible death. However, as Jesus was alone in his final *(28:16)*

1. See Luke Timothy Johnson, *The Acts of the Apostles*, Sacra pagina 5 (Collegeville, MN: Liturgical Press, 1992), 464–65; Joseph A. Fitzmyer, *The Acts of the Apostles*, Anchor Bible 31 (New York: Doubleday, 1998), 787–88.

imprisonment, Luke no longer mentions that any of Paul's travel companions continue to support him once he is placed under house arrest in Rome. He is **by himself, with the soldier who was guarding him**.

Luke does, however, mention that Paul has visitors. And Paul's Letters indicate that, at least in some of his imprisonments, other Christians were fellow prisoners with him (see sidebar).

Reflection and Application (28:11–16)

The pagans of Malta were particularly impressed by Paul's miraculous survival from a poisonous snakebite and by the many healings the sick experienced at his hands. Evangelization in earliest Christianity, following the example of Jesus' own ministry, was immensely aided by healings and other miracles, which effectively invited faith from those who witnessed them. As I was writing this chapter, I was visited by a former doctoral student who recently felt called by God to join a team with a worldwide mission. They travel especially to India and Africa for evangelistic preaching to crowds as many as hundreds of thousands. What makes their message particularly persuasive are the many healings that occur through their preaching and prayer with the sick. I was surprised to be reminded that numerous healings like those of Paul on Malta are still occurring, often in developing countries where people are more aware

Paul's Fellow Prisoners

BIBLICAL BACKGROUND

In the prison from which Paul wrote his letter to Philemon, he was not alone: "Epaphras, my fellow prisoner in Christ Jesus, greets you" (Philem 23). Also in Colossians, Paul includes greetings from a fellow prisoner named Aristarchus, as well as from Luke (Col 4:10, 14). Neither of these letters makes clear where Paul is imprisoned.

The Second Letter to Timothy, however, clearly says that Paul is imprisoned in Rome (1:8, 17). Paul states, "Luke is the only one with me" (4:11), and requests that Mark be sent and that Timothy himself come before winter (4:11, 13, 21). But Paul also maintains that he was abandoned in his first trial (as Jesus was): "At my first defense no one appeared on my behalf, but everyone deserted me" (2 Tim 4:16). Although Paul, unlike Jesus, sometimes had human helpers with him in prison and at his hearings, at least once his letters mention that he shared in his Lord Jesus' experience of abandonment during his trial.

of their need for God's help and have not raised rationalist barriers to divine intervention. The Acts of the Apostles, and Paul's example in particular, challenge contemporary Christian witnesses to open ourselves more completely to faith in God's power to heal and convert members of "every nation, tribe, tongue, and people" (Rev 14:6).

Even among Christians in developed nations, the tendency is to rely on modern medicine rather than God. However, all genuine healing comes from God (Ps 103:3), whether through medical means, directly through prayer, or through a combination of both. The teaching of Scripture about how to respond to sickness remains valid (Sir 38:1–12; James 5:14–16); Jesus' promise about healing through the laying on of hands still holds (Mark 16:17–20). Even if evangelization in some situations may not emphasize healing as much as among poorer peoples, it still depends on God for its effectiveness. We still need to call on God's power for whatever ministry he has given us to carry out.

Testimony in Rome

Acts 28:17–31

Paul's final testimony to Jesus takes place in Rome, where he is under house arrest but allowed to have visitors. Paul speaks mainly to the leaders of the Jews. He makes every effort to reassure them that although he is a prisoner, he is innocent of any offense against either Jewish or Roman laws or customs. He insists also that his only reason for appealing to the Roman emperor is because his opponents objected to his being set free (25:10–12). But he did not turn to Rome out of any animosity toward his fellow Jews.

Paul's lengthy exposition of his beliefs persuades some Jews, but not others. When they leave, unable to agree among themselves, Paul quotes Isa 6:9–10, which prophesied that God's people would not be receptive to the prophetic message. Therefore, Paul announces, this salvation will be offered to the Gentiles, who will be responsive.

Acts ends without reporting what happened to Paul after the "two full years" of his detention. Luke maintains his focus, which is not on Paul's life and career but on the spread of God's word. Acts ends on a high note, with Paul's testimony to the gospel bold and unhindered, despite his chains. By implication, readers are invited to continue such bold witness and, like Paul, refuse to be deterred by any obstacles.

Testimony to Jews in Rome (28:17–31)

[17]Three days later he called together the leaders of the Jews. When they had gathered he said to them, "My brothers, although I had done nothing

against our people or our ancestral customs, I was handed over to the Romans as a prisoner from Jerusalem. [18]After trying my case the Romans wanted to release me, because they found nothing against me deserving the death penalty. [19]But when the Jews objected, I was obliged to appeal to Caesar, even though I had no accusation to make against my own nation. [20]This is the reason, then, I have requested to see you and to speak with you, for it is on account of the hope of Israel that I wear these chains." [21]They answered him, "We have received no letters from Judea about you, nor has any of the brothers arrived with a damaging report or rumor about you. [22]But we should like to hear you present your views, for we know that this sect is denounced everywhere."

[23]So they arranged a day with him and came to his lodgings in great numbers. From early morning until evening, he expounded his position to them, bearing witness to the kingdom of God and trying to convince them about Jesus from the law of Moses and the prophets. [24]Some were convinced by what he had said, while others did not believe. [25]Without reaching any agreement among themselves they began to leave; then Paul made one final statement. "Well did the holy Spirit speak to your ancestors through the prophet Isaiah, saying:

> [26]'Go to this people and say:
> You shall indeed hear but not understand.
> You shall indeed look but never see.
> [27]Gross is the heart of this people;
> they will not hear with their ears;
> they have closed their eyes,
> so they may not see with their eyes
> and hear with their ears
> and understand with their heart and be converted,
> and I heal them.'

[28]Let it be known to you that this salvation of God has been sent to the Gentiles; they will listen." [29] [30]He remained for two full years in his lodgings. He received all who came to him, [31]and with complete assurance and without hindrance he proclaimed the kingdom of God and taught about the Lord Jesus Christ.

OT: Isa 6:9–10; 49:6

NT: Mark 16:8; Luke 8:10; John 12:40; Acts 1:1–3; 23:6

Catechism: universality of sin, salvation needed by all, 402, 588

Lectionary: Acts 28:11–16, 30–31: Dedication of the Basilicas of Saints Peter and Paul, Apostles

28:17–19   Because he is kept in custody while awaiting his trial, Paul is unable to visit synagogues or public places. However, because he is not considered to be a threat to Roman order, he is held under house arrest and allowed the freedom to invite people to his lodgings and speak with them there. There is no mention of Paul's meeting with Christians of Rome. The only interactions with Roman Christians that Luke reports took place as Paul was arriving (28:15), though we may assume that the Christians who went out of their way to welcome Paul maintained contact with him.

Three days after arriving, Paul invites the leaders of the Jews. This accords with his normal pattern of reaching out to Jews first, then to Gentiles (Acts 13:5, 14–49; see Luke 4:16, 44). Paul does not begin by evangelizing individual Jews haphazardly but addresses their leadership, perhaps in the interest of reaching more of the Jewish community in Rome. He explains why they should listen to him in three points: first, he remains a loyal Jew, having **done nothing against** his **people** or their **ancestral customs**; second, he is not a criminal by Roman standards, and for this reason **the Romans wanted to release** him; third, it was only because of objections to his release by Jews in Jerusalem that he was forced to **appeal to Caesar**. Paul, however, remains loyal to his **own nation** and has filed **no accusation** against them.

28:20   Paul declares that the only reason he is in **chains** is **the hope of Israel**, that is, hope for resurrection from the dead, a doctrine that the Jews of Rome likely share. Paul has professed this hope repeatedly (Acts 23:6; 24:15). Readers, however, realize that for Paul, the hope of Israel is inseparably linked to the resurrected Jewish Messiah, Jesus, whom Paul proclaims.

28:21   The Jewish leaders' answer is surprising in view of the negative rumors about Paul circulating in Jerusalem (21:21) and the relentless prosecution of Paul by the Jewish authorities there. The Roman Jews have **received no letters from Judea** about him, nor any **damaging** oral **report or rumor**. It is possible that a negative report from Jerusalem had not yet reached Rome simply due to the hazardous winter sailing conditions.

28:22   These Jewish leaders in Rome show a certain fair-mindedness: they want to hear Paul despite the fact that they have heard of Christianity, which they regard as a Jewish **sect**, being **denounced everywhere**. Perhaps Paul's credentials as a rabbi who had studied in Jerusalem earned him some credibility (22:3). They must know of the Christian community in Rome to which Paul wrote some five years earlier, but they seem not to be well acquainted with it.

28:23–24   The Jewish leaders therefore arrange a follow-up date to return to Paul's **lodgings**. Somehow the residence is large enough to receive the **great numbers** who come. Paul's presentation of the gospel is quite protracted, lasting from **early morning until evening**. Doubtless it is no monologue, since in the Jewish culture of the day, religious topics occasioned vigorous and often passionate discussion. Paul's exposition includes two elements: **bearing witness to** (the Greek connotes a solemn testimony, even warning about) **the kingdom of God**, the main subject of Jesus' own preaching (as in Luke 4:43), and seeking to persuade them about **Jesus**. Ever since the death and resurrection of Jesus, the gospel message of the kingdom is also a message about the anointed king himself, Jesus.

Since Luke does not detail the content, we may assume that Paul follows the pattern of his preaching to Jewish audiences, as in his synagogue sermon in Pisidian Antioch (13:16–41) and in his speeches to the Jews of Jerusalem and King Agrippa (Acts 22; 26). He bases his arguments on **the law of Moses and the prophets**, Luke's shorthand for the Old Testament. The results are mixed, as his preaching to Jews has usually been throughout Acts. **Some** listeners are **convinced**, while **others** do **not believe**.

The Jews fail to come to **any agreement among themselves**, and as they are leaving, Paul's **final statement** reminds them of the appropriateness of what the **holy Spirit** spoke to their **ancestors** through the prophet **Isaiah** (6:9–10). In three of the Gospels a quotation of this same prophecy provides a prominent explanation for how Jesus the Messiah could have been rejected by his own people (Matt 13:14–15; Mark 4:12; John 12:40). Luke's Gospel, however, cites the passage only in an abbreviated form: "they may look but not see, and hear but not understand" (8:10). Luke waits to quote Isa 6:9–10 more fully until this climactic moment at the end of Acts, the end of his entire two-volume work. **28:25**

At his calling to be a prophet to Israel, Isaiah was given the sobering announcement that his message would be rejected. The people will **hear** his message **but not understand** it because they do not want to heed it. Their **heart** is **gross** (or "dull," RSV; "torpid," NJB). Like many people who become addicted to sinful ways, they are in denial: **they have closed their eyes, so they may not see**, nor hear, nor **understand**. By their refusal they will frustrate God's gracious plan, which is that they **be converted** so he can **heal them**. This biblical quotation warns Paul's Jewish compatriots of the danger of imitating their ancestors by refusing to heed God's call to them through Paul. The distressing fact that many Jews did not accept the good news about their Messiah Jesus is thus shown to have been foreshadowed by God's word through Isaiah. **28:26–27**

Paul announces to his Jewish listeners, **"This salvation of God has been sent to the Gentiles."** This conclusion is similar to Paul's teaching in Rom 11:30–31 **28:28**

Does God Harden Hearts?

BIBLICAL BACKGROUND

Acts quotes the †Septuagint Greek version of Isa 6:9–10 rather than the Hebrew. In the original Hebrew version, God commands the prophet to harden the people: "Make the heart of this people sluggish, dull their ears and close their eyes" (Isa 6:10). Taken literally, this seems grossly unjust. But wherever Scripture speaks of God's hardening someone's heart (such as Pharaoh's in Exod 7:3–5), it is a way of expressing the truth that God allows people to experience the consequences of their own choices. Other biblical passages put more emphasis on humans' responsibility in their own wrongdoing.

The †Septuagint Greek translation of the Hebrew Bible, which was completed during the third to first centuries BC, often adds theological clarifications. The Greek of Isa 6:9–10, which is what Luke quotes in Acts, simply states that the people are unreceptive, not that God or the prophet made them so. Instead of "Make the heart of this people sluggish," it says, "Gross is the heart of this people." This translation shows a nuanced understanding: although God upholds everything in existence, human beings have free will and are responsible for their choices.

that *because* Jews rejected the gospel, the Gentiles were given the opportunity to receive it. Isaiah had already prophesied that God's salvation is to extend to every nation of the earth (42:6; 49:6). Paul goes on to predict that the Gentiles **will listen**. This does not mean that the evangelization of Jews is ended and replaced by outreach exclusively to Gentiles, or that all Gentiles will heed the message. Not all of them have accepted it in the course of Acts. Paul's two previous statements about turning to Gentiles (Acts 13:46; 18:6) were followed by continued outreach to Jews, and there is no indication that Jews cease to be among **all who came** to Paul (28:30) in his house arrest.

The pattern already evident in Acts will continue beyond the ending of the book. Luke has repeatedly reported mixed Jewish reception of the gospel, followed by large numbers of Gentiles taking the message to heart. At the time Luke writes, there are many Gentile Christians in addition to the original Jewish foundation of the Church featured in Acts 1–6.

28:30   Acts ends with the declaration that Paul **remained for two full years** under house arrest. For Luke to state a definite time of two full years, most scholars agree, he must have known what happened at the end of that period even though he does not say. Was Paul martyred at that time, or was he freed to continue further missionary travels? The letter to Titus (1:5) mentions Paul's evangelizing Crete (which does not fit the travels mentioned in Acts), and about AD 95 Clement of Rome wrote that Paul took the gospel to the limits of the west, which seems to imply Spain.[2] Although these reports lack historical certainty, they are probable. However, if Paul was freed after these two years, the Christian tradition is strong that not many years later he was beheaded in Rome under Nero.

During these two years, Paul stays **in his lodgings**: the Greek literally says "at his own expense." For Paul's Roman captors, an advantage of house arrest is that he bears the expense of his detention. An advantage for Paul is that he is able to continue his ministry. Although his movement is restricted, he is able to meet with **all who came to him**.

Despite his house arrest, Paul **proclaimed the kingdom of God and taught**   **28:31**
about the Lord Jesus Christ, the same two realities at the center of his message in verse 23. The entire narrative of Acts is thus bracketed by teaching about the kingdom of God—by the risen Jesus at the beginning (1:3) and by his disciple Paul at the end. This frame or †*inclusio* underscores that fact that the risen Jesus continues to speak and act through his disciples empowered by the Spirit (see 1:1 RSV, NIV).

Thus Acts ends on a triumphal note. The final two words in Greek are literally "boldness" and "unhindered." Although a prisoner, Paul continues to proclaim the gospel **with complete assurance and without hindrance**. Even if the messenger is chained, the message is not (see 2 Tim 2:9). Here lies the reason why Luke does not tell us what happened to Paul at the end of the two full years. Though Luke knows what happened to Paul, his narrative is not primarily about Paul but about the spread of the good news of Jesus Christ.

Reflection and Application (28:17–31)

As a faithful Jew who had come to believe that Jesus was the Jewish Messiah, Paul wanted the best for his fellow Jews. At the end of Acts, Luke shows Paul as trying to explain himself to the leaders of the Roman Jewish community. Paul's poignant love and concern for his fellow Jews is even more movingly expressed in his Letter to the Romans, chapters 9–11. Paul provides a good example for us today. When someone becomes a Catholic, for instance, it is fitting to be grateful for the graces one has received through one's previous faith community and to maintain good relationships with the people in it, insofar as possible.

2. *First Clement* 5.7.

Luke ends his two-volume work on a high note: Paul is proclaiming the kingdom and teaching about the Lord Jesus Christ "with complete assurance and without hindrance." This open-ended conclusion implies a challenge to us, his readers. The examples of Peter, John, Stephen, Philip, Barnabas, and Paul summon us too to be daring witnesses to Jesus. It is now up to us to continue the proclamation of the gospel boldly and without hindrance, no matter what obstacles we may encounter.

Suggested Resources

From the Christian Tradition

Martin, Francis, and Evan Smith, eds. *Acts*. Ancient Christian Commentary on Scripture: New Testament 5. Downers Grove, IL: InterVarsity, 2006. This series offers rich selections from patristic writings on every passage of the biblical text.

Venerable Bede, The. *The Venerable Bede Commentary on the Acts of the Apostles*. Translated by Lawrence T. Martin. Cistercian Studies Series 117. Kalamazoo, MI: Cistercian Publications, 1989. Delightful and insightful patristic commentary that some Bible study groups have found helpful.

Scholarly Commentaries

Fitzmyer, Joseph A. *The Acts of the Apostles*. Anchor Bible 31. New York: Doubleday, 1998. Thorough interaction with secondary literature and heavy emphasis on historical information; more useful as a reference book than to be read through.

Johnson, Luke Timothy. *The Acts of the Apostles*. Sacra pagina 5. Collegeville, MN: Liturgical Press, 1992. Scholarly but well-written commentary focusing especially on primary texts rather than secondary literature. Johnson also wrote the Sacra pagina volume on the Gospel of Luke, and the matching commentaries provide excellent insights into Luke's use of the Old Testament as well as the relationship between Luke and Acts.

Tannehill, Robert C. *The Narrative Unity of Luke-Acts: A Literary Interpretation*. 2 vols. Philadelphia: Fortress, 1986–90. Very readable and helpful commentary by a Methodist author, stressing the narrative of Luke and Acts more than historical criticism.

Popular Commentaries or Study Bibles

Casciaro, Jose Maria, et al., eds. *The Navarre Bible: The Acts of the Apostles.* Dublin: Four Courts, 1989 (Spanish original, 1984). The commentary includes the RSVCE translation of the biblical text (1965–66), with expositions and quotations from Church documents and writings of popes and saints, especially St. Josemaría Escrivá, founder of Opus Dei.

Hahn, Scott, and Curtis Mitch. *The Acts of the Apostles.* Ignatius Catholic Study Bible. San Francisco: Ignatius Press, 2002. RSVCE biblical text, supplemented with succinct and informative footnotes, often citing the Fathers or Church doctrine.

Kurz, William. *Following Jesus: A Disciple's Guide to Luke and Acts.* Ann Arbor, MI: Charis Books, 2003. Popular pastoral meditations on both Luke and Acts.

Perrotta, Kevin, and Gerald Darring. *Acts: The Good News of the Holy Spirit.* Catholic Perspectives: Six Weeks with the Bible. Chicago: Loyola Press, 2004. A Bible study for teens, with questions to help youths discern what Scripture means for their lives today.

Special Studies

Cadbury, Henry J. *The Making of Luke-Acts.* London: SPCK, 1961. Hendrickson Publishers issued a newer imprint with introduction by Paul N. Anderson in 1999. A classic and still a most insightful treatment of how Luke wrote Luke and Acts as two volumes.

Cassidy, Richard J. *Paul in Chains.* New York: Crossroad, 2001. A fascinating historical and theological study of Paul's imprisonments based on data in Acts and the Letters of Paul.

Marguerat, Daniel. *The First Christian Historian: Writing the "Acts of the Apostles."* Translated by Ken McKinney, Gregory J. Laughery, and Richard Bauckham. Port Chester, NY: Cambridge University Press, 2002. Scholarly literary and theological explanation of how Luke wrote Luke and Acts as a narrative of Christian beginnings, integrating Jewish and Hellenistic cultures, with special chapters on the God of Acts and the work of the Spirit.

Montague, George. *The Holy Spirit: Growth of a Biblical Tradition.* 2nd ed. Eugene, OR: Wipf & Stock, 2006. A rich and thoughtful exploration of all the major biblical texts dealing with the Holy Spirit, with two chapters on Acts.

Pope Benedict XVI. *The Apostles: The Origin of the Church and Their Co-Workers.* Huntington, IN: Our Sunday Visitor, 2010. Papal reflections on the continuity between the apostles and their successors, using Acts and other sources.

Glossary

apocalyptic (from Greek *apokalypsis*, "revelation"): a distinctive type of ancient Jewish and Christian literature that uses symbols and strange imagery to describe end-times events or heavenly realities. Prominent biblical examples of apocalypses are the books of Daniel and Revelation.

Aramaic: a Semitic language related to Hebrew, adopted by Jews after their exile in Babylon and spoken by most Jews in first-century Palestine.

brothers: a term used by Christians to refer to fellow Christians and by Jews to refer to fellow Jews. In most contexts its meaning is inclusive of both men and women.

Christ (Greek *Christos*): see Messiah.

Christology: doctrine or understanding of the identity and mission of Jesus Christ.

covenant: a sacred kinship bond between God and his people, which God established with Abraham and later with his descendants, the people of Israel, through Moses (Acts 3:25). Through his passion and resurrection, Jesus established the new and eternal covenant that fulfills the old (see Jer 31:31–33; Mark 14:24).

Diaspora: the "scattering" of Jews outside their homeland of Palestine, which began with the Assyrian and Babylonian exiles. By the first century AD, there were communities of Diaspora Jews in most cities throughout the Roman Empire.

divine passive: the use of the passive form of a verb to imply that God is the subject of the action, as in Acts 13:49.

ecclesiology: doctrine or understanding of the Church.

eisegesis: reading into a text a meaning that is not actually there but originates from the interpreter's own ideas or biases.

eschatological: having to do with the last things: God's decisive intervention in history to bring the former age to an end and inaugurate the new and final age of salvation history. For the New Testament, the end has already begun with Jesus' passion and resurrection. See sidebar, p. 52.

Gentile: a person of non-Jewish descent. Much of Acts is concerned with God's extension of the blessings of salvation to the Gentiles.

Gnosticism: a common early Christian heresy claiming that matter is evil and that salvation comes through *gnōsis* (knowledge).

God-fearer: a Gentile who believed in the one God of Israel and adopted some Jewish practices but without actually becoming a Jewish convert, like Cornelius in Acts 10 and Lydia in Acts 16. Also called a worshiper of God.

Hellenists: Jews who had lived outside of Palestine in Hellenistic cultures and who spoke Greek, some of whom had immigrated back to Palestine.

inclusio: a literary technique in which similar material or phrasing is placed at the beginning and end of a section, forming a frame around it.

intertestamental writings: Jewish writings composed between the periods of the Old and New Testaments (roughly 400 BC to AD 50).

Jerusalem Council: a gathering of the apostles and elders in Jerusalem, narrated in Acts 15, to decide a question of major importance for the future of the Church: do Gentile Christian converts need to be circumcised and keep the law of Moses?

Judaizers: early Christians who held that Gentile converts need to keep the law of Moses to be saved, including having the males circumcised. The early Church rejected this claim at the Jerusalem Council in Acts 15.

kerygma: the core or essential content of the good news preached by Christians, which has intrinsic power to awaken faith in the hearers.

Messiah (from Hebrew *mashiakh*, "anointed one"): the anointed descendant of King David promised by God, who would come to restore the kingdom of Israel and for whom Jews waited with expectant hope. The Christian proclamation is that *Jesus* is the Messiah.

monotheism: the belief that there is only one God—the foundational doctrine of both Judaism and Christianity.

Nazirite vow: a form of consecration to God for Israelite laypeople that included abstention from alcohol and from cutting one's hair. See sidebar, p. 286.

parousia: Jesus' promised return in glory at the end of the world (Acts 1:11).

presbyter (Greek *presbyteros*, "elder"): church leaders, often mentioned in Acts, who were appointed by apostles to lead local churches. This term gradually came to be understood as signifying a share in Christ's priestly ministry; hence it is the origin of the English word "priest."

prophet like Moses: a future wonder-working prophet and leader promised by God in Deut 18:15; the early Church proclaimed that Jesus is that prophet (see Acts 3:22–23).

rhetoric: the art of persuasive speech or writing, a highly prized skill in the ancient world.

Sadducees: members of the Jewish priestly aristocracy, who were often among the early Christians' fiercest opponents. They accepted only the Torah as Scripture and denied the resurrection of the dead, reward or punishment after death, and the existence of angels and demons. See sidebar p. 337.

Sanhedrin: the supreme judicial council of the Jewish people, consisting of seventy members, including elders, priests, and scribes, plus the high priest as chair.

Septuagint (abbreviated LXX): a translation of the Hebrew Bible made around 250 BC by Jews in Alexandria, Egypt.

synoptic (Greek for "seeing together"): a term referring to the Gospels of Matthew, Mark, and Luke because they contain very similar material.

theophany (Greek for "divine appearance"): a perceptible manifestation of God's holy presence, which causes human awe, fear, and trembling.

type: a biblical person, thing, or event at an earlier stage of salvation history prefiguring the way God accomplishes his future purposes, especially the culmination of his plan in Jesus Christ.

Way: the earliest name for Christianity, alluding to the fact that following Jesus is a whole way of life. See Acts 9:2.

worshiper of God: *see* God-fearer.

Index of Pastoral Topics

This index indicates where topics are mentioned in Acts that may be useful for evangelization, catechesis, apologetics, or other forms of pastoral ministry.

Index of Sidebars